MOTIVATION of HUMAN and ANIMAL BEHAVIOR

BEHAVIORAL SCIENCE SERIES

MOTIVATION OF HUMAN AND ANIMAL BEHAVIOR
An Ethological View

Konrad Lorenz   Paul Leyhausen

Translated by B. A. Tonkin

BEHAVIORAL SCIENCE SERIES

VAN NOSTRAND REINHOLD COMPANY
New York Cincinnati Toronto London Melbourne

Van Nostrand Reinhold Company Regional Offices:
New York Cincinnati Chicago Millbrae Dallas

Van Nostrand Reinhold Company International Offices:
London Toronto Melbourne

Copyright © 1973 by Litton Educational Publishing, Inc.

Library of Congress Catalog Card Number: 72-1460
ISBN: 0-442-24885-7

Manufactured in the United States of America

Published by Van Nostrand Reinhold Company
450 West 33rd Street, New York, N.Y. 10001

Published simultaneously in Canada by Van Nostrand Reinhold Ltd.

15 14 13 12 11 10 9 8 7 6 5 4 3 2 1

Figures 1, 2, 5, 6, 7, 9, 10, 11, 15, 16 and 19 were adapted from the original photographs by Hermann Kacher.

Library of Congress Cataloging in Publication Data

Lorenz, Konrad.
  Motivation of human and animal behavior.

  (Behavioral science series)
  Translation of Antriebe tierischen und menschlichen Verhaltens.
  Bibliography: p.
  1. Psychology, Comparative. I. Leyhausen, Paul.
II. Title. [DNLM: 1. Psychology, Comparative.
BF 673 L869a 1973]
BF673.L613   156   72-1460
ISBN 0-442-24885-7

BEHAVIORAL SCIENCE SERIES

The Van Nostrand Reinhold Behavioral Science Series will publish a broad range of books on animal and human behavior from an ethological perspective. Although presently observable behavior is the focus of this series, the development of behavior in individuals, as well as the evolutionary history in various species, will also be considered. It is felt that such an holistic approach is needed to come to a fuller understanding of behavior in general. This series is a contribution toward this goal.

Erich Klinghammer, Consulting Editor
Purdue University

Foreword

In the past decade ethology has become vastly better known in the United States than it was previously. There has come to be an increasingly greater acceptance and use of ethological methods and concepts in application to human and animal behavior. Progress has consequently been made toward a better understanding of the biological bases of animal behavior.

The growth of ethology and of the awareness of ethology in the United States has given rise to a pressing need for greater availability of the writings of European ethologists. Konrad Lorenz has become quite familiar to Americans. His *King Solomon's Ring* and *On Aggression* have both sold widely, and two entire translated volumes of his scholarly papers were published recently. Yet there is still much in the body of European ethological literature that is unknown here. Paul Leyhausen's work is one of the most important lacunae in this respect. Few people have heard of him and even among those familiar with him he is often regarded as a "cat" man. In fact, however, Leyhausen is more than a specialist in cat behavior and has made material contributions to the whole field of ethology for over twenty years. His logical analyses of extremely difficult ethological concepts have not reached American scholars, with the result that he is probably the least appreciated among significant ethologists. Hopefully this volume, containing ten papers by Leyhausen, will begin to rectify this situation.

Not only will this volume help to bring Paul Leyhausen his deserved recognition but it will also do much to clear up some common misconceptions regarding ethological research and to add further dimensions to what is presently known of ethology in this country. These tasks are especially important at the present time, since some current books which deal with animal behavior or with ethology have either given an incomplete presentation of the ethological viewpoint or have presented it in a biased form. Lorenz's and Leyhausen's writings will enable readers to discover for themselves the nature of the data collected by ethologists and how they utilize these data in interpreting behavioral phenomena.

One reason for ethology's importance is that in the last few years its application to human behavior has begun to expand and to give us some vital insights about ourselves. Human ethology is making us aware that we have a very ancient animal heritage and that the biological bases of our behavior are of extreme significance. Indeed, once these biological bases are appreciated, it becomes apparent that the social and individual problems of mankind cannot be solved by disregarding them. Genetics, developmental factors in relation to experiential ones, ecology, physiology, nutrition, drives and motivation, and so on, form an intricate behavior foundation which is presently only little understood. It is at great peril to ourselves that we remain ignorant of them.

Humans are animals—a special species, to be sure, but *thoroughly* animals. Charles Darwin had an ethological approach to the expression of emotions in man and animals (1872) and the modern ethological study of human beings has been conducted for over two decades, as shown by Leyhausen's work, since even his earliest writing in this volume involves human ethology. Furthermore, Lorenz's 1939 article, reprinted here, includes a discussion of behavior rudiments in man as involving serious social and personal problems. Problems such as these are clearly ones that must be dealt with if progress is to be made in improving the human condition.

In one sense, then, human ethology is not new at all. But it is new in the sense that only recently have we become really aware of it. It is my hope that this volume will do much to stimulate and encourage the considerable research needed in this area. Not all of us are completely willing to look at ourselves as we really are. But we must do so if we are to discern the total causal bases of our behavior and to discover how to prevent social psychopathology. Leyhausen's discussions of the effects of population density upon human behavior are good examples of the necessity of understanding the importance of adequate environmental provision for the optimal satisfaction of biologically based needs. The genetic programming within members of the human species must be taken into account and dealt with if human problems are to be solved. For ethology does not permit us to adopt fatalistic attitudes, but calls us to action.

Eckhard H. Hess
The University of Chicago

Preface

When two volumes of my early papers were reissued as a collected edition, the interest they aroused was a surprise to both the publishers and myself. The fact that they could become positive best sellers demands some explanation. As literature they are not at all distinguished, so that cannot be the reason. Nor could it be a love of animals, for this finds no satisfaction in dry science, however much it deals with animals. Their success can, then, only be due to the highly gratifying fact that many people have actually understood the deeper significance of the comparative study of behavior. Without any doubt, very many of the specific regularities to be found in animal behavior are also present in our own human conduct, and descriptions of animal behavior therefore arouse human interest. Not that man is "a mere animal"; for as a result of many of his qualities and capabilities he towers high above all other creatures. As the Chinese sage once said, not all the human is there in animals, but certainly all the animal is in humans.

Among those who have "grown into" comparative ethology, i.e. graduated to it from zoology, Paul Leyhausen is the only one who is also fully trained in human psychology. Furthermore, he is the only one of us to have dedicated his life's work to the investigation of a group of higher mammals, namely the felid carnivores. That these intelligent animals are far less easy to understand and interpret in their behavior than Jackdaws and Graylag Geese will soon become clear to the reader. But equally soon he will perceive that knowledge gained from higher mammals is of far greater, or at least more direct, use in helping to understand humans.

Konrad Lorenz

Seewiesen

Preface

In January, 1941, I was a student of twenty-four and the Institute of Comparative Psychology of the University of Koenigsberg—three small rooms and a somewhat larger aquarium—had just been founded. When I somewhat diffidently told the newly appointed Professor of Psychology, Konrad Lorenz, that I would appreciate his advice as I was interested in animal psychology, his abrupt answer, "There is only *one* psychology!" shocked me profoundly. For I had been brought up in the traditional idea that man was something quite apart and that any direct comparison with animals practically bordered on sacrilege. Lorenz must have noticed my shock, for he said little more to me. Instead he simply took me by the arm, led me to his aquarium tanks— and first taught me to see. Later he gave me some things to read, including the Rostock lecture which, at my particular request, is the first of the chapters reprinted in this volume. Considered objectively, this paper is certainly not the most significant of Lorenz's writings which appeared up to 1940. Yet, no other has impressed and convinced me as much as this one did, nor, as far as I am aware, has anything I read or heard before or since so strongly shaped my way of learning and thinking and my research. It is not particularly easy to read and in some parts is even self-contradictory. But this only goes to show how hesitantly the early ethologist felt his way along and how often he wavered when he found himself up against formidable, long-established schools of thought and research.

From that time onward, however, it was clear to me that if the ethologists wanted to achieve more precise and far-reaching bases for comparison in the direction of human behavior they would have to look to the mammals, and particularly the highly developed ones, more than hitherto. This is more easily said than done; for most higher mammals are rather large and have a significantly longer developmental cycle than the small birds, fishes, and insects ethologists prefer. Observing them—or, even more so, keeping and breeding them in large numbers—requires a disproportionately large expenditure in terms of time, money, and space, and results take so much longer to come. Thus, those of us who are principally engaged in investigating the behavior of larger mammals are still only a small minority even today. That in the end the results can nevertheless justify the expenditure and, moreover, also make some contribution to the interpretation of human behavior and its crises is something I hope to demonstrate by means of this collection of articles.

Nowadays critical observers sometimes aver that ethology is preparing to swallow human psychology in its entirety along with social psychology, psychiatry, cultural anthropology, and a whole series of other related disciplines, and even, with the presumptuousness of natural science, not merely to rattle the sacred foundations of those purely humane-philosophical disciplines, cognition theory and ethics, but quite simply to replace them. Now, the fact that in all these neighboring sciences our findings are attracting more and more attention (and sometimes, to our dismay, being rather inadequately assimilated) naturally fills us with pleasure and—I fear—with pride. Apart from this, the implied suspicion is based on a misunderstanding: All that we are doing is to add a new, or at least totally neglected, dimension to these disciplines—the dimension of one or two billion years of evolution. Not that philosophers, psychologists, and sociologists had not heard of this in the hundred years since Darwin, and the number of more or less speculative attempts to find evolutionistic explanations for human behavior is legion. What is new about ethology is that it has succeeded—at least to the extent of highly promising first steps—in getting a grip in terms of *method* on this vast and awe-inspiring dimension. Thus, evolution as a *current reality* can no longer be pushed aside as too speculative or operationally intangible. It is now a *compelling obligation* for every single science which has in any way to do with human behavior to take this dimension into account also.

The chapters which follow attempt to demonstrate how important this "fourth dimension" is to the interpretation of human behavior, by way of three themes: motivational theory as the hard core of any "general psychology," expression and impression as the first system of interindividual communication organisms had, and the role of space in social behavior and social organization. The papers are in chronological and not thematic sequence, so that the second and last articles are devoted to the theme of expression, the sixth and eighth to social organization, and all the others to various aspects of motivation. In order to give some idea of how comparative research proceeds in detail and, not least, to show how much hard and patient grind this kind of investigation demands, the present volume contains a paper ("Relative hierarchy of moods," p. 144) which could threaten to tire the reader, particularly one not favorably disposed in advance, with the mass of detailed descriptions in the first part; I can only hope that the second part may more or less compensate him for this.

The *Felidae* are only a small group, containing some 40 species. Among mammals, they occupy what one might call a medium level of evolution, and are thus well suited to bridging the gap still left in our knowledge of mammalian behavior between the well-studied small rodents and the nowadays equally intensively studied higher primates. As carnivores, they offer the student one motivational system in particular which is of a very high complexity and which at the same time lends itself well to experimentation, since the prey object constitutes a natural "independent variable" of equal complexity which can be replaced by dummies of various kinds in an experimental situation. The analysis of the phylogeny and ontogeny of this motivational system revealed basic principles of organization which are, I think, to be found in the motivational make-up of all higher mammals and therefore also of man.

The second and third chapters were my first shaky steps toward direct comparison between human and mammalian behavior. If they are reprinted here despite weaknesses that are all too obvious today, this is for two reasons: Firstly, they contain the first mention of hypotheses concerning the relationship between expression and impression and concerning the interplay between the individual propensities and their internal, gradually changing balance, hypotheses which have been confirmed in full by later investigations (see ninth and eleventh chapters); and secondly, it seems to me that the practical applications in education I recommended then are still valid today. This last claim I would also make—contrary to the current trend—on behalf of the conclusions drawn in the seventh article concerning sex education and early sexual enlightenment.

The motivational theory developed step by step in the other chapters is largely physiologically orientated. For this reason it will doubt-less be disapproved of by those human psychologists who cling to the belief that the psyche may only be explained psychologically, i.e. on the basis of psychical processes. I can do nothing about this; the belief may have been consecrated by a long tradition of thought, but it is nonetheless false. If there is one place where we certainly shall not find the explanation for the psychical occurrence and experience, it is in the psyche itself, and for the same reasons as we find the explanation for digestion not in the digestive processes but in the particular ecological conditions which, about a billion years ago, exposed a number of organisms to a selection pressure which induced them to absorb nutrients of an organic nature instead of assimilating only anorganic nutrients. The psychical processes are functions with life- and species-preserving value which have likewise appeared as a result of selection pressure, and the explanation for them precedes them in every sense (this is also true of actualization, see p. 282). Whether we shall ever *find* this explanation is uncertain, but, if we do, it will only be via the model of a motivational system which does not already presuppose the psychical but demands it as an additional integrating function in the course of its further development. It was in the search for such a model that the present chapters originated. Any reader who takes the trouble to collate the overall picture from them, without overlooking a single detail, will find himself faced with an extremely complex, perhaps even confusing, functional ap-paratus. August simplicity is something the astronomer or atomic physicist may discover. For us in the middle walks of Nature, the august simplicity of the elephant ceases the moment we look under its skin.

Paul Leyhausen

Wuppertal-Elberfeld

Contents

KONRAD LORENZ

1 The Comparative Study of Behavior (1939)

I. THE INSTINCTIVE BEHAVIOR PATTERN IN PHYLOGENY

In some quarters zoological taxonomy is rather looked down upon nowadays as something which has ground to a standstill and been outlived. People tend to forget that it was on the basis of zoological taxonomy that the thought developed which more than any other promoted the adoption of a dynamic theory of life: It is to comparative morphology, which classifies the animate world according to increasing and decreasing similarities, that we owe that knowledge of evolutive species mutation which today is of greater importance to our personal and social conduct than any other scientific knowledge. Even if this should prove to have already been the greatest and finest gift comparative morphology is capable of bestowing on us, with somewhat modified propositions and in synthesis with genetics we may still look to it for vital information about the causes of species mutation. In addition, however, there is a large field of biological research which has not yet benefited to the same degree as morphology from an approach which combines evolutionary aspects with comparative methods. By this I mean the investigation of animal and human *behavior*. That human psychology is also in need of comparative phylogenetic research has long been clearly recognized, even as far back as Wundt (1882). In their psychological make-up too all living creatures are historical creatures, and without insight into their evolutionary history it is utterly impossible to understand all the facts about them. However complete the typology of the present creature may be, as long as this neglects the historical development it can never satisfy our quest for causality. What particularly the researcher into animal and human behavior misses above all in a purely typological classification is a place for the fact which cannot be understood in terms of finality *but only* in terms of history, a place for yesterday's adaptation, the *rudiment* which gets completely overlooked—one of the worst consequences of carrying a biased finalistic way of thinking to excess, as is nowadays so common. Yet, the "dysteleological" effect of old mental structures is not only of theoretical importance but in fact one of the most urgent practical problems of the present day, particularly in the case of Man who, more than any other living creature before him, has changed his whole ecology and sociology in the shortest period of time. The fact that some taxes and instincts inherited from the distant past are "no longer appropriate" today, and above all come into conflict with the continuously increasing demands made by society on the individual, has such an obtrusively disturbing effect that the naive assume the influence of an "evil enemy," a devil, while psychoanalysis, no less naively but with far less excuse, postulates a specific "death wish." Yet, with the most modest knowledge about the conservative nature of instinctive movements in phylogeny and about the physiology of their endogenous self-stimulation precisely these phenomena become not merely intelligible but even self-evident and theoretically indispensable.

Nevertheless, until very recent times exceedingly little use has been made of the comparative method. There are several reasons for this. The scholastic idea of the general protean variability of animal behavior was partly to blame for the fact that to most people it seemed hopeless to search for hereditary characters which did not vary from individual to individual and were thus accessible to consideration from a phylogenetic viewpoint. In this the mechanistic behaviorists, with their explanatory monism based on the conditioned reflex, were in complete agreement with the finalistic vitalists, whose dogmatic belief in the purposiveness of every animal act prohibited them from assuming the existence of constant elements. In addition, however, the lack of a genuinely comparative method of research in psychology has a much simpler explanation: It can be neither learned from a book nor pursued in theory, but demands practical training on the object. Evaluating phylogenetic relationships involves so many highly complex functions of "taxonomic feel" that in very many cases the actual scientific work is the self-analysis which must first tell us on which single characters in an otherwise unanalyzed complex our judgment was based. Although a judgment formed on the basis of unanalyzed complex qualities is scientifically invalid, its intuitive apperception is indispensable when choosing precisely which analytical approach is to be adopted. Only someone with a thorough practical knowledge of the object can develop a proper sense of taxonomic feel and thus truly appreciate the value and validity of the theory of descent—but never a theoretician and still less a philosopher.

Thus it was a zoologist and not a psychologist who was the first to approach the phenomena of animal behavior from a genuinely comparative phylogenetic viewpoint. And he immediately discovered something the existence of which is still being denied even today by some psychologists, namely the hereditary invariants in animal behavior which render phylogenetic comparison from species to species, from genus to genus, possible as well as indeed essential to an explanation of their particular form. This was Charles Otis Whitman, who as far back as 1898 wrote the words, "Instincts and organs are to be studied from the common viewpoint of phyletic descent." Whitman did not state this theoretical demand and leave it at that, but instead produced a most precise comparative work on a clearly defined group of animals, namely pigeons (1919). In this work the hereditary behavior pattern is subjected to consideration as *one* taxonomic character alongside all available morphological ones, and in the process the instinctive act quite clearly emerges as a character possessing marked phylogenetic constancy and thus taxonomic rank. If morphological characters alone are used, the order of pigeons, for example, can be defined only by means of a complicated combination of these characters: nidicolous carinates with a weak, soft-skinned, vesicularly swollen beak, medium-long pointed wings, low perching feet or spreading toes, etc. To every one of the characters mentioned there are exceptions. *Goura* is not nidicolous and furthermore has rounded wings similar to those of a chicken, *Didunculus* has quite a different beak, and so on. If on the other hand one defines the order by means of one single behavioral character, namely that when pigeons drink, the water is pumped up by peristalsis of the esophagus, not one exception to this can be found; however, the only other group which displays the same behavior, namely the *Pteroclidae*, moves closer to the pigeons through possessing just this indubitably very old characteristic than on account of many morphological characters pointing in the same direction.

Independently of Whitman, Heinroth had at that time consciously introduced the approach of comparative zoology into the study of behavior. In his work "Concerning certain motor patterns in vertebrates" (1930) he broadened this viewpoint to include far larger taxa and showed that the taxonomic significance of a particular movement, e.g. scratching the head with the hind foot, familiar to us all from dogs, is equal to that of the very oldest morphological characters of the tetrapods, for instance the construction of the hind limb out of femur, tibia, and fibula. The way in which this movement is performed within the class of birds shows that its details are governed exclusively by historical and not at all by functional factors. The majority of birds performs the scratching movement in the manner characteristic of amphibians, reptiles, and mammals, in that the scratching hind foot moves laterally past the forelimb in the direction of the head; in other words the wing has to be *brought back* into the position peculiar to four-footed animals before the movement can be discharged. Now this procedure, explicable only historically through the class mutation (if I may use the expression) of the reptilian arm, has been abandoned by individual groups in the process of phylogenesis in favor of the functionally self-explanatory method of leaving the wing, which is in any case not in the way of the scratching foot, lying on the back and scratching themselves "round the front." Scratching round-the-front or round-the-back is distributed in the system without any relation whatever to function, long- or short-leggedness, shape of foot and the like, but depends exclusively on which group the bird belongs to. *Chionis* evidences its puzzling and isolated systematic position by performing a movement intermediate between scratching round the front and round the back; it spreads its wing as though it would scratch itself round the back, but then brings the foot medially past the wing to the head, a form of behavior really intelligible only in historical terms. Other motor patterns such as yawning, stretching, shaking, etc., display a similarly wide distribution in the system.

In addition to this work, in which he pursued single characters so to speak through their whole phylogenetic development, Heinroth also applied the second method of comparative research to the study of behavior and, like Whitman, but in an even more thoroughgoing manner, worked on a narrowly defined group of animals, the *Anatidae*, on the basis of the widest collection of observational material covering all behavioral characters which could be taxonomically evaluated. Heinroth's taxonomic conclusions (1910) were impressively confirmed by the investigations of Poll (1910), who took the degree of infertility in hybrids as a measure of phylogenetic relationship: in all cases in which the two researchers diverged from the traditional arrangement of the groups, they were in agreement with one another.[1]

Neither Whitman nor Heinroth ever employs the expression "homology," and yet their works are based on the assumption that the *concept of homology* in use in morphology is just as applicable to hereditary motor patterns as to anatomical characters. The persuasive power of their results proves how right this working hypothesis was. Now we ask *what* is actually being compared and homologized. Neither of the scientists gives a precise definition of the concept of instinct, and both treat every hereditary innate behavior pattern as a manifestation of instinct. Nowadays when we speak of innate adaptive motor processes we make a distinction between two kinds which are strictly separated fundamentally, i.e. physiologically, from one another: the automatic functions of the central nervous system dependent on endogenous excitatory processes, for which alone I use the expression "instinctive act," and the orienting reactions dependent on direction from external stimuli, which in common with Kühn (1919) we call "taxes." This conceptual distinction based on physiological facts with which we shall deal in greater detail shortly cannot be found in so many words in the work of the two pioneers of comparative ethology. Yet, with their fine intuitive feeling for taxonomy they both understood one important effect of the physiological differences between the two processes: the instinctive behavior pattern, already coordinated in the central nervous system itself, its form independent of external stimuli, understandably has greater taxonomic usefulness than the innate orienting reaction which depends on direction from specific external stimuli. Insofar as questions of taxonomy are concerned, both Heinroth and Whitman almost exclusively employ as characters movements coordinated in the central nervous system, first and foremost the instinctive movements of courtship, which involve particularly few taxes. It is important to emphasize this, *because the comparative phylogenetic observations made by Whitman and Heinroth were precisely what drew attention to the stability of the instinctive act.* If they with their comparative descriptions had not established this remarkable fact—which moreover is denied by so many psychologists—we should never have discovered that the instinctive act as an endogenous automatic function is something different in *physiology* and *origin* from all individually variable behavior patterns.

At first there were few similar papers, and these dealt mainly with birds. I would mention the names of Verwey (1930), Tinbergen (1936, 1937, 1938), Goethe (1937), Makkink (1931, 1936). So far scarcely anyone has worked with mammals, for the papers by Carpenter (1934, 1935) on platyrhine monkeys contain but few comparative considerations, and the investigation of *Mustelidae* by Goethe (1940 b) is not yet complete.

In view of this situation I planned a comparative investigation intended to deal in a particularly thorough manner with a clearly defined group of animals. A system of actions of every single form belonging to the group was to be recorded as completely as possible, and at the same time as many taxonomically important forms as possible should be represented so that the individual behavioral characters and the individual species would be susceptible of tabular arrangement, thus enabling one to see where in the group a particular feature was present or missing, and also to compare the complexes of features characterizing the species with one another by registering the features statistically. Naturally my aim was not to limit myself to behavioral features but at the same time to take all available morphological characters into consideration as well. Only a very small taxonomic unit could be considered for such a painstaking investigation. The demands on the object, some of them purely technical, decided the choice. The group must already have been thoroughly investigated taxonomically and morphologically, had to be rich in forms which differed as widely as possible in their degrees of relationship, i.e. included the maximum possible number of smooth transitions between species and race, genus and species, must be rich in taxis-free instinctive acts, and finally these had to be easy to record on film, the only objective method of registering complex movements. The *Anatinae* fitted these stipulations better than any other group. Furthermore, a good number of "true species" can produce fertile hybrids among themselves, thus making it obvious to try to combine the comparative investigation, planned on a broad basis of as many features as possible, with the genetic investigation of these features. What particularly interested me was the question whether obviously homologous behavioral features in two species would always prove homogenetical when these species were hybridized. If they behaved in this respect in the same way as anatomical features, this would be strong justification for applying the concept of homology to innate motor patterns. We selected sixteen clearly recognizable and definable instinctive acts connected with courtship which are present as definite homologous entities in most of the species, and indeed in such different stages of development and differentiation that statements as to the *direction* their evolution had taken attained a high degree of probability. Leaving aside a few exceptions, which in fact opened up instructive new perspectives, the distribution of these features and their degree of differentiation coincide astonishingly consistently with one another and with all anatomical characters considered, above all the degree of development of the tracheal drum of the drake. The classification which emerges from the sum total of these features differs considerably, however, from the generally accepted classification of Hartert, and above all renders Hartert's genus *Anas* obsolete. Here, of course, I cannot give even an outline of the details and will therefore content myself with two examples. In the Mallard group, *Anas platyrhynchos, poecilorhyncha, melleri, obscura, superciliosa, undulata*, etc., as with many other *Anatinae*, the male sex performs chin-raising, an action which, as comparative research teaches us, is a phylogenetic derivative of a symbolic drinking movement. The females perform an action still more widely distributed in the group, namely "inciting," a symbolic threatening back over the shoulder. The two actions are functionally paired to form a "ceremony," in that they elicit one another mutually and are therefore usually performed simultaneously by a bonded pair. Widgeon pairs, both *Mareca penelope* and *sibilatrix*, are distinct from the Mallard group in that both members of the pair possess a movement corresponding to that of the Mallard drake. "Inciting" over the shoulder is missing in the female, and the stimulus situation in which mutual chin-raising is performed—namely always after an agonistic bout with other pond residents, particularly with other widgeon pairs—is rather more reminiscent of the analogous (not homologous) ceremony of the *Anserinae*, what is called the "triumph ceremony." In comparison with that performed by the Mallard group, this chin-raising is more highly differentiated and its connection with display drinking no longer obvious, whereas in the case of the Mallard drake drinking is "still" indicated by a brief tap on the surface of the water. I should not dare to claim homology between the two forms of chin-raising were it not for the fact that the gadwall, *Chaulelasmus streperus*, represents an indisputable link between them. In the case of this species, as with the widgeon, both sexes possess chin-raising, but the female additionally possesses the movement of "inciting" back over the shoulder, like the female Mallard. Bill-raising is performed simultaneously by both members of the pair, as with the widgeon, but by the female it is omitted almost exactly every second time and replaced by the "inciting" movement. In this way a characteristic movement rhythm results, to which the rhythm of the vocalization accompanying the ceremony also corresponds. In contrast to the Mallard species, the "triumph ceremony" significance is clear, if not as pronounced as in the case of the widgeon. Even the downy young already possess the corresponding motor pattern, which leads me to assume care of the young by the drake and close family cohesion, such as we find in the case of geese and *Casarcinae*. At a high intensity of reaction the adult male gadwall taps the surface of the water prior to chin-raising just as the Mallard drake does, so that through a knowledge of the gadwall the homology between the chin-raising of the Mallard drake and that of both sexes of the widgeon would seem to be confirmed. We are strengthened in this assumption by the fact that the gadwall clearly occupies a position midway between *Anas* and *Mareca*, not only morphologically but also in the fertility of its hybrids with both the other genera. In *Anas-Mareca* hybrids spermatogenesis comes to a halt before the first meiotic division (Poll 1910). As opposed to this the gadwall produces physiologically fertile hybrids with both the other genera. What is positively astounding, however, is that the conclusions indicated by the facts I have described so far have been confirmed by research into hybridization: A pair of hybrids between Mallard and *Mareca sibilatrix* kindly presented to me by the Berlin Zoological Garden astonishingly enough displayed *precisely the same synthesis* between the described behavioral features of the parent species as we find in the gadwall, where it is a differentiation which has developed during phylogeny! A second example: The gadwall displays two courtship acts in inseparable combination which in the case of the Mallard are performed separately and unconnected with one another. Various circumstances permit the assumption that the behavior of the Mallard is the phylogenetically older of the two. Now, I possess a strain of domestic ducks called Kaki-Campbells, and in these the same obligatory combination of the two automatic functions occurs as in the case of the gadwall, but is a mutation resulting from domestication. Hybridization experiments are planned.

I should not wish to conclude this section on the behavior of the instinctive act in phylogeny without mentioning briefly that a second source of knowledge from morphological phylogenetics may also be exploited for the purpose of its investigation, namely the temporary appearance during ontogenesis of phylogenetically old features. We know of many cases in which a form of behavior, generally distributed and certainly original in some groups of animals, occurs in related groups also, but here is displayed only by the juveniles and no longer by the adults. Thus some kinds of passerines, which do not hop on both legs simultaneously like most members of the family but walk on alternate legs, possess as juveniles the coordination of hopping characteristic of the family. This can be seen particularly clearly when as yet unfledged nestlings are persuaded to move on foot. Recently Ahlquist (1937) has published a most important observation on young *Laridae*. The genus *Larus*, which may be considered as a typical representative of the group, possesses a particular form of movement for fishing from the surface of the water. In the case of the subgenus *Chroicocephalus* (Laughing Gulls) and the genus *Stercorarius* (Skuas), which have become differentiated in various directions from the general and certainly older gull type, this instinctive act is *missing* in the adult bird but appears in the "play" of the juvenile bird in the typical form otherwise peculiar to the group.

II. THE PHYSIOLOGY OF THE INSTINCTIVE ACT

From the results of comparative research the *constancy of form* of the instinctive act emerges clearly. It is not the success of the motor pattern which remains the same (this is a false generalization of specific regularities valid in respect of orienting reactions and purposive behavior) but the form of coordination of the movement. This constancy of form, remarkable in view of the diversity of external stimuli, poses the question of the physiological reasons for it and suggests the idea of a link between the movement and internal structural systems in the central nervous system. The first explanation thought of was, understandably enough, *reflex chains,* a theory which Ziegler (1920) has represented with clarity.

Various arguments were presented in objection to the reflex chain theory, such as the self-regulating capacity of motor coordinations investigated by Bethe (1931) and Bethe and Fischer (1931). One difficulty in accepting the idea of simple reflex chains which we must discuss here consists of the *varying degrees of intensity* of the instinctive act. These are governed mainly by the opposite of an "all or none law." If the excitation associated with an instinctive act reaches only a level too low to permit the full discharge which alone would have adaptive value, then the movement is not *omitted* but appears in purposeless, incomplete form. Starting from barely perceptible beginnings of actions, which are known as "intention movements" because they reveal the direction the expected activity will take, there are all possible transitional forms up to complete effective discharge. Statistically speaking, purposeless discharge occurs more frequently than effective discharge. A Graylag Goose or a Herring Gull, for example, performs incomplete versions of certain nest-building actions the whole year through, but it is only when the hormonally and seasonally governed maximum intensity is reached that these harmonize into the systematic function which they have been differentiated during phylogeny to fulfil. The actions belonging together in *one* sequence of steps, each of which is higher in intensity than the foregoing, can sometimes be *very different in appearance*. As the intention to fly mounts, a wild goose first stretches its neck long, then it utters a particular sound, then with its beak it performs circular shaking movements, only now does the beginning of the actual flight movements become visible in the form of an unfolding of the wings and preparations for the spring into the air, then finally come the spring and wing-beats as it flies off. All these differences in the form of the action are not, however, in essence an argument against their having reflex nature. Their actual explanation would, namely, also be conceivable on this basis. From the investigations of von Holst (1935 b, c) we know that the "all or none law" is fully valid with regard to the motor element of movements coordinated in the central nervous system, in that the differences in intensity depend on the *number* of elements reacting, and this fluctuates according to the intensity of excitation. The differences of form between different levels of intensity are explained by the fact that different motor patterns have different threshold levels for the *same* kind of excitation. Beak-shaking in the goose simply sets in at lower values than does the preparation for the spring. All this could still be the case if the reflex were the basis of instinctive acts.

There are, however, other phenomena which cannot be explained in terms of the reflex chain theory, namely certain fluctuations in the intensity of instinctive acts which obey one very particular rule. This rule may be roughly summarized as follows: The longer an instinctive act has not been elicited, the greater the intensity with which it reacts to a given stimulus situation. Considered from the point of view of the stimulus, this same specific regularity expresses itself in the fact that the longer the time which has elapsed since an instinctive act was last elicited, the slighter the stimulus which is capable of eliciting it. Analagous behavior can be found in the case of reflexes, it is true, where via proprioceptoral processes the *level of content of hollow organs* (bladder, seminal vesicle) relieves the external stimuli of part of their releaser work and in this way lowers their threshold. A corresponding process also exists in the case of *states of deficiency* which provoke stimulation of the proprioceptors, often in a roundabout way via quite complicated indicators—e.g. thirst via the perceived sensation of a dry mucous membrane of the throat—and thus achieve their effect in the way I have hinted. But *without* such additional mechanisms which procure an accumulation of internal stimulation, this regular fluctuation of intensity and reactivity is missing in the reflex as well as in the orienting reaction composed of reflexes. If one turns a beetle on its back and thus elicits its tropotactic "turning" reaction, this experiment can be repeated until the organism as a whole or at least its effectors are exhausted, and the same is true of the menotactic light-compass reaction of a wandering ant; in all these cases the exhaustibility of the experimenter will reveal itself sooner than that of the experimental object. Conversely, however, the reflex can lie idle like an unused machine for unlimited lengths of time without any change whatever in its intensity or reactivity. Our patellar-tendon reflex does not react more easily for not having been elicited for a long time. It is quite a different matter with the instinctive act. For example, if one elicits the behavior pattern of "feigning injury" in a warbler by coming threateningly close to the nest, this will succeed once, twice; a third time the reaction is already noticeably weaker, a fourth time it may come after a short pause or even not at all. This *specific exhaustibility,* fundamentally characteristic of all instinctive acts, in fact already suggests the idea of a *reservoir* of action-specific energy,[2] the emptying of which results in the organism no longer having the behavior pattern in question "at its disposal" long before it is exhausted itself as a whole or in its effectors. The same idea of an *accumulation* of action-specific energy becomes even more obtrusive if we make the converse experiment and "dam up" the instinctive act instead of "pumping it out," i.e. reduce it to a state of permanent rest by removing all external stimuli. Now the instinctive act does something which the reflex, in accordance with the essential nature which accounts for its name, cannot do: It "strives for an outlet." This it expresses in the fact that, as already described, the threshold for the eliciting stimuli drops, and furthermore in the fact that, if accumulation becomes considerable, it sets the whole organism in a state of motoric unrest, which viewed objectively increases the probability that eliciting stimulus situations will be met, but which subjectively manifests itself as searching for these stimulus situations. Finally, however, the internal pressure of the accumulating action-specific energy reaches such proportions that it bursts through all the inhibitions imposed upon it, the reduction of threshold value for eliciting stimuli reaches zero and the motor pattern "goes off of its own accord" without any demonstrable external stimulus. Such vacuum discharge of often very highly differentiated sequences of movements makes it possible in many cases to pick out very precisely the automatic functions of an instinctive nature built into complex and partly taxis-directed motor processes. In addition, however, it is of the greatest theoretical interest that highly differentiated behavior patterns of great survival value can in this way *prove themselves to be totally independent of the animal's receptors.* Animal psychologists fixated on finality, who see in every animal movement without exception the pursuit of a goal to which the subject strives, make the dependence of the chain of actions on direction from additional stimuli positively the critical proof of their viewpoint. Arguing in favor of the purposivity of all animal behavior, Tolman (1932) made the extraordinary statement that "Animal behavior cannot go off in vacuo." By thus attempting to reduce the assumption of non-purposive behavior patterns to an absurdity, he demands that proof of their existence which we are able to offer most convincingly in the form of "vacuum activities." Even the initiated time and again find it impressive and surprising when, for instance, a starling which was hand-reared from an early age and has never caught a flying insect in its life suddenly performs the appropriate motor patterns in all their tiniest details, including beating the non-existent prey dead and swallowing it; or when a hummingbird in a cage begins to perform highly differentiated movements of wrapping non-existent nest material around a branch, and so on. Lashley (1915, 1938), who looks to the receptors for the principal explanation of all innately purposive behavior patterns, is astonished at the fact that rats can still perform complex instinctive acts after being deprived of all their main sensory organs. As we shall see, not only such a peripheral "deafferentation" but even one in the central nervous system itself fails to destroy the coordination of instinctual automatic functions.

The phenomena of accumulation of action-specific energy and its consumption in discharge of a motor pattern have long been known to physiology, although under a different name—Sherrington's *spinal contrast* (1906). One example of this phenomenon: A sea horse, *Hippocampus,* is decapitated and artificial respiration administered to the spinal animal. After a while the dorsal fin has adopted a particular, half-erected balance position. If tactile stimuli are now applied by means of pressure in the "neck" region of the fish, the fin is lowered completely, only to rise higher than before when the inhibiting stimulus diminishes again, thus explaining the name "contrast." When inhibiting stimuli have been applied for a fairly long time and are then discontinued, the fin will not only be spread to the maximum but will also begin to beat sideways for a short while. This soon ceases again and the fin gradually sinks back to the position of balance. The sideways beat does not appear until a higher level of the *same* kind of excitation has been reached than that corresponding to the erection of the fin. Both movements consume the same action-specific energy. When the fin stands "at half mast" consumption maintains a balance with the continuous production of energy, and every time consumption is prevented the result is an accumulation and consequently an intensification of erection when the obstacle is removed. Long inhibition, however, raises the level of excitation to the threshold value necessary for the beating movement. Probably more complex processes of a kind such as that of the Graylag Goose described on p. 10 are also capable of being explained in an analogous manner.

We were brought a considerable step closer to an understanding of the origin of these facts arguing so clearly against instinctive acts having reflex nature by the works of von Holst (1936 a, b, c, 1937), which were unknown to me when I first described this phenomenon. Von Holst showed that many highly differentiated and adaptive motor processes, which until then had been generally considered as reflex chains, also run off undisturbed in form and coordination even when the central nervous system of the animal concerned has been deprived of all afferent nerves and thus of the possibility of registering reflex-eliciting and directing stimuli. In the ventral nerve-cord of earthworms, just as in the spinal cord of the widest variety of teleost fishes, the motor impulses occur automatically and in rhythmic succession just like the endogenous self-stimulation occurring in the heart. Furthermore the coordination of these into adaptively ordered movements takes place, *independent of receptors,* including proprioceptors, right back in the central nervous system. Here we need not go into the processes affecting this central nervous coordination, which von Holst analyzed very precisely. We need retain only one fact: So many parallels exist between the instinctive act and excitatory processes with central nervous coordination of their impulse rhythms analyzed by von Holst that the following assumption is an amply justified working hypothesis: Wherever a species-specific motor sequence displays lowering of threshold, vacuum discharge, and, conversely, exhaustibility of action-specific energy, then endogenous excitatory processes are involved.

The range of phenomena which can be provided with an explanation of their origin through the above assumption is very wide. One must remember that it makes precisely those phenomena which have resisted all other attempts at explanation, and which are for this reason constantly and unjustly doubted, not only intelligible but even a theoretical necessity. Still wider is the range of phenomena in the study of which specific, regular fluctuations of the "current level" of action-specific energy must be taken into consideration in order to eliminate a source of error. Thus the effectiveness of *every* stimulus is quantitatively and qualitatively dependent on the current level of one or more reactions which can be elicited by it. A Mallard duck may treat an in fact neutral dummy of a flying bird at one time as a predator, at another as a conspecific male, depending on whether specific courtship actions or specific escape actions are particularly low in threshold at that moment; without knowledge of the specific regularities on which the behavior is based, this can create an impression of completely voluntary, "intra-central nervous" changes of attitude. The enormous subjective inconstancy of things in an animal's environment, as well as of the various "shadings" (Uexküll 1921) of objects, have their objective physiological correlate in the processes I have described.

III. AUTOMATIC FUNCTION AND REFLEX

The assumption that the centrally coordinated nervous automatism of the instinctive action is a clearly delineated process and above all one basically different from the reflex compels us to clarify its relationships to the reflex as well as to other not yet analyzed functions of the central nervous system. To begin with we must be clear as to which processes we still have to explain by means of the reflex element. Considered from a purely functional point of view, every process by means of which an organism gets to grips with a factor in its environment is a "reflex," in the broad sense that a stimulus coming from without is answered in a specifically regular manner. In this sense all orienting reactions which establish a relationship between the organism and the spatial conditions of its environment are also reflexes, whether these are simple and recognizable as such analytically, or as yet unanalyzed "peak" functions of the central nervous system. In the same way all those *releaser processes* via which the automatic functions otherwise kept constantly under inhibition by the influence of the higher nerve centers are set free at the biologically correct moment are also reflexes. Such a "cloak of reflexes," as von Holst (1936 b, 1937) expresses it, interposes itself as a mediator between the inflexible automatic functions and the hard conditions of the external world. In places the reflex superimposes itself, in the form of a perhaps very limited adaptation, on the movement dictated by the automatic function coordinated in the central nervous system and softens its contours, like a covering of snow on a roof. Thus from the point of view of being able to analyze the superimposed components there is as little justification for speaking of a plasticity of the instinctive act as of a "plasticity" of the shape of the roof.

A. Taxis and instinctive act

In the literature of animal psychology much fruitless strife has resulted from the fact that the concept of "instinct" was employed indiscriminately for both taxis and automatic function of the central nervous system. Thus Russel (1934) says of innate behavior simply that "it is continued until either the goal is achieved or the animal is exhausted," which is true only of taxes. McDougall (1912), arguing against the false premise *Animal non agit, agitur,* says, "The healthy animal is up and doing," which may be perfectly correct for a dog, a raven, or any other organism rich in instinctive acts, but certainly not for any reflex animal endowed with few automatic functions such as an ant-lion, a toad, or any other lower animal adapted to sitting and waiting for its prey.

The vital element which is innate in the case of the *taxis* is not a *movement* norm as with the instinctive act but a norm of *reaction to external stimuli,* which in all cases analyzed with precision so far consists of a system of reflexes in a state of readiness. Breaking down all innate behavior patterns into the reflexes and automatic functions composing them, in the right sequence, compels us to define not only the concept of the instinctive act but also that of the taxis rather more narrowly than has hitherto been usual. When we say that an organism has a "positive phototaxis," for example an asphyxiating tadpole, what we are designating with this term is in effect already a *system* of movements made up of directing reflex and automatic function, an "interlocking" of reflex and instinctive act. The snakelike locomotory movement of the tail (although investigated so far only in fishes but, as far as I know, never in amphibians) is quite certainly caused by an endogenous automatic function. The guiding turn toward the light, as well as the regular repetition of this on a smaller scale as often as the animal deviates from the direction, is reflexlike in its nature even in those cases where it is based on far more complex "peak" functions of the central nervous system. So firmly am I of the opinion that this turn, with its *stimulus-regulated dimensions,* is the vital point about the taxis, or more precisely the *topotaxis,* that it is just this process I mean when for the sake of brevity I speak simply of "taxis" in the following text.

Thus, considered precisely, the "pure" orienting movement, i.e.

one striving after an optimum, is already an interlocking of taxis and automatic function, a *system* which appears uniform but is in fact welded together out of two component parts with different origins. The same is naturally true of many, if not all, other complicated and highly differentiated innate behavior patterns, whose composition out of reflex and automatic function is for the time being accessible to analysis only in the very simplest of cases. One such case—the egg-retrieving movement of the Graylag Goose—has been investigated by Tinbergen and myself (1939). In this innate motor pattern, whose purpose is to roll any egg which has got out of the nest hollow back into it, an instinctive act and an orienting reaction work on two planes set at right angles to one another. Bending the neck, the means by which the egg is pulled in, takes place on the vertical plane. From the constancy of the strength and form of the movement, as well as from the fact that vacuum performance can easily be elicited experimentally, it follows clearly that this movement is coordinated in the central nervous system. In contrast, the small, balancing sideways movements which, all the way along, keep the egg from deviating from the nestward direction are governed by thigmotaxis, as could be proved by very simple experiments.

In another equally typical and in fact more frequent case of interlocking, the relationships between taxis and instinctive act are more complicated. The presence of a high level of specific energy associated with one particular instinctive act is expressed not only passively by a lowering of threshold for the action and its increased readiness to react; in addition it *actively* forces the higher levels of the central nervous system to be aware of it, perhaps through the fact that the automatic function requires an ever-increasing amount of energy to be devoted to maintaining the inhibition imposed upon it. In the simplest case, internal tension of this kind expresses itself in motoric unrest and, as I have already hinted, in actually undirected "searching" for the releaser stimulus situation. Usually, however, very specific taxes are built into the system of innate behavior patterns at this point which are activated only by the presence of the high current level of specific energy. Just as, for instance, the light stimulus, disregarded at other times, exerts a specific effect on a tadpole in the case of O_2 deficiency, so particular stimulus situations, often very complicated in structure, are answered by strong positive taxes *only* when there is quite a high accumulation of action-specific energy. Often, though certainly not always, once they have achieved a particular spatial situational relationship these stimulus combinations eliciting a specific taxis are also the releaser for the instinctive act. *Taxes of this kind, which are dependent on the current level value of a particular instinctive act, are called "drives."*

Expressing this in subjective terms, we may say that in such cases an orienting reaction seeks as its goal a stimulus situation through which a particular instinctive act will be specifically elicited. This type of interlocking is extremely frequent and is familiar to us all. In everyday language this means that the animal has an "appetite" for a particular instinctive act, for example eating, copulation, etc. This goal function of the instinctive act, which is of tremendous significance to an understanding of the motivation of animal and human actions, was clearly recognized for the first time by Wallace Craig (1918). In his paper, "Appetites and aversions as constituents of instincts," Craig made a sharp conceptual distinction between the two basically different parts of such chains of actions, namely the more or less variable *purposive* action which proceeds under the influence of the drive, and the purely instinctual consummatory action *satisfying* it. Like Craig, we call purposive behavior which has as its goal a stimulus situation eliciting an instinctive act *"appetitive behavior."* In the case of the analagously functioning systems composed of appetitive acts and consequent instinctive act in various animals, a specifically regular quantitative difference, which depends on the level of their mental capacities, exists between the roles assigned to each of these two single functions: The higher the mental level attained by the organism, the higher the goal which can be set the variable purposive action component. Let us consider two extreme examples of the acquisition of food—in a bird of prey and in a human being. In the former case the appetitive behavior is limited to an extremely primitive searching, containing at best a little self-conditioning, until the prey is sighted; leaving aside extremely simple guiding taxes, this is followed only by instinctive acts which actually already represent the emotive goal of the appetitive behavior striven after from the subjective point of view of the animal. In the case of a man working only with the motivation of earning his bread, however, the behavior directed at this end encompasses practically all the higher mental functions of which he is capable; the motive, the instinctive act of "breaking and eating" striven after as goal, has withdrawn a long way to the end of the series of actions, but without in any way disowning its basic instinctive nature in the process. In fact, out of the characters which make meals more "appetizing" it is quite possible to analyze the optimal, non-conditioned releasing stimuli for the instinctive acts of chewing, swallowing, etc. Thus, in man's case too the subjective purpose toward which the appetence strives is in no way identical with the objective biological success of the chain of actions. In view of this, it is positively astonishing how obstinately some animal psychologists fixated on finality persist in confusing these concepts which Craig had already clearly separated in 1918.

The gradual "withdrawal" of the instinctive act described above probably corresponds to the phylogenetic process during the "mental ascendance" of an animal form. In contrast to the opinion which prevailed for a long time and was upheld by Spencer, Lloyd Morgan, and others—that the "instinct" is the ontogenetic and phylogenetic step preceding higher mental capacity—we must clearly realize that appetitive behavior, in its capacity as sole root of all "variable" behavior, is not only something fundamentally different physiologically from the automatic function of the instinctive act, but that the two different processes also appear vicariously in that the higher development of the one renders the other unnecessary and excludes it. In a sequence of actions having the same function, the attainment of higher capacity is always accompanied by a reduction in the number of automatic functions involved, as I have discussed in my paper "The establishment of the instinct concept."[3, 4]

Considered from a subjective point of view, in cases of very complex interlocking the instinctive act may occur on one occasion, for example in the optimum taxis (p. 16) and in appetitive behavior (p. 17), as the *means,* on another occasion (p. 17) as the *end.* This has led some authors to the incorrect assumption that there are two different kinds of instinctive act (first-order drives, second-order drives, etc.). However, the objective difference between the instinctive movement functioning as end and that functioning as means lies only in the quantitative relationships between tempo of production of specific energy and probability or frequency of its elicitation. Some automatic functions, such as copulation, nest-building, etc., are elicited only rarely in the lifetime of the organism, whereas others, such as the breast-fin stroke of the Labroid Fish, the hopping of a small bird, etc., are almost continuously in motion. In the case of homologous actions, the production of action-specific energy also varies from species to species and is adapted to the daily rate of consumption: The fin-stroke of a Labroid Fish hovering freely in the water continues virtually without interruption, even in the deafferented spinal animal, whereas the corresponding fin-stroke of the (usually perched) sea horse has to be "saved up for" by means of inhibition before it can appear at all through spinal contrast (p. 12). Still greater, understandably enough, are the quantitative differences between instinctive acts differing widely in function, for instance a mode of locomotion, the extreme example of an everyday "tool" activity, and copulation, the extreme example of a self-rewarding instinctive act. In closest correlation with this difference in tempo of production of action-specific energy for these two typical forms of instinctive act stands the *selectivity* of the releasing mechanisms activating them. The automatic functions belonging to everyday tool activities are not set in motion only by fairly unspecific and frequently occurring stimulus situations; instead, every single one of these motor patterns can be activated by *very many* and very varied mechanisms in the central nervous system, ranging from simplest unconditioned reflex to completely unanalyzed "voluntary" disinhibition. The *applicability* of these simple motor elements is correspondingly manifold. In contrast, the self-rewarding instinctive act which is seldom required virtually never has more than *one single,* highly specific function, and accordingly only one releasing mechanism, usually a system of unconditioned reflexes (what is called an "innate schema"), which rigorously selects the sole biologically correct situation. Instinctive acts such as this can never be "voluntarily" disinhibited. On the basis of these, in every respect only gradual differences, even the most extreme contrasts between tool activity and self-rewarding instinctive act can be freely explained: In spite of their rapid production of endogenous excitation, the tool actions, just because they are so easy to elicit, normally never accumulate so strongly that they give rise to action-specific urge and appetitive behavior. A dog easily finds occasion to run, or a mouse something to gnaw, etc. However, because its stimulus requirements are so specialized, the seldom required instinctive act which has been developed as a special function will never be able to appear except after a more or less clearly observable appetitive act or at least a positive taxis toward the releasing stimulus situation. That it should be elicited by chance before an accumulation of action-specific energy has activated the drive toward it is generally unlikely though basically possible. Conversely it is possible to turn any tool activity into a drive goal at any time through the simplest of experiments, by depriving the animal of any opportunity of transforming the internally produced excitation of the automatic function concerned into movement and thus discharging it. In such a case, not only does the everyday motor pattern almost immediately display a lowering of threshold and vacuum discharge, but it also becomes just as much the goal of a positively irresistible subjective striving as does any self-rewarding instinctive act in the free-ranging animal. In excellent experiments, Luther (verbal communication) has proved that mice given the possibility of discharging their locomotory automatic functions on a wheel made absolutely no attempt to gnaw their way out of their confined quarters, but that they did so at once when he made the wheel immovable. The same is correspondingly true of the running of dogs, the flying of the raven, etc.

The automatic functions serving the tool activities, particularly those of all locomotory movements, which with their almost inexhaustible production are at the disposal of any orienting reaction and any other kind of appetitive behavior, are usually regarded as *voluntary actions.* Herein lies a source of error, even in those cases in which the highest levels of the central nervous system do in fact directly control the release of the automatic functions. In accordance with the foregoing, there is absolutely no sharp dividing line between the more frequently occurring instinctive movements which may be unspecifically elicited and the rarer ones requiring more specific stimuli: Likewise the "same" homologous motor pattern in two animals, e.g. flying, may be closer to the first type in the one case (for instance, in a small passerine bird) and to the second type in the other (for instance, in the Graylag Goose). If one presents the passerine bird with a detour problem requiring flying for its solution, on account of its extremely high endogenous production one may safely ignore the current state of its action-specific energy and assume that the higher levels of the central nervous system have this motor pattern at their disposal to a fairly constant degree. But if one sets a similar task to the Graylag Goose, in whose case flying is one of the rarer motor patterns, then the current level of the automatic function certainly must be taken into consideration if one is not to arrive at completely misleading results regarding the higher mental capacities of the bird. In a detour experiment requiring the use of the wings, after a period of time roughly constant in relation to the experimental conditions the goose will, it is true, manifest its "insight" into the situation by going to a spot best suited to take-off and there making intention movements of flying off. But when it actually *will* fly off no longer lies with the higher levels of its central nervous system. The goose *wants* to fly, it "tries to put itself in the mood for take-off," and anyone familiar with geese can predict the moment when it will fly from the intensity of its intention movements. This is dependent, however, not on the will but on the current level of action-specific excitation. Geese which, immediately after a long, continuous flight which has considerably reduced this level, find themselves in a situation obliging them to fly over a fence, often display "insight" and intention movements of flight after only a few seconds, but they do not actually manage to take off for many hours or even until next day. Experience and a knowledge of the obstacle alter nothing: The same bird which has often accomplished the task before will still fail when the automatic function of flight is exhausted. Since analogous processes are widely distributed throughout the animal kingdom, when making learning and intelligence experiments one must always take into consideration the "degree of voluntary availability" or the current level of the required instinctive act.

B. The releasing schema

One function of the "cloak of reflexes" clearly separable from spatial orientation is the *release* of innate behavior patterns in particular situations in which they fulfil their biological purpose. The pricking act of the common tick is a reaction to the simple combined effect of the temperature stimulus of 37°C and a chemical stimulus from butyric acid. Simple though this stimulus combination is, it suffices to effect the strict selection of those biological situations in which the motor pattern "fits." Under natural circumstances it is almost infinitely unlikely that an object which is *not* the appropriate host, namely a mammal, should transmit these two sign stimuli and cause the tick to prick by mistake. Such a sensory correlate to a combination of stimuli eliciting unconditioned reflexes *characterizes* a particular biological situation by means of a *simplified* rendering of its most significant features, which is why we call it an innate *schema*. Not only instinctive acts but also taxes, as well as behavior patterns with a complicated structure made up of both, may be linked to innate schemata which are the releasing mechanisms determining the choice of the appropriate occasion. Tinbergen and Kuenen (1939), in their investigation of the gaping reaction of Blackbird nestlings, have shown that the automatic functions and directional mechanisms involved in this reaction are activated *independently of one another* by completely *different* stimulus combinations. It is quite possible experimentally to separate the stimuli causing a nestling to sit up and open its beak from those which direct the gaping action toward the head of the parent bird. In accordance with Tinbergen's findings, in all investigations of this kind the stimulus situations eliciting the instinctive act and those determining the direction must be considered quite separately from one another for they are by no means automatically identical. *One* schema belongs to *one* reaction, and since dealing with one and the same object usually involves a whole number, a *system,* of taxes and automatic functions, it is actually a misuse of the term to speak of *the* "innate schema" of *the* conspecific, sexual partner, prey, etc., as has become usual, and for which I unfortunately am largely to blame. One cannot actually say that the sum of the sensory correlates referring to one object produces a "total schema" of the object: Experimentally every action dependent on its own releasing schema may be elicited completely independently of all other reactions intended for the same object.

The method of investigating innate schemata is the *experiment with dummies,* for which, as Koehler (1933) has shown, two paths lie open: the reduction of features, starting from the natural, adequate object, and conversely reconstruction, which starts with the simplest dummies and progresses to equality of effectiveness between dummy and natural object. Since a human can best control the presence of optical stimuli in an experimental setup, most people investigating rather highly organized innate schemata take schemata of an optical nature as their subject. Thus, Goethe (1940 a) found that in response to a dummy bird of prey pulled along on a wire young capercaillie produced a reaction which clearly differed quantitatively from their reaction to other, only slightly simpler dummies. It is interesting that already in the 20-day-old chicks this reaction differed according to sex, in that the hen chicks took to cover but the cock adopted a defensive posture. Tinbergen and I now attempted to develop such experiments further and subjected practically all the young birds available in Altenberg in the spring of 1937 to predator dummies which were moved along a wire hung between two tall trees. Graylag Geese did not themselves react to predator dummies until from approximately their eighth week onward; up till then, in natural conditions, they are induced to perform the same actions by the alarm call of the parent birds. Thus, even when the opportunity to acquire the bird of prey schema by means of individual learning is there, the reaction still matures of its own accord at a particular time independent of experience and the example of the parent birds. The features which a dummy must have if it is to elicit the reaction of *taking cover* in its full intensity indicate that this is intended for one very particular bird of prey, namely the White-tailed Eagle. The general bird shape of the dummy is of little significance. What is important, however, is that the object outlined against the sky *moves forward only slowly in relation to its size,* in other words *measured in its own body lengths.* This is interesting because we humans also judge the size of a bird flying high in the sky by the same criterion. In spite of their smallness, feathers floating past are always stared at by Graylag Geese, but never small birds flying quickly overhead. A dummy, roughly the size of a starling and symmetrical fore and aft, which could be pulled to and fro infinitely often, elicited the most intensive alert postures, alarm calls, and withdrawal in the direction of cover if it was moved across slowly. But when, the next moment, it was pulled back swiftly, not one eye held onto it, although every single goose was still looking skyward. It was particularly clear that the slow dummy was perceived, as it were, projected high into the air, but the fast-moving one only as a small bird flying low. Pigeons, which would come gliding very slowly into view in the sky when there was a strong wind against them, could elicit the reaction to the White-tailed Eagle, but only as long as they *did not flap their wings*. As soon as they did so, reassurance became evident. Calm gliding may, therefore, unconditionally be taken as a feature of the innate schema. It is different in the case of ducks. Year after year in spring these birds react to the newly arrived Swifts by going on the alert or even by looking for cover (negative phototaxis), whereas the geese take no notice of them. On the other hand, ducks are much less afraid of airplanes than geese are. This renders even more probable the assumption that the releasing schema for the escape reaction of the geese is intended primarily for the White-tailed Eagle, that of the ducks, however, for falcons. Our experiments with the geese were brought to a premature but amusing end by the undesired development of conditioned reflexes. After a considerable period of experimentation, the geese began to perform the eagle reaction as soon as Tinbergen or I took a waist-jump onto the lowest branch of the tree where the wire hung. In fact, a waist-jump onto any tree was sufficient to make them look suspiciously skyward and make off for the nearest cover. For experiments concerning the innate schema one should really have fresh young birds every time, with which one can be certain that one is working on "virgin soil."

Whereas in the case of Graylag Geese and also ducklings (with adult, hand-reared ducks we were unable to experiment for technical reasons) the shape of the dummy is not important to its effect, or at least not in a statistically clear manner, we were able to prove that the opposite is true in the case of turkeys. For these experiments we relied on the observation made by Heinroth, that domestic chicken fear short-necked, long-tailed birds more than long-necked ones. We produced a dummy which had one pair of wings symmetrical fore and aft and, in the longitudinal axis, at one end a short and at the other a longer extension which looked like head or tail depending on the direction of movement. And in effect the turkeys reacted far more strongly when the dummy was moved with the short end at the front, as could easily be quantified from the number of alarm calls uttered.[5]

Innate schemata attain their highest differentiation where a conspecific is the adequate object of the reaction. In all other cases a limit is imposed on the differentiation of the schema resulting from the number and type of perceptible characteristics the object possesses. The lock cannot be developed further than the key, and this latter is in general not subject to the developmental processes of the species concerned but is a fixed factor of the external world. It is different when the object of the reaction is a conspecific. Then the possibility exists of progressively differentiating the stimulus transmitters and the innate schemata simultaneously, coupled together in a significant, effective unit. To put it quite bluntly, a Pike cannot "arrange" for an additional signal to develop on its prey which would keep it from discharging its predatory reaction on the wrong object; but in phylogenetic terms *Poephila gouldiae*, for example, was able to attach a little signal lantern to the corner of the beak of the young bird and simultaneously develop a sensory correlate to it in the parent bird. Stimulus transmitters of this kind we call "releasers." They may consist of morphological differentiations or conspicuous motor patterns, but usually they are a system built up out of both. Releasers can be developed in connection with any of the senses—tactile, like the love-dart of the *Pulmonata;* olfactory, like so many scent-producing organs; acoustic, like absolutely all the differentiations serving the production of sound. For reasons I have already mentioned, the best experimental objects are those transmitting optical stimuli. The entire sociology of higher animals is built up on the basis of releasers and innate schemata, and the thin putty of acquired behavior patterns is relatively so unimportant that as a basic principle any sociological investigation should start by analyzing the two innate elements mentioned above. The first good analyses in this field came from G. W. and E. G. Peckham (1889), who as far back as the middle of the last century were making genuine dummy experiments with spiders. It is true that the spiders they used were of a different species from that of their dummies, but their discussion of the effectiveness of the individual features is thoroughly discerning and exemplary. In the meantime a whole series of investigations has appeared, innumerable valuable observations by Heinroth (1910, 1930), the painstaking investigations of Sticklebacks by Pelkwijk and Tinbergen (1937), experiments on Herring Gulls by Goethe (1937), on the

Fighting Fish by Lissmann (1932), the investigation of the mating behavior of *Sepia* by L. Tinbergen (1939), and many others.

Differentiations serving the transmission of releaser stimuli are many. Of these, instinctive movements command particular interest since they are the only ones which have so far provided us with some insight into their *phylogenetic development*. As comparative research shows, almost all these signals are derived from actions which originally had a practical use, and the derivation has taken one of two possible paths. The one kind is represented by intention movements, which became releasers and in the process have undergone a particular kind of formalization and expressive over-accentuation, thereby increasing their stimulus transmitting effect but in some cases changing them so much as to make them unrecognizable. To this kind of releaser I have given the name *symbolic act*. The second phylogenetic way in which releaser instinctive movements have originated is based on the fact that, when the general level of excitation is high, certain automatic functions such as walking become easily disinhibited. For example, a man displays the nervous tension of giving a lecture by walking to and fro. Now, with some specific types of excitation it can happen that in a quite specifically regular and predictable manner the excitation "sparks over" onto the disinhibition mechanisms of other automatic functions. This phenomenon, discovered by Tinbergen (1940) and Kortlandt (1938) independently of one another, has likewise led to the creation of releasers, whereby the actions activated by the displacement of excitation may undergo a change through formalization and over-accentuation similar to that undergone by the symbolic act. The fact that they have originated from displacement activities explains the singular change of meaning of some actions. Thus a formalized preening behind the wing signifies an introduction to mating in the case of the domestic pigeon, threat in the case of the crane, and so on. According to Makkink (1936), the sleeping-posture of the avocet has even become a gesture of threat!

The systems of innate schemata are a splendid field for comparative phylogenetic research because in an investigation of these we can virtually rule out the phenomenon of *convergence*. The particular form of movements which have been ceremonially over-accentuated and then become stereotyped cannot be explained by their function but exclusively in terms of their historical origin. As a result, just as in the case of human speech symbols, if two signaling systems found in different animal groups living separately are identical, this always signifies homology. Otherwise it could only be explained by pure coincidence, which is almost infinitely improbable. These circumstances often permit us to clarify phylogenetic relationships with a degree of probability seldom granted to purely morphological research.

The existence of highly complicated systems of releasers and of innate schemata is of great interest when discussing the Darwinian view of sexual selection (1871). Bright colors and shapes, such as are displayed in the courtship of many birds, reptiles, and teleost fish, *naturally occur in other releasers as well,* which is quite easily explained by their function as a signal. It is, however, thoroughly erroneous to quote the way in which these non-sexual releasers function as an argument in favor of the assumption that such conspicuous differentiations could not also have been bred as a result of sexual selection in the narrowest Darwinian sense. Quite to the contrary, we now know that the most extreme male display markings occur precisely in the case of those animals the males of which do not fight but have a social form of courtship, during which they are selected in a process of active mate-choosing by the female. Thus the Mandarin Duck, which has the most colorful male display markings of all ducks, is precisely the species in which social courtship is most highly developed and the female most active in mate-choosing. The facts are similar in the case of the Bird of Paradise, the Ruff, the Peacock, and so on. All these striking display markings have certainly originated as a result of sexual selection in the narrowest sense.

One question of interest to psychology is whether one may call innate schemata "gestalts." The functionally uniform and purposeful behavior an animal displays toward an object characterized by innate schemata, for instance a conspecific, all too easily causes the observer to overlook the fact that this uniformity has its bases not in the acting subject but in a combination of eliciting features in the object. The subject performs each one of the reactions involved just as readily in response to a dummy which transmits solely the stimuli belonging to the releasing schema of this one reaction alone. The stimulus combinations which elicit unconditioned reflexes and whose sensory correlates we call innate schemata are never *complex qualities.* This is in sharp contrast to those stimulus situations which elicit actions on the basis of acquired conditioned reflexes. Even the most primitive cases of self-conditioning in animals quite low on the intellectual scale are wont to be linked to a positively incalculable abundance of features in the eliciting situation. It is a source of continual surprise that a small and apparently irrelevant change, which one did not even think the animal would notice, can so alter the complex quality of a situation as a whole for the animal that its conditioning no longer works. In the case of birds, for example, the smallest change in their familiar surroundings suffices to unbalance completely all behavior patterns linked to habit; a path need only be strewn with a different kind of sand to prevent cranes or Graylag Geese from alighting on it as usual. In the case of the innate schema, however, the most incredible and, to our eyes, the most important features of the situation as a whole may be omitted; if only the few stimuli "provided for" in the schema are present, the reaction is discharged just as intensively in response to the simplified dummy as to the normal situation. This is also true of organisms which in their reaction to conditioned releaser situations display the discernment described above in their perception of complex qualities. A Jackdaw is capable of distinguishing about 20 conspecifics individually from one another by means of minute differences in the complex qualities of the physiognomy, yet it discharges its social defensive reaction with equal intensity whether the object seized before its eyes is one of its personal friends from the Jackdaw colony or a pair of black bathing trunks! The words written by Demoll more than 20 years ago (1933), "The hereditary nature of the instinct gives cause to expect automatically that it may be elicited only by the simplest stimuli," are fully valid even today, provided we substitute for "instinct" our concept of the schema.

A good comparison for the function of the innate schema is provided by the verbal *description* of an object. This can never convey the complex quality of the sensory perception but only a total of individual features. Now, if we assume that the number of individual features in the object to be identified from a verbal description is restricted, and further that the receiver of the description is somewhat limited and capable of identifying only very clear, absolute features in the actual object but not of making distinctions of a relative or quantitative nature, then we have before us a model of the function of the innate schema which is in complete accord with the facts. Let us assume that by means of a description in words we have to designate, let us say, a female gadwall so clearly to someone with no knowledge of the subject that he is capable of distinguishing her from all other female Dabbling Ducks. This will be possible only by taking those few features which have been differentiated by the species as releasers and which therefore display the distinctiveness and simplicity typical of such organs. In the case of the duck these are solely the colors of the speculum and their distribution. If we exclude this sole releaser the duck possesses from our consideration and think of her, say, swimming, when her wings are closed and the speculum is hidden, then designation by means of mere description is virtually impossible. It is as easy to train even someone with only moderate intelligence to recognize the *complex quality* of a swimming female gadwall as it is difficult, even impossible, to convey this ability to him by means of summative description. Even a nature lover who unhesitatingly names the duck correctly will scarcely be able to name the features which guide him in his decision. In contrast, an animal in whose external form *releasers* play an important part can always be designated easily by means of summative description as well. This circumstance also drew our attention to the relative *simplicity* of the stimulus combinations which is so tremendously characteristic of all genuine releasers, and to the limitations of the function of the innate schemata being discussed here. *If the innate schema were able, like the conditioned reflex, to react selectively to complex qualities, then releasers would not need to exist!* Taking these considerations, based on the nature of the releaser and on a few chance observations, as our point of departure, we first undertook experiments on Mallards to find out to what extent the presence of releasers is decisive for the innate recognition of the conspecific. The following result emerged: A female which I reared from the egg in company with pintails and isolated from its own conspecifics never showed even the slightest sexual reaction toward a male pintail. When, however, contrary to my intentions, she caught sight of a male Mallard for the first time in the neighboring enclosure through a gap between two boards, a highly impressive explosive outburst of female courtship actions resulted. In contrast, however, a male Mallard, isolated from its conspecifics and reared with pintails, was converted to the other species in its mating reactions, but it is interesting to note that it mounted both male and female pintails indiscriminately. For social courtship it sought out male Mallards. Thus, the reaction to the releasers in the male display markings was innate to it also, but not the complex quality of the female plumage. Seitz has analyzed the same phenomenon even more clearly in the cichlid fish, *Astatotilapia*. If one tries to elicit fighting reactions in a male that has been reared normally in the company of its conspecifics, imitation of the releasers of one of its own sex will achieve this without difficulty. The blue color of the display markings, the sheen on the scales, and more especially the movement features of the threat display are important, analogous to the findings of Pelkwijk and Tinbergen (1937) in the male Stickleback. If one tries, however, to elicit courtship in the cichlid by means of a dummy, in contrast to the Stickleback this does not work. The dummy must be a faithful copy of a female in every detail and a certain lowering of the threshold for the reaction must be present, and even then all that is achieved are a few half-hearted indications of courtship movements. In contrast to the female Stickleback a female *Astatotilapia* possesses *no specific releaser.* This extremely high selectivity of the courtship reaction is based on the fact that it reacts to a complex quality in the female which is learned. A male reared in isolation courted any dummy whatsoever, but in its reaction to combinations of stimuli eliciting fighting it did not differ at all from the normal control animals. Thus for *Astatotilapia* it is also proven that only the simple, distinctive stimuli of the releaser are matched by innate sensory correlates, but that the reaction to complex qualities must be acquired in the form of conditioned reactions. All these findings are in sharp contrast to the so-called archetype theory of Jung (1938), which was quoted to an extensive degree by Alverdes (1937) to explain innate behavior patterns and which proceeds from the assumption of innate gestalt images, rather like pictures perceived, and indeed assumes that a "projection" of such pictures into the motor system can take place!

It is perhaps possible with certain reservations to regard the individual features of an innate schema as "gestalts": The short-neckedness of the bird-of-prey schema of the turkey, the relative head size, transposable into various absolute sizes, of the gaping schema of the young blackbird, have certain characteristics of the gestalt. Quite certainly, however, the relation to and alongside one another of the *various* features characterizing a stimulus situation or an object has neither wholeness nor gestalt. Above all its eliciting effect is in fact *summative,* as Seitz has shown in his so far unpublished work on cichlids. In this he speaks specifically of a law of stimulus summation. This states quite simply that no single feature of a releasing stimulus combination is qualitatively indispensable to its effect, but that the strong total effect of the adequate object or of a dummy transmitting all vital stimuli is based on summation. The effect of the individual features in this sum is *quantifiable,* if only roughly and relatively. If one omits the blue sheen from a fighting dummy for *Astatotilapia,* then particular movement releasers must be copied more precisely; in the case of the Stickleback the color red is approximately as important to the following reaction of the female as all features of shape, i.e. without red the dummy must otherwise be very precise, *with* red a plasticine ball is sufficient. When one weighs the relative effect of individual releasing features against one another in this way, *movement features*—in other words, all instinctive acts having effect as releasers—regularly prove vastly to outweigh all others quantitatively, so much so that in certain circumstances they become "indispensable." Thus in the case of the Stickleback a particular instinctive act by the male, which Leiner (1929) has called the "zigzag dance," can scarcely be omitted without the following reaction of the female sinking to minimal intensity or failing to appear altogether. The same is correspondingly true of movement releasers in the case of *Astatotilapia*.

The existence of the phenomenon of stimulus summation in the innate schemata renders it possible to quantify in a dual manner in the case of every process eliciting an instinctive act. One can, as Lissmann (1932) did with the Fighting Fish, take the duration of the reaction as a measure of the effectiveness of the dummy presented. The experimental animal goes on reacting until the threshold level for elicitation has risen above the value necessary for reaction to the dummy. After the dummy, the fully adequate stimulus situation is always presented in order to find out "how much was left," for the current level of action-specific energy is dependent on many factors and cannot be forecast with certainty from the length of accumulation alone. Scarcely perceptible physical damage, for example, is already sufficient to slow down accumulation considerably. Allowing for these sources of error, one can also quantify successfully in the *converse* direction, by taking as a measure of the effectiveness of a dummy the length of time a reaction must be dammed up before this dummy is able to release it. Both methods may be employed to investigate the relative speed of specific energy production, e.g. in the case of different individuals or races, or in the case of one individual and different temperatures, etc. Related to one another in this way, the phenomena of the relative effectiveness of features and the continuous lowering of the action-specific stimulus threshold create the positive impression of possessing specific regularities, whereas the behavior of the animal, above all the changeability of its reaction to constant stimulus situations, *appears* to be completely and chaotically unpredictable if one is unaware of the *two* specific regularities on which it is based. As a matter of fact, just these phenomena have been quoted in the most widely varying quarters as examples of what cannot be rationalized. Despite the existence of technical sources of error, which is expressly admitted here, the effects of the phenomena just described are so regular that from certain inconsistencies between the two specific regularities when superimposed on one another Seitz (1940) succeeded in deducing a third—that of the so-called "inertia phenomenon" of the instinctive act. If one takes an animal which at that moment does not react to a particular object because the current level of some action-specific energy or other is too low, leaves this animal with the object and waits for the lowering of threshold which leads to eventual reaction, then from a theoretical point of view one would expect that once the threshold level for the given object is reached the instinctive act would begin to "trickle out" slowly at minimum intensity, as is in fact the case, for example, with the spinal sea horse, discussed on p. 12. In the intact animal, however, once the instinctive act has begun to react it continues to do so for longer than would be expected in accordance with the above considerations, thereby causing the threshold of the current level of its specific energy to sink below the height of the threshold at which the instinctive act began to react from a state of rest. The more intensively the reaction "got going," the greater this span is, as Seitz was able to show from the differences in the length of time elapsing before the next reaction came. Other details of these phenomena also suggest the conceptual model of an "initial friction" and a "reaction inertia."

It is not the task of the present paper to convince anyone of the correctness of the viewpoints represented here. Without exception they must be regarded as working hypotheses, and we are well aware what crass simplifications of reality they are. Nor do we believe that with the few phenomena we have begun to analyze we can prepare a system which explains everything. We have a proper respect both for the proven findings of others, including those investigating the conditioned reflex, as well as for what as yet remains unanalyzed. In the foregoing I have myself repeatedly used the word "voluntary," which is a useful but likewise dangerous omnibus designation for the not-yet-analyzed and the supposedly impossible-to-rationalize in animal and human behavior. One fact I hope, however, to have demonstrated to some extent: The comparative study of behavior offers an enormous field for genuine holistic causal analysis, a field in which descriptive-comparative research and the experimentation which so far is only in its preparatory stages have yet to begin to set a limit on the speculation still generally customary even today. Neither with philosophical speculations nor with anticipatory explanatory principles, such as the "vitalist fantasy" of Buytendijk (1933) or the "archetypes" of Jung (1930), shall we make any substantial progress in knowledge, but exclusively by means of the modest and, unfortunately, in our case particularly protracted and costly daily grind of inductive research. The objects of this research, however, are deep-rooted and ancient structures, including those of *our own mind*, about which we are sadly in need of knowledge.

PAUL LEYHAUSEN

2 Introduction to the Study of Impression (1951)

One vital aid a teacher has to help him form a judgment of children is the study of expression. This branch of modern psychology founded by Klages (1936) is based on two conditions.
1. Any emotional activity in us can be experienced by another person only to the extent that it results in bodily processes.
2. All our movements, however mechanically and single-mindedly they are performed, always contain a quantity of subtle details which are not explained by the purpose of the movement but are indicative of both our permanent mental peculiarities and our momentary emotional state.

These facts are common knowledge. Yet researchers into expression have so far almost completely overlooked one fact which is as crucial to the possibility of making a science out of expression as are the laws of expression themselves: namely, the fact that expression acquires significance in the social life of humans (and thus as a means of forming a judgment of people) only when it becomes *impression*, i.e. when someone is capable of perceiving and recognizing expression as such. This may seem self-evident but is far from being so. Klages himself has seen the problem already and speaks of the "polarity of expression and impression." However, whereas research into expression has blossomed and flourished, human psychology has as yet made no research worth mentioning into impression. In contrast to

32

this, animal psychologists have done a great deal of work in recent times which belongs under the heading of impression research, only in this context one speaks of the investigation of "innate releasing schemata" or, adopting the Anglo-Saxon usage, "innate releasing mechanisms" (hereafter abbreviated to IRMs) (Lorenz 1943 a).

In the case of animals, behavior toward food and enemies, during mating and the care of offspring, and in the herd community is largely regulated by an innate comprehension of the situation which is quite independent of experience and learning, with the result that a particular form of behavior is reliably elicited at the "biologically correct" moment. We must, however, beware of incautious generalizations: Not all the behavior of animals is determined from the start by such hereditary mechanisms and there are often considerable differences from species to species in this respect. Where one species possesses an IRM, its nearest relative may be obliged to rely on individual experience.

Of particular importance in our context are those IRMs which regulate social intercourse among animals of the same species. In these cases, not only must an apparatus (the IRM) be available in the perceptual capacities of the individual animal which on arrival of specific stimuli releases the activity corresponding to the situation ("lock-key relationship"): The sign stimuli, which usually consist of specific, conspicuous shapes, colors, and motor patterns in the partner animal, are likewise subject to a form of phylogenetic selection aimed at rendering them increasingly conspicuous and impossible to confuse with other natural processes. The spread tail of turkey and peacock, the splendid colors of male ducks, the curious movements of a male pigeon cooing, the arched back of a cat, the tail-wagging of a dog, and much else owe their origin and present-day form largely to the influence exerted on breeding by the corresponding IRMs.

One example: A herd of deer is grazing in a woodland clearing. Suddenly one animal raises its head, scents the air briefly, and bounds off. As it does so it spreads into an ellipse the wreath of white hairs which decorate the behinds of these animals and are almost invisible when they are relaxed. In next to no time all the other animals are up and away, too. This so-called "sympathetic induction of mood" is far from self-explanatory. Klages is much mistaken when he considers that the movement of one animal always arouses a tendency to perform the same movement in any conspecifics watching. When several cats are kept together, if one runs away suddenly, the others are not in the least concerned if they cannot themselves perceive the reason.

Now, many experiments have shown that these IRMs obey different rules from those governing that comprehension of situation we have acquired through experience and learning which is designated as perception in the narrower sense. The sign stimuli essential for the arousal of an IRM do not, namely, combine in their effect to a whole or a perceptual gestalt, but achieve their effect purely through their summation; incompleteness achieves solely a quantitative diminution of the releaser effect but not a qualitative change in it, as is automatically the case with a perceptual gestalt if one of the conditions essential to its creation is changed or even omitted altogether.

Taking laughing and the movements of human intimidation display and threat as their examples, Wolfgang Schmidt (1951) and the author (unpublished) were able to prove that immediate comprehension of expression by humans is also subject to the law of summation of heterogeneous stimuli. As a result, man must also possess innate comprehension, i.e. IRMs, at least for a whole series of facial expressive movements and bodily gestures.

The fact that IRMs are involved in the general impression we receive from another person has particular consequences. Firstly, IRMs supply impressions at a speed at which not even the most practiced connoisseur of people can arrive at a judgment based on conscious observation. We react immediately and without being able to account for it to the finest nuances of expression in a partner. The evaluation of sensory data in the IRM probably takes place not via the optical cortex and other components of the cerebral cortex but directly in the mid-brain.[1] Speaking in psychological terms this means that without considerations, comparisons, conclusions, and judgments being involved they are transformed instantly into emotional reactions and tendencies to movement (own expression!). In this way, we have already adopted an emotional attitude toward the other person which, being impossible to justify rationally, is all the more resistant to any criticism based on insight. Since furthermore it arrives sooner than any judgment founded upon conscious observation, it exercises a kind of censorship and prejudices our objectivity toward the observational material provided by the partner (or the experimental subject).

It would be wrong to regard this fact only as a disadvantage. As we have seen, in the case of animals the IRMs largely guarantee "correct" behavior toward a conspecific. In our case, too, the emotional attitude adopted toward another person is often far more "correct" than our judgment of him we deduce rationally. Unfortunately, however, our IRMs no longer operate with the same reliability as those of animals; above all, individual people are gifted to differing degrees in this respect—in fact, cases of almost complete "impression blindness" exist.

I should like to mention briefly one of the possible malfunctions of IRMs. Lersch (1943) points to the difference between "lasting traces of expression" in the face and "facial architecture" (i.e. individual peculiarities with an anatomical basis) and warns against regarding facial architecture as having expressive content. He does not, however, ask himself how we arrive at such a misunderstanding in the first place. In animals (with the exception of our domestic animals, which occupy a special position), anatomical features frequently represent a measure of health and thus of social acceptability; I have already mentioned that anatomical and behavioral features enter the IRMs of animals with equal rights. Originally things must undoubtedly have been the same with humans. Somewhere along his developmental path, however, man has partly lost that harmony between external appearance and internal value. Yet his IRMs have not been able to adapt so quickly to the changed conditions. This is the reason why it is particularly difficult for us to adopt and maintain an objective attitude toward people who are strikingly beautiful or ugly. Likewise our IRM is incapable of distinguishing between a face that is broad and round by nature and one that is broadened by the expression of benevolence and smiling kindliness. It is the features as such which create an effect on the IRM without concern for their origin (Lorenz 1940, 1943 a, 1950 b).

What practical interest do these facts have for a teacher? Let us take the following consideration: Even under ideal school conditions and with the most extensive psychological training, a teacher has no choice but to base his judgment of a child largely on the general impression he has of him, and this is particularly true nowadays when classes everywhere contain far too many pupils. In this "general impression" there is a usually uncontrolled and often uncontrollable mixture of conscious observation and "intuitive perception." This so-called intuition consists for its part of (1) observations which were made more or less "on the edge of consciousness" when the attention was fixed on something else and which, instead of undergoing conscious evaluation, were relegated to some near-, sub-, or unconsciousness; (2) emotional attitudes elicited by IRMs.

Now it must already have happened to every teacher with some experience that his consciously founded judgment and his emotional attitude have come into open conflict. He is then faced with the choice of adopting the one or the other. If he represses his "personal feelings" in order not to do the child an injustice, it can easily happen that these feelings will be justified later. But it can just as soon turn out to be a serious mistake if he follows his "hunch." I believe, however, that the possibility exists of making the choice not according to principle or inclination but with just discrimination.

As I see it, there are three possible methods of checking. The teacher should

1. Take the external appearance and conduct of the child in question item by item (in other words, *not as a whole*) and note the emotional effect which each single one has on him. In this way it is possible to discover which details evoke the attitude which is contrary to the rest of the judgment, and one can then decide how much genuine expression these contain. This procedure can be employed with real success, however, only by people who possess a certain amount of self-knowledge and practice in self-observation. Anyone else will find that he cannot discover one single feature which appears to be responsible for the emotional attitude.

2. Look for people who arouse the same or a similar emotional reaction as the person to be judged. Then by means of comparison it is often relatively simple to establish the common factor and its expressive value. Here it should be noted, however, that the factor common to the persons being compared may be purely external and have a different expressive value in each case, although the value of the impression is the same throughout.

3. Observe carefully the relationship between the child in question and those of his fellow pupils in whose case a judgment seems easiest and most clear-cut. This often makes it possible to arrive at specific conclusions concerning the justifiability of one's own emotional attitude.

Anyone who employs these three methods conscientiously will in most cases receive confirmation of his emotional attitude which can now also be rationalized, or discover that it was evoked by mere external appearances without any real expressive value. In the latter case the more or less obscure feeling is replaced by a rationally justifiable judgment which corrects the previous evaluation by taking new experiences and insight into consideration. The IRM, however, remains "blind," and in individual cases we shall always have to check anew whether it is fooling us with external appearances, or whether it is pointing out to us fundamentals of the personality which have so far remained hidden to our consciously observing eye.

3 The Relationship Between Drive and Will in its Significance to Educational Theory

(1952)

I. THE AUTONOMOUS SYSTEM OF DRIVES[1]

Since time immemorial the question of the relationship between drive and will and how far it is possible to exercise educational influence on both has been at the core of every theory of education. This is understandable, for receptivity to educational matter of every kind is determined—apart from intellectual ability—first and foremost by the type and inclination of the driving forces active in a person. The answer to the question how and to what extent these forces themselves prove accessible to the molding and orienting endeavors of a teacher is crucial to the basic attitude with which the teacher approaches his task, and thus largely also to his success. In the past the question has received biased answers, both in the affirmative and the negative, and good arguments could be found for both. As a result, for the moment the idea that it is a "bit of both" has prevailed: It is assumed that disposition largely determines the development of motivation but still leaves enough room for profound educational influence. By itself this compromise formula has not removed the existing uncertainty. As far as I know, namely, there has not been one acceptable attempt at an analysis which would tell us which aspects of our motivational nature it is impossible to influence and which may be more or less molded by means of external influences.

Yet, we need just this knowledge if success is to be in reasonable relation to the outlay in educational means. As we shall see, there are motivational structures which are truly inflexible and inaccessible to influence. Furthermore, the degree to which it is possible to mold those structures which are plastic does not remain constant, but is dependent on the most varied developmental rhythms superimposed on one another; about these relationships, however, the teacher needs to be better informed than hitherto in order to be able to apply pressure at the right point and at the right time. This is possible only if the motivational nature is not lumped together as a "whole." On the contrary, ever subtler functional details must be recognized, for only by means of an analytical procedure of this kind can the possibilities of a causally effective character training be fully exploited. The present article is an attempt in this direction. The viewpoints expressed may seem strange, indeed unsuitable, to some; but I believe it is time to oppose the all too biased school of thought based on subjective phenomenology at present dominant with another which should, for its part, not be regarded as absolute either, but which likewise may not be neglected as it has been hitherto if we are to hope to widen our knowledge.

In order to clarify the relationship between drive and will, we must first investigate what "drive" actually is. To this end a consideration of the physiological aspect of the phenomenon is necessary. It is not that I want to explain away the mental experience of "inner compulsion," of "feeling compelled" to do something, by means of physiological processes: As yet insurmountable barriers are set on our experience between the world of the physiological phenomenon and the world of mental experience. And yet the objective mutual dependence of both spheres of phenomena cannot be overlooked. Whether I interpret this in the sense of a psychophysical parallelism or conclude that we are dealing only with different aspects, accessible to external and internal experience respectively, of one and the same process, in neither case can what occurs physiologically be of indifference to the psychologist. About the physiological aspect of the drive occurrence, however, we know a good deal more than about the mental aspect. Internal experience conceals from us much that the observation of physiological processes makes plain.

Further, for a considerable part of the way we shall be concentrating on conditions in animals. Animals make it possible to recognize with model clarity many things which, if we did not have the comparative method of procedure, would be difficult or even impossible to analyze in man on account of his incomparably more complex structure. Man does not become degraded in the process; for comparison brings out all the more clearly not only the common factors but also the specific differences.

Originally, i.e. in the primitive animal, drive and motoric function are closely coupled with one another; a particular discharge of activity has its own specific source of energy within the central nervous system. The drive roughly represents an "accumulator," which is exhausted each time the associated drive activity is discharged and becomes "recharged" during the pauses. The behavior patterns concerned are elicited as a rule by specific "sign stimuli," which stimulate an "innate releasing mechanism" (see below). The drive energy is, however, not absolutely dependent on being elicited in this way. If, namely, the accumulation of energy exceeds a particular level without the eliciting situation having occurred, the drive activity can go off without external cause, in the absence of the object normally necessary.

Here are two examples: A young elephant moved its trunk in the air, just as elephants normally do to roll a bundle of hay together, then brought its trunk to its jaws in the typical manner as if it were putting something in. As this was repeated several times, I was able to establish beyond doubt that in fact not the tiniest particle of food was taken up.

Human babies, awake or asleep, frequently make sucking movements "on nothing," i.e. no recognizable external stimulus is having effect.

We cannot, however, observe such overflow discharge[2] in the case of all instinctive movements, not even when every possibility of discharging them normally has been eliminated. The reason for this is as follows: Not every individual instinctive movement possesses its own excitatory center with automatic production of energy; frequently chains of instinctive movements having many links are supplied from a common excitatory center, whereby the next link in the chain is always discharged at a higher level of excitation than the preceding one was. Thus the fighting activities of the small fish *Astatotilapia strigigena* mount in five steps (Seitz 1940):

First step: Two males meet, and instantly they begin to change color and adopt what are known as their display markings (which these animals, similar to the proverbial chameleons, are able to do as a result of complicated systems of skin cells containing color pigments and supplied with nerves).

Second step: Both animals spread all their fins and adopt a parallel position, the head of the one beside the tail-fin of the other.

Third step: Folds of skin in the bottom of the mouth are protruded, thus—seen from the side—considerably enlarging the outline of the head.

Fourth step: Alternately the fishes perform a characteristically slow, quite emphatic stroke with the tail-fin before the nose of the opponent. As this simultaneously results in a forward thrust, the fishes begin to circle one another slowly.

Fifth step: Suddenly one, its tooth-filled jaws wide open, attempts to ram the other in the flank. The other tries to ram for its own part, thereby simultaneously withdrawing its flank from its opponent. Eventually one of them gives up and is chased off by the other.

The fact that these various "levels of intensity" of the fighting actions of this fish are dependent on *one common* "action-specific energy" has been established experimentally (Seitz 1940). When this energy accumulates, the lowest steps tend to be the first to display overflow discharge. In this way, however, an outlet is opened for the drive energy which (here, as in very many other cases) is sufficient to offset the constant input of tension. Thus overflow discharge of the higher steps does not occur. An *Astatotilapia* male kept in social isolation for a long time displays nothing more in the way of overflow discharge of fighting actions than display coloration and, at the most, fin-spreading.

This rhythmically automatic charging of the drive energies and the fact that they accumulate and strive of their own accord for discharge is of the highest significance. On this, namely, is based the *entire spontaneous activity* of the organism. If animal and human are not, as was at one time assumed in all seriousness, pure reflex machines, obliged always to reply to specific external stimulation with the same stereotyped reaction, it is due to this automatic drive production.

A unit consisting of rhythmically self-charging drive energy and a fixed and inflexible motor pattern, as I have described it above, we call an instinct. This is innate and cannot be influenced in its form by the animal's environment or its individual experience. As a result of its internal dynamics, the actual drive goal is *not,* as is frequently assumed even today, the *attainment of an external object or state, but as smooth and uninhibited a discharge of the instinctive act as possible,* thereby eliminating the internal tension. Thus, instincts cannot be classified and analyzed according to external goals, as the older investigators of instinct mostly tried to do. The behavior of many lower animals is largely governed by a small or larger number of such instincts. Furthermore, in general it is only *one* drive which determines the behavior of the lower animal at any given moment.

Thus conflict between drives is scarcely possible in these cases. But as soon as we come to the higher animal, and above all to man, it is rare for one drive to have exclusive control, even temporarily. In humans such conditions are abnormal and, if the disposition is permanent, pathological. Before we go into this more closely, however, we must stay with the animals a little longer.

Independent of one another as the various instincts of an animal may be with respect to the speed with which their action-specific energy recharges, they do not, however, exist as isolated units alongside one another. They form an inter-connecting system, in that accumulation or exhaustion of one can increase or decrease the reactivity (threshold) of another. Thus, the instinct-specific energies form a "floating equilibrium" among themselves which is constantly subject to disruption, for one reason because of the different speeds at which the individual drive energies recharge themselves and, for another, because of the effect of external stimuli. One might compare the relationship between the individual instinct-specific energies in the case of lower animals to a parliament in which nothing is referred to committees but on every subject a decision is taken and immediately carried out. This floating equilibrium of drives among themselves resembles the equilibrium of the internal secretory glands. We may, in fact, assume with certainty that the accumulation of drive energy is also based on the production of excitatory substances in particular parts of the brain. There is likewise no doubt as to the close connection between motivational rhythm and internal secretory function.

A particular developmental path is taken by this periodicity of accumulation of instinct-specific energy and chain of instinctive acts in the case of higher animals and above all mammals. Here, namely, the inflexible sequence of the individual links in the chain of action disintegrates. A lower animal cannot pick any link it wishes out of a whole sequence and produce it on its own. Without leading up to it by means of the preceding stages, our little fish, *Astatotilapia,* is incapable of taking up the parallel position or beating its tail. But mammals *can* do the equivalent. The antagonistic actions of a cat toward another it does not know consist of a chain of specific motor patterns just as with *Astatotilapia:* The animal's hair stands on end, particularly on the back and tail, and the tail forms a stiff downward crook (by this I do not mean the arched back, which is adopted only toward a predator, for example a dog). Now with growls, hisses, and spits the animals progress slowly, crab-wise and stiff-legged, toward one another; finally one shoots forward, and blows land on nose and forehead. If one turns to flee, the other follows, deals it paw-blows behind the ears, and tries to grasp it diagonally from behind and pull it to the ground. Thereupon the escapee throws itself on its back, retracts its neck in order to protect its endangered throat, and defends itself with tooth and claw. However, if one keeps several adult cats together it will probably never be possible to observe this sequence in its entirety. If the conspecific is a *familiar* one, a cat can, quite out of sequence, merely hiss at it, deal it a paw-blow, or even fall on it suddenly from behind, and all this with or without its hair standing on end. This may at first sight seem unimportant, but is in fact highly significant: only mammals are capable of combining individual links from various instinctive acts with one another in play, thus "discovering" completely new sequences of movement (Lorenz 1935, 1937 b, 1940, 1943 a, 1950 b).

This availability of the instinctive movements in other connections increases continually as the mammal series ascends, and increasingly subtle movement details become dissociable from their original connection. At the top end of the process stands the boundless multiplicity and complexity of human movement, where it is no longer possible to see that it has anything to do with fixed links in a chain of instinctive movements. This disintegration of the complete instinctive discharge *does not, however, destroy the original connection.* On the contrary, this is retained as a *possibility,* and at the appropriate moment can run off uninterruptedly and with complete inflexibility just as in the case of any lower animal.

II. THE REACTIVE RELEASING MECHANISMS

At this point, however, even at the risk of exhausting the patience of any readers not interested in specialist animal psychology, I fear we must go back and take yet another look at conditions in lower animals. So far, namely, we have dealt only with the independent internal dynamics of the drive processes, with the fact that they are in principle independent of external stimuli. It is plain, however, that the survival of the species and of the individual is guaranteed only because these internal dynamics are adjusted to external situations which occur with a certain regularity. Thus already at a purely physiological level devices exist which synchronize external cause and internal dynamics with one another, with the result, for example, that under natural conditions the parental behavior of a song-bird is discharged when, and only when, there are young in the nest. The animal or the "parliament of drives" in it must, therefore, somehow be able to "interpret" the environmental event. And in many instances the capacity to do so cannot be learned in the course of the individual animal's life, for many animals possess instinctive acts which are performed only once in a lifetime, and so the animal has to "get it right" the very first time. In animal perception there are "templates" for a whole series of important events in life which are kept more or less in a state of readiness, and if a perceptual object or a process in the environment fits such a template the corresponding drive activity will be released (provided that the drive energy concerned is adequately charged). We call these templates "innate releasing mechanisms," and from numerous animal experiments we have already acquired a good deal of information about their properties and functional peculiarities. The innate releasing mechanisms (IRMs) roughly represent the "keyboard" by means of which the environment plays on the "organ of drives," or—seen from the point of view of the animal—the IRMs sort the stimuli impinging on the animal from its environment under the headings "vital to existence," "less important," or "of no consequence." Of importance in our context are those IRMs which regulate the social life of animals in troops, herds, colonies, and the like. Here I must first add that not only drive activities are elicited by IRMs but also reactions of other kinds, such as directing mechanisms (taxes) and—something which is particularly important in the social context—also inhibitions. In the field of social life IRMs determine not only *when* something will be done but also when something may *not* be done! Thus they form a kind of "moral code" below the level of genuine morals. For example: Ravens hack with preference at shining objects, and thus at the eyes when they are dealing with prey. In relation to a conspecific they possess a specific inhibition preventing them from coming too close to its eyes with their beak. And since a tame raven transfers this inhibition to the human with whom it is friendly, it is possible to force it to perform the most comical contortions of the neck by constantly trying to bring one's eye close to the tip of its beak. Furthermore, many animals having some form of social life possess specific body postures which interrupt fights before they can inflict serious damage on one another. Often it is precisely the most vulnerable part of the body which is thus proffered to the superior opponent. And now the latter becomes incapable of doing what it has just been trying eagerly to do while fighting. namely, to bite, hack, ram, or whatever other movements the species in question possesses for killing and fighting, at just that point. Some fishes stand upright and thus expose the belly to the opponent. Turkeycocks lie flat on the ground and stretch their necks out, thus exposing the vulnerable upper side of the cranium. In fights between peacock and turkey such as occasionally occur in poultry farmyards, the turkey usually comes off worst as a result of the different fighting methods of the two species. If, by adopting the "submissive posture" described above, it indicates that it wants to abandon the fight, this makes no impression whatever on the peacock, as the peacock has no corresponding IRM and so no fighting inhibition can be elicited. On the contrary, it only hacks all the more energetically at the motionless turkey, and the turkey consequently becomes increasingly confirmed in its "submissive gesture." Expressed in human terms: It cannot imagine that anyone would be so mean as to kill a defenseless creature. The social IRMs do in fact afford a kind of "evaluation" of the conspecific and its behavior. And basically different as this capacity is from a genuine sense of values, it is nonetheless—let me say this straight away—the indisputable prerequisite for one and for the formation of all those esthetic, ethical, moral, and religious valuations which constitute the essence of human culture and moral codes.

III. WILL, FREEDOM, CONSCIENCE

The more comprehensive and sophisticated an animal's organs become in the process of its phylogenetic development, the richer the choice of environmental stimuli which can be registered and "internally processed." The IRM, however, cannot become unlimitedly complicated, and there is also apparently a limit on the number of IRMs possible for any one species. Thus, the diversity of what can be perceived and experienced in the environment faces a set of IRMs in the animal which is limited in number and capacity. Yet, only via these can it gain access to the internal forces of the organism! It is the task of learning, experience, insight, and reflection to translate the diversity of the environment into the simple "formulae" of the IRMs and thus make it comprehensible to the "parliament of drives." Here, then, something happens which—as I have already said—is not possible in the case of a more simply organized animal: Insight and experience represent, so to speak, the "committees of experts" of the drive parliament. In these the situation is "discussed" on the basis of all available details, and the result is returned in the form of a short report to the parliament, which can now make its decision. In this way an animal learns that a situation which does not actually contain any impression for the IRMs can nevertheless be of interest, for instance because it contains the possibility of activating the drive in another form, or because specific actions can convert it into one of drive usefulness. This possibility of mobilizing the drive forces also in conditions not specific to them, the capacity to classify the diversity of the external world and to reduce it to relatively few formulae, valuations, articles of belief, rules of behavior and principles, which for their part can then be connected up via an unconscious process to the much simpler battery of IRMs—all this reaches in man its highest development, one which leaves every other animal far behind.

This highly complex functional interplay is one aspect of the process of the will (we shall deal with another later). What is known as "strength of will" is therefore a function of the strength of the individual drives and their combined effect. The practices frequently resorted to as a means of strengthening the will, such as cold showers, physical exercises, and the like, do not have an electively specific effect on "the will," but serve to increase tonus and step up the metabolism in general, thereby naturally also increasing the endogenous motivational production. On the relative strength of the individual drives, however, all this has no influence at all.

The will is then—by no means a new discovery—not a particular factor or any other kind of "something" which can be singled out in the mental apparatus. Instead it draws all its strength from the drives and can function properly only when drives and IRMs have remained more or less in harmony. But if this foundation is disrupted, then a clear will formation is no longer possible. And if one deprives it of this foundation altogether (though of course this experiment would presumably be possible only in theory) we are left with pure reason, which by itself is a lifeless calculating machine with nothing to motivate it and nothing to set its goals.

Now we know that it is virtually impossible to effect adaptive modification of the drive equipment during its development by means of environmental influence (and thus teaching).[3] It is useless to hope to alter the relative balance of strength between the individual drives by teaching methods, for this balance has been laid down by developmental processes resistant to modification ("peristostable"; cf. p. 296). This does not, however, mean to say that the strength of a drive remains the same throughout a whole lifetime. Every drive has its own developmental curve, a time of maturation, of culmination, and also of gradual extinction. The differences between these curves are the reason why the balance of strength of the drives can change completely several times in a lifetime. Puberty is a particularly impressive example of this, but by no means the only one. Shifts in emphasis of this kind within the drive system take place not only according to general rules applying to everyone, as in the above example; similar processes of an individual nature occur simultaneously and variously interwoven with the events of general development. This needs to be particularly emphasized, for such a purely endogenous change in balance between the drives, which often proceeds quite gradually, can look like the effect of training whereas what in fact has taken place is a maturation process independent of all external influence.

It cannot be emphasized strongly enough that the moment at which a particular characteristic or a particular capacity appears is no indication as to the extent to which the developmental processes involved are accessible to environmental influences or not. Thus, the literature of psychology in particular is haunted time and again by an idea without any foundation in genetic facts, namely that everything in behavior which is inaccessible to environmental influence must already be present in a functional state at birth (e.g. Remplein 1950). What use immediately after birth are functionally mature nest-building instincts to a young sparrow, mating instincts to a foal, or the instinct of the struggle for social rank to a lion cub? I leave it to the reader to imagine corresponding human parallels.

People are often loath to recognize the dependence of will on the drives and their associated releasing mechanisms. The objections raised are often passionate rather than reasonable. They ask: "If all our aspirations, thoughts, and deeds are really dependent on some surreptitious drive machinery which is subject only to its own specific regularities and as remote from the grasp of our will as the stars above us, must we not become fatalists? What is the point of all endeavors to form the character and the will if there is no real freedom from which man's decisions spring?!"

Certainly being equipped with hereditary features which virtually cannot be influenced represents a considerable limitation on our objective freedom. This has nothing to do with fatalism, however. Or should we call it that when man accepts without a murmur the facts of his physical construction? Considered objectively, the fact that our knee-joint can only move like a hinge and not freely in all directions represents a considerable restriction on our freedom (of movement). Imagine what freedom of movement our legs would gain if the knee-joint permitted the lower leg to turn in all directions, as for example the spines of a sea-urchin can! "The amoeba is less of a machine than the horse," Jacob von Uexküll once said. The amoeba can turn its slimy body into almost any shape. It can flow through a small gap as a narrow tape and revert to its original shape on the other side.

Try to imagine this with a horse! Yet just these many, purely mechanical parts which are built into the body of the horse and determine its fixed shape allow it to lift itself "free" of the ground, to stand upright on its legs, and to cover long distances in the time it takes the amoeba to roll the length of its own body. "Freedom is the purpose of constraint" is a quotation which also fits this case. Along the path of development from amoeba to horse (and to man) nature has, to express it in anthropomorphic terms, continually sacrificed lower order freedoms in order to develop higher orders of freedom, more multiform and more versatile functional systems. The internal drive dynamics cloud the objectivity of our view and force our thought and judgment in particular directions according to the momentary state of balance of the drive system as a whole. Depth psychology has produced a wealth of material to show how incredibly far this can go, how mistaken we can often be about our real motives. On the one hand this is, I repeat, a considerable and, in its effects, often very regrettable limitation on our freedom. On the other hand, however, these autonomous drive dynamics make a decisive contribution to freedom. *They alone are responsible for that independence from the external situation which makes spontaneous activity possible.* The bonds of our drives free us from enslavement to the physical world around us, and for this reason the concepts of "field" and "vector" which some gestalt psychologists have introduced into psychology are quite out of place. For here already begins the freedom, "the spontaneity of the Ego which determines its own goals" (Katz 1948), of which more later.

The "keyboard" of the IRMs also involves, on the one hand, a limitation on the "universal receptivity" of the organism. Anything which cannot be reduced in some form or other to these norms for the perception of the external world remains in the end outside the bounds of perception. In this way the IRMs are also the indispensable prerequisite for all higher forms of apperception and evaluation of the world around us. That does *not* mean—and to avoid misunderstandings I would expressly emphasize this—that all higher ideals and values consist of IRMs or can be traced back to these *in content.* But only through their link with IRMs do they gain influence over the discharge of our motivational forces and thus over our behavior. However, those ultimate emotional evaluations which we cannot explain rationally, and which often tell us with amazing precision what one can still just do as a "decent person" and what not, are all *direct functions of IRMs. They are the divine voice within us, the daimonion of Socrates, they are the foundation stones of our conscience im-*

mutably innate, inexplicable—and therefore also incorrodible—by reason. No one should take exception when we as natural scientists see in them physiological mechanisms which may legitimately be investigated with the help of our methodology. For precisely in what is innate and cannot be learned or guided by reason we see a much more direct gift from the Creator to His creation than in reason, which has been unjustly overrated for so long, and in all that is or can be learned. One thing is certain: Without these pre-programmed norms of apperception of the external world and of our actions in it, we should be the most helpless creatures under the sun, truly abandoned to the supposed "inundation of stimuli" of which Gehlen (1941) speaks, *and without any prospect of ever bringing order into the chaos sweeping over us.* Instincts and IRMs are "formulae of order," the IRMs intended for perception (in the broader sense), the instincts for actions. By themselves they are not sufficient to enable the human being to master the world around him, as we shall shortly see, but they are what makes this possible in the first place. Thus we should not disavow them as shackles and limitations on our freedom, but revere them as one of the most precious of divine gifts. A teacher should also share this estimation; for even if he cannot shape the innate at will and it limits his influence on the young, nevertheless it is, on the other hand, a form of protection for them against manifold deleterious influences. To put it bluntly: Even in his most optimistic moments, a thoughtful and experienced teacher will admit that very many children grow into good and useful adults *not because of, but in spite of the training they receive* (training is meant here in the broadest sense, as a general term for all influences at home, in school, in the streets, etc.). Thus, while the teacher cannot make any improvements in these innate foundations of character, he can console himself with the thought (for he, too, is only an imperfect and sometimes erring human) that he cannot do anything to spoil them either!

IV. IMPRINTING AND DOMESTICATION

It is, however, necessary to qualify the foregoing sentence in respect of one important point, or rather to guard against one possible misunderstanding. The IRMs of *some* innate behavior patterns are, namely, not very precise and they become matched precisely to the "correct" object by means of an extraordinary kind of learning process which differs from normal learning in that it cannot be unlearned again, at least not without enormous difficulties. We call this process "imprinting" (Lorenz 1935). It is possible only during a partic-ular phase of development, *but this phase may fall at different times for the various IRMs.* A young Graylag Goose, for example, regards the first large moving body it sees after hatching from the egg as its mother and follows it everywhere. Normally this will indeed be its mother. In this way, however, a Graylag Goose hatched in an incuba-tor can without difficulty be imprinted to accept a human as its "mother." It then follows this human everywhere and nothing will persuade it to attach itself to a Graylag Goose leading chicks. The imprinting process itself lasts only a few moments and sensitivity to imprinting lasts only a short while after hatching. Some other im-printing processes in other species take considerably longer, and in these cases *within* the sensitive period re-orientation from one im-printing object to another is possible, if with difficulty. Once the imprinting period is over such a re-orientation is, so far as we yet know, totally impossible. In the case of many birds, the objects of imprinting include the "parental companion," the "sexual compan-ion," and, for gregarious species, the "flight companion."

As far as mammals and humans are concerned this question has so far scarcely been investigated. Yet, precisely in man's case the suspi-cion exists that imprinting processes play a decisive role. During a period of sensitivity to imprinting the young animal seems positively to be searching for appropriate imprinting sensory impressions, and this is something we can observe most clearly in growing humans, particularly during puberty and post-puberty: a constant searching for someone they can model themselves on. And we know how power-less all good teaching can be at such times, and how tremendous the influence for good as well as for bad the person taken as an idol can have. It seems to me that during this period the guiding principles which determine the ethics and social behavior of humans for the rest of their lives are imprinted in accordance with the example of older people who are in some way revered, loved, or "idolized"[4]; the process in which this is effected would be similar in principle to the imprinting of the young Graylag Goose to its mother. The responsibil-ity which anyone entering into a close relationship with a young per-son in this phase of development is obliged to accept cannot be emphasized too strongly (Baumgarten 1950).

Now, I have already said that in man's case the equipment of hereditary social behavior patterns is not sufficient to cope with the many forms of social structure we have today. There are two main reasons for this: 1. In what for evolutionary processes is a very short time, Neanderthal man has developed into modern civilized man. The hereditary behavior patterns have not been able to offer appropriate differentiations in reply to this precipitate external development. They have remained more or less as they were originally, and may well be adequate to regulate the social relationships of a small tribe roaming like animals through bush and steppe, but not those of a citizen of one of our modern, technological forms of society with their extremely complicated history and conventions. 2. Not only has the system of innate behavior patterns been unable to keep pace with the cultural development, but it has on the contrary undergone certain degenerative changes, such as also occur in a comparable manner in man's domestic animals and may be studied in them as a model. These changes are, therefore, known as "consequences of domestication"—though this is perhaps not a particularly happy choice of name. As far as the drives are concerned, the most important of these are faulty development ranging up to complete loss (atrophy of instinct) on the one hand, and over-development (hypertrophy of instinct) on the other. It will be obvious that this situation considerably disturbs the original balance between the drives. This accounts for the fact that we regard some drives as bad, namely those with a tendency to over-development, and conversely esteem extremely highly those drives tending to atrophy and, as a result of this high esteem, often refuse to acknowledge their drive character.

The IRMs have likewise suffered losses. In the case of IRMs equipped with numerous single features, the finer features are particularly liable to be lost, thereby reducing the selectivity of the IRM affected. Here the losses can progress to such an extent that precisely circumscribed blindness to impression and values can result. Even if he is highly intelligent, a person having a defect in this respect is not in a position *genuinely to experience* a particular sphere of values as such, even if he can be brought to observe and respect them in his outward behavior.

Here I should like to say a few words of explanation about heredity.[5] The individuals of an animal species living in the wilds look broadly (if not completely) similar to one another in external features and functions. Thus, they also correspond in their hereditary behavior patterns. Man, however, (like his domestic animals) possesses much more manifold variants and, as a result, two humans are far less alike than, say, two tigers. Thus, the innate patterns of behavior and experience of one human are sometimes very different from those of another, often even of his nearest relatives. *This does not, however, mean that they are less stable (more modifiable) in the individual than those of wild animals!*

V. THE STABILIZING SYSTEMS

Now we can go in greater detail into the question, touched on above, of the actual function of the will. *First I would remind readers once more that all that has been said about drives and IRMs refers to physiological mechanisms. These are not themselves the content of our consciousness, i.e. they cannot be consciously experienced.* At the basis of our consciously experienced feelings of compulsion, wishes, longings, motives, guiding principles, and ideals, there always lies a highly complex interplay between these and other physiological functions. And I have already said that one of the most important tasks of reason, if not *the* most important of all, is, so to speak, to "convert" our complicated social situations, which now hardly ever register with one of the IRMs in full, direct strength, into the much simpler "formula language" of the IRMs. The following is an example of this: A human, and particularly a man, quite certainly possesses an IRM which reacts to the situation of "woman brutally attacked by strange man." Assuming that the situation arrives unheralded and the spectacle is sufficiently violent, any man who does not immediately respond with unreflected and energetic protective and fighting reactions has a serious innate defect. But if a female factory worker in a room with several others is obliged to sit out her eight-hour day on a stool without any means of adjusting the height, without a comfortable seat and without a back-rest, this situation creates no such direct effect as the previous one. Here the data have to be processed by the understanding before the facts "woman in situation which is dangerous and, in the long run, severely damaging to health" can be abstracted from the much more complex situation as a whole and, going on from there, be fed into the IRM described above. For this reason, too, the IRM itself will respond with less strength and, as a result, our reaction is less impulsive and more open to competition from other impulses.

In this way, one single drive will hardly ever be stimulated alone. For situations are ambiguous, and herein lies a *further and decisive possibility of freedom: Nothing determines beforehand which particulate complexes of a situation will emerge from a diffuse whole as a gestalt, which ideals and moral principles will be stimulated by it and, as a further consequence, in what strength ratio the various drives will be activated.* The current internal state of excitation of the drives does, it is true, have a directing and selecting influence in this, but only in borderline cases—in extraordinary situations, or where pathological individuals are concerned—is this so all-powerful that it is decisive by itself. Thus, at a fairly high developmental level the drives are compelled to make compromises. And thanks to the fact that, as mentioned above, the individual motoric components can be variously combined, the drive compromise can also lead to a compromise formula in the behavior manifested. This compromise nature is highly characteristic of many processes of the will and is probably not absent even where it seems to be a matter of pure decisions between alternatives.

It is largely a question of training to ensure that certain stand-points are given priority in a situation. And this is also the real problem and real point of departure of will-*formation*. Let no one think this is putting too niggardly a limitation on the field. In truth, it is an enormous amount: If I spoke earlier of how the shackles of the drives free us from enslavement to the physical world, it is here that, via the detour described, the physical world *wins back just as much influence as is necessary to loosen the shackles of the drives and to make a "may" out of a "must"! Thus Nature plays two inflexible, predetermined mechanisms off against one another in order to create from them freedom.*

I should like to point out expressly that here we are speaking only of objective freedom, not of subjective consciousness of freedom, which in part has quite different sources and with which we need not deal here.

The *organization of the elicitation of drives* through the processing of a situation by means of conscious understanding reaches a further and higher stage as a result of the fact that not only the present situational content is taken into consideration but also the future development of the situation as well as the consequences of one's own behavior. In this way a person can set himself long-range goals which, because of their complex nature, stimulate several drives. Thus "stabilizing systems" are formed[6] which can provide a person's behavior with a practically even supply of energy over a long period of time, since the rhythmical fluctuations in the individual drives can be largely compensated by their differences in rhythm. These relatively steady "stabilizing systems" with their relatively constant supply of energy are, incidentally, the basis for the assumption that something like a general drive exists which is primarily undirected and is only guided into specific channels by stimuli or will. This idea must be decisively contradicted. The availability of a more or less constant "amount" of drive is a thoroughly derivative phenomenon and is consequently highly liable to upset. If this were not so, it would, for example, be quite impossible to explain why during puberty a young person goes through such an upheaval of his whole personality after this had already acquired a fairly stable form in late childhood. If all that the maturation of sexual drives did was to open up new outlets for the general reservoir of drives, it could never lead to such profound changes. As it is, however, the more or less steady stabilizing systems into which the drives have already integrated themselves disintegrate again. Since the sexual drives bring forces of a new kind pulling in a new direction, the internal balance of drives itself must be worked out anew. Only when this genuine metamorphosis is complete can the new stabilizing systems which represent the vital core of the later, mature personality gradually form.

Thus, within certain limits stabilizing systems of this kind are also capable of compensating in particular for disharmonies in the innate disposition such as were mentioned briefly above. Here, however, I would expressly emphasize that this regulating function of the stabilizing systems is neither in a position to compensate fully for serious defects in the innate equipment, nor does it have sufficient carrying capacity to stand up to extreme conditions. The ultimate, unpremeditated decision in the face of an extreme emergency, the greatest danger, the final triumph, is something a person always takes instinctively, on the basis of his innate behavioral norm. Thus, it has frequently happened that the "plucky" soldier, who was the pride of his officers in barracks, broke down completely under the demands of battle, while another who was not at all plucky sometimes surprised everyone with his amazing composure. Thus our teachers are faced with the task of *correctly assessing and exploiting the possibilities* left to them by the hereditary behavioral structures they cannot influence.

To sum up:—

Drives are specific motivational factors; their production is rhythmically automatic and leads to internal states of tension which, of their own accord and without external cause, strive to be discharged. They are thus *the* source of spontaneous behavior. During ontogeny they obey their own developmental laws and are practically inaccessible to the influence of a teacher.

IRMs are inherited mechanisms for the release of a drive in the biologically "correct" situation. They constitute among other things the indispensable prerequisite for the development of a system of higher values. They are likewise impossible to influence through teaching, but some are subject in the course of their development to an imprinting process which accomplishes itself basically on "idols" of the person's own choice. *These* IRMs the teacher is largely capable of molding, by pointing out suitable examples in history, but above all by his own exemplary conduct. The specific nature of the imprinting process makes it impossible to retrieve an opportunity once neglected and virtually impossible to put right what has once been spoiled.

Will is the balancing function of the drives, constructed with the aid of reason, intellect, and the sense of higher values reached via IRMs; self-control means control of drives by drives. The aspects of will which have been dealt with here are: the apperception of the ambiguity of a situation, which only by this means attains effectiveness; the possibility of compromise behavior; the steadiness brought to motivation by the formation of stabilizing systems. Since it is purely drive-determined, the dynamic substance of the will cannot be affected by training,[3] but, broadly speaking, a person's interpretation of situation and the "will-goals" dependent on his sense of values can.

VI. CONCLUSIONS

In conclusion I shall attempt to show how the views expressed here can be applied practically in education.

The first obvious disturbance of the balance in a child's motivational nature occurs in what it known as the "first difficult age." A new drive takes up its function, and the consequence is a temporary disharmony with positive tendency to overflow discharge of the new drive, which must first establish mutual dynamic relationships with the other drives already functioning before a new state of balance can be achieved. Herein lies the phenomenological similarity to the second "difficult period" which induced Schmeing (1939), in his certainly clever and fundamentally accurate "three stages theory," to conclude that the internal processes are identical in nature because of the similarity of their external appearance: In the first difficult period he sees the ontogenetic "recapitulation" of a puberty which actually took place at this age at an earlier stage of human evolution (which is extremely unlikely, if only because maturity occurs a good deal later in the anthropoid apes, e.g. in chimpanzees at about the age of eight at the earliest). Here, however, it is a question of drives of self-assertion which at first, in a completely undirected and unspecific manner, simply take everything as an excuse for appearing. A child *positively makes it his object* to find opposition. And in fact *insurmountable* opposition. The drive is, to a certain extent, sounding out where the socially acceptable limits lie, and the remedy generally tried—namely, of ignoring the fits of defiance of this age and over-coming them by distraction—is then out of place. With his defiant behavior, the child is looking for socially staked-out limits, i.e. for social foundation and social assurance. If the adults only give way every time, this is just as "frightful," i.e. frightening, to the child as it is to us when we tread on nothing where we thought there was a step. Depriving the child here of opposition, if necessary forcible, means doing serious and probably permanent damage to his capacity for social orientation later. The kind of "opposition" the adult must provide depends largely on the individual nature of the child. Often restraint consistently applied suffices. At the risk of hurting delicate feelings, I must, however, state that restraint is not always enough. In certain cases it is not only permissible to slap a child but positively essential for its mental health and subsequent development. It should not be frequent and certainly not particularly hard, and in most cases it need not even hurt. But it must be done *immediately*. The basic rule that one should not punish a child in rage is quite wrong *in this connection:* That is what the rage "is there for," in order to punish in it! And just as a slap of this kind represents an immediate and genuine instinctive act on the part of the adult, so the child, too, has a finely tuned innate comprehension of this, and in most cases is at once virtually transformed. The child's love is not diminished in the least by this—rather the opposite—and no child bears ill will for punishment he has deliberately provoked himself. All that matters is the right moment. That "childhood traumata" which poison the whole of later life should result from punishment of this kind is pure non-sense. As far as I am aware, no psychotherapist or depth psychologist who is to be taken seriously holds this view any longer.

From the foregoing it will be clear that the first difficult age should not be considered as the very first appearance of "will." It would be wrong to deny any will whatever in a child of the first phase. Just watch with what tenacity it tries time and again to reach an object outside its playpen, and then say it has no "will." But in the difficult age this "willing" takes on a new direction through the awakening of a new drive. Naturally the actual functions of the will, as described above, undergo further development which, once the new organiza-tion of the drive system is complete, in other words not really until after the actual difficult period has been overcome, then manifests itself as more or less pronounced rapid progress.

In puberty things are considerably more complicated. This is brought about in the first place by the fact that not merely *one* drive but a whole group puts in a new appearance. In the case of boys, the first to appear are the fighting drives characterized by the words "rivalry" and "social hierarchy"; it is they that call forth the phenomena of the second difficult period, and thus the rebellion of the adolescent is correspondingly different from that of the small child. The next to announce itself is the actual sexual drive, the aim of which is physical communion with the opposite sex. Almost simultaneously with it, the drives stimulating courtship, tenderness, and protectiveness toward the partner which, for good or bad, are lumped together under the heading of romantic love appear on the scene. The situation is further complicated by the fact that fighting drives and love are genuinely maturing drives which are now becoming functional for the first time, whereas the sexual drive has long been functionally mature but its specific motivational energy has been under inhibition until now. This explains the relative independence of their speeds of development, which has led to the misconception that hormones have less influence on the development of love than on that of sexuality. It is important, if the course of puberty is to be normal, that the disinhibition of sexuality should happen not at one blow but gradually, so that the simultaneous maturation of the releasing mechanisms which are common to love and sexuality is completed in time to prevent aimless outbursts of sexuality. It is the fact that the releasing mechanisms are common to both, namely, which later steers sexuality and love toward the same object, thus causing their effective unity. If for some reason the releasing mechanisms are subject to developmental disturbance, the result may be the naive romantic type, or the Don Juan incapable of faithfulness, according to whether one component or another predominates. If sexuality is disinhibited too early, it lacks firstly the inhibitions which later become established when sexuality is teamed with love, and secondly the exacting selectivity which is a function of the fully matured IRM. The sexual drive then directs itself without inhibition toward any attainable "object," and as a result of its "unsureness of aim" can be tempted particularly easily into perversions. We know of an almost precise parallel to human circumstances in the case of the Graylag Goose. Graylag Geese ideally mate for life. The actual mating is preceded by lengthy courtship and engagement ceremonies. The gander normally reaches sexual maturity after two years. In stunted animals, however, the unadorned copulatory reactions already appear during the second year, whereas the maturation of the instinctive behavior of courtship and pair-bonding does not take place until later than in normal animals. Certain occurrences during the postwar period now in fact seem to reveal comparable cases in humans. A few years after World War II ended, namely, incidents of rape by youths began to increase. Almost without exception the youths concerned were not particularly powerful but positively puny types. It does not seem right to attribute this merely to the state of utter neglect many youths endured in the chaos of the postwar period; for it is striking that the accumulation of cases did not occur until a time when conditions were already fairly well on the way to normalization. The suspicion which suggests itself instead is that the youths concerned had suffered some physiological damage at the time of the worst food shortage when they were just in the stage of late childhood and early adolescence. As in the case of the stunted Graylag Goose, a premature disinhibition of the sexual drive seems to have taken place, while maturation of the associated "brakes" was delayed. Punishment therefore does these youths hardly any service. What one should give them, however, is the possibility of "catching up" with their maturation in peace in conditions which make further lapses physically impossible. Pedagogic influence exerted on them would not need to be different from that usual in the case of normal children, except that their retarded tempo of development in the respect described would have to be taken into consideration. In conjunction with this I should just like to indicate briefly that the value of the precautions recommended for the period of puberty, such as distraction from over-much brooding, toughening, and a good deal of movement and sport in the fresh air, comes perhaps less from their pedagogic results than from their physiological effectiveness in promoting health. From numerous experiences with animals we know that precisely the system of innate drives and releasing mechanisms is the most sensitive indicator of minute, otherwise scarcely perceptible physiological damage. From this point of view, the old saying, *Mens sana in corpore sano,* acquires a new sense.

From what has been said, it follows that during actual puberty the main skill of a teacher consists of being able to bide his time quietly and let maturation take its course, of keeping sources of trouble at a distance as inconspicuously as possible, and of an equally inconspicuous care for the health of the adolescent. He can expand his activities as an example and an instructor again during postpuberty. For it is then, as I have already described, that the ideals and principles crucial to the acquisition of a sense of values are imprinted, the stabilizing systems essential to the character formed and—once the difficulties involved in the internal rearrangement of drives and the readjustment of their balance have been overcome—the forces freed for the ultimate mastering of the external world.

In conclusion I would expressly emphasize that the representation of conditions outlined here is in every respect a rough and schematic simplification, not only as regards the considerable gaps still left in our knowledge, but also as far as the present state of established knowledge is concerned. A more detailed consideration of all the known individual facts, however, would not only have gone beyond the framework of this article but would only have created confusion in a preliminary introduction to the way in which this complex of questions may be considered from our viewpoint, which is in general fairly unfamiliar to educational psychology. I have, however, endeavored to keep this simplification down to "proper proportions" and thus avoid biased distortions of the picture as a whole. I can scarcely hope to have been totally successful in this. Let each one extract from the models offered whatever seems of practical use, and may the rest be a stimulus to him to get to grips himself with the existing theories and, as far as possible, to devote more attention than before to the phenomena in practice.

4 Theoretical Considerations in Criticism of the Concept of the "Displacement Movement"

(1952)

I. INTRODUCTION

In a detailed paper, N. Tinbergen (1940) has described a number of activities in animals which, following Kortlandt (1938), he has designated collectively as "displacement movements." The characteristic common to these is said to consist of the fact that a specific instinct energy which has already been elicited (an "urge") is prevented by internal or external factors from discharging itself along its proper ("autochthonous") motor paths and now seeks an outlet along "allochthonous" paths which normally serve the discharge of other action-specific energies. The phenomenon itself is striking enough and no doubt to be found in any species of animal if one looks closely enough; the physiological explanation for it, actually originating from Kortlandt, which is offered in the concept of a "sparking-over" of action-specific energy seems so convincing that to my knowledge no one has so far cast any doubt on it or, indeed, subjected it to critical examination. In fact, however, even some of the material quoted by Tinbergen is contradictory to the hypothesis. Viewed in conjunction with some new observations, and taking into consideration certain facts so far considered "irrelevant," this occasioned the following reflections.

II. THE THREE FORMS OF DISPLACEMENT MOVEMENT

According to Tinbergen there are three general situations in which displacement movements may occur:

1. Where there is conflict between two urges: Two mutually exclusive tendencies are aroused by the same situation. This is particularly frequent in antagonistic situations, in which attack and escape are elicited simultaneously.
2. If the "goal" is attained too suddenly (for example, sexual displacement movements by the Cormorant when its fighting opponent suddenly flees; many post-copulatory activities).
3. When the adequate stimulus "expected" next in a chain of actions fails to materialize (nest-building movements by a courting Stickleback when the female fails to follow to the nest).

In the case of all three forms, two internal conditions are essential if the displacement movement is to occur: (a) an urge already activated finds its autochthonous motor paths blocked; (b) the urge thus blocked can be discharged only via a motor pattern which is normally driven by an action-specific energy of its own.[1]

III. OBJECTIONS TO THE ASSUMPTION OF A "SPARKING-OVER" OF ENERGY

(a) If the urge already activated were really expended immediately in the allochthonous movement, this would necessarily lead to a precise correspondence between accumulation of urge and intensity of displacement movement. Since in case 1 (conflict) two urges have been activated, the fact of their flowing simultaneously into *one* allochthonous motor path should result in particularly intensive displacement movements. Very often, however, displacement digging by the Stickleback, pretense pecking by cocks, and all comparable displacement movements in other animals are of noticeably weak intensity.

(b) Displacement threat movements of this kind do not use up the action-specific energy of fighting activities, or at least not to an extent worth mentioning; on the contrary, further accumulation occurs. This results in the opponents suddenly rushing at one another and beginning to fight "autochthonously." After a certain amount of time the fight is interrupted and the opponents stand threatening one another anew. In two cocks in this situation it is possible to see clearly that they are fairly exhausted by the fight, and the displacement movement of pretense pecking not only has threat function but also signifies a *breathing space*. Just at the moment of the changeover to displacement movement, then, there is no particular accumulation of action-specific energy for the fighting movements. Instead, it is considerably depleted and is now recharging slowly for the next round. And this *at a time when the displacement movement is increasing in intensity and should, therefore, if the hypothesis of a sparking-over of energy were correct, be using up fighting energy in increasing amounts*. This fact—namely that under certain circumstances a displacement movement not only does *not* discharge the activated urge but, on the contrary, stimulates it still further—Tinbergen himself has already expressly emphasized, but without seeing in it an objection to the sparking-over hypothesis.

(c) If the appearance of the "displacement" movement really signified an outpouring of energy through alien channels, it would be difficult to understand why the only motor patterns suitable for the purpose are of a kind normally driven by an action-specific energy, but not "pure reactions" which only become active in response to external stimuli.

(d) According to the hypothesis, in case 2 (too sudden attainment of the goal) and case 3 (failure of a stimulus to materialize which would have conveyed the chain of action further) loss of the adequate external stimulus is so strong an inhibition on the autochthonous motor patterns that the energy already activated bursts through the "insulation" and drives an allochthonous movement which, for its part, is then discharged in the absence of an object or an external stimulus, in other words more or less spontaneously. Viewed in this way, displacement activities are certainly a kind of overflow activity. Here, however, the question inevitably arises why the urge which has already been "activated," i.e. is already hovering on the threshold of the autochthonous motor path, cannot surmount the obstacles lying in this, its very own path, more easily than those in a strange path. After all, the adequate object for both the autochthonous and the allochthonous movement is missing. Why then is this "inhibition" not more easily overcome autochthonously than allochthonously? Here the hypothesis of a direct sparking-over of energy from the autochthonous to the allochthonous motor path finally breaks down: If, namely, it were really easier for the action-specific energy to penetrate into the allochthonous rather than the autochthonous path, how then could autochthonous movements ever occur? All the energy would surely already have been exhausted in allochthonous movements! On the other hand, the energy available is undoubtedly insufficient to produce autochthonous overflow activity. This is clearly shown by one of my own experiments: I brought an approximately eighteen-month-old tomcat, which with certainty had not seen live prey for over a year, into a cage in which there were several sparrows. The sparrows immediately fluttered up and hung under the roof of the cage. In this situation—"prey quite close but unattainable"—cats generally display two displacement movements, namely lip-licking and "chattering" (a characteristically spasmodic, rapid up-and-down movement of the lower jaw without the mouth being closed completely, and with the corners of the mouth pulled well back). At first the cat did both, but then a storm of prey-catching actions, an absolute paroxysm of paw-blows and bites broke out, and what they were performed on was a lump of earth! The displacement movements clearly emerged *before* activation of prey-catching movements had reached a degree allowing "reaction to a substitute object." For the reasons given, instead of "displacement movement" I should like to propose the term *"alternative movement,"* which does not already contain physiological implications.

IV. THE STIMULATION OF "EXHAUSTED" ACTION CENTERS

Tinbergen describes how a Graylag Goose, whose egg-retrieving movement he had elicited several times in succession, did not roll in the next egg set down at the rim of the nest, but instead performed a nest-building movement. Since, however, the criterion "inhibition on discharge of a strongly activated urge" obviously does not apply here, he is unwilling to accept this as a case of "displacement." To me, however, closer analysis of such examples seems likely to throw new light on the whole question. I shall explain this by means of the example of "alternative washing" by the cat.

A cat sits there quietly and watches me approach. It makes a more or less clear intention movement to stand up and come to meet me, but then remains seated and licks a few times from its shoulder down to its elbow with emphatic strokes. There is nothing to stop the cat from coming to meet me except perhaps a certain "initial friction," which cannot be very great. In human terms, the animal is simply too lazy. Yet, the alternative movement is often very energetic. There is also no doubt that it was the intention to get up which set the washing movement in motion. One cannot, however, say that, as with the alternative nest-building movement of the Graylag Goose, the discussion of this behavior does not belong here; for between the case I have just described and an alternative washing which is quite certainly a "genuine" displacement movement every possible transitional stage exists. In the case of the cat, washing occurs as an alternative movement extremely frequently and in all possible situations, for example after killing prey, after briefly running away, or when an animal would like to go somewhere but dares not pass a higher-ranking animal standing in its way—to name but three occasions.

Elicitation of one particular alternative movement by the most varied "urges" seems to me, incidentally, to be far less rare than Tinbergen's description would lead one to assume. In the domestic cat, apart from washing there is nose-licking (as opposed to lip-licking), in the Mallard duck there is "tail-wagging" (Weidmann 1956). L. Koenig (1953) describes how the Bee-eater's movement of beating to death can be discharged as an alternative movement for the widest variety of reasons, which does not prevent it from being built into the bird's courtship behavior at one point, where it is obligatory and ritualized.

As Tinbergen has already emphasized, alternative movements are usually instinctive acts of a kind which display a particularly high production of action-specific energy of their own. This is also true of the motor patterns I have just described. These circumstances seem to me to imply a form of allochthonous elicitation of movement which, however, no longer fits into the definition of the displacement movement and which, therefore, has not so far been taken into consideration by any author who has contributed to our knowledge of alternative movements and their theoretical interpretation.

V. APPETITIVE MOVEMENTS

In the cases just mentioned, the consumption of the action-specific energy stimulating the alternative movement is often not clearly discernible. However, we know of many examples in which, if the adequate situation is missing, the excitation of one mood stimulates another "subordinate" mood, whereupon the movement associated with the latter is discharged. A hungry animal gets on the move and "searches" for something edible. However, the urge to eat is not discharged by moving around, but instead continues to increase. *Thus, eventually the whole range of possible appetitive actions can, so to speak, be lifted over the internal stimulus threshold by the mood, by the urge toward the "consummatory act," without there being any decrease in the urge itself.* Now, the appetitive actions frequently include genuine instinctive movements which, when the "balance of moods" is different, are themselves quite capable of being striven after as "consummatory acts" and can activate appetitive behavior for their own part. This is even true of the automatic functions of locomotion, which serve so often as appetitive behavior for other moods that their independent status as an instinctive movement is frequently overlooked (Lorenz 1939). All the phenomena designated here as alternative movements may also be understood as special cases in the interplay of moods.

We will take as our point of departure Tinbergen's (1951) diagram of the hierarchy of moods, and to be precise the diagram of the third level centers (moods), since what Tinbergen takes to be first and second level centers are of no consequence to our considerations (Fig. 1).

Let us assume that the state of tension in a mood center (i.e. its "current state") exerts on every other center of the same level an influence which, according to the "state of co-action" (see p. 77), signifies either inhibition or promotion (similar to the way in which "magnetic influence" between two of the automatisms described by von Holst can cause "inhibition" or "facilitation"). In that case discharge of a mood along autochthonous paths would entail a rearrangement of the entire balance of moods: The moods as yet kept under inhibition by the one now—wholly or partly—discharged would mount and thus approach their own threshhold, whereas those which had been promoted by it would be more strongly exposed to the inhibiting influence of other centers. Under these conditions, a mounting mood should be able to lift another mounting mood, which it has facilitated and which is currently not far below its threshold of elicitation, over this threshold *before actually crossing its own*. This would account for appetitive behavior and make it conceivable that stimulation of an exhausted mood can still "coax out" just enough to bring another mood which has almost reached its threshold to the point of discharge. This would also automatically explain the usually very short duration of alternative movements following the stimulation of exhausted moods. Now let us try applying this functional picture to the actual displacement movements:

(a) (p. 60): When two conflicting moods mutually inhibit one another, they raise each other's stimulus threshold to such an extent that, despite strong internal tension, none of their autochthonous motor patterns is capable of being released. However, a third mood facilitated by them would be able to surmount its threshold and now go off, so to speak, as "overflow activity." It is easy to see that

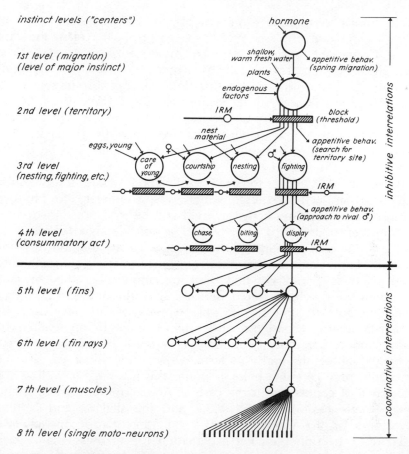

Fig. 1 The hierarchical system of "centers" underlying a major instinct, viz. the reproductive instinct of the male three-spined stickleback. Adapted from the German edition of "The study of instinct," by permission of Prof. N. Tinbergen.

facilitation would then inevitably increase as the tension between the conflicting moods mounted without involving any consumption of action-specific energy worth mentioning, for, of course, the actual motive force of the alternative movement would in fact be supplied by its own autochthonous mood. This would simultaneously provide an explanation for (b) (see p. 60): since the release of an alternative movement does not involve any particular consumption of the action-specific energies of the conflicting drives, these can be accumulated still further.

The reason for (c) (see p. 61) is that alternative movements too are driven by their own action-specific energy. Thus "pure reactions" cannot appear as alternative movements, for they are dependent on external stimulation (but see p. 338 et seq., p. 383). Yet in the case of the Cormorant, sexual alternative movements occur at a time when autochthonous sexual activity is quiescent. However, it is not necessary to assume that during this time there is absolutely no endogenous production of sexual instinct energy. During sexual quiescence sexual drive energies are recharged at so low a rate that the tension does not suffice to release its own appetitive behavior. But through the influence of other mood centers it could still be briefly lifted over its threshold.

(d) (see p. 61): Here, too, the explanation would follow quite simply that an activated urge which was insufficient to produce autochthonous overflow activity would still be in a position to activate another urge which already had a considerable tendency to overflow discharge. In addition, however, as an explanation of many processes Lorenz's idea that they are phenomena comparable to spinal contrast would certainly also be applicable here. In fact, the prerequisites I have stated demand that alternative movements should be able to appear not only when they are facilitated by another mounting mood but also when the inhibition exerted by another mood is removed suddenly as a result of this latter being discharged autochthonously. Alternative washing by a cat after it has caught prey certainly belongs under this heading, as well as the occurrence of copulation in the case of Arenaria after sudden frightening experiences (Armstrong 1950) and the shaking and bathing movements of the Cormorant after intention escape movements.

According to Tinbergen the explanation for all these examples is as follows: An instinctive act is initially elicited, but the stimuli necessary to its continuation are missing. The urge which has already been activated and partially fed into its autochthonous motor paths (intention movements!) finds its way blocked and vents itself along the allochthonous paths of the displacement movement.

My interpretation would be different: Intention movements also consume action-specific energy; this frees an alternative movement for an instant from the inhibition imposed by high level readiness for escape, and so it can spring into action. The fact that on one occasion the animal ruffles its feathers and shakes itself and on another performs bathing movements fits very well with this idea, for the mood which is then lifted over its threshold is, of course, whichever one was already closest to it at the time.

Finally, the hypothesis expounded here makes it comprehensible if a particular motor pattern, which can no longer be elicited as appetitive behavior, still reacts with full intensity to autochthonous stimulation. After Drees (1952) had repeatedly presented saltatory spiders with dummies of their prey, he was no longer able to stimulate them to run toward the dummies. In a "phototaxis experiment," however, the running movement proved to be virtually inexhaustible. Drees believes that the conclusion to be drawn is that there is no action-specific energy for locomotion. In the prey dummy experiment, however, it was not locomotion but predation which had been exhausted and was then incapable of lifting locomotion over the threshold.

VI. THE ROLE OF THE AFFERENT IMPULSES

A movement driven by an action-specific energy and coordinated in the central nervous system causes afferent impulses through stimulation of the proprioceptors of the limbs moved. These afferent impulses certainly do not only pass their message to the activated coordination center as "reafferent impulses" (von Holst and Mittelstaedt 1950), but likewise convey it as "exafferent impulses" to all others more or less in a state of rest at the time. In this we may perhaps see one of the reasons why all other motor patterns are normally excluded as soon as one particular motor coordination begins discharge. Afferent impulses from proprioceptors which notify the coordination center of a sequence of muscular contractions and slackenings other than its own characteristic one signify inhibition. Perhaps the converse is also true: If by chance these afferent impulses correspond more or less precisely to the reafferent impulses flowing back when this coordination center itself is active, this could bring about facilitation. Here we no doubt discover the grain of truth in the James-Lange theory, which as is well known considered all emotions to be peripherally induced. This at least seems to me how many alternative movements come about: as Tinbergen has already emphasized, the egg-rolling movement and the nest-building movement which appears when it is exhausted (see p. 62) have a beginning which is common to both, namely the forward stretching of neck and beak. Similar connections can frequently be observed. Cocks facing one another ready for attack are in a posture very similar to that adopted for food intake. As far as displacement washing by the cat is concerned, the cat's position at the time influences how the movement is performed: If the animal is standing or sitting, it usually licks down over its shoulder in the manner already described; if, however, the cat is walking, it can stop and likewise wash down one side, but more often it brings the forepaw it has just raised up as far as its mouth and licks it, or it swings the hind-leg which was just moving forward farther forward and up, sitting down abruptly as it does so and starting to wash the hind-leg. At any event it seems certain that the afferent impulses constantly arriving likewise influence the balance of moods and may on occasion contribute to the release of a particular alternative movement.

VII. THE QUESTION OF RITUALIZATION

If it has sounded in the foregoing section as if the excitation releasing an alternative movement were too weak itself to flow into its autochthonous paths, this is not quite correct. The normal procedure when action-specific energy is activated comprises three things:
1. the movement coordinated in the central nervous system;
2. specific changes in tonus distribution, which must be distinguished from the hereditary coordination in the same sense as von Holst made a distinction between the "motoric" and the rhythmic function in the spinal cord of a fish; and
3. directing taxis components.
In the case of action-specific energies which may express themselves motorically in several consecutive levels of intensity with a chain of actions having qualitatively different links, the lower levels are almost always of a purely tonic nature. Thus of the five steps by which the fighting actions of *Astatotilapia strigigena* proceed, as described by Seitz (1940), the first two—display coloration and fin-spreading—are tonic. In very many cases, the strength of the activated urge is sufficient to evoke the changes in tonus before it elicits the alternative movement, but is incapable of setting its own higher levels of intensity—namely the autochthonous motor activity—in motion. Often the associated taxes are also elicited, since they, of course, are dependent on the stimulus object. Thus, when an alternative movement starts up it frequently finds itself in a curious, so to speak, unaccustomed situation: The tonus distribution in the musculature is quite different from what it would be in the case of genuine, adequate release of the alternative movement (as autochthonous movement) simply under the influence of its own tonicity and its own directing taxes. Quite obviously the resulting distortion of the movement offers a favorable foothold to a selection pressure aimed at ritualization of alternative movements as "signals" (see p. 303).

VIII. CONCLUSION

The hypothesis of a "sparking-over" of energy offering a simple explanation for a limited range of facts has proved inadequate. The new conceptual model developed here as a working hypothesis for further investigations has the following advantages:

1. It covers all processes so far designated as "displacement movements."
2. It makes both these and a series of other peculiarities of the central nervous "self-management" of excitations intelligible on the basis of uniform functional principles.
3. It assumes that the same functional principles are valid for the processes in the higher "centers" of the central nervous system as for those in the lower ones (cf. Fig. 1).
4. The new hypothesis may be summarized as follows:

The action-specific energies of an animal have a constant mutual relationship of inhibition and facilitation toward one another. Further, they can mutually raise or lower each other's internal threshold of elicitation. None of these mutual effects is determined for all time; they are all constantly changing, either gradually or abruptly, according to the "state of coaction" (von Holst 1936 b,c, 1937, 1939 a,b,c) of the system as a whole at any given time. The influence exerted on a specific excitation and the associated threshold need not necessarily be oriented in the same direction. Here we have a dualism of the same kind as that between the automatic and motoric elements of the spinal cord demonstrated by von Holst, and as that expressed in terms of method in the dual quantification of external stimulus and internal excitation first employed by Seitz (1940)[2] (see p. 29, 306).

Thus "activated urges" whose own motor system cannot be set in motion are able to promote others or lower their threshold to such an extent that they now become motorically active. If this leads to the removal of the obstacle blocking the originally activated instinctive movement, or to a situation which is more favorable to it, we call the secondarily activated behavior *appetitive behavior;* if it does not and so seems not to fit into the situation as a whole, we call it a "displacement" or, better, an "alternative" movement. The internal mechanism, however, is identical in principle. Stimuli acting on proprioceptors as well as on exteroceptors may to some extent help to determine which movements will be activated in this roundabout way.

5 The Discovery of Relative Coordination

A Contribution Toward Bridging the Gap Between Physiology and Psychology (1954)

I. INTRODUCTION

Around the turn of the century the dispute between the older, atomistic psychology and the new school of gestalt psychology flared up. Atomistic psychology was based on theories on the functioning of the central nervous system which were so commonly accepted at the time that they could almost be called classical and which have survived unchanged in essence until quite recently. The laws of mental processes newly discovered by the school of gestalt psychologists seemed incompatible with these physiological concepts. It can, therefore, easily be understood that the gestalt psychologists in their enthusiasm for the new discoveries had no time for the conceptual framework of classical neurophysiology and tried to develop their own concepts of how the central nervous system might work gestaltwise. However, they did not try to test these concepts by way of neurophysiological experiments, but based their ideas on in part very vague physical analogies. Nowadays, however, we see a completely new picture emerging of the functional integration within the central nervous system. On the one hand this new picture permits the established facts of "classical" neurophysiology to be classified as special cases in a more general set of functional laws, and on the other it reveals a host of functional parallels with the findings of gestalt psychology. Thus, we may hope that this new neurophysiology heralds a more auspicious and fruitful cooperation between physiology and psychology than resulted from earlier attempts. Despite some reservations, it might therefore be worthwhile to review the basic importance of the new findings, which so far have received little appreciation even from physiologists and have, as far as I can see, been completely overlooked by the psychologists.

II. THE "CLASSICAL" CONCEPT OF CENTRAL NERVOUS FUNCTION

Following Abderhalden (1941) and Rein (1948), I shall first briefly summarize what in this context I call the classical concept of central nervous function.

The central nervous system is connected with the periphery of the body by nerve fibers which end there in either receptors or effectors. When a stimulus activates a receptor, it sends impulses via the connecting fiber to a center. There nervous excitation is transmitted to an effector neuron, sometimes after passing a number of intermediary neurons (switching cells), and eventually reaches an effector, either muscle or gland, thus inciting it to activity. The nervous pathway through which the excitation is relayed is called a "reflex arc" and the process itself is called a "reflex." The simplest example of the reflex is the proprioceptive muscle reflex which, according to many researchers, passes its excitation immediately from the sensory to the motor neuron of the same somatic segment without any intermediary neurons. In contrast, coordinated reflexes always include intermediary neurons in the spinal cord and/or the brain. The receptors and the effectors involved in this case may belong to widely separate parts of the body and not to the same or even adjacent segments. The excitation can pass on from very few receptors to many different effectors and the excitation of a number of different and widely distributed receptors may be channeled to a single effector organ.

All movements of an animal are supposed merely to be combinations of such reflexes. As a rule one reflex is thought to produce the stimulus which will elicit a subsequent reflex ("chain reflex"). Other reflexes may either inhibit or facilitate each other, i.e. the elicitation of one reflex may at the same time diminish or increase the excitability of other reflex arcs. In any case, it is believed that in the intact animal a reflex can without exception be started only on stimulation of a receptor. The original eliciting stimulus is specific to each reflex arc and is innately determined ("unconditioned reflex"). Under certain conditions new reflex arcs can be established: 1. A new stimulus can acquire the power to elicit a certain reflex movement (choice of stimulus). 2. A new motor sequence can be connected to a given stimulus (choice of reaction). Both processes can occur in combination. Such newly acquired sequences of reactions are called "conditioned reflexes." Their formation obeys the laws of association. On the physiological level it is thought either that new connections between neurons are formed or that connections already in existence need to be strengthened through frequent use or strong stimuli, while others develop an increased internal resistance or inhibition through disuse.

Conditioned reflexes almost always involve higher levels of the central nervous system. Through their own activity their functional characteristics are continuously modified; their particular form at a given moment, therefore, is determined not only by impulses currently arriving but also to a certain extent by those previously received. In addition, certain parts of the central nervous system are capable of storing excitation received in such a way that a stimulus need not immediately be followed by a reaction.

Many researchers, e.g. Ziehen (1914), firmly believed that the account of central nervous function given above was quite sufficient to explain all the physiological facts, and even claimed that it also provided useful and completely adequate models of the functional properties of the "soul."

The gestalt psychologists (for review, see Petermann 1929) refuted any such conceptual framework, while the physiologists clung to it tenaciously. Thus, today we find both disciplines existing side by side with almost no mutual communication. However, the physiologists are now beginning to depart from their old, beloved concepts. Although many details must still be clarified and investigated, a very new picture of central nervous functioning is emerging which, as already mentioned, seems to cover both the facts of classical physiology and the findings of the new psychology. The most important contribution to this new picture was made by Erich von Holst, whose results I shall try to review briefly in the following pages. For details of the experimental setup I must for the sake of brevity refer readers to the original papers (1935 a, b, c, 1936 a, b, c, 1937, 1938, 1939 a, b, c, 1943, 1948, 1950 a, b).

III. THE RESULTS OF VON HOLST'S EXPERIMENTS[1]

Studies on the chain reflex first suggested to von Holst an entirely new series of experiments. According to classical theory the snakelike swimming movements of an eel, for instance, were supposed to be produced in such a way that contraction of one muscular segment influences the tension of the next segment, in this way stimulates the proprioceptors of that segment and thus in turn elicits from its segmental reflex arc a contraction similar to that produced by the previous segment, and vice versa with relaxation. Consequently a well-coordinated swimming movement should be impossible if all dorsal roots of the spinal cord were severed and in this way all input from peripheral receptors were literally cut off. In the actual experiment, however, von Holst was able to show that such an operation does not interfere in any way with the undulating swimming movements. If the middle section of a deafferented spinal eel is fixed in such a way that it cannot itself undulate, a wave starting in the front section will appear in the rear section after exactly the amount of time it would have needed for passing through the middle section if this could have moved. The progress of the wave along the body of the eel cannot, therefore, be explained on gross mechanical principles. Both these observations force us to conclude that the swimming movement cannot be based on chain reflexes, but that central factors achieve the coordination of the undulating swimming movement even when receptors and the segmental reflex arcs cannot participate. The fact that the undulation starts and stops simultaneously over the whole animal is also incompatible with the chain reflex hypothesis: A wave does not start at the front end and peter out at the rear before stopping. In other words, there is not a wave of impulses running synchronously with the phases of the wave along the body of the eel, but it looks as if each somatic segment pulsates in its own rhythm with a certain phase interval to both the anterior and posterior segments.

Von Holst's next step was to look for the factors responsible for such central coordination. As experimental subjects he chose fishes which normally swim not with an undulating movement of the whole body but with rhythmic alternating movements of their fins while the body is kept more or less rigid. The medulla of the fish (of the family *Labridae*) was severed between the 3rd and the 10th cranial nerves. The fish was then put in swimming posture into a shallow basin containing water, and fresh breathing water was continuously fed into its mouth by means of an inserted tube. The fins were geared to writing pens by a system of very light levers which showed only negligible inertia. Thus all fin movements could be recorded simultaneously.

A functional level of arousal of the spinal cord returns within 2 to 10 hours after the operation. Rhythmic fin movements set in spontaneously, though they can be elicited some time before this by external stimulation. The recorded graphs look very similar to sinoidal waves. If only one fin is oscillating, the recorded curve is quite regular, but when several fins move simultaneously the curves show modifications of varying degree and kind. Thus, there is some interdependence between the rhythm of one fin and that of others. This is based on central nervous factors, for if one moves a resting fin experimentally this has no modifying effect whatever on the form of movement of a fin already in motion. Such periodic modifications cannot, therefore, be explained as reflexes or as being caused by the mechanical pressure of water waves.

Two fins oscillating can influence each other mutually to the same degree, or one of them may appear quite uninfluenced, keeping its own unmodified rhythm while the rhythm of the other shows periodic modifications. In such a case we speak of an "independent" or "dominant" rhythm and a "dependent" rhythm. Between the two extremes mentioned—that is, equal mutual interdependence or dominance and complete dependence—there are all gradations to be found. Absolutely independent rhythms are found very rarely; various degrees of mutual dependence seem to be the rule.

The influence exerted by one rhythm on another expresses itself in the recorded curves in two ways, which will be described by taking the example of the most simple case, i.e. the influence of a dominant rhythm on a dependent rhythm.

Each fin endeavors to keep its own rhythm unaltered (perseverant tendency). This primary rhythm is modified by external stimulation and by internal physiological change, but if physiological conditions are kept constant it remains constant also. The independent rhythm forces its own frequency on the dependent one with varying success. The degree of influence it can exert changes periodically with the phase interval between the two rhythms. If in their phasic relationship the dependent rhythm gets ahead of the independent, it is slowed down, and if the dependent rhythm lags behind, the independent one accelerates it. Since when both rhythms have different frequencies the phasic relationship changes periodically, the dependent rhythm shows an alternating acceleration and slackening of its frequency. If the effect of the independent rhythm on the dependent one is very strong, it eventually succeeds in forcing the latter to adopt the frequency of the independent rhythm. This can be effected by gradual shifts, but more often the change is by abrupt saltation. What makes the independent rhythm attract the frequency of the dependent one, or makes two rhythms mutually dependent, von Holst calls "magnetic influence" or "magnetic effect."

A second way in which the dependent rhythm can be influenced by the independent one is called "superposition." In this case, the curves recorded from the dependent rhythm look as if the two basic rhythms—the independent one and the unadulterated dependent one —were added together numerically, analogous to the addition of two pure sine waves. The resultant curves, in addition to periodicity of frequency, also show an alternating periodicity of amplitude. In this way, too, the dependent rhythm can eventually be forced into the frequency of the independent one.

Pure magnetic influence on the one hand and pure superposition on the other are rare phenomena; as a rule we find combinations of the two. Magnetic influence and superposition thus each "seek" to force the dependent rhythm, against its own perseverant tendency, to adopt the same frequency as the independent rhythm. If this is achieved, the consequence is that both rhythms now have a fixed, unchanging phasic relationship (absolute coordination). However, if the two influences are not sufficiently powerful to succeed in this completely, the phasic relationships are subject to periodic, but certainly not wholly irregular, changes. This von Holst calls "relative coordination."

In terrestrial animals relative coordination is certainly less prominent than the absolute form, but is still probably far more frequent than it would seem at first glance. Relative coordination has been proved to exist between the gait of fore- and hind-limbs in mammals, between breathing and sucking rhythms in babies, and experimentally even between the movements of the two arms in adult humans (von Holst 1938).

A number of data suggest that the motoneurons of the anterior horn of the spinal cord relay the impulses to the musculature but do not themselves generate them. For instance, it is possible to enhance the amplitude of the rhythm of a pectoral fin via reflex without simultaneously enhancing the effect on the dependent rhythm of the dorsal fin. This can only be explained if it is possible to change the activity of the motoneuron via a reflex without at the same time affecting the rhythmic generation of impulses, i.e. if the rhythm itself does not originate in the motoneurons. Likewise, by exerting slight pressure on the tail fin it is possible to decrease the amplitude of the dorsal fin. If in this case the strength of the rhythmic impulses is also partially diminished, the influence exerted by the dominant pectoral fin rhythm ought to increase proportionately; again, this is not the case. From these and a number of other such data, von Holst concluded that the rhythm must originate in special neurons in the spinal cord. As they can become active of their own accord without any externally directed stimulation and coordination, he called them "automatic neurons" or "automatic cells." Since each fin owns a typically characteristic basic rhythm, it follows that the musculature of each fin must be governed by a specific group of automatic neurons. Such a group is called by von Holst a "central nervous automatism." A single fin, however, does not oscillate as a rigid plane but undulates. This is particularly striking in fishes which have a long-stretched dorsal fin, but it can also be observed in all other fins. "Undulating movement," however, means only that the spines in each fin do not act synergistically but that each follows the action of the previous one with a characteristic, minute phasic delay. Von Holst now applied the same method of observation he had employed in observing the activity of two different fins to different spines of the same fin. He found that the coordination of two such spines obeys basically the same principles as the activity relationship between two whole fins. It follows that a central nervous automatism is not a rigid unit, but is built up of a number of segmental sub-groups corresponding exactly to the number of muscles innervated by the motoneurons of the same segment; even the antagonistic muscles of one spine are each rhythmically activated by their own automatic sub-groups. In this, the link between the synergistic muscles of different spines is stricter than that between the antagonistic muscles of the same spine.

As a rule, the magnetic influence coordinates the sub-groups of a given automatism more forcefully and intimately than two or more whole central nervous automatisms. The rule within an automatism is, therefore, absolute coordination. Even so, within the automatism each sub-group exerts magnetic influence on each other sub-group and in turn receives such influence from them, and the same applies to the functional relationships of all automatisms among themselves. As a result, we find that a complex rhythmic periodicity pervades the whole of the spinal cord which is itself the result of innumerable individual rhythms influencing each other. The degree to which an individual rhythm is influenced by this total process depends on its frequency and tendency to persevere, and on the total activity balance of the whole system at any given moment; one could speak, therefore, of the individual rhythm possessing a "resonant capacity."

According to this overall picture, it is possible to explain the phenomenon of superposition as a special case of magnetic influence.

Each automatic sub-group has to fend for itself when meeting the magnetic influence of another central nervous automatism. Some sub-groups may yield completely to this foreign influence sooner than others, so that at a given time the dependent automatism may, so to speak, be divided into two factions, one of which is still resisting the magnetic influence of the independent rhythm while the other has already completely surrendered. These two factions superimpose their impulses on the motoneurons, and thus a resultant curve can be obtained in the experiment. It is even very probable that each automatic cell within an automatic sub-group is tied to synergism with the other neighboring automatic cells only by the same magnetic influence. As soon as its perseverant tendency is overcome, such a cell obeys the strongest magnetic influence present, and this is not always the one exerted by the most proximal automatic cells. Under certain conditions, which are not well understood as yet, the strongest influence can be exerted by automatic groups fairly distantly situated in the nervous system.

It is also not quite clear yet which influences determine the phasic relationship which two automatic units tend to preserve between themselves (their "specific state of co-action"). As long as conditions remain constant, this phasic relationship also stays unchanged, but it may be very different between different rhythms and it is different between the same automatic units at different times. All possibilities, from complete phasic coincidence (synergism) to a phasic delay from one to the other of .5 (antagonism), can be found. Precise antagonistic innervation, therefore, is a special case, and incidentally a very rare one, for even with movements which are usually explained as the function of antagonistic muscles (e.g. in the movement of a leg when walking) the limb is moved not up and down in a simple, hingelike fashion but in a rather complicated curve. The muscles involved work together in an ordered time sequence, not in a strictly alternating way.

IV. THE PLACE OF THE FINDINGS OF "CLASSICAL" NEUROPHYSIOLOGY

What, then, is the role of peripheral stimulation if the coordination and organization of complex movements is in essence a function of the central nervous system which is in principle independent of peripheral direction? In other words, what is left of the old reflex concept?

First I should like to remind the reader of a few facts of receptor function. To this day, current notions see the receptor as something inactive until a stimulus "awakens" it. Von Holst (1950 a, b), however, was able to prove that the statolithic maculae of fishes continuously emit impulses of a definite frequency when not being stimulated. The effect of stimulation is a modulation of this frequency either upward or downward. At the same time O. Löwenstein proved the continuous automatic activity of the static sense receptors by recording their action potentials. This had already been established earlier with respect to a number of other types of receptors, e.g. the pressor receptors of the circulatory system (papers of Adrian and O. Löwenstein, which I have hitherto not seen in the original).

Adrian (1950) also found automatic continuous activity in what are known as the "accessory" cells of the olfactory bulb. A so-called "basic potential" has also been recorded from the vertebrate eye in absolute darkness, which makes it very probable that the retina is also continuously active. On the whole, one would seem to be justified, therefore, in assuming quite generally a continuous automatic activity for all receptor types, the frequency of which is only modulated by stimulation. Thus it is not just excitation which the stimulated receptor transmits to its sensory center, but changes in the beat frequencies of this.

The central nervous automatisms of the spinal cord become active only when general central arousal has reached a certain level. In preparations with transections anterior to the medulla, this level is kept up by excitation generated in the reticular formation of the medulla, without any additional peripheral stimulation. As mentioned earlier, peripheral stimulation, however, is capable of eliciting the automatic activity of the spinal cord before the reticular formation has recovered sufficiently. This means that, although the central nervous automatisms are in principle independent of external stimulation, they are not impervious to it. In reflex experiments with transection of the spinal cord at lower levels, the higher centers and their effects—namely spontaneous central nervous reorganization and spontaneous activation of the automatisms—are cut off. In this way, a fair constancy of the physiological conditions within the spinal cord is secured, and for this reason a certain proportionality between stimulus and reaction is achieved. In the medullary preparations or even the intact animal, however, the relationship is in no way determined by quality and quantity of stimulus alone. Quite to the contrary, the effect of stimulation is also dependent on the current balance of activities within the central nervous system at a given moment. In von Holst's experiments, for instance, shutting off the breathing water may have the following different effects on one and the same preparation:

1. the maximally active right pectoral fin becomes increasingly inhibited;
2. the incipient activity of the left pectoral fin is enhanced up to maximum activity and then stops very abruptly;
3. the currently inactive dorsal fin starts to oscillate slowly, its activity soon reaches its maximum point, then decreases again and peters out.

The so-called "reflex laws" must, therefore, be considered as marginal cases of more general regularities.

Peripheral stimulation, however, not only influences the automatic cells directly, but also largely controls the sensitivity of the motor cells to the rhythmical discharge from the automatic cells. This, of course, helps considerably to shape the externally observable form of the movement, since the amplitude of the movement is thus dependent not only on the number of automatic cells active but also, and to a large degree, on the physiological readiness (tonicity) of the motor cells. The frequency of a rhythmic movement, however, is exclusively a function of the automatic cells.

Above we have seen that the same stimulus may affect different automatisms in different ways related to their varying physiological state. Likewise the reaction of the motor and the automatic cells which control the movements of the same muscle may react differently to the same stimulus, and do so in many instances in an exactly opposite way. The same stimulus at the same time may considerably inhibit the excitability of the motor cells and increase the activity of the automatic cells, and vice versa.

In this context von Holst remarks that the old concepts of "inhibition" and "facilitation" are no longer suitable to describe the central nervous function. What means inhibition to one automatism means excitation to another. Even the same automatism is either facilitated or inhibited by the same stimulation at different times, depending on its current state. Inhibition can even lead to action in the opposite direction if superposition is very strong. Facilitation is a combined effect of magnetic influence and superposition which can even set in motion muscles whose automatisms are themselves inactive. All this leads to an entirely new picture of the internal functional relationships within the motor system.

V. THE ROLE OF THE CENTRAL NERVOUS AUTOMATISMS IN THE MOTOR SYSTEM

Reflexes in the old "classical" sense can no longer be regarded as the basic elements of complex movements. On the contrary, they are "complex and rather artificial, functional fragments which are of little use in analyzing the individual causal factors of central coordination." The apparently strict relationships between stimulus and reaction which reflex physiology produced were found only in experiments with preparations in which the spinal cord had been severed at a lower level. As already mentioned, the continuous rise in central arousal produced in the medulla and consequently the spontaneous onset of the central nervous automatisms cannot be observed in such cases. Monosynaptic reflexes, above all, need not be considered here. As far as we know, these are present only in animals with a pyramidal tract, i.e. in mammals. They least of all, therefore, could be primordial elements of the motor system since they appear only so late in evolution. But it is they which obey the reflexological laws in the strictest way. If we must look for a basic element of motor coordination, it can only be the segmental unit of a central nervous automatism. Something of this kind already appeared in Wacholder's (1925) conclusions regarding the so-called "recoil phenomenon" which follows single, arhythmic thrusts of movement; however, he interprets the fact that a fast movement of a limb in one direction never fails to elicit a movement in the opposite direction, which cannot be completely suppressed, as a "proprioceptive reflex." Yet he insists that the original form of movement in a baby is the alternating movement and that the baby has to learn to produce only one section of it. An observant person, however, can easily see that a baby's movements do not, in fact, alternate in a hingelike way but go in circles, ellipses, figures-of-eight, and even more complicated curves. These movements are therefore characterized by regular, though complicated, phasic relationships between the components and strict antagonism is only one possibility among many. These conclusions are corroborated by investigations of the movement of the mammalian fetus by Barcroft and Barron (1939).

The first fetal movements which can be elicited are jerky. At first they occur singly, but soon in rhythm. In the course of ontogenetic development the locally elicited rhythmic excitation usually irradiates over the whole fetus, due doubtless to the spread of magnetic influence. It may be remembered that the musculature of a dependent rhythm starts working at low amplitude in the rhythm of the dominating automatism when its own automatism stops. Later in ontogeny, centers in the inter-brain, which Barcroft and Barron were able to identify, acquire a capacity for limiting the spread of magnetic influence so that definite stimuli again elicit more localized responses. At first, however, all movement continues to be rhythmic. The movements of the fetus and the new-born baby have often been described, especially in American literature, as "mass activity." Gesell (1929) has already opposed this view and stated that the movements of a baby are typical for each phase of development. This can only mean that for each phase they reveal a typical form of coordination. They may be without aim or goal, but they are certainly not without order. The rhythms of central nervous automatisms fit this description: They need no aim or goal and no direction from external stimuli in order to produce well-ordered, recognizable patterns of movement.

To recapitulate: The elementary nervous unit underlying any movement can only be the individual group of synergistically working automatic cells in the spinal cord. However, their activities cannot go on in isolation in a vacuum. They affect one another continuously by magnetic influence, and the degree to which an automatic group of cells succumbs to the sum of magnetic influence exerted on it depends not only on the strength of that influence but also on its own capacity for perseverance.

However, the countless number of theoretically possible relationships between all automatic cell groups are not actualized with equal probability. There are certain rules. These caused von Holst to draw certain parallels between central nervous automatic functions and some basic phenomena of gestalt psychology. The periodical changes in rhythm and amplitude which occur under the rule of relative coordination of movements do not have equal chance but display differential stability. The stability of the interdependence of two or more rhythms increases proportionally with the simplicity of their frequency ratios. The most stable conjunction is, therefore, absolute coordination, 1 : 1, followed by 1 : 2, 1 : 3, 2 : 3, and so on (for 3 rhythms, 1 : 2 : 2, 1 : 2 : 3, 2 : 3 : 4, and so on; similarly for more than 3 rhythms). This is in accordance with the "law of prägnanz" (the tendency of a gestalt toward meaningfulness, completeness, and relative simplicity) of the gestalt psychologists in its tendency toward definite, discrete modes of performance. In terrestrial animals absolute coordination is admittedly more useful and its prevalence intelligible without recourse to gestalt theory. This, however, does not apply to the various forms of relative coordination in aquatic animals. A frequency ratio of 1 : 2 between the rhythms of the pectoral fins and tail-fin has no advantage over a ratio of, say, 1 : 3 or 1 : 4. The greater stability of the more simple ratio is, therefore, not adaptive but can only be related to the internal properties of the functional mechanism producing it.

The stability of such a total activity pattern to which several automatisms contribute expresses itself also in the fact that any gradual or sudden change in a condition extraneous to the pattern itself does not necessarily bring about a corresponding change in the pattern; as long as changes in the extraneous condition do not exceed certain limits, the pattern perseveres in its form. Only when the change exceeds this limit may the pattern suddenly change its internal coordination and relationships completely. It is only a special case of this general rule if, as mentioned earlier, the transition from relative to absolute coordination almost always sets in quite abruptly and not gradually. In this way the stabilized mutual frequency and phase relationship of two or more automatisms represents a relatively autonomous whole set off against the rest of the functional relationships within the spinal cord. In this respect, it closely resembles the "dynamic configurations" of gestalt psychology.

Finally, "the strictly determined *relationship between each part activity* and every other at a given moment *cannot be explained on the basis of the forces acting at this same moment.* The relationship between the automatisms if regarded at any cross section in time (as obtained in the recorded curve by considering all the points of each curve coinciding in time) is very often—and with very complex functional systems *almost always*—a *disequilibrium* which itself tends toward a *different* set of relationships; in other words the disequilibrium existing at any given time is compensated for periodically by an antagonistic complementary disequilibrium. The periodicity of all these functional relationships therefore forms a configuration in time *(Zeitgestalt)* within which temporally distant parts affect each other" (1939 a).

In addition to these three parallels between the configurations of psychology and the functional properties of the central nervous automatisms which von Holst himself has already pointed out, I should myself like to emphasize a fourth similarity, which can be demonstrated by a particularly illuminating example. The motor configurations produced by the automatisms can be transposed. This is a direct consequence of the fact that, when an automatism changes its frequency, the phasic relationships of its automatic sub-groups remain stable. This means, for instance, that if, say, the automatism of the dorsal fin increases its frequency, the waves running along the fin become faster but their configuration, i.e. their wavelength and amplitude, remains the same. The *phase delay* between each two neighboring fin spines remains the same, but the *time-lag* changes in such a way that it keeps the same proportion to the total duration of a complete cycle. The example referred to is the one given by Künnapas, quoted after Katz (1948). His experimental subjects found it quite natural to produce a certain rhythm, for instance by knocking with the finger, more slowly or more quickly. The relative time-lag between the single knocks was kept with amazing accuracy and reliability. Knowing von Holst's results, this is only to be expected. Experiments concerning transposition of more complex movements show even more striking correspondence. The activity chosen for the experiment was handwriting, and the experimental persons were asked to change both the size of the letters and the speed of writing. The size of the letters could be either diminished or increased in the ratio of 1 : 5 as against the normal letter size of the writer without any change in the total time the writer needed for a word or a single letter. Within these limits, writing speed is therefore independent of letter size. This corresponds closely to the fact, already mentioned, that amplitude of movement depends mainly on the tonicity of the *motor* cells employed and can, therefore, be changed without any influence on the *rhythm of the movement*. The habitual rhythm of writing shows high stability independent of the absolute speed with which the writing hand moves and which, of course, is much greater when the letters are big than when they are small. If, however, in another experiment the experimental person changes the speed of writing, the relative proportion of time needed for each letter remains *constant* in relation to the time needed for the whole word, regardless of whether the writing speed is increased or slowed down. This means that the time differences between the muscles which effect the writing movement stay *the same in proportion to the total duration* of a rhythmic period (= cycle). The phase lags remain *the same* with respect to the cycle as a whole, just as described above in respect of the action of the muscles which move a single spine of a fin. Thus the transposability of a complete movement, a motoric gestalt, is an immediate consequence of the laws of central nervous coordination!

Here I must mention a type of complex movement possessing all the properties emphasized by von Holst, namely the instinct movement. Lorenz (1932, 1937 a, b), independent of von Holst, found that the intensity of an instinct movement is not dependent solely on the strength of the releasing stimulus but also on the current "mood" of the animal. Hence he speaks of the "dual quantifiability of internal and external stimulation." Likewise, the automatisms of an experimental preparation in different states of readiness react differently to one and the same stimulus. Lorenz settled the controversy as to whether an instinct movement was in some way plastic or rigid in favor of rigidity (1937 a, b). He was able to demonstrate constant, strictly innate elements in the various, often very complex instinct actions of animals which are so characteristic of the species that they are of as much or even better use in taxonomy than anatomical characteristics. The rigidity of instinct movements emphasized by Lorenz, however, must not be taken as implying a machinelike, unvarying performance of the movement, as for instance Schwangart (1940) does when writing that he doubted "even the existence of unconditionally rigid behavioral elements." Lorenz himself describes different intensities of instinct movements and his definition of an instinct movement as a "hereditary coordination" in particular makes it clear what the term rigidity refers to, namely the phase relationships between all muscles employed in that particular movement. The gestalt of the movement itself can be transposed with respect to amplitude and frequency, but it always remains identifiable, regardless of whether it runs off at its highest intensity from beginning to end or reveals itself only in a fleeting intention movement. As far as transposition is concerned, therefore, an instinctive movement is plastic in the Lorenzian definition, too, but as a given configuration it is rigid and invariable. Furthermore, this rigidity can be maintained only under "physiological" conditions, i.e. within the more or less intact organism. As already mentioned, stable systems of coordination retain their form only within certain limits, but beyond these they may jump abruptly into a different form of coordination. These limits are, of course, reached and surpassed if one removes several pairs of legs from a millipede or a bug or the hind-legs from a dog experimentally. Coordination of the remaining limbs changes abruptly. This is not to say that the central nervous system is plastic in the sense that in such cases the requirements of peripheral function could create new functional organizations within the center. The adaptedness of such regulations can be adequately explained by the fact that in the course of a long phylogeny mutilations and even losses of limbs were sufficiently frequent in the life of animals for evolution to prepare a second line of patterns on which the mutilated animal could fall back. In addition, the resulting changes in coordination proved not quite so adaptive in all experiments. Sperry (1945) therefore sums up the results of all relevant investigations in the following way: "For practical purposes it would seem best, on the basis of the evidence now available, to relinquish altogether any hope that immediate spontaneous reorganization will effect correction of function after nerve misdirection or muscle transposition." And further: "that the re-educative adjustments are not effected in the primary motor or sensory nuclei but involve the higher association centers, and that it is not merely a simple localized switching of anatomical connections which occurs but an operationally organized readjustment of the sort involved in ordinary learning under normal conditions."

Furthermore, the instinct movement is proof that within the central nervous system there must be centers above the level of the spinal cord which are able to exert a stabilizing influence on those patterned movements which are coordinated within the spinal cord. As mentioned earlier, it is the magnetic influence and the strength of perserverance of two respective automatisms which determine the coordination and relationship between the two. For the orderly performance of instinctive movements these two factors governing the functional relationship between the central nervous automatisms employed are genetically determined. However, since the medullary preparations do not show any instinct movements more complex than the locomotory automatisms, it follows that instinct coordination must be located in higher centers. Location and functioning of some of these higher centers have been investigated by W. R. Hess and his collaborators (Hess 1943 b, Hess and Brügger 1943).

Let us briefly review the new picture of motoric function: In the spinal cord there are groups of automatically functioning cells distributed segmentally which emit their impulses rhythmically to the corresponding motor cells. They determine the frequency and, probably through the number of cells being activated at a given time, partly also the amplitude of a muscular movement. The amplitude is, however, mainly determined by the tonicity of the motor cells. The segmental automatic units combine to form larger action units (automatisms), which are responsible for the movement of a limb or fin. The functional relationships both between the segmental groups of an automatism and between different automatisms are governed by their strength of perserverance and the mutually exerted magnetic influences. In this way, the most diverse forms of coordination can be produced without any need of peripheral direction. The automatisms are activated by excitation originating in higher order centers (spontaneous movements) or at the periphery (reflex movements, basic reflexes, coordinated reflexes). The resultant movement, apart from depending on the nature of the impulses arriving, is essentially dependent on the momentary functional readiness of the nervous elements involved. The functional relationships between the single segmental automatic groups of an automatism and also between automatisms as wholes tend toward definite frequency ratios distinguished by their simplicity. Such systems are, within certain limits, persistent in the face of changes in external conditions, and they maintain their equilibrium by means of a rhythmical sequence of disequilibria canceling each other out. They are temporal gestalts which can be transposed with respect to frequency and amplitude. Certain more complex movement sequences have such functional relationships of the automatic units involved fixed genetically and located in higher centers (instinct movements).

VI. VOLUNTARY MOVEMENTS AND THE CONDITIONED REFLEX

Within the framework thus established, the so-called "voluntary motor system" does not appear to be motorically independent but is rather a means of interfering in the complex web of interacting magnetic influences and perseverance tendencies in such a way that it is able to retain for a certain time a relationship between various rhythms which otherwise would not be stable. In the course of phylogeny, this is possible at first only between larger units of sequential movements. Thus whole instinct movements or large parts of them become available in contexts outside that of the original complex activity, as exemplified by a dog giving a paw. In this the dog is not able to alter part elements of the whole movement voluntarily, e.g. by moving a single toe separately. However, in the further course of phylogeny voluntary influence reaches ever smaller parts of the whole sequence. This finds anatomical expression in the progressive development of the motor cortex and the pyramidal tracts in mammals. Finally, in the highest mammals and man an immediate influence on single segmental automatic units seems possible. If the hypothesis outlined here is correct, voluntary movement always depends on the cooperation of automatic elements and therefore on parts of the central nervous system which traditionally have been attributed to the extra-pyramidal motor system.

Recent investigations by Lloyd (1944) have proved that the axons of the pyramidal motor cells do *not*, as was assumed until then, form a direct synapse with the motor cells of the anterior horn of the spinal cord, but only with the interneurons (what are sometimes called correlating neurons). Since the axons of the pyramidal cells have a comparatively slow speed of impulse transmission, impulses originating in the motor cortex arrive at a certain segment of the spinal cord faster by way of extra-pyramidal fibers, to which the impulses are already diverted in the mid-brain through collaterals of the pyramidal fibers. These findings fit the hypothesis outlined above excellently. Further corroboration can be found in the long known fact that in

the case of partial paralysis of the motor cortex the voluntary movement of muscles not immediately afflicted by the paralysis is able
to cause the affected muscles to produce complicated and well-
coordinated corresponding movements.

According to the hypothesis, the processes when learning a new
motor sequence or pattern would have to be approximately of the
following type:— Stage 1: Voluntary innervation forces a number of
central nervous automatisms to produce a sequence of disharmonious
and in part discontinuous actions by forcibly retaining unstable functional coordination between them, as described above. The resultant
flow of the movement is uncertain, often jerky, and transitions in
particular seem labored. In stage 2 the voluntary motor system exerts
direction by way of negative feedback from the success of the movement, while underneath this voluntary supervision the automatic elements strive toward an internal coordination of their own which is in
itself stable yet still produces the desired effect of the movement. In
accordance with the functional properties of central nervous coordination already explained, the transition from the first pattern of the
movement, which in most of its details is directed by voluntary control, into a habituated, automatized form is often abrupt; and even
where at first glance we gain the impression of continuous progress
toward ever better performance, close scrutiny reveals that progress
is actually achieved in a number of smaller steps. At first only certain
phases of the performance become smooth, or the whole sequence
changes its pattern several times, each change bringing it closer to
smooth performance, i.e. a more stable internal organization. Anyone
who needs to learn very special techniques of movement for his
activity, e.g. many craftsmen and sportsmen, will on consideration
confirm that the learning process does indeed progress in this way.
In every case the habituated movement pattern eventually has very
little in common with the original movement voluntarily produced in
all its parts, apart from its final effect. Thus the pattern finally established is a new and stable system ordered according to the internal
functional conditions of the spinal cord (and higher centers as the
case may be) and the voluntary control over the whole system is only
that of a push-button device. As we have seen exemplified by handwriting, the pattern is, then, a configuration which can be transposed
within certain very wide limits. And nothing can demonstrate better
than handwriting the complete diversity of internal organization between the writing movement of the beginner, which in all its parts
is performed voluntarily, and the smooth performance of a practiced
writer.

This change in nature of the motor coordination which accompanies accomplishment of a new motor pattern is also responsible for the fact that, after the new pattern has been established, it becomes increasingly difficult to exert voluntary influence on single elements, and that any attempt to do so will at first only disrupt the whole. The rhythmic automatic nature of the activity of the spinal cord also explains why such new patterns, once established, need only be activated and will then go on without any further voluntary impulse. Very often it even needs a conscious effort to stop them. A further consequence of all this is that the rhythmic, periodic self-differentiation of such a complex movement pattern comes about more easily and quickly if, where possible, one starts by training the whole sequence or pattern and not parts of it separately. Part movements habituated separately form a stable system in themselves, and if they are to be combined into a complex whole system they have each to be *re*-formed—their internal equilibrium has to be broken up and a new total equilibrium found (see above p. 81–2). This is the reason why learning parts of a sequence separately is very often not only not beneficial but directly detrimental to learning the whole. All this has long been known to psychology and has found its expression in practice—for instance, in teaching beginners to write (whole word method). Von Holst's findings only provided us with an understanding of the underlying physiological processes.

VII. SOME PARALLELS BETWEEN GESTALTIST LEARNING THEORY AND THE PHENOMENA OF CENTRAL NERVOUS COORDINATION

From what has been said so far, it may be safely concluded that the old concept of the conditioned reflex, at least as far as the motor or efferent part is concerned, is no more an adequate description of what actually goes on than is the principle of the reflex in general. It is, however, now possible to draw a few tentative conclusions concerning the phenomena of associative processing of data and perception. Von Holst himself realized the close correspondence between his own results and the curves recorded from action potentials obtained from different areas of the cortex by means of unipolar electrodes. In the meantime work by Jung (1939 a, 1941) and Hugger (1941) has shown that the mechanisms coordinating the functions of the cortex are of the same nature as those of the spinal cord. In each case rhythmic automatic activity of groups of nerve cells is found and the action potentials of different areas of the cortex reveal the same kind of coordination and phasic relations as do the automatisms of the spinal cord.

The cooperation and interplay between perseverant tendency and magnetic influence function in a manner exactly analogous to the association mechanisms which played such an omnipotent role in the theory of older psychology. It must be borne in mind, then, that the concept of magnetic influence, like that of association, is purely descriptive in nature, and at first glance it might seem questionable whether there is any advantage in using one name instead of the other. However, the concept of magnetic influence makes it possible to explain not only the laws of association but also a number of phenomena apparently contradictory to them on the basis of the same causal network. Again we find a far-reaching correspondence between the physiological model and the hypotheses of the gestaltists concerning the processes of learning, thinking, and memory. Von Holst's models make it possible for us to understand why sometimes a single instance suffices while in other cases very long practice is required in order to learn material presenting the same degree of difficulty, even though it is not possible to assume differences in stimulation or "learning drive" in these cases. A certain melody, for instance, which one hardly noticed while viewing a film and quite certainly did not intend to learn, may insistently haunt one's consciousness for days. Assuming that the automatisms of the brain which play a part in this particular learning activity may, according to their different state of activity at the moment, form a stable new equilibrium either at once and at one stroke or in several smaller steps, or even, in rare cases, by a smooth gradual change, as the case may be, then it is clear that the kind of stimulation can by itself have only a very restricted influence on learning success.

Likewise, it is easy to imagine that the automatisms, if left to themselves (while conscious control is at rest), may achieve coordination patterns to which there are no corresponding stimulation patterns in the environment and which, therefore, also cannot be derived from experience. This opens up at least some possibility of understanding creative fantasy on a physiological basis. The sudden intuition which allows us to find the solution to a difficult problem may also be explained in this way. "One concentrates on a number of conditions which must be fulfilled, twists and turns the available data before one's mental eye—and then (sometimes) suddenly has the solution, as if it had been inaudibly whispered into one's ear. For such a process I could find no better simple model than the abrupt appearance of new configurations of rhythm in the spinal cord of a fish during an experiment in which the experimenter gradually and slowly changes external conditions. For in both cases the emergence of something new depends both on the internal coordinating mechanisms and on the external situation. If one knows only about the external part, the result must look like spontaneous intuition" (von Holst 1948). In any case, we are capable of experiencing only such conditions and relationships as can be expressed by patterns which the central coordinating mechanisms are capable of forming.

Furthermore, magnetic influence helps us understand why the direction of association influences the actual path association takes. If a is associated with both b and c, it is still possible that in a given case a will elicit the memory of c exclusively, despite the fact that the association between a and b may be stronger in absolute terms. The reason is that the association between a and c has been acquired in a situation resembling the present case. This corresponds exactly to the fact, mentioned already, that in a periodical pattern of rhythm parts distant in time may influence each other. There is likewise a physiological model for the process of associative inhibition closely corresponding to the explanation for it given by the gestaltists: If a pattern a is linked with a pattern b by magnetic influence, the two together form a new unit—a compound process or period ab—which, when encountering a new influence c, shows greater resistance or stability than each of the still independent elementary patterns a and b could muster.

The close correspondence between the ideas on the physiology of learning processes which can be derived from von Holst's results— if so far only in a purely hypothetical way—and the respective ideas of the gestaltists does, however, encounter one very important reservation: The gestaltists think that no learning process exists which is absolutely useless or senseless. When typing, however, if one repeatedly and consistently mistypes, for instance, the suffix "-ably" as "-alby" or "-baly," this is certainly not the result of a direct intention to learn and it also makes no sense in any other way. On the contrary, such mistyping must be ascribed exclusively to the internal nature of the coordinating mechanisms. It seems that the sequence -a-l-b-y-, for instance, falls more easily into a stable phase relationship as soon as conscious control relaxes than the correct -a-b-l-y-. Every teacher knows how diffcult it can be to eradicate a similar mistake (for instance in pronouncing a word in a foreign language) once it has occurred.

VIII. PHENOMENA CORRESPONDING TO THE FINDINGS OF PERCEPTION PSYCHOLOGY

For the sake of argument, let us assume that not only those receptors mentioned on p. 78 but quite simply all receptors are continuously and automatically active. In this case a number of basic phenomena produced by our sensory systems become intelligible. For instance, the subjective experience of a darkish gray which we have in complete darkness could be explained by the automatic activity of the light receptors. It is significantly different from the "nothing" experienced after some part of the retina has been destroyed. Futhermore, it becomes quite clear why our sensory systems respond not to absolute stimulus quantities but to fluctuations in stimulus intensity, i.e. it is differences in stimulation which are being perceived. This is necessary, since the automatic activity of the sensory cells is physiologically subject to fluctuations, and if the more central part of the sensory system reacted to absolute frequencies of impulses they could not differentiate between slight stimulation superimposed on a low frequency automatic activity and an unstimulated state with enhanced automatic activity. Reaction to intensity differences or fluctuations, however, means that it is relationships or ratios which are being evaluated. The increase or decrease in the basic frequency elicited by stimulation is compared with the previous frequency shown by the same receptor and also with those of the neighboring receptors. If a stimulus is applied to one receptor but not to its neighbor, it can easily be understood why the relationship between the two does not seem to have undergone a *unilateral* change but that subjectively the impression of mutual influence prevails.

Relativity of influence of this kind could already be proved by Motikawa (1950) for receptors within the retina: the pecularities he found quite patently form the physiological basis of a host of regularities found in gestalt perception (e.g. the tendency toward wholeness which makes us perceive a complete gestalt when the actual stimulus material is in some way defective) and in some optical illusions (e.g. Müller-Lyer illusion). Likewise, simultaneous color contrast would not only be explained but would automatically follow, and the same is true of negative and positive after-images. Since, according to our model, the more centrally situated sensory centers also have their own automatic activity which tends toward a stable mutual relationship, the "creeping in" phenomenon under low intensity stimulation could be explained. Up to certain limits the stable equilibrium, once achieved, remains insensitive toward arriving impulses. Stimulus threshold and differential threshold spring from the same biological basis. If our model of central sensory coordination is applicable, some constancy phenomena—namely brightness constancy and color constancy—could also be explained, since it is frequency ratios and not absolute intensities, i.e. frequencies, which matter. Constancy of space, size, and objects, however, is based on far more complex processes, which cannot be dealt with further here but which have already at least partially been analyzed by von Holst and Mittelstaedt (1950). The transposability of perceived configurations can be explained in an analagous way to what has been said about melodies and motor coordinations. Since impulses originating from receptors meet impulse waves in the sensory centers which have already stabilized themselves in different ways and which react to disturbance of their equilibrium by jumping abruptly into another stable form of coordination, this seems to represent a good model for what is called the "tendency toward gestalt perception." Finally it must be assumed that on their way from the sensory cells to the higher centers the impulses already interact in various and complicated ways and that what actually arrives at the centers are in many cases more or less complicated superpositions of the original individual receptor impulses. The reaction to such integrated processes probably follows the principle of resonance (see above p. 76) and one can therefore imagine that the sensory impulse complex reaching the higher centers may be analyzed by these into elements different from those which established them originally. This could easily account for another part of sensory illusions. Last but not least, the completion of incomplete stimulus complexes into a whole according to "gestalt tendency" would find a physiological model in that magnetic influence could co-activate rhythms which had not been reached directly by the impulse waves originating from the receptors.

IX. THE RELATIONSHIP BETWEEN THE PHYSIOLOGICAL MODEL DEVELOPED ABOVE AND GESTALT THEORY

As has been pointed out, the findings of von Holst and the physiological models derived from them parallel the findings of gestalt psychology in all essential points. In many respects the models are admittedly still hypothetical, but this does not apply to the motor functions. It may, therefore, be permissible, proceeding from this firm foundation, to contribute some critical remarks on the gestalt theory derived from the findings of the gestalt psychologists.

Von Holst has already voiced criticism of the much-quoted dictum that the whole is more than the sum of its parts. He demonstrates that this is not true of the gestalt of motor sequences analyzed by him, if the temporal and spatial relationships between the components are properly included in the equation. "If this coordination is taken into account, then all that is necessary is to add up the corresponding, recorded data, and nothing but the gestalt (or whole) itself results." (1939 a.) The same holds true for the so-called "physical gestalts" of Wolfgang Köhler. If one takes into account the form and material of an isolated conductor, then without any further data it is possible to calculate the equilibrium of the electrical charge distributed over it, i.e. it can be analyzed according to summation and ratios. That this is also possible with the gestalt of motor sequences should require no further explanation. However, two examples will be given to demonstrate the emergence of such gestalts in steps:

1. The periodical fluctuations of frequency which magnetic influence produces in a dependent rhythm are generated within its automatic cells. The fluctuations in frequency and amplitude which are due to superposition, however, do not form until one relay station further, namely through superposition of the impulses of different frequencies emerging from "schizoid" automatic subgroups (see above, p. 77) in the motor neurons. Within the automatic subgroup, part of which is still working at its original autonomous frequency while its other part has joined the rhythm of the dominant automatism, we still see the two positions of a simple addition. If in the total movement magnetic influence and superposition are combined, the result is a gestalt motor sequence which is integrated on different levels from a number of different forming factors. This in no way alters the wholeness of the resulting gestalt of the movement.

2. The innate releasing mechanisms (Lorenz 1943 a) of animals are based on their reacting innately to certain combinations of stimuli. The individual elements of these stimulus combinations consist of simple relationships, colors, movements—in short, they have the characteristics of very simple gestalts. However, in the perception of the animals they do not lose their individuality in a whole gestalt: Their releasing power can be measured individually, and they are able to replace each other in a random way (e.g. *a-c-d* in place of *a-b-c*, or *a-a-b* in place of *a-b-c*). This is known as the law of summation of heterogeneous stimuli and has been con-

firmed in a great number of animal experiments. The phenomenon can only be interpreted in such a way that the "gestalt components" (=single features) are measured individually and added up to a sum of eliciting power in some intermediary center before they can be integrated into a whole gestalt in some higher sensory center. This, more than anything else, seems to me proof that our perception builds up gestalts in steps, even if we never become conscious of the process.

The reluctance of the gestalt theorist to acknowledge such reasoning stems, I think, from a methodological error. The study of phenomenology, which is almost the only method used by the gestaltists, easily induces the researcher to *identify the inner experience with the conditions which make it possible and govern its course.* Many gestaltists see no difference between the *experience of a gestalt* and the *origin of a gestalt.* Some of them would even deny that gestalts have an origin at all. Inner experience simply does not tell us anything about how it originates, and herein lies a constitutional weakness of phenomenological analysis. We must assume that any experience, even the phenomenologically most elementary one, is produced by a very complex interaction of a widely differing number of central nervous processes. Even in pure mathematics it is not possible to find out by mere calculation which harmonious curves in particular form a given superposition curve of regular periodicity unless at least part of the original harmonics is known. Any such complex curve can in theory have originated from the combination of an infinite number of different harmonics. In an analogous way, I think we are encountering here a vital barrier which limits the results it would be possible to obtain by way of phenomenological analysis. To use a simple mechanical analogy, the phenomenologist finds himself in a similar position to someone who has been asked to analyze the mechanical conditions of film projection from what he can see on the screen.

Against this view two arguments are usually raised:
1. that an analysis not founded on phenomenology is no longer dealing with the mind or anything psychological, and
2. that the high value of phenomenological study of psychic processes is thereby completely underestimated.

Both arguments I should like to counter with a new paradigm which is, however, as always arguable: A physicist faced with a physical mixture of substances may, by employing the means of physical analysis, be able to segregate the ingredients and determine which they are. Thus far phenomenological analysis will take us. If our physicist wants to probe more deeply into the nature of the ingredients, he must employ chemical methods. In the process of chemical analysis, the physical properties of the ingredients get lost, but only in this way is he able to gain knowledge of their inner nature.

In this process it may become apparent that substances with very similar physical properties are not in the least related chemically and, vice versa, that substances having a very similar chemical make-up reveal widely different physical properties. Similarly, in psychology it often emerges that phenomena which look very similar or even identical are quite heterogeneous if analyzed genetically and causally, as has been shown above with regard to the different phenomena commonly subsumed under the heading "constancy phenomena." In the more recent studies of animal behavior, many a misunderstanding between researchers could have been avoided and much could have been recognized as a purely semantic problem far sooner if one had always been aware of the fact that, for instance, the "subjective environmentology" (*Umweltlehre* 1909) of von Uexküll is phenomenologically oriented, whereas the comparative ethology of Konrad Lorenz has its methodological basis in genetical and causal analysis. The concept of the "functional system," or "major instinct" in the terminology of Tinbergen, is, therefore, a phenomenological concept and comprises behavior components which originated from very different roots of widely differing phylogenetic age; this in no way disrupts their smooth cooperation within the functional context. The concept of the instinct movement, however, was formed inductively from causal analysis, and instinct movements originating from the same phylogenetic root may be integrated fully into very different functional systems.

The point I am trying to make is that, *for all its limitations, no one would claim that a physical investigation of ingredients is inadequate and that the only road to knowledge is chemistry. Of course, a psychologist must employ phenomenological analysis, but*—and this is essential—*he must not stop there.* To return to our first example: Anyone wanting to analyze the mechanical conditions producing pictures seen on the screen must turn away from the screen and start to investigate the projection apparatus. The psychologist simply must not shy away from crossing the logical abyss which opens up between the world of inner experience and the world of physiological processes. The specifically psychic will, at first at least, disappear in this process. However, he gains abundantly in understanding the basic conditions which underlie it even if our knowledge in this respect is still very incomplete and fragmentary.

The situation is comparable to that in biological systematics. Linné formed his *systema naturae,* so to speak, along phenomenological lines. To our way of thinking, it is a matter of course to replace this gradually by a system based on natural, i.e. phylogenetic, relationships. But this is at all possible only because and after the phenomenological inventory has been assembled. Likewise in psychology the phenomenological procedure can only supply us with a description and classification of conscious processes according to their apparent and functional similarity (this corresponds to the concept of analogy in comparative anatomy). Neither the biologist nor the psychologist, however, can be satisfied with this but must investigate the genetical and causal conditions of these processes. For the psychologist this is impossible without delving rather deeply into physiology and trying to use physiological data for the interpretation of psychological experiences and processes. Time and again this very procedure is discredited as an illegitimate crossing of borderlines. But crossing the borderline—namely the borderline between inner and external experience—is just what I insist must be tried. And "illegitimate"? As far as I know, there is not a psychologist left in the world who bases his interpretation solely on the one purely psychological means of research, i.e. introspection. Without exception, *any* other psychological method deals in the first place with physiological and not psychological facts, and these facts are then psychologically interpreted on the basis of the researcher's own introspective experience and on the introspective experiences of other people, which themselves can be transmitted only by way of other physiological processes. No one has the slightest doubt that *this* is necessary. But who, then, would venture to prohibit a researcher from proceeding in the opposite direction? Only by using both methods can the psychologist hope to eschew theoretical bias, and only in this way may we hope to achieve some working knowledge of those most highly integrated functions of the organism which are *not themselves divided according to the categories of our experience.*

I should like to make one more comment on gestalt theory. It appears to me that gestalt theory has one trait in common with the atomistic schools it tries so hard to fight, and that is that it has an exaggerated idea of the organism's dependence on external conditions. The extreme representatives of atomistic psychology regard the organism as a reflex machine which has no kind of autonomy whatsoever in relation to its external conditions. In developing the "field theory" and "topological vector psychology" (Lewin 1926) gestalt psychology commits quite the same kind of sin, though under an entirely different name. From both viewpoints it is hardly intelligible why organisms should be treated as special natural bodies, different from crystals and other inanimate physical matter, by a science all of their own. Kuo (1929) says, "Every movement is a forced movement," and Giese (in Elsenhans-Giese 1939) writes: "We are approaching now a kind of objective psychology, a psychology of the field and field effects," or elsewhere, "At no moment is there a quasi personally determined endogenous condition of the mind." Here both the behaviorists and the gestaltists express an essentially identical basic attitude which makes it very difficult, if not impossible, to appreciate adequately the autonomy of the organism in relation to its physical environment. The results of von Holst represent a contribution toward rediscovering this autonomy in all living beings which cannot be misunderstood and must not be overlooked. He has proved that the movements of animals need not be coordinated by external factors but are formed by factors endogenous to the animal itself, which in principle can act independently of external stimuli. In the same way Lorenz (1937 b) newly defines instinct by quite expressly excluding the external goal and eliciting stimuli from the definition and he supports his new concept of instinct with a mass of data from observation and experimentation. Lorenz emphasizes that both the primary release and the primary goal of instinctive acts must be sought in the animal itself. Of course, the majority of biologists agree that the autonomy of the organism as understood here can only be relative, but certainly its scope is far wider than the gestaltists' field theory appears to allow. Modern psychology and comparative ethology leave more room for the "spontaneity of the ego, that determines its own goals" (Katz 1948) than modern gestalt psychology does.

At the end of the work quoted here, Katz poses the question, "Will gestalt psychology in the near future arrive at the synthesis with the older atomistic psychology which would be expected on the grounds of Hegelian logics?" As has been pointed out, the results of von Holst allow us to integrate the data of reflex physiology, and, accordingly, those of atomistic psychology that are based on reflex physiology, into a more general functional picture of the nervous system, within which they represent special cases. On the other hand, von Holst's results show amazing concordances, covering many details, with the reliable results of gestalt psychology. Thus, it may not be premature to hope that in the very near future the antagonism between atomistic psychology and gestalt psychology will resolve itself in a broader, more comprehensive theoretical system.

6 A Comparison Between Territoriality in Animals and the Need for Space in Humans (1954)

Even in recent times human behavior is still being presented as a contrast to all that is animal. It is said not to display any innate elements, to be lacking in instinct, to create itself according to its own (extranatural) laws (Petzelt 1951), to be "universally receptive" ("*weltoffen*," Gehlen 1941). Yet, the comparative study of behavior increasingly supports the opposite view: However different human behavior, seen from a phenomenological point of view, may seem to be from that of even the highest mammals, at the basis of the most variable modes of human behavior lie peristostable "instinctive" elements (Baumgarten 1951, Kramer 1950, Leyhausen 1952, Lorenz 1940, 1943 a, b, 1950 b, c). Here comparative ethology concurs with views expressed in the field of psychiatry (Kretschmer 1946, 1948). Very much of human behavior is simply not intelligible on the basis of the life history of the individual, but only against the background of the long history of the species *Homo sapiens,* a history which for enormous periods of time was shared with the mammals and all other vertebrates. Thus a comparative study of animal behavior gives us insight into the phylogenetic development of human behavior. And the viewpoints of comparative morphology and physiology also prove their great heuristic value in the comparative investigation of animal and human behavior. We are, therefore, fully justified in speaking of homologous behavior patterns in the same sense as the comparative anatomist speaks of homologous organs. Here, too, the establishment of homology does not signify that the behaviors compared must be identical in either form or function. It seems essential to emphasize this as strongly as possible in view of frequent misunderstandings on the part of psychologists, sociologists, and philosophers.

From what I have said above, the justification for the narrow definition of our problem will be evident: What is the comparative study of behavior already capable of telling us about the relationship between man and the space around him, and what further questions can we expect it to answer?

Animals in what is known as their "natural state of freedom" never, as far as we yet know, enjoy the unconstrained and carefree freedom which a sentimental view of nature ascribes to them. No free-ranging animal, whether it belongs to a species living gregariously or spends the greater part of its life in solitude, has freedom of movement, i.e. moves as it pleases and at random. Already through its organization it is bound to a limited living space which offers it the conditions necessary for life. Even where this area is fairly large and provides these conditions uniformly well throughout, the animal is still not independent in its movement. Instead it limits itself to one or more small areas, known as its range; this it does not normally leave except from dire necessity. Within its range, too, the animal does not move at random, but only along particular paths and according to a fairly fixed schedule (Hediger 1949). Like the animal's preferred paths, this schedule may change with seasonal conditions; a herd of deer, for example, keeps more to rye and wheat fields in early summer and to oat fields later in the year. The range (or territory)[1] is, however, always divided up by permanent paths. Within it there are places which are particularly favorable for a particular activity (searching for food, resting). The safest and most comfortable resting-place enjoys the animal's especial preference as "home." Some animals also have separate territories for living and for hunting or finding food. Whereas in such cases the living territory is dominated mostly by solitary animals or pairs, the feeding territory may belong to many neighbors in common. The variations here are very numerous and the functions which being more or less strictly bound to a locality fulfils in the life of the different animal species are likewise manifold. This is not the place to enumerate them all; a detailed review containing examples of each of the forms of territorial behavior mentioned is provided by Nice (1941).

What determines the outer limits of a territory? Even when an animal species is so rare that the individual specimens practically never meet in the living space at their disposal,[2] the range does not generally exceed a specific size. If, however, population density grows, the ranges of neighboring individuals soon become adjacent, and if the increase in population continues they must inevitably have a restricting effect on one another. It does sometimes happen that they overlap and that the border areas of two territories are used by two neighbors in common. Usually, however, every territory owner tries to seclude and defend its territory from its neighbors and to extend it at their expense. When the overall population grows, the individual territories become increasingly cramped. There is, however, a limit on the increase of "density of habitation"; the effect of this is that particularly favorable habitats have a density of habitation which always remains constant, while fluctuations in total population numbers are accommodated by less favored habitats (L. Tinbergen and Kluyver 1953). The conditions prevailing in the case of defended territories may best be illustrated by comparing the "home" part of the territory with an energy center which has a repulsive effect on all like energy centers; the boundary between two runs along a line where their respective fields of effect cancel one another out. This type of territory behaves like a flexible or elastic disc which, along with many other identical discs, is squeezed into a box—the total amount of space available for use in the locality. The territory owner defends the "center" most of all, while its courage—if the expression is permissible—diminishes as the distance from this center increases. Conversely the neighbor's readiness to fight increases the nearer it is to *its* home. Most song-birds and fishes which defend a territory behave according to this schema. In fact, these "fields of force" are demonstrated in positively classical manner in the boundary fights of some fishes. If one *Etroplus maculatus* oversteps the territorial boundary of its opponent, its pectoral fins switch to "counterstroke," while the tail-fin continues to produce forward propulsion; the strength of the tail-stroke decreases continually and that of the pectoral fins increases, so that the fish gradually comes to a standstill and is then propelled backward once more, whereas its opponent, which had at first withdrawn, now moves forward as a result of the reciprocal process. In this way, the two fighters can swing backward and forward over the territorial boundary for minutes on end. All this implies that within its territory, and particularly in the vicinity of its "center," an animal is superior in fighting strength to almost any conspecific, even the strongest. Only in very few cases has it ever been observed that an animal already firmly settled in its territory was driven out of it by an overpowerful neighbor or stranger (Lack 1939).

It is difficult to say what this fact is due to in detail. *One* factor is certainly the animal's familiarity with its surroundings; all higher animals are unsure and anxious in unfamiliar surroundings and reach complete assurance only after they have exhaustively investigated them. If one animal has only a slight lead, this can be decisive. If two cichlid fishes in a state of readiness to fight are put into a strange aquarium, the one put in first will be unequivocally dominant, at least at the start of the fight, even if it is the weaker of the two and only a few seconds elapsed before the second fish was put in. It is, however, questionable whether this factor alone can explain the development of territoriality in vertebrates and the different forms it takes.

Frequently, as with many song-birds, the elastic nature of the territory is evident only at the beginning of territorial occupation. Once the territorial boundaries have been settled in the course of fights between neighbors, they are respected after a certain time by all concerned. Boundary disputes then occur only occasionally when two neighbors meet by chance too close to the boundary. Neighboring animals no longer strive to extend their territory; each keeps peacefully within its own boundaries, ignoring the neighbor, and thus the immediate incentive for boundary fights is removed. In some cases, even a kind of friendly neighborliness has been observed, in that a neighbor is temporarily tolerated on a particular stretch at the edge of another's area without eliciting any fighting reaction in the territorial owner. This does not, however, signify a general relaxation of the readiness to fight. Any strange animal which happens to trespass is still immediately attacked and fought with maximum violence. The tendency to expand is also only latent. If an animal or a pair moves away or dies, within a short space of time its territory has been divided up among the others. Under certain circumstances this can result in the entire distribution of territory in a small habitat being disrupted and rearranged. If the vacated territory is relatively large, it is sometimes not shared out completely among the neighbors, but one part is left unoccupied. This is further proof of the fact that, even in the absence of competition from conspecifics, the size of a territory is limited and the animal does not extend its range indefinitely.

Territorial behavior varies tremendously according to the way of life of the individual animal species and particularly according to the form of its social life. We find that animals living chiefly alone and only during the mating period in pairs have territories which are more or less identical to the kind I have just described. Animals living in social communities often have very large territories with less clearly delineated boundaries. The animals no longer have complete visual control over them and cannot, therefore, always defend them effectively. In addition to this, large animals living in herds are compelled by the considerable food requirements for their numbers to move around constantly in their territory. As a result they cannot become tied to one locality as their home to the same extent as animals living singly or in pairs. Herds of deer, for example, do, it is true, prefer a particular kind of thicket in their territory as a resting-place, but the location can vary considerably insofar as this is at all possible from the point of view of the vegetation the territory offers. Furthermore seasonal fluctuations in vegetation frequently cause seasonal migrations of these animals within their territory or from a summer to a winter territory.

An intermediate position between the two forms mentioned above is occupied by animals living in family groups. Here the group is still small enough to enable it to adhere to a home, but on the other hand the size of the group stipulates a territory which is correspondingly larger and cannot, therefore, be kept under constant visual control and defended at all times. Among mammals, conditions of this kind exist, for example, in the case of the wolf, about whose family life and territorial behavior we have a good deal of information (Murie 1944).

Food requirements and social structure are not, however, the only factors governing the territorial behavior of an animal species. Internal factors independent of environmental conditions also play a part, as is demonstrated by a South and Central American family of cuckoos (Davis 1942). The family of the *Crotophaginae* consists of four species whose areas of distribution partially overlap and, broadly speaking, offer the same living conditions throughout. Yet, the four species differ clearly from one another in their territorial and social behavior. The species *Guira guira,* which probably represents the phylogenetically oldest stage, lives in fairly large groups, and each group defends a territory. During the breeding season, however, this group territory is mostly divided up among the individual pairs which form. Now, within the group territory each pair defends its little breeding territory against the neighboring pairs. However, both the group territory and the breeding territories are relatively weakly defended. *Crotophaga major* defends the group territory with noticeably greater intensity. During the breeding season pairs do not detach themselves from the group but build *one* common nest, in which all the females lay their eggs. Finally the species *C. ani* and *C. sulcirostris* defend their group territory with the most extreme vigor; pairs, however, are no longer formed at all and promiscuity reigns between the sexes. Here, too, there is only one common nest for all.

So far we know very little about the territories of higher mammals. Certainly they are often less sharply delineated than the territories of birds and fishes. Overlapping seems to be quite frequent. The only precise observations we have in this respect are on the behavior of the North American wolf (Murie 1944). Here a family group numbering on an average two to eight adult animals and several young occupy a hunting territory during the summer, within which a "living area" of about two kilometers in diameter is marked off. The den is situated somewhere in this area but is inhabited in the main only by the young and the nursing females. The hunting area, which is many square kilometers in size, overlaps at the edges with the hunting areas of neighboring families. Relations between neighbors are generally friendly and the crossing of a boundary does not elicit animosity; but in contrast, strange wolves passing through are repelled forcibly. It can, however, happen that after first being repelled strangers still manage to attach themselves to the group.

Our knowledge of the relevant behavior in monkeys and particularly the anthropoid apes is unfortunately extremely fragmentary so far. In these cases, too, family groups or fairly large bands seem in general to dominate a particular living area. We know scarcely anything, however, about how this area is separated and, if need be, defended from neighboring groups. In the case of the South American Howler Monkeys, similar to song-birds, the voice serves to designate ownership of the territory; the animals of a group are constantly in vocal contact and likewise the various groups within the living area (Carpenter 1934). The relations between neighbors are, as far as we know, very peaceful. Chimpanzees wander in small or somewhat larger troops through their habitat. In the evening each member of the troop builds itself a sleeping nest in a tree; mothers take their babies into the nest with them and juveniles probably also sleep occasionally in twos (Nissen 1931).

Although the information we have about the life of the anthropoid apes in the wilds is so far only scanty, it does reveal some striking correspondences with the social life of primitive hunting and food-gathering peoples. In the latter case, too, the main social community is the family or a tribe consisting of three or four families who find their living together in a clearly delineated area. Relations between neighboring tribes are in general quite friendly, though boundary infringements are at once resisted with force, usually by attack from the rear without warning, sometimes bringing about violent fighting between the neighboring groups. Communal life within the tribes proceeds in circumstances of relatively loose spatial connection. The individuals, or the individual families, roam and camp together, but always at a certain distance from one another. Every evening each individual family erects a windshield for the night. The Andaman people live in conditions which are sufficiently favorable to enable a group to stay a fairly long time in one place. In their case already one large hut is built in which the whole group is accommodated. Yet these huts clearly reveal how they have originated, namely by moving individual windshields closer together. Each family builds only its own part of the hut, has exclusive responsibility for repairing damage to it, and stakes out the room belonging to it inside the hut by laying pieces of wood, stones, and the like on the ground (Immenroth 1933, Nippold 1954, Schmidt 1937).

In the course of higher cultural development, these simple spatial relationships in human community life have changed greatly, and yet certain features recur time and again. Especially common is the way that every social community, small or large, and particularly the individual or the head of family, strives to reserve one certain area as its property and to repel any intrusion by others. Larger group territories (tribal land, "fatherland," etc.) can be identified with which there is a considerable emotional bond. It is true that this bond with the particular area concerned and some of its peculiarities is established by means of training and tradition, but these factors still do not create the *possibility* of such a fixation, nor do they explain it. Instead it is pre-programmed into the disposition of every single human, just like the many forms in which this bond finds expression. "Homesickness" as such is certainly not something which has to be learned. Within the various group territories each individual seeks to build his own private kingdom, and the greater the density of habitation the stronger this need to stake out limits: The fences become more impenetrable, the walls higher and higher. Furthermore most people like to occupy particular places wherever they frequently spend their time—in the streetcar or the lecture hall, on the beach, and so on ("'my' corner," "'my' seat"). On summer vacation one automatically asks to have "the same room as last year." And if one of these places is already occupied when we arrive, every one of us feels somehow put out; if the opportunity arises, some people even become aggressive toward the person who has in all innocence taken the place before them. A person's desk at the office or father's writing desk at home are positively sacred objects, defended with a depth of emotion which certainly does not seem to be adequately explained or justified purely by any untidiness which may have been caused. Every teacher knows, too, with what tenacity the pupils in a class usually adhere to a seating plan once it has been worked out. And here the vital factor is not always personal links between children sitting in neighboring seats. Frequently it is simply a matter of holding onto the "place." This also plays its part even in cases where the personal links are more apparent.

All these phenomena become particularly clear, however, in unusual community situations. If a fairly large number of prisoners-of-war is moved to a new camp, the very first thing every single man does is seek his place for sleeping and living (insofar as one can use the term in this context), occupy it as fast as possible, and defend it bitterly against all other claims. Characteristically, this attitude of the individual has the fundamental approval of all the others, naturally with the exception of anyone who would have liked to have that particular place himself. Each one divides off the place he has occupied from his neighbors as well as is humanly possible with the means available, such as blankets, cardboard, string, etc., and takes jealous care that no one enters this "home" without his special permission. Within a short space of time the distribution of places has become an accepted fact, respected by all, even if in some cases envy of the lucky occupant of a really, or only supposedly, better place never quite dies and may take on the most extraordinary forms of expression. Others proceed with extreme cunning on the principle of "creeping infiltration"; they extend their space gradually at the cost of their nearest neighbors and indignantly deny—often no doubt fully convinced of their own honesty—any intention of the kind when they are caught out.

In animals, defense of territory plays a particular role in singling out and clearly designating ("individualizing," Kramer 1950) certain animals for their conspecifics. In the case of many animals, namely, all social interplay is elicited by stimuli emanating from the social partner, and these stimuli may be quite different for each individual social reaction. The acting animal need not associate all these various stimuli with one individual animal in its perception. Even without this the "biological purpose" will be achieved. This may be illustrated in the following manner: Let us imagine a man sitting in a completely dark room before a row of levers. When a red light shines he is supposed to press one lever, and when a green light shines another, and so on. Now, it may be that these signals light up in an ordered sequence on a machine whose operation is governed by the pressing of the levers, but this remains hidden from our imaginary experimental person. He sees only what seem to him completely separate, apparently unconnected signals lighting up at various points in the room and responds to them in a specific and each time different manner. In the animal kingdom realization that the various sign stimuli emanating from a social partner all belong to one individual animal comes only at a relatively late stage and is varyingly successful in the various social contexts: One and the same animal may in one context behave similarly to the "model" just described and in another have precise knowledge of the individual members of its social group (Lorenz 1931). In the case of animals with a fixed territory, this "process of individualization" seems to perfect itself more easily. This is perhaps explained by the very good memory for places possessed by most vertebrates, since memories bound up with places are of great significance to them. A neighbor linked to a locality is no doubt easier to recognize as "always the same one." Now, if in man's case, and particularly in the early days of our own civilization, it was (and is) perfectly usual to call people after their locality, after the farm on which they lived, after the village from which they originated, it certainly does not seem absolutely out of the question that this is based on similar internal connections. This no doubt explains why even today a large percentage of our family names still indicates where their bearers originally came from.

In the case of some animals living in social communities, the individual members to a certain extent carry the "elastic disc" of their "private" territory around with them constantly. Wherever the highest ranking male of a herd of Rhesus Monkeys goes, the other members of the herd keep at a "social distance" from it. This distance has a radius of about one or two meters and apart from the "favorite wife" no other dares, or is allowed to dare, to come closer. If the "chieftain" sits down somewhere, the monkeys nearby also sit down roughly in a circle and all faces are turned toward it. The social distance is also transferred to the favorite female: If she joins a group of monkeys huddling close together for warmth when the weather is cool, one after another they gradually leave the gathering, which soon forms up again some distance away, leaving the favorite female alone once more (Chance 1953). In the case of the Hamadryas Baboon, several females always surround the "despot" at a suitable distance. If it moves around, they move around too, some preceding it, some following. None approaches within about a meter of it without adopting a "submissive attitude." Thus, already at the most primitive level, "leadership" on the one hand lifts the individual out of the mass, but on the other sentences it to considerable social isolation. As the above example of the favorite Rhesus female shows, even at this level isolation is not always particularly pleasant. Impressive parallels in human behavior are so numerous I hardly need to quote them specifically.

Inadequate as our knowledge is of territorial behavior in both higher mammals and primitive man, this much can still be concluded from it: Originally, it is true, man did live gregariously, but neither in large communities nor in confined space. Social gathering by the small family groups of hunters and food-collectors is confined to the night hours and to one or two special occasions. During the daily search for food, however, the individual members are scattered apart; only the small children accompany the mothers, while the older youths stay with the fathers.

In the course of the development of civilization, the number of people per ground unit has increased many times. Generally speaking, however, man's instinctual equipment has without any doubt—apart from phenomena of loss and degeneration caused by domestication—remained unchanged (Lorenz 1940, 1950 b, c). This is certainly also true of the space and social distance the individual needs for his happiness and contentment. With increasing population density in an area there is, as I have already mentioned, also an increase in the tendency of the individual or the family to mark off all the more distinctly what space is left to it, to erect fences and walls around land and build permanent living quarters, to bolt house doors and to greet any intrusion by strangers—"unauthorized persons," as it is so tastefully expressed—with distrust, even with open antagonism. Under such circumstances the instinctive reaction of defense of territory is continually exposed to excessive stimulation by the "unbiologically" close and constant proximity of one's neighbor and by strangers frequently passing through one's territory. The constraint exercised by social conventions, however, prevents or proscribes almost any open expression of this. In the long run, therefore, mental damage is unavoidable. This is again shown with particular clarity in the prisoner-of-war camp. The nature of the accommodation here determines the fact that each individual can win for himself only a very, very small "home" (see above). The only space he can occupy as his own is usually his bed, or what serves as such. The space before and beside it he is obliged to share with at least some of those in the neighboring beds. This may seem quite natural and certainly any reasonable prisoner accepts the situation. But if it continues for a long time it leads to intolerable tensions, even between people with the best of intentions who in normal civilized conditions would have got on wonderfully together throughout years of untroubled friendship. The irritation caused by continual, obtrusive, and irremovable proximity of the person in the neighboring bed accumulates subliminally to a significant level. In the end the most insignificant things can lead to bitter quarrels and even to blows. Just as typical as the insignificance of the cause and the violence of the outbreak is the speed and the at least superficial completeness with which the quarrelers are usually reconciled. Yet, nothing can stop the next quarrel from breaking out. Equally understandably each one seeks the cause only in the malicious character of the other, and this can build up into paranoid suspiciousness. But if one sees in contrast, as we prisoners-of-war in Canada did, how helpful, welcoming, and good-natured people are when their nearest neighbor lives a day's journey or even further away, and how a whole series of social difficulties is simply incomprehensible to such people, then it really is scarcely possible to avoid attributing much greater significance to space as a social factor than has generally been the case so far.

Murie's studies (1944) on the life of wolves in the wilds and the detailed observations which Schenkel (1947) carried out on these animals in the zoos of Basle and Berne offer a picture which corresponds in many details to that just drawn of human conditions. The members of a family of wolves in the wilds are friendly toward one another, the ranking order is recognizable but seldom emphasized, biting bouts virtually do not occur, food is willingly shared with others. The animals kept in a confined space in captivity, however, behaved quite differently. Here the strictest ranking order was observed, which allowed only the top animal unrestrained activity. Almost continuously there were serious biting bouts, and scarcely one of the animals could ever relax completely.

Even if the conditions of our civilized existence today are not as extreme as those in a prisoner-of-war camp, they are already bad enough, particularly in our big cities. Many often incredible-sounding reports about the behavior of an endemic population toward refugees who have been allocated accommodation in their homes only show all too clearly with what force resistance to such "intruders" can prevail over all insight and reason, how deep in the instinctive core of the human character it must be rooted.

Excessive social demands are continually being made on modern man as regards tolerating others, often many others, in the sphere of his own direct need for territory and space. This already begins in the kindergarten, where attempts are nowadays being made to counteract the threat of emotional damage ("hospitalism") by means of the "room-division method" (Klimpfinger 1952). Many social difficulties, indeed neuroses, in individuals are basically no more than the mental effects of lack of space. The same people who often scarcely greet one another when they meet daily on the staircase of an apartment house, frequently only stare at each other balefully, and will quarrel loudly over the smallest difficulty in the house, would love each other dearly if they were still each other's "nearest neighbors" but miles apart.

It should be emphasized that all that has been said is only intended to draw attention to the present problematical situation. It is certain that the behavior patterns of animals and humans described above have the same homologous (in the real sense of the word) root. As regards the details, to what extent we are dealing with genuine homologies, with convergencies, or with pure analogies, is something about which we can as yet make only more or less likely assumptions. The extent to which man has the possibility of compensating, of counteracting with means of a different nature is likewise something which can only be guessed at. All that is certain is that here as elsewhere compensation has its limits and is by no means omnipotent. *Our individual and social need for space has been laid down by our phylogenetic history and is therefore a basic characteristic of the genus,* i.e. within certain limits it is an *immutable natural right*.

Of course, there can be no question of breaking up the modern mass communities completely. From the point of view of our technical and economic development, they are quite simply a necessity. On the other hand, however, something must be done to mitigate as far as possible the excessive social demands on the individual described above. For too long we have relied on the fact that human beings are social creatures and believed that this automatically makes it possible to pack them together in as little space as we like provided that the questions of food and physical health are cared for. Without the slightest doubt this is an error. If it is being calculated today that with adequate exploitation of all sources of production the earth can feed ten or even more billion people, *it is high time we also asked the question whether this world will still be worth experiencing for the ten billion,* or whether we shall not be feeding ten billion mentally crippled, neurotic, unhappy people. This question is, I believe, one of the most urgent of our time. We should not hesitate to employ every means at the disposal of modern research to seek the answer to it and then act accordingly.

7 *On the Choice of a Sexual Partner by Animals* *(1955)*

Man has always been wont to contemplate the behavior of animals with the idea that this could help to throw light on human modes of behavior and experience. Yet, this is actually true only if the comparability of the phenomena is based on true kinship such as results from the fact of common phylogenetic development. There is, however, a considerable difference in length between the stretches of evolution common to the individual animal species and man, as well as between those common to the various animal species in relation to one another. It is on account of this difference in length of the common evolutionary path even among the various animals that "the animal" as a uniform entity diametrically opposed to "man" cannot exist. That concept is the invention of people who do not really *know* any animals.

Emphasizing the common nature of the phenomena does not, however, mean putting them on an equal, as is frequently insinuated. In the everyday jargon of our science we do, it is true, call homologous organs, organic functions, and behavior patterns "the same," but do *not* mean this to indicate that they are *identical*. A human behavior pattern is still a *human* behavior pattern, even when we establish its homology with a behavior pattern of a particular animal, and likewise the behavior pattern of this animal still remains specific to the animal, be it cat, dog, elephant, or anything else. Yet, the

110

latter is in no case "animal" in the sense that from the very first it is strictly distinguished from the human equivalent. If we speak of "animal" in this category, it can only be in contrast to "vegetable," i.e. "human," being a subordinate concept, must at all events be included in "animal."

Let us briefly consider the general picture which comparative ethology draws for us of the internal functional connections throughout animal behavior. The central concept we meet here is the "instinctive movement." By this we mean specific motor patterns typical of the animal species concerned, the coordination of which is hereditary and cannot be influenced by individual experience. In the normal course of events, these motor patterns appear to be directed toward the attainment of particular external, biologically significant goals, and during phylogenetic development the attainment or non-attainment of this external "goal" was and is the point at which natural selection begins to function. These goals have, however, proved not to be what motivates performance of the movement by the individual; instead, the movement itself possesses a *central nervous excitatory process of its own* which operates in accordance with its own characteristic rhythm and independent of external stimuli. By this means the readiness to perform the instinctive movement concerned increases with a specific regularity the longer the movement has not been performed. Thus, the instinctive movements have their own internal dynamics, and so in the case of long accumulation of readiness may *burst out spontaneously* in situations other than the "biologically correct" ones. There is every reason to assume that all spontaneous activity of animals (including man) is based on the endogenous rhythms of central nervous excitatory processes of the kind described (Leyhausen 1952, 1954 a, Lorenz 1937 b, 1943 a, Tinbergen 1951).

The excitatory processes associated with the individual instinctive movements are not separate and unrelated to one another, but form a counterbalancing system in which the strengthening or weakening of one component influences the relationships among all others in a specifically regular manner. Degree and direction of this influence, however, depend on the state of activity of each individual excitatory center, so that one and the same influence may have an inhibiting effect in one case and a facilitating effect in another. This system has many functional characteristics in common with the system of endocrine glands. In physiological terms it is highly probable that the counterbalancing of the system of instincts involves corresponding chemical processes. Within the system, too, relationships are not uniform, but groups are formed which are closely connected among themselves. Tinbergen therefore speaks of a *hierarchical system of instincts* (Leyhausen 1952, 1954 a, Tinbergen 1951).

The particular nature of this hierarchically ordered system of instincts and of the mutual influence exerted by the individual instincts on one another, which varies according to internal situation, is responsible for the fact that the actions performed by an animal at any given moment are seldom governed by one single instinct alone. It only appeared that this was so as long as the objects of investigation were mainly lower vertebrates. However, investigation of higher vertebrates and particularly mammals shows with increasing clarity that the normal event is for *several instincts to be superimposed on one another* in an animal's actions, even if one more or less clearly occupies a leading position. The observation of this phenomenon opened our eyes to the fact that in the behavior of lower vertebrates, too, such a superimposition represents the rule and the absolute sovereignty of one single instinct an exception. An exceptional case of this kind may be evoked by an abnormal external situation, or it may be the expression of a permanent internal disposition, in which case it must be regarded as pathological in higher animals also, just as in man.

The endogenous excitatory processes endow the system of instincts with relative *independence from external stimuli* and thus the behavior of the animal with a certain *autonomy;* on the other hand there must, of course, be some synchronization between the instinct expressed and the external situation if the biological goal of an instinctive act and with it adaptive benefit to the survival of the species are to be attained. Thus, in general the specific rhythm of an instinct is well tuned to the frequency of occurrence of the adequate stimulus situation in "natural" living conditions; accumulation of the instinct seldom reaches a level which results in "reaction to a substitute object" and "overflow activity." Furthermore, within the context of the adequate stimulus situation the elicitation of the instinctive movement concerned must take place at precisely the right moment. This is achieved by *specific sets of disinhibitory apparatus in the central nervous system* which are assigned to the individual instinctive movements and are likewise innate (innate schema = innate releasing mechanism = IRM). They react to specific details in the external biological situation concerned and it is possible to discover experimentally which details of the entire situation these are. They are known as *sign stimuli* and always consist of features which in normal circumstances *clearly designate* the appropriate situation in the animal's environment. Their effect, however, is purely summative and completely independent of being integrated into the situation as a whole (gestalt). Thus, it is easy to imitate and isolate them in an experiment with dummies and in this way elicit the animal's reaction under completely different circumstances and in a manner devoid of biological purpose. In many cases, however, this succeeds only when the animal has not yet become acquainted from its own experience with the complete biological situation concerned (Leyhausen 1951, Lorenz 1943 a, Tinbergen 1951).

Not all releasing mechanisms are hereditarily adjusted to particular sign stimuli. Indeed, this is possible only when the biological situation concerned can be characterized in a clear and unmistakable way by means of only a few features. In the case of the Mallard, for example, the display plumage of the drake is distinguished by a few strong colors on relatively large areas. These colors and their arrangement therefore serve also as sign stimuli for the instinctive actions of the duck in relation to the drake and of the drake in relation to rivals, i.e. "knowledge" of the *male* Mallard is equally innate to both male and female. The plumage of the Mallard *duck,* however, has quite an insignificant pattern of an almost plain grayish brown. There is nothing about her which could produce a sign stimulus, and as a result a Mallard drake reared *without access to any conspecifics* does not "know" what its female must look like. Later it then tries to mate any other kind of duck which is not a Mallard drake like itself, in other words, not only female Mallards but also indiscriminately males and females of other species of duck.

Mallard drakes reared by a Mallard mother duck, however, never make a mistake when choosing a female. Thus, the image of the mother in its many details must be *imprinted* at an early stage on the young male so that it later recognizes a strange female Mallard for what it is. "Imprinting processes" (Lorenz 1935) such as this have proved to have very specific prerequisites. Firstly, a certain limit is set by the IRMs on what is suitable as an imprinting object. A young Graylag Goose, for example, regards whatever large, dark, and moving body it sees first after hatching out of the egg as its "mother" and follows this unconditionally everywhere. Large, dark, and moving are, therefore, the qualities in response to which the IRM can disinhibit the following reaction of the Graylag chick for the first time. Secondly, the stimulus concerned must create its effect within a particular period of time. In the case of the Graylag chick just mentioned, this period lasts only a few hours after hatching. In other cases, however, this period may fall in other phases of juvenile development. Frequently, too, imprinting takes place long before the associated reaction can be elicited for the first time. In the case of the young Graylag Goose, imprinting requires only a few minutes. Thereafter no change is possible; the process is *irreversible,* which clearly distinguishes it from the formation of conditioned reflexes and from learning. In other cases the period during which imprinting occurs is not so short; here, too, however, once this period has elapsed the result cannot be altered any more. An example of this which has become famous is the jackdaw, Tschok, which was cared for by Lorenz and imprinted to him as its parental companion. Later Tschok flew with a flock of Hooded Crows it met on its first flight; thereafter it was incapable of attaching itself to a flock of jackdaws. Finally, at the time when it became sexually mature it courted a girl who had been in service in Lorenz's house a year before but who now lived in a village several kilometers away. Parental care, however, was displayed by Tschok only toward a strange young jackdaw. The images of the parental companion, the flight companion, and the sexual companion must, therefore, have been imprinted independently of one another at various times, but the red gaping mouth of the young jackdaw was effective as a sign stimulus without any previous experience (Lorenz 1931).

Finally, there are in addition instinctive movements which are not elicited by an IRM associated with the adequate object itself. A young jackdaw, for example, does not know what it needs to fear and to flee from. Initially its escape behavior is elicited solely by the warning behavior of adult jackdaws. Which objects are to be feared is something it first has to learn from the behavior of the older animals. The ways in which it is possible to elicit an instinctive act are, therefore, very numerous. Thus, every mode of behavior represents an extremely complicated interplay between various instinctive acts, the various ways in which these may be elicited or inhibited, and behavioral components of other kinds which cannot, however, be discussed in greater detail here. This is also true of the way sexual partners come together, as will be demonstrated by two examples: the courtship and pair-formation of the Mallard duck (Lorenz 1952 a), and the pairing of the European hamster (Eibl-Eibesfeldt 1953 a).

In the case of the Mallards, after the autumn molt the drakes assemble in small communities on open water. The ducks, in part guided by the call-note of the courting drakes, fall in with them and form a circle around them. The courtship mood is announced by the drakes shaking themselves initially. This is followed by the first actual courtship movement, namely the "grunt whistle." The next, and higher, level of excitation is expressed in two further movements: The "down-up movement" and the subsequent "Räb-räb Palaver" occur when courtship and fighting excitation are superimposed on one another. If the latter is missing, the much rarer movement known as "head-up tail-up" occurs. Subsequently the drake concerned swims around a particular duck making abrupt movements with its neck flattened out, stops suddenly, stretches its neck up and turns the back of its head toward the duck ("nod-swimming"). A further measure of the mounting excitation of courtship is the frequency with which several drakes simultaneously perform one of the motor patterns described. After this communal courtship by the Mallard males has continued for several weeks, the females at last begin to choose their partner from among them. A duck swims up to a particular drake and tries to win its affections by performing the "inciting movement." If the drake is inclined to accept the duck's courtship, it replies either with "chin-raising" and "Räb-räb Palaver" or with "displacement preening." If, however, the drake does not react to the inciting movement of the duck, she often tries to "incite" another drake to attack the one which has just rejected her. If "inciting" and a positive reaction on the part of the drake follow one another several times in the same two birds, the pairing is confirmed. Now these birds keep together and separate themselves from the rest of the flock. Actual copulation does not occur until the spring, when both partners express their willingness to mate by communal "pumping" movements, which mutually stimulate each other to increasing intensity. Finally the duck announces her readiness for coition by lying quite flat on the water. Frequently the drake makes further pumping movements before accepting the invitation of the duck. Thus, the method of leading up to mating through weeks and months of courtship and preliminary overtures as well as the sequel to mating which now follows are both highly developed processes.

In the case of the European hamster matters are fundamentally different. Throughout the year this rodent lives alone and defends its territory vigorously against any conspecific irrespective of sex. In the mating season, the male hamsters leave their territories and search for females. In a female's territory they mark tufts of grass and similar objects by rubbing off on them the secretion from the glands on their flanks, and in this way take a kind of possession of the strange territory. The first meeting with the female demands extreme caution, for initially readiness to escape and resistance to the intruder predominate in her. Time and again the female runs away and the male follows patiently, withdrawing a little as soon as the female turns around. In time, however, the behavior of the female becomes more yielding; now she runs away only hesitantly, stopping at once if the male ceases to follow, and in the end she follows the male herself. The next phase of the approach consists of cautiously circling and sniffing one another, the forepaws raised in readiness for defense. Eventually the male follows the female into her burrow and here he gradually succeeds in overcoming her timidity and achieving copulation. After a few days the two part again. The rearing of the young is cared for exclusively by the female.

This, then, is how complicated the interplay of the various constituents of animals' innate behavior can be before the consummation of the actual sexual act is reached. The reactivity of the IRMs to "stimulus summation" leads in this context to a choice of partner according to quality. For in the case of wild animals the strongest and most "beautiful" are also the healthiest and most "acceptable" in the sense of their sexual and social function. In man as well as his domestic animals, however, this link between "beautiful" and "good" has been more or less destroyed. The "keyboard" of the IRMs, however, has not kept pace with this development and consequently beautiful people attract love and sympathy without effort whereas qualities of character alone have much greater difficulty in gaining recognition and love. Here we find one of the reasons why so-called "marriages of convenience" are sometimes happier than pure "love matches" (Leyhausen 1951, Lorenz 1940, 1943 a). One frequently hears the opinion expressed that only the coarsely sensual constituents of sexual life are of a drive nature and thus hereditary, whereas all the finer, tender details as well as the inhibitions are conditioned by experience and teaching. This idea is quite certainly wrong. "The sexual drive" is anything but a uniform mechanism. Its various constituent parts mature during different phases of ontogeny and at widely differing speeds. But they are all hereditary and largely inaccessible to influence by experience and teaching. Nevertheless, the differentially developed constituents of behavior (and experience) are rather susceptible to disturbance: It is very easy for them to be simply "swept aside" when the above-mentioned accumulation of specific instinct energies exceeds a certain level; they are the first casualties of increasing variation within a population, such as we find in man and his domestic animals under the influence of the domestication process; and finally, they are also the first to be affected if physiological development is impaired. Young Graylag Geese, for example, normally become paired in their third year. The courtship period, which may vary in length, concludes with both partners performing the "triumph ceremony" together, whereupon the marriage is settled—and for life (at least ideally). In the case of young ganders which have suffered developmental damage ("runts") the appearance of ceremonial courtship is considerably delayed; copulation reactions, however, which never appear in a normal bird until after the conclusion of courtship, put in an appearance in the runts not later but prematurely, namely already during the second year. No lasting bond with the partner results. Now, to my knowledge in the years 1948–1951 there was an accumulation of cases in which fifteen- to seventeen-year-old youths attempted or actually committed rape and in some instances subsequently murdered the victim. In all the cases where I was able to learn details, those involved were not particularly well-developed youths in "sexual need" as a result of maturing early, but decidedly puny types. Already at that time I expressed the opinion that it was a matter of loss of inhibition caused by physiological damage during development (Leyhausen 1952). This assumption becomes plausible when one considers that the youths concerned were just in the prepuberal stage at the time of the worst food shortage toward the end of the war and in the first postwar years. The observations are not, however, sufficiently numerous to render the assumed connection statistically certain. Here I should just like to point out the possibility of such connections and suggest that they should be followed up.

If I emphasized above how differentially developed and manifold the hereditary constituents of behavior, particularly of sexual behavior, may be and in man's case certainly are, this does not mean that inhibitions of other kinds, particularly social, cannot likewise affect this behavior. I am aware how greatly the form of the social community life of higher monkeys helps to mold their sexual behavior and how, conversely, the social structure of the monkey group is governed by the sexual sphere (Chance and Mead 1953). Without the slightest doubt, both aspects are also valid as far as man is concerned. But social inhibitions are capable only of imposing limitations according to place and time, of repressing, but not of creating anything new in the actual field of love and sexuality, or of modifying this in essence. The variation in individual phenotypes mentioned above may often make this appear to be so; in addition, it seems that imprinting processes, which most certainly take place long before puberty, later exert a decisive influence on the choice of partner or object and also contribute to variability.

Although it is necessary to look with great caution on over-hasty application of the results of behavioral research on animals to human conditions, the following conclusions may nevertheless be drawn:

Nowadays it is (once again) fashionable to regard the possible influence of education and experience on character, and particularly on the development of sexual life, as very great. It is impossible to share this optimism about education. Precisely in this respect the last generations have had to put up with the most varied and contrasting educational systems, and if the influence of education were really so great people could not have remained as basically similar over the generations as they in fact are. In nature, highly important functions are not left to such "chance occurrences," just because these functions have developed through chance, i.e. in natural selection *against* chance in the course of phylogeny. The "survival of the fittest" requires stability and resistance in relation to any environmental factors which are subject to all too great and irregular fluctuations, and certainly "education" (in the broadest sense) is one such factor. Thus the relevant developmental processes are *frequently shielded* from being influenced too profoundly by such external factors. However, not only do these safety factors largely eliminate bad influence, but they also allow good influence little prospect of success. One practical conclusion, among others, to be drawn from this is that nowadays as far as sexual education is concerned far too much effort is expended on discussions about "smutty publications" and keeping them away from children. In fact, these influences are greatly exaggerated. To avoid misunderstanding let me add that this qualification does not refer to that section of "children's books" and films which deals with the glamorization of criminals; it is quite impossible to exaggerate the amount of influence these may have even on children who have no "criminal tendencies" whatsoever. For here, namely, it is a question of social behavior patterns and standards, and these appear to be largely molded by imprinting processes of the kind described above.

The normal development of the sexual and romantic behavior patterns of the capacity for love, tenderness, courtship, and also of love's inhibitions is, however, such a complicated sequence of *finely tuned* processes (Leyhausen 1952) and so little is yet known in detail about it that any attempt at intervention looks clumsy from the start —rather like taking a hammer and wrench to repair the works of a lady's wristwatch. In an extreme case one may have no choice, and sometimes the procedure is even successful. Only one should not build too much on these successes: One never really knows precisely what they are actually due to, and thus they remain chance successes *with minimum probability*. What emerges instead is a very serious warning about all too early instruction in sexual matters. I have a strong impression that this does more harm than good. These are things which cannot be expressed in words, even the most well intended and well chosen, without hurting the maturing child's feelings, which are hypersensitive on this point. The shyness of most parents about discussing this topic with their children is, therefore, only too well founded and should not be set aside by force. One thing at least is certain: if the instruction is to be of any use, or at least not do any harm, *the moment for it must be very precisely chosen;* for as far as the actual sexual processes are concerned the maturing drive itself instructs the child, and here it is absolutely necessary to wait until the child's "eyes open" for themselves; any prompting is harmful, and for precisely the same reason as it is wrong to encourage babies to walk upright before they do so spontaneously and of their own accord. The objection— that if instruction about sex does not come in time from "authorized" quarters, the "gutter" will take care of things—is quite unsound: No one kills his child "in time" with a morphine injection because it might otherwise be the victim of a traffic accident! Instead, this is a field, though a limited one, in which the old habit of parents of "sheltering" their children—so much in discredit now but considered quite natural more than two generations ago—would be an ideal to wish for today as well. Being taught the facts of life by its parents can but help a child to fit its new inner experiences into the general world picture and practical social behavior, but it will help only if the process of maturation has already progressed far enough for the child to *comprehend properly* what it is that has to be fitted in. This demand for precise timing of any attempt at instruction rules out straight away any *mass sex education,* such as in school, for it can never happen that all children in a class or an age group have exactly the same "developmental age." And no instruction at all is in any case better than bad, or than instruction however good but imparted at a bad time. The best sex education children can have is a relaxed family life in which nakedness is too normal to require explanation and thus does not provoke questions at an inappropriate time.

It may appear to some that I have not paid sufficient heed to my own warning about the over-hasty application of the results of comparative ethology to human conditions. However, within the narrow limitations of this article it is impossible to present a convincing justification of the conclusions drawn (for this I must refer readers to the literature quoted). The purpose of this exposition is rather to draw the attention of any doctor or research worker interested in sexual problems to a field of *research* which has important material for comparison to offer and is certainly also capable of contributing to the solution of many human sexual problems.

8 Social Organization and Density Tolerance in Mammals *(1965)*

I. INTRODUCTION

Normally we do not think of solitary animals as forming a community of any kind except for the very limited purposes and periods of propagation. Perhaps this is true of a great number of species, even some mammals, as for example the hamster, the red squirrel, the badger (Eibl-Eibesfeldt 1950, 1953 b, 1958 a) and the wolverine (Krott 1959). However, if we want to examine more closely what relationships might possibly exist between individuals of an allegedly solitary mammalian species, we are in a very bad position indeed. For the main reason why so many mammals are said to be solitary seems to be that they can only be shot one at a time. Very little field work has been done on such species; field workers—for reasons not to be discussed here—have concentrated on mammals living in social groups or herds. Hence some of my arguments will be of a highly speculative nature. The only justification is my hope that they may help to arouse more interest in the life of solitary mammals and that more field observations will be made over long periods of time and in sufficient detail.[1]

II. MAMMALIAN TERRITORIES

As far as I know, the existence of a social pattern into which individual, solitary lives might be woven has never seriously been considered. The basis for any such pattern could be found in territorial behavior. This was first observed in birds, and bird territories have been studied most fully. When similar behavior was discovered in other vertebrates as well, the characteristics of bird territories were at first thought to apply universally. They have been thoroughly listed and reviewed by Nice (1941).

If we exclude colony breeders from our considerations, it may broadly be stated that the breeding territories of most birds—and for that matter fishes—start from a center which is occupied by the owner, who afterward stakes out his claim in serious or ritualized fights with occupants of nearby centers, so that after a while territory boundaries can be mapped out quite precisely, each territory owner as a rule keeping to his own boundaries (Curio 1959, Greenberg 1947, Kirchshofer 1953, Kluyver 1955, O. Koenig 1951, Lind 1961, Tinbergen & Kluyver 1953).

Hediger (1949) pointed out that, to mammals, it is not so much an occupied area which is important as a number of points of interest—first-order homes, second-order homes, places for feeding, rubbing, resting, sunbathing, etc. All these places are connected by an elaborate network of paths, along which the territory owner travels according to a more or less strict daily, or seasonal, or otherwise determined routine. The areas enclosed by the pathways, though more or less familiar, are seldom or never used. These concepts have been corroborated and elaborated in detail by the studies of Dasmann & Taber (1956) and Graf (1956) on territorialism in North American deer.

The distinction made by Burt (1943) between home range as an area regularly used by the animal and territory as an area (usually smaller than and situated within the home range) defended against intruding or trespassing conspecifics is not borne out by free-ranging domestic cats, because they behave inconsistently; for a full discussion of these concepts see Kaufmann (1962). The terminology adopted for the purpose of this paper is a synthesis between that of Hediger and of Kaufmann.

One outstanding feature of most mamalian territories—the only exception I know being that of the hamster (Eibl-Eibesfeldt 1958 a)— is that mammals are not usually in a position to survey the whole of their territory all the time and to spot intruders or trespassers almost instantaneously, because of the nature of the habitat and of inferior methods of locomotion (as compared with birds). This is usually thought to be sufficient explanation for the often considerable overlap of adjacent territories and the shared use of paths running through border areas (Hediger 1948, 1949, 1951, Eibl-Eibesfeldt 1958 a, Krott 1959, Krott & Krott 1963, Hall 1962, a, b, L. Koenig 1960, Kaufmann 1962, Wynne-Edwards 1962).

Gustav Kramer (1950) was the first to point out that in territorial animals the fixation of an individual in a definite locality obviously facilitates the recognition of this individual by its neighbors. All territorial animals have a good memory for localities and their spatial relationships. Hence they probably "label" the conspecifics encountered by the locality where the encounter took place. This is perhaps of minor importance in species like most song-birds, where neighbors are in almost continuous vocal/auditory contact, but is likely to play a major role under conditions prevailing for solitary mammals, as described above.

Attention has always been focused on the fact that territories in general owe their existence to repulsive forces within the animals, which tend to space out individuals as far apart as possible, and students of territory and territorial behavior have been almost completely absorbed by studying hostile or agonistic behavior. However, it has long been known that in cases where there is a small population of territorial birds inhabiting a very wide area that is well suited to all conceivable needs of the species, the individuals or pairs are not spaced out evenly as far from each other as the inhabitable area would allow. Clearly there is, in many species at least, not only a minimum but also a maximum size of territory (Kluyver 1955, O. Koenig 1951, Tinbergen & Kluyver 1953; for review see Wynne-Edwards 1962). Many authors have noted the fact and expressed their belief that there must be some agent which keeps a population from dispersing beyond any possibility of contact, but although, as I have already mentioned, dispersing forces have been studied intensively, there has as yet been no attempt to make a close study of the counteracting forces and modes of behavior which allow a population of solitary individuals to retain contact with each other. Fights, threat displays, and the like are very conspicuous and therefore more easily observed in the field than hypothetical centripetal tendencies which, if they can be affirmed, are certainly of a less theatrical nature. To detect them, it would be necessary to make an uninterrupted, continuous day-and-night record of a selected population of solitary mammals. As far as I know, this has so far never been done, and the only people who ever seriously set out to do it were my collaborator R. Wolff and myself—on free-ranging domestic cats! The result of this little survey has been published elsewhere (Leyhausen & Wolff 1959).

As measured against the standards set out above, we failed: It was an impossible task. To follow a single cat around day and night without losing sight of it, and keep a complete record of all its movements, encounters, etc., requires at least three well-trained, physically fit, and inexhaustible observers, plus a lot more equipment than we could command at the time. We carefully selected an isolated farmhouse situated in a clearing in a very hilly region. There were two resident cats, and another one in a farm some 600 yards away. Sufficient data were collected for only one of the residents, to form a picture from which we hope no essential feature is missing: but even this was not complete. When we had finished the study, we did not feel it amounted to much in itself and only reluctantly published it, mainly in order to elicit comment and to interest other field workers with perhaps better resources and more time to spend.

However, both of us had previously made extensive observations on cat populations under free-ranging conditions, Wolff in two suburbs of Hamburg,[2] myself in the gardens facing the back of my parents' home in Bonn, of some cats in Wales, of a small population in a garden area of Zurich where I lived for approximately two and a half years, and of some individually known cats which night after night populated a small square on the outskirts of Paris. Combined, this was a sizable amount of data, and our observations confirmed each other in most details. Part of our data fitted well with traditional theories, but some simply did not seem to make sense. However, when we compared these with the data from the little field study and with old and recent observations and experiments on caged cats, the once odd and ill-fitting pieces suddenly fell into place, and what had previously seemed contradictory became comprehensible. Hence I am quite confident that the picture I shall outline briefly is correct in its essentials.

III. SOCIAL AND TERRITORIAL BEHAVIOR OF THE DOMESTIC CAT

Individual cats own a territory which tallies roughly with Hediger's description (loc. cit.) of the average mammalian territory: a first-order home, usually a room or even a special corner in a room of the house where they live, and a home range which consists of a varying number of more or less regularly visited localities connected by an elaborate network of pathways. To draw a line through the outer points of this network and call this the boundary of the home range would be a purely abstract procedure. The concept of such a boundary cannot be based on the actual behavior of the animals, as we shall see in due course. The immediate surroundings of the first-order home, as for example the house and the garden, are entirely familiar to the resident cat, it uses practically every part of them and there are usually several places in them for resting, sunbathing, keeping watch, etc. Beyond this limited home area the paths mentioned above lead to places for hunting, courting, contests and fighting, and other activities. To each of these places there is usually more than one path. The areas between the paths are rarely used, if at all. The places the paths lead to must not, of course, be thought of as mere points. Hunting grounds, for example, like clearings in a wood or freshly cut wheat fields where mice are abundant, may cover areas bigger than the home area, and in the course of time the cat investigates them thoroughly.

There are two snags, however, in our attempt to use observations on free-ranging domestic cats as a kind of substitute for the observation of true wild solitary mammals: (i) Domestic cats are not allowed to choose or control their own density of numbers, and as a rule they are not allowed to select their first-order home freely; (ii) their behavior has been changed in various respects during the course of domestication. Important with regard to territorial behavior is the fact that domestic cats are less repulsive to one another than their wild relatives and in most cases can be brought to share a home area and often even the first-order home with one or more other cats (Leyhausen 1956 a, 1962 a). At first this might seem to be a serious disadvantage, but probably it is simply that the special circumstances mentioned above have brought out more clearly the cohesive factors within the population which are certainly at work in wild populations as well.

As stated above, it is quite normal for the pathway-network of neighboring cats to overlap, and overlap in this case means the common use of pathways and also of hunting grounds and sometimes other commodities such as sites for sunbathing and lookout posts. However, common use normally does not mean simultaneous use. In their daily routine, the animals avoid direct encounters, and even cats sharing a home keep separate in the field. According to Hediger (loc. cit.) many species achieve this by following a rather definite timetable, scheduled like a railway timetable so as to make collisions unlikely. Wolff's and my observations have so far failed to produce any positive evidence that the daily routine of domestic cats is subject to such a definite schedule. Where there is a strong tendency toward being in a certain place at the same time every day, this is usually due to human influence, e.g. feeding time. Thus, the cat population (up to a dozen or more) of the Welsh farms I saw gathered about milking time at the barn door or the cowshed to collect their daily ration of milk. Of course, this does show that cats are quite capable of keeping to a time schedule. Our failure to observe anything of the kind in free-ranging cats which are not influenced by human time-fixing does not mean that it could not occur—and, indeed, it does occur in captive groups (see below).

Cats seem to regulate their traffic mainly by visual contact. It is often possible to observe one cat watching another moving along a path some distance away—say anything from thirty to one hundred yards—until it is out of sight. Some time afterward, the watching cat can usually be seen using the same path. On occasion I have observed two cats approaching a kind of cat crossroads from different directions. If they had gone on they would have met almost precisely at the crossing. Both sat down and stared at each other, looking deliberately away from time to time. The deadlock is eventually broken, either by one cat moving on toward the crossing while the other is looking away, hesitantly at first, then speeding up and trotting hastily away as soon as it has passed the point nearest to the other cat; or after a while both move off almost simultaneously in the direction from which they originally came. In all these remote visual-contact (or control) cases, it is very rare indeed for one of the animals to walk right up to the other in order to drive it way or, if it does not move, to attack it. If, however, the animals suddenly and unexpectedly find themselves face to face, a clash of some sort may result. In this way a ranking order is established between neighbors. There is rarely more than one serious fight between any two adult animals; usually any subsequent close-range encounter will develop almost at once into a chase, with the animal which had been defeated in the previous fight taking to flight, and the victorious one chasing and slashing out at the other if it gets close enough. Females are, on the whole, less tolerant of each other than males.

However, the kind of ranking order thus produced does not develop into a rigid social hierarchy within the population. Although the victorious cat is sometimes permitted to visit and inspect the territory and even the first-order home of the defeated one unchallenged, it does not make a habit of this and it does not take over the other's home range. Nor is its superiority valid at any place and at any time. If the inferior cat has already entered a commonly used passage before the superior cat arrives on the scene, the latter will sit down and wait until the road is clear; if it does not, its superiority may be challenged successfully. In one case, for example, two females had established homes in two adjacent rooms of the house. The normally superior one had kittens, which enhanced her superiority still further. She wanted to cross into the adjacent room but her neighbor was sitting in the doorway, and when she tried to pass, the other spat at her and blocked her path. So she did not fight, but retreated a little way and waited. After a while her neighbor moved away from the doorway, the mother cat crossed and was afterward tolerated by the resident and in no way inhibited in her investigation of the room. Likewise a superior cat will not normally drive away an inferior one which is already occupying the superior cat's favorite resting place or lookout post.

Sometimes the clashes and chasings involved in establishing a locality-priority-dependent hierarchy produce a lasting and irreconcilable hate between two neighbors, so that the superior one chases and hits the other on sight. But this is by no means the rule. Not only is the superior animal allowed to pay visits to the home area of the inferior one, but the latter may also trespass on the former's ground. They may hunt over the same area at the same time, keeping on an average some 50 yards apart, depending on the ground and the vegetation. They do so deliberately, even when there is no other reason for being so close together. This was particularly obvious in the Welsh farm populations. After collecting their daily milk, the animals walked off one by one to their hunting grounds. Normally they were not fed by the farmers but had to sustain themselves, largely by catching and eating rabbits which lived in vast numbers in the hedges bordering the fields. Although rabbits seemed to abound everywhere, it was usual to see two or three cats hunting within 30 to 70 yards of each other, rather than one lone cat.

At nightfall there is often something which I can only describe as a social gathering. Males and females come to a meeting place adjacent to or situated within the fringe of their territories and just sit around. This has no connection with the mating season, which I am excluding from my description throughout. They sit, not far apart—2 to 5 yards or even less—some individuals even in actual contact, sometimes licking and grooming each other. There is very little sound, the faces are friendly and only occasionally an ear flattens or a small hiss or growl is heard when an animal closes in too much on a shy member of the gathering. Apart from this there is certainly no general hostility, no threat displays can be seen except perhaps for a tom parading a little just for fun. I could observe this particularly well and on many occasions in the Paris population. The gathering would go on for hours, sometimes (probably as a forewarning of the mating season) all night. But usually by about midnight or shortly after the cats had retired to their respective sleeping quarters. There can be no doubt that these meetings were on a friendly, social footing, although members of these same populations could at other times be seen chasing each other wildly or even fighting. Indeed, such an urge for social "togetherness" exists also in those wild species in which, according to all available observations, mutual repulsion is much stronger than it is in domestic cats. They are, therefore, better capable of close friendship with humans than with conspecifics. A human with sufficient knowledge and understanding can have all the social attractiveness of a conspecific without necessarily possessing its repulsiveness (Leyhausen 1956 a).

IV. THE TOMCAT BROTHERHOOD

So far I have been dealing mainly with the behavior of the females. Resident males are different in that, normally, they are even more tolerant toward trespassers. Their aggressiveness is, of course, accentuated during the mating season, but this has no relation to territory or home range in the proper sense. Fierce defense of the home and the home area is usually exhibited only by females rearing a litter. Adult tomcats meeting for the first time are liable to engage in fierce fighting regardless of the season. But once it has been decided which is the stronger or the more tenacious, courageous fighter of the two, they settle their arguments thereafter by display and avoid serious fighting. It is therefore possible to put several adult tomcats, so far strangers to one another, with a number of females in a comparatively small cage, and after a few days of bitter fights there is peace, even when one or more females come on heat. The males may show their threat display but they will rarely engage in actual fighting. Several times I have seen a shifting of rank between the two top cats of such a caged crowd effected by display alone. In an earlier paper (1956 a) I interpreted all this as a consequence of the animals being forced to live so close together all day that they expended their aggressiveness in "small change" all the time and therefore had no opportunity to build up an aggressive urge strong enough to lead to and sustain actual fighting. This may still play a part, but I am quite certain that a similar process occurs in free-ranging tomcats and that, after some initial fighting, those who pass the test and are not completely defeated and reduced to pariahs form a kind of order or establishment, ruling a great area in brotherhood. They gather in friendly convention as described above, and even in the mating season seldom fight to the bitter end. Such fights as take place between members of the establishment seem mostly to have a mock or *pro forma* quality.

The picture is strikingly different if, within the established neighborhood, there is a young tom just crossing the line from adolescence to maturity. The established tomcats of the vicinity, singly or in twos and threes, will come to his home and yell their challenge to him to come out and join the brotherhood, but first to go through the initiation rites. The challenge is not the piercing, up-and-down caterwauling of the threat display but rather softer and seems to have a good deal of purr in it, as if it were not merely challenging but also coaxing. In fact, the sound is hardly discernible from the call by which a tom tries to entice a female on heat to meet him. If the youngster lets himself be persuaded, hard and prolonged fighting ensues. This is in fact the situation in which most really bitter fights occur. And since the novice, who feels his strength growing from day to day, will not accept defeat as any sensible adult would, he will at first be beaten up and often more or less badly injured. But the wounds have hardly closed before he hurries to battle again. After a year or so, if he survives and is not beaten into total submission, he will have won his place within the order and the respect of his brethren and now sets out in his own turn to "teach the young heroes a lesson."

It should be remembered that, whereas the "status" accorded an individual animal as a result of territorial fighting is relative, rival fights between tomcats mostly take place on neutral ground and the resulting hierarchy is, therefore, absolute like that of herding animals.

For the sake of clarity, I will summarize the basic principles of an absolute hierarchy: Schjelderup-Ebbe was the first to realize that the hens of a barnyard do not by any means have equal rights, but establish among themselves a "peck-order" in which each individual is allocated a definite place on the social ladder which it is normally unable to alter. Usually a subordinate does not even try to fight a superior animal even if grossly provoked. When it does, it is almost invariably quickly subdued. Very rarely, and only after prolonged and bitter fighting, does an inferior animal succeed in improving its social position by degrading a formerly superior one. The resulting ranking order is mostly linear: Hen A pecks B but is not pecked by her, B pecks C but is not pecked by her, C is thus automatically inferior to A, and so on throughout the whole flock. Quarreling usually occurs only between individuals separated by not more than one step of the social ladder; an inferior animal never dares so much as to look straight at an animal two or more steps its superior; and an animal so vastly superior cannot be bothered to notice the existence of the ones far below—she has enough to do to keep her nearest rival in check and to avoid the relentless attacks of her immediate superior, by which she is punished if she inadvertently comes too close. Occasionally, relationships may be somewhat more complicated, for instance in a triangle where A may peck B and B may peck C, but C in turn pecks A. Very occasionally even four-cornered relationships occur. However, this does not alter the main principle: The resulting social hierarchy is very rigid, and it is absolute, meaning that the ranking between any two given individuals of the flock, once established, is observed at all times, in all places, and under all circumstances. Throughout this article, therefore, it will be called "absolute social hierarchy." The main prerequisite for its proper functioning is, of course, that all the members of a community know each other individually. This kind of social hierarchy largely prevails in the case of all vertebrates normally living together in groups, herds, and similarly organized societies. Thus the strongest animal enjoys uncontested "top rank" in a group and knows how to exploit it.

The strongest tomcat in an area, however, normally does not, as is often assumed, become a tyrant, dominating and excluding all others from courting and mating, if for no other reason than that choice of partner is something which is almost always decided by the female. I have known female cats, free ranging and in cage situations, remaining faithful to inferior males from one heat period to the next for years. And at least with the caged animals I know for certain that the dominant male never made any serious attempt to interfere. Furthermore, however, the "brotherhood" does not, of course, represent a permanent band. The members separate again at intervals and each returns to its individual territory, where the weaker ones enjoy the advantages of relative hierarchy once more. The whole social system as described above seems to me designed to ensure that the greatest possible number of strong and healthy males has an almost equal chance of reproduction, rather than to favor a single dominating individual exclusively. Such a situation could arise only if one male were so overpoweringly superior, in both physique and energy, that no other tomcat dared to challenge his dominance. This may happen in individual cases, but is extremely rare, particularly in areas where the cats still have considerable freedom of movement out of doors and a relatively "natural" environment. What I rather poetically described above as the "brotherhood" is in fact nothing mythical, but rests on a very real balance of power, risks, and deterrents. It can be formed only if there are several males of almost equal strength, so that victories and defeats are decided by a narrow margin and it might cost a higher-ranking male his superiority if he provoked an inferior so far as to make him actually fight.

V. MARKING THE TERRITORY

Before describing the interaction of the hierarchial dichotomy in caged-cat societies, I must make a few remarks on what is called territory marking. Many authors have described how territorial mammals mark their territories by scent, sound, scratching posts, etc. The usual interpretation attributed to this sort of behavior is that the animal is setting up a warning signal, with the intention of scaring away trespassers and potential intruders. I do not know whether this scaring-off function of an olfactory mark has been established beyond doubt in a species of solitary mammal. In cats I have certainly never observed anything suggesting such an interpretation. Cats, predominantly males but also most females, have a habit of spraying their urine against trees, poles, shrubs, walls, etc., and afterward they often rub their face in it and then the face against other things. No cat has been observed to go up to the mark made by another, sniff it, and then retreat. What they almost invariably do is sniff the mark carefully and at leisure, and then either move on quite unconcernedly or put their own mark over it. There is not the slightest hint that the original marking has had anything like an intimidating effect. Of course, this is no proof that this is never the case; but there must be at least one other function if not more. One may be to avoid unexpected encounters and sudden clashes, another to tell who is ahead on the road and how far, and whether he can be met if required. However, this is pure speculation and my data do not so far allow me to single out or reject any of the possibilities. The odds are that all of them play their part depending on the situation. But I should like to stress the point that we must not deny territorial behavior to cats because their markings do not, or only moderately, function as deterrents.

VI. CAGED COMMUNITIES

When I first (1956 a) described the structure of artificial cat societies in cages, I found that there was usually a dominant male
and frequently, though not always, one or two animals, male or
female, which were so subdued that they hardly dared breathe,
and which I called "pariahs." There was some ranking order among
the rest of the population, but it seemed very indefinite and unstable. My explanation then was that cats, as essentially solitary
animals, simply lack the capacity to build a stable society. When
the existence of two different types of ranking dawned upon me,
two facts emerged:

1. It is actually possible to find evidence for such a dualism. At
the food bowl, for example, an absolute rank order is observed.
Narrow passages and preferred resting places may, in a sense, belong
to top cats, and inferior cats often leave them when the superior
one approaches, but if they do not there is no quarrel; and, in
particular, the cat already in a passage has the right of way regardless of its status within the absolute hierarchy. Also, there is sometimes a prerogative related to the time of day. Some cats, for
example, make full use of the floor for running and playing in the
morning, others in the evening, and it is "their" time, when they
are superior to all others which happen to come their way, again
regardless of their absolute ranking.

2. There is a direct relationship between the balance of absolute
and relative hierarchy, and population density. The more crowded
the cage is, the less relative hierarchy there is. Eventually a despot
emerges, "pariahs" appear, driven to frenzy and all kinds of neurotic
behavior by continuous and pitiless attack by all the others; the
community turns into a spiteful mob. They all seldom relax, they
never look at ease, and there is continuous hissing, growling, and
even fighting. Play stops altogether and locomotion and exercise are
reduced to a minimum.

VII. SOCIAL STRUCTURE AMONG OTHER MAMMALS

There are many indications that the basic dualism of social hierarchy described here is present in many other mammals and that
it alone accounts for much in their behavior and ecology. The interaction of the two and the possibility of the weight shifting from
one to the other lies at the root of the ability of some species to
lead solitary, territorial lives in one area and to live in small or

even quite large groups in another. But as individual territories shrink and the group emerges, a group territory is formed. Davis (1942) found that the social behavior of various species of the family of *Crotophaginae* represents successive steps in a phylogenetic change from individual to group territory.

However, the change need not be brought about by a slow, phylogenetic process. Marler (1955 a, b, 1956, 1957) has found that in the chaffinch there is a *seasonally* governed shift from territorial behavior with relative hierarchy in the breeding season to flocking behavior with absolute hierarchy in winter, and in between times a mixture of transitional stages. I also agree with Marler's opinion that it is not a question of different kinds of fighting behavior but of different internal and external factors eliciting this. It seems that in the case of the chaffinch these factors, and particularly the internal ones, change their relative importance along with the seasonally governed shift in hormonal balance, but that in mammals they can co-exist constantly. Thus the individuals of many mammalian species are equally capable of leading a solitary or a gregarious life. In each particular case ecological and other physical circumstances of the area concerned no doubt determine what kind of social structure a population will have. The North African lion (since exterminated) was, as far as one can make out from the reports of hunters and travelers, a solitary animal living at the most in pairs. This seems also to be true of the West African lion in many regions. Yet in the East African plains lions live in groups sometimes numbering more than twenty (Guggisberg 1961).

The same principle also seems to govern the life—both within the group and among the groups—of species such as the yellow-bellied marmot (Armitage 1962) and the wolf (Murie 1944), which habitually live in small groups. Murie in particular gives examples of strong leadership at times and of relative tolerance and indulgence at others when the rights of the weak are well and, I might almost say, deliberately respected by the strong. In striking contrast are the observations of Schenkel (1947), who describes the social behavior of wolves in an overcrowded captivity situation in exactly the same way as I have for the overcrowded cat community.

I should also like to suggest that the fact that territorial dominance in mammals depends on locality and time might help to settle controversies between various observers with regard to territoriality in some species. Hediger (1951) reports territorial behavior in bull hippopotamuses; Grzimek (1956) and Verheyen (1954) deny this. Likewise it has always been assumed, and has also been confirmed by field observations, that black and brown bears are territorial animals (Meehan 1961, Meyer-Holzapfel 1957). Yet Krott & Krott (1963) frantically deny even the remotest possibility of territoriality in bears and describe the species as being "socially indifferent" *(sozial neutral)*. It has, I hope, become sufficiently clear from the above that the only mammal one could conceivably speak of as being socially indifferent is a dead one. Apart from this ill-chosen term, I think once again that the controversy may find its solution in the way I have already explained. Only after studying a population for a long period and following the individuals at all times and through all situations will one be able to make a correct and proportional assessment of their social interaction and relationships.

Just as mammals that normally live solitary lives often seem to have a faculty for changing to some form of group life, so many, if not all, mammals normally living in groups and even large herds seem to me to possess a faculty in the reverse direction. The wapiti, for example, is territorial in some habitats and non-territorial in others (Altmann 1952, Graf 1956). I therefore believe that, even in mammals living in herds and not occupying territories in the strict sense, both forms of social hierarchy could be traced, if only the attention of observers were focused on the point. And in that case I should predict that the bigger the herd and the less there is a tendency to subdivide it into small groups, the more absolute rank order would predominate over relative rank order.

VIII. HUMAN DENSITY PROBLEMS

Although I have no special knowledge of the social life of monkeys and apes, I suggest that here again the hierarchical dichotomy could be found. There would be perhaps almost exclusive predominance of absolute hierarchy in monkeys living in large bands, like the rhesus (Chance 1959, Chance and Mead 1953), and a more proportionate balance between the two in monkeys living in smaller groups, like the South Indian Macaque (Nolte 1955) or the langur (Jay 1962, 1963). Whatever the results of pertinent observation of monkey life may be, I feel sure that the dichotomy exists basically in man and can be observed in all kinds of human social organizations; I am also convinced that the well-being and even the survival of our species depends on a proper balance between the two types of hierarchy.

In an earlier paper (1954 b) I gave numerous examples of the fact that in all sorts of human social organization territorial behavior in various forms, both unadorned and sublimated, plays a role which it would be hard to overestimate (Meyer-Holzapfel 1952, Nippold 1954, Schmidt 1937). I described in some detail that, under the conditions of overcrowding prevailing in prisoner-of-war camps, exactly the same symptoms developed as those described above in overcrowded captive cat and wolf communities. I showed that the same symptoms are becoming increasingly conspicuous in modern mass communities. In that sense, the cynical definition of psychoanalysis, as the main symptom of the illness of which it pretends to be the cure, is 100 percent correct. My conclusion was that space in its physical or—if I may say so—biological form, not in a sublimated or figurative sense only, is indispensable for the biological, and particularly for the psychological and mental health of humans in a human society. For these reasons overcrowding is a menace to mankind long before general and insurmountable food shortage sets in. The increase in human numbers is not primarily a food problem, it is a psychological, sociological, mental health problem—in short, a humanist problem. And we have to realize that human nature sets a far narrower limit to human adaptability to overcrowding than is commonly believed today.

This I could see as a fact in 1954, but at that time I had no idea why it should be so. The key was given me by Wynne-Edwards (1962) when he formulated and elaborated the principle that natural selection has produced various kinds of social organization because they replace direct competition for the basic needs of life by competition for other goals (i.e. social goals in the widest sense). He considers that this social competition controls population density *before* such basic necessities of life as food, etc., become scarce and that generally speaking, and over a period of years, it keeps the numbers of exploiter and exploited—carnivores and their prey, herbivorous animals and their fodder, and so on—at an optimum level.

It is, of course, a debatable point whether interspecific limitation of numbers and density was the only factor in natural selection which has produced the enormous variety of social systems and "conventional competition," as Wynne-Edwards calls it. Certainly many other factors, including directly operating ecological ones, are involved in the natural limitation of population numbers. If one or more of these factors became inoperative, it is doubtful whether the mechanism described by Wynne-Edwards could stem the tide of overreproduction unaided. However, in view of the overwhelming profusion of evidence he puts forward, it is impossible to deny that "conventional competition" at least plays a vital part in the natural limitation of population numbers as well as of density. How important this part is depends no doubt on how much difference in periodicity there is between the life cycles of exploiter and exploited organism. Short-lived animals, with a high rate of reproduction and corresponding elimination, probably find it easier to adapt directly and almost without delay to fluctuations in ecological conditions, for example in the availability of food and water, than do long-lived species with a low rate of reproduction. For example, if in a good year for mice the foxes were to reproduce as much as the available food permitted, in a subsequent bad year hordes of them would have to starve (assuming that mice are the fox's sole source of food; and in fact they are its main source, despite all folklore association of ideas with other more nourishing animals). Before this happened, however, they would also have found and eaten practically the last mouse. The mouse population would then be incapable of recovering quickly, and even more foxes would have to die of hunger. Thus it is clear that once overexploitation has begun it is scarcely possible to call a halt to it again, and in this way the exploiter automatically destroys itself as well. The slower generation sequence of the fox therefore compels it to adapt its population somehow or other to the average number of mice available *every* year.

Now, no single component part of nature is quite perfect, including this mechanism of adaptation. Thus, in reality slightly more foxes will be reared in a year when there are plenty of mice, and to balance this a few more are eliminated in the subsequent winter. These fluctuations in the fox population, however, bear no relation to the vastly greater fluctuations in the mouse population, even taking into account that other predators as well live partly or even mainly on mice.

It will, then, be seen that all those ecological factors which, among other things, help to keep the population numbers and density of an animal species stable in the long term are mutually inter-dependent and have, so to speak, been taken into account in the process of evolving the "homeostatic machine" so that they are practically working parts of it. If one or even several of them drop out, the remainder cannot by themselves maintain the *necessary equilibrium* between birth and death, and any *constant increase in total population, however small this may be when expressed as a percentage, must in the long run destroy this ecological equilibrium and with it eventually the overfertile species as well.* Enough such cases are already known: Game reserves in which all predators have been exterminated, or which are far too small and invaded by far too much big game from neighboring areas where hunting is allowed. Hippopotamuses, elephants, and other kinds of big game have already had to be shot in their thousands in the reserves because with their excessive numbers they are threatening to destroy their own sources of nourishment completely and irrevocably.

Similarly, but to a much more hideous extent, the system of ecological factors which once kept human population within tolerable limits has been destroyed, and for a long while we were blind enough to think this was good. A constant increase in the human population seemed not only to comply with God's will, but it also seemed to mean an increasingly better world.

The other point I did not realize in 1954 was the dichotomy of social hierarchy described here for the first time. It is to this that the rest of this article will be devoted, because in its effective working in humans I see a non-material factor determining the mental hygiene and health of the individual and of the human race as a whole which theologians, philosophers, psychologists, sociologists, politicians, and economists have so far failed to recognize and which has, therefore, remained totally neglected.

IX. MAN—THE TERMITE?

Man is supposed to be the all-round adaptable animal. Yet, in modern times an ever-increasing number of medical, psychological, and social workers is concerned with the care, and if possible the cure, of an even more rapidly growing number of socially ill-adapted, maladjusted individuals. According to common belief, Man is also an essentially social animal. However, beliefs vary widely as to how Man as a social being should behave. Thus, it is hard to define conclusively the individual's place in the community.

People undoubtedly display territorial behavior in many forms and in many spheres of their lives. Klimpfinger (1952) has shown that it starts in the nursery. Garden walls, no-trespassing posters, the "my home—my castle" attitude of mind, the way people and especially children are quick to stake out their claims on the holiday beach and resent all "intruders," are clear examples of this all-pervading tendency to territorial behavior. There is, on the other hand, hardly any need to point out examples of absolute social hierarchy in human societies, ancient or recent, primitive or evolved: Chieftains, princes, kings, and the carefully elaborate hierarchies of their courts, armies, and the management of modern big business, as well as teen-age gangs, are only a few.

What it may lead to if territorial behavior runs free of any control by a superimposed absolute order can be amply illustrated, for instance, from the history of exploration and settlement in North America. At the other extreme, the result of unchecked absolute hierarchy is tyranny, when individuals or organizations have acquired excessive power and succeeded in reducing individual liberty more and more in favor of the "common good." In crowded societies, the two have a strong tendency to combine and to squash the individual into an anonymous cipher. Sometimes the problem of crowding has been solved socially by the emergence of an élite of "free citizens" or princes, who established among themselves a community based on proper balance between relative and absolute dominance, reducing the rest of the population to the status of mere domestic animals. Striking examples of this were the city-states of ancient Greece and the medieval princedoms of central Europe. Whenever the absolute hierarchy grew too oppressive, rebellions and revolutions were the inevitable course of events. And the coercion exerted by the underlying mechanism described can hardly be better illustrated than by the fact that the great revolution rising in the name of *liberté, égalité, fraternité* set up its own tyranny as soon as it had won victory. This was not because of the wickedness of some of the revolutionary leaders, but was the inevitable consequence of crowding and crowd management, and it is not by chance that under similar circumstances wicked leaders are almost automatically swept into power.

I do not want to oversimplify matters. There is no question of hierarchical antagonism being the one and only agent of human history. All I wish to stress is that it has been *one* agent, and that the fact it has a biological foundation and forms an indispensable and indestructible part of human nature has hitherto been utterly neglected. The shift of balance between the two orders of dominance is only possible within limits. The range of such a shift is species-specific and represents the density tolerance of a species as defined by this particular mechanism. Unfortunately, as will be shown in greater detail below, the density tolerance limit is not written clearly on our foreheads for everyone to see. In combined interaction with the other ecological factors it may all too easily be "outvoted," unobtrusively overstepped, without the resulting damage being dramatic or easy to diagnose. What we lack are adequate scientific investigations into *where* the tolerance limits lie in man's case and what could be regarded as "optimum density of habitation" and optimum world population for our species. The only thing that is certain is that we *have* long since overstepped all tolerable limits.

Observing autistic patients, Esser (1964, 1965) in New York and Grant (1965) in Birmingham, knowing nothing of one another or of my theories, found a dichotomy of absolute and relative hierarchy practically identical to what I observed in crowded domestic cat communities. As such patients have virtually none of the social inhibitions which prevent normal people from giving vent to undisguised aggressiveness, their display of dominance and territoriality (Esser's terms for absolute and relative hierarchy respectively) was almost brutally uninhibited, though this does not mean that the basic mechanisms involved are in themselves abnormal.

Nearly five years in prisoner-of-war camps taught me that overcrowded human societies reflect the symptoms of overcrowded wolf, cat, goat, mouse, rat, or rabbit communities to the last detail and that all differences are merely species-specific; the basic forces of social interaction and of organization are *in principle* identical and there is true homology between man and animal throughout the whole range of vertebrates. To recognize such an internal balance in man between absolute and relative social hierarchy, brought about by evolution as part of a density-control mechanism, *which limits the adaptability of the individual,* is not to deny that adaptability. What it does mean, however, is that the mental health of the individual is in danger and will eventually break down if adaptability is stretched too far beyond the limits set by evolutionary adaptation. If this happens to enough individuals to constitute a sizable proportion of a community, then that community ceases to be stable, healthy, and fit for humans to inhabit. Density surreptitiously creeping beyond the tolerance limits (for in a species like ours there is certainly also a minimum limit, though this is not of such general importance at present because we are not in acute danger of underpopulation) may create symptoms which cannot be directly and easily traced back to it as their cause but are often attributed to factors which are merely contributory or symptomatic in themselves. The resulting constant subliminal tension will lower the individual's resistance toward other disturbing factors. Thus, I have no doubt whatever that a great number of neuroses and social maladjustments are partially or totally, directly or indirectly, caused by overcrowding.

Calhoun (1962, 1963 a, b) and others have shown that crowded conditions seriously disturb maternal care in rats and mice. Likewise human mothers, according to Spitz (1964), are deeply influenced by population density: They often cannot form and maintain the proper emotional bonds toward their babies; this in turn interferes with the child's "ego formation," with its whole character development in which early youth and proper maternal care and affection are so vastly important. Nothing shows better than this what far-reaching damage can be done indirectly to future generations by the parent generations being too densely packed.

This is our situation now, and we have already been in it a long while. What every normal man wants for himself and his family is a detached house in an adequate garden, with neighbors close enough to be found if needed or one feels like a social call, yet far enough away to be avoided at other times. What we see instead is the cancerous growth of the huge blocks of flats of so-called satellite cities creeping out into the countryside, and very soon we shall reach the point where individuals simply cannot any longer be allowed to acquire a piece of land of their own and erect a single family house on it: In the interest of the Common Good the block of flats will have to become compulsory. Our civilization is marching with banners flying from battery hen to battery consumer.

Where captive wild animals are concerned, suitable subdivision and furnishing of the space available can to a certain degree compensate for its lack of extent (Hediger 1961). The architect Richard Neutra (1956) won world-wide acceptance for this viewpoint in the structuring of human living accommodation, housing estates, and artificial landscapes. But if Neutra considers that his techniques offer a cure and not merely temporary relief from the symptoms, I cannot agree with him. A soundproof wall may obscure the fact that there is no tree or meadow between us and the next neighbor, and may for a while even console us for the lack, but it is *no substitute* for them.

X. SOCIO-POLITICAL CONSEQUENCES

In recent years there has been growing concern about the so-called population explosion and the measures to be taken to avoid overcrowding. However, this is mostly understood to mean that an attempt should be made only to slow down the population increase so that the production of supplies, predominantly food, can catch up, and if this is achieved everything will be fine—or so many of those in political, social, and economic authority seem to think.

Reasoning on these lines makes it look as if controlling the population growth were mainly a problem of the underdeveloped countries: Our own affluence distracts from the fact that we *are* already overcrowded. We recommend birth control to the underdeveloped nations, but in our own overpopulated countries we still encourage large families with tax relief and even handsome allowances.

Contrary to current discussion, the danger of overpopulation does not rest solely on the need for food and shelter. It lies in whether the population will exceed the limits of human tolerance toward the presence of other humans. These limits have been set by evolutionary processes over millions of years. They cannot, therefore, be altered and trained differently within a few generations, nor can they be neglected, repressed, or overstepped without seriously disrupting the internal harmony of the species and with it the vital core of human nature itself.

It will be argued that my assertions run contrary to almost everything which is regarded as scientifically safe in modern psychology and sociology. The concept of adjustment is almost invariably understood as pertaining to the adjustment of individuals to environment, especially social environment. Hence, where disharmony between individual and social environment is found, this is generally explained as failure of the individual to adjust. True as this is in some cases, it overlooks the fact that in many respects the environment fails to be adjusted to the proper needs of the individual. Modern psychologists have, in many instances at least, been so amazed and overwhelmed by the enormous range of variation found among human personalities and behavior patterns that they have largely forgotten that all variations are but variations on the one theme, the species. Nothing can happen to or become of the individual which is not within the range of the characteristics defining the species. But today most psychologists are so sure of the omnipotence of individual adaptability and learning that they are blind to the facts which would help to reveal exactly what is the role of genetic—that is phylogenetic—information in all the different types of human behavior.

Yet, along with the learning psychologist, our social psychologists and sociologists are so convinced that everything in social behavior can, and therefore must, be trained, learned, institutionalized, that they fail to see a very plain fact: Traditions and institutions would never be stable if they did not rest on an innate behavioral basis. To the student of evolutionary processes, all changes in cultural, traditional, educational, religious, philosophical, and institutional attitudes appear to stir the surface only. The very core of human nature and conduct has evidently remained unchanged throughout known human history.

One of the age-old characteristics of the human species is that it is adapted to social life in a small group where each member knows each of the others personally, having a need for larger social gatherings from time to time but not too often, feeling a need to be by himself quite often, and reacting to continued oversocialization with all sorts of frustrations, repressions, aggressions, and fears which soon develop into genuine neuroses. As it is a species characteristic it does not matter whether we like or regret the fact. *We have to live with it* and create conditions which allow us to live with it in comparative health, wealth, and sanity.

That it is, for instance, possible to rear and train children so that they become habituated to oversocialized conditions until they are unable to feel safe and happy outside a crowd of their own kind certainly does not invalidate my point. Children and even adults can be trained or habituated to avoid everything good and healthy, to see their only source of contentment and even happiness in regularly overeating all sorts of palatable but unbalanced food, in continually seeking unsuitable and demoralizing amusements, in all kinds of perversions and addictions, and similarly in living continuously in a crowd. Robbed of these conditions, the afflicted individual will feel thoroughly dejected and miserable. Yet, this "adjustment" to mass communities does the human species no more good than drug addiction or alcoholism. As mentioned earlier, all *structurally* organized vertebrate communities depend for their internal structure and function on the individuals being personally acquainted with each other. This is the most fundamental difference between such communities, which therefore rightly deserve to be called societies, and the highly organized communities of bees, ants, and termites, in which individuals in the sense of known personalities are wholly unimportant and, as a matter of fact, not to be found: Any given individual will do for a certain function provided it is of the right "caste" or in the right phase of its life cycle. In a vertebrate community, however, which is not solely governed by absolute social hierarchy, the individual not only acquires personality, he also has some place, some preserve, where he is superior to all other members of the community. No matter how big or small the territory may be, and no matter what the ranking of the individual in the various absolute hierarchies of the community, as territory owner he is equal among his equals. In this capacity, and in this capacity alone, the human individual is able to enter, as a responsible, participating, cooperating, independent, self-respecting, and self-supporting citizen, the type of communal organization we call a democracy. Overcrowded conditions are thus a danger to true democracy which it is impossible to exaggerate. Tyranny is the almost inevitable result, whether it be exercised by personal tyrants or by an abstract principle like the Common Good, which is no longer any good at all to the mass of individuals. *For this is an unalterable law:* As long as density is tolerable, sacrifices made for a common cause will, one way or another, pay dividends to the individual and contribute to his own fulfilment. Beyond this point, however, the demands of the Common Good rise steeply, and what is taken away from the individual is gone for good; he cannot even see that it goes in any sizable amount to others, for they are likewise robbed without reward.

If, in accordance with Wynne-Edwards's theories, the innate balance of relative and absolute social hierarchy once served as density control mechanism and thus ensured that social life did not develop into unbearable social pressure, why has it now apparently ceased to function in man? To the biologist the answer is obvious; hardly any biological mechanism works independently of others and faultlessly. Thus density tolerance in humans is adapted to a certain (i.e. high) level of child mortality, to a generally far shorter life expectation than is usual nowadays.

Scientific and technical progress has altered all this, but it could not and has not altered the basis of human social behavior and happiness which has been built into each individual by at least five hundred million years of vertebrate evolution. This cannot be altered in harmony with the whole except by that same, slow process of evolution, taking countless generations, and any attempt to force it will only result in the destruction of our own species. But the density control mechanism described here at length can be revived and brought into its natural and beneficial function again if we use our rational powers to restore the equilibrium, and use them swiftly and efficiently. It is no longer a question of forestalling future overpopulation: we must not only call a halt to further increase, we must find ethically and psychologically acceptable means of slowly shrinking numbers back to less than the present, to a sane density level. There is no time to be lost.

At present most people seem paralyzed by fear of The Bomb, but the bomb in itself is no danger. The only real danger to Man is men, too many men. Statisticians have forecast that by 2040 the world population will have reached 22 billion. By then production may possibly be capable of feeding, clothing, and battery-keeping these numbers; but then nobody will be able to move without being impeded by numbers of other people moving, and without interfering irritatingly with their movements. At least half the population will have to be psychiatrists tending the neuroses of the other half. To this future population, the bomb will no longer be a threat but a temptation: It will appear as the salvation from all evil.

I think we all agree that we want neither the extinction of our species, or at least of many future billions, through the bomb, nor the re-establishment of the old, cruel methods by which nature balanced our numbers. Thus, the only way remaining is human density control —birth control. It can be done. Automation, if properly used, can allow us to keep and even enhance our living standard with a slowly decreasing number of young working people. At present, under the influence of an economic theory which regards ever-growing expansion as the aim of all economy and automation as a means of stepping it up even further and faster, it can end only as all unchecked positive feedback mechanisms end: in catastrophe. The choice is still ours: Do we want rational regulation and—for some time—reduction of numbers, or unrestricted procreation and The Bomb as Ultima Ratio? There can be no turning back. Those who bear the responsibility (and as voters that includes each and every one of us) should make no mistake about it—it is no longer five minutes to midnight, but already a quarter past. . . .

9 On the Function of the Relative Hierarchy of Moods

(As Exemplified by the Phylogenetic and Ontogenetic Development of Prey-Catching in Carnivores)[1] (1965)

I. INTRODUCTION

In "Verhaltensstudien" (a study of cat behavior) (1956 a) I gave a detailed description of the prey-catching of cats—mainly domestic cats. In simple experiments I analyzed the releasing mechanisms, taxes, and instinctive movements involved. It proved impossible to interpret the coordination and sequence of the last-named in accordance with the inflexible, one-directional hierarchical systems described by Baerends (1941) and Tinbergen (1950) (see Fig. on p. 65); this led to the formulation of the principle of the "relative hierarchy of moods" by association with von Holst's concept of "relative coordination" (1936 a, Leyhausen 1955 a, 1956 a). At that time I was able to discuss only briefly and incompletely the ontogenetic development of prey-catching actions and the contribution made by experience and learning and I was unable to compare more than a few species.

Observations and experiments in recent years on a series of further species kept in something approaching ideal conditions make it possible to add considerably to the previously published results, and in part to correct them.[2]

II. MATERIAL AND METHOD

A total of 47 animals belonging to 15 species was available for study. Depending on size and compatibility, the animals live singly, in pairs

Fig. 1 West-African genet with dorsal mane and tail hairs (a) flat, (b) erected.

or in groups, in indoor cages of 12 square meters in size adjoined by outdoor enclosures varying in size from 30 to 200 square meters and containing grass, bushes, and small trees.

Many experiments, and as far as possible all first encounters between an animal and a particular kind of prey, were filmed; where this was not possible for technical reasons, at least copious series of photographs were made. All observations were dictated directly onto tape. For details of animal keeping, lay-out, and technical facilities see Leyhausen (1962 b).

The following report is based on more than 20,000 individual observations, approximately 2,000 meters of 16-mm film and hundreds of photographs. The results have been only qualitatively evaluated and a quantitative analysis is not the intention of this work.

For reasons of space I must assume a knowledge of the results and ideas contained in the paper of 1956 a. To make the reader's task easier, the page number in *"Verhaltensstudien"* referred to is indicated in square brackets. However, since precisely those nuances which get lost when material is presented in a statistical, graphic, or tabular form can be of decisive importance to qualitative analysis and discussions, detailed—and sometimes perhaps wearisome—descriptions of individual cases are unavoidable. Only by this means can the reader gain anything like an adequate impression of the range and nature of the phenomena.

Since the observations made on the individual animals are to be discussed in various connections, I shall first enumerate them separately according to species and, where necessary, individually, and shall refer back accordingly in the discussion section.

Simpson's nomenclature and systematics (1945), which are nowadays almost generally accepted in mammalogy, do not seem to me appropriate in the case of the family of the *Felidae*. In naming the species enumerated here, therefore, I have adopted the system proposed by Pocock (1917) as improved by Haltenorfh (1953) and Weigel (1961). The reasons for this may be found in detail in Leyhausen (1956 b, 1963) and Weigel (1961).

III. RESULTS

1. *Genetta felina felina* Thunberg

(West-African genet; Westafrikanische Ginsterkatze)

Previous history: 1 ♀, "Netti," caught as adult in 1954 in the Wilhelmstal district of Southwest Africa, in my possession since January 11, 1956. *Genetta felina* belongs to a group of West African genets which, in contrast to both their East and Central African relatives and the North African-European *Genetta genetta*, have considerably elongated hairs on their back and tail which they erect when excited (Fig. 1); this makes the close relationship between genets and civets much more obvious than it is in the case of the shorthaired species.

In my possession Netti has received day-old chicks, mice, golden hamsters, rats, and guinea pigs in large numbers, in recent years always live; thus, her killing method could be observed daily from once to several times according to the size of the prey. The process was filmed 27 times, mostly in slow motion (16 chicks, 11 white rats weighing between 200 and 400 grams).

In contrast to Dücker's genets (1957) *(Genetta genetta suahelica)*, my animal displays neither lying in wait [2] nor typical stalking [3]. Instead, she walks toward her prey, at most slightly crouched and hesitantly, but usually fast, and, if it is a chick, usually catches it as she goes, without stopping or even pausing. She approaches mam-

Fig. 2   Genet seizes chick by the middle of its back as she runs.

mals in the same way, but pauses just in front of them, pulls her head up and back and her chin in, her nose pointing toward the prey animal, then brings it down fast almost like a heron. Normally she grasps chicks in the back (Fig. 2), mammals over or even behind the shoulder; direct nape bites are rare (in the films only once). Insofar, then, her method of catching chicks is completely identical to the behavior described by Dücker (1957) in the case of *Viverricula*, but not that of cats (cf. *Viverra*, p. 153). Certainly my animal must also be able to lie in wait and stalk, only the threshold for this is probably higher than it was in Dücker's animals; whether this is a matter of species or comes from the fact that Dücker was observing young animals cannot for the moment be decided. Even when I gave my genet a fully grown brown rat for the first time, she approached this in the same way, though much more slowly and cautiously than with white rats, sniffing uninterruptedly and making great play with her ears.

If Netti has grasped the chick by the back, she adjusts her grip forward in the direction of the head with 2 to 4 snapping movements until she has the head in her mouth and chews this off; when making these adjusting snaps she may toss the chick up a little each time, catching it again before it falls to the ground. She does not help herself in this by using her paws. Before the adjusting snaps she sometimes gives the chick a brief shake (see below).

Her rat-catching is more dramatic. Netti grasps the rat in the shoulder region, pressing it down with her snout, lays a forepaw over its hindquarters and tries to pull these backward. Then with her teeth she pulls the prey upward, and as she does so her paw eventually slides off. Often she gives the rat a brief shake before pressing it down again and, as she does so, snapping or adjusting her grip in the direction of its head. This is repeated one or more times until Netti has the rat by the neck between shoulder and head; only then does she kill it by taking several repeat bites and each time pressing it down. If the rat offers considerable resistance, Netti either lets it go again, withdraws a little or turns through 360° and attacks anew, or she encircles the rat with her two forepaws and pulls it backward under her own body or throws herself onto one shoulder (Fig. 3). The *shaking* she gives it is always very brief—once, at the most twice. In the process Netti's head swings only to one side, never back over the median to the other (Fig. 4f-k). Occasionally she makes her adjusting snap at the side turning-point of the shaking movement instead of on returning to the median (Fig. 4 l-n).

In contrast to *adjusting snaps,* I call it *repeat biting* when Netti does not quite free her teeth from the prey animal (repeat biting, Eibl-Eibesfeldt 1956; repeat munching, Goethe 1950). I subsequently investigated some of the rats and guinea pigs killed by her. In the neck skin I usually found only 4 perforations corresponding to the 4 canine teeth. The neck musculature underneath, however, was always totally bitten through and squashed in a way that could never have happened with one single bite. Thus, in after-biting Netti must open her fangs far enough to pull them out of the musculature but not out of the loose neck skin. In all cases, the cervical vertebrae were severed at at least one or two points; only once was a vertebra crushed.

Golden hamsters are usually much more ready to defend themselves than white laboratory rats and are not so easy to take by surprise from the rear. Netti never uses her forepaws, as a cat would, to strike down or pull around a prey animal of this sort that is standing upright in defensive posture [17]. Instead, she always withdraws a little and waits until the hamster tires and drops onto all fours again, when she makes a fresh lightning attack; this she repeats until eventually she is successful. Furthermore, with animals willing to defend themselves she aims much more precisely at the nape and only rarely grasps them as far to the rear as she does with prey animals that are sitting motionless or running away.

Netti grasped a small chicken on the run with both forepaws (as

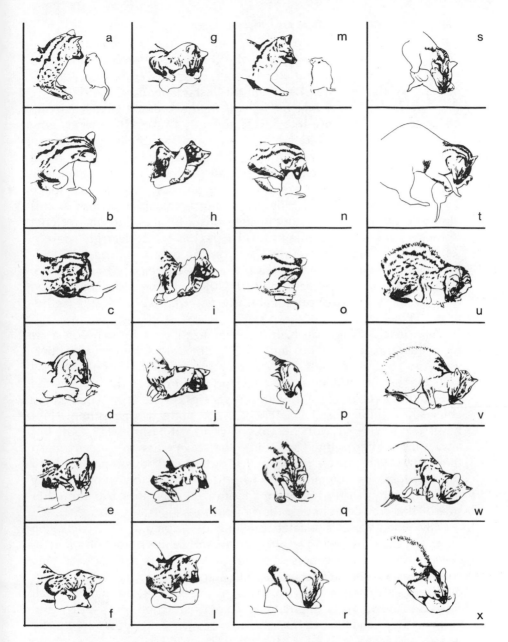

Fig. 3 Genet catches rat: a) Pauses before biting, b) bites, c-e) reaches over rat's hindquarters with one forepaw and pulls these backward, d-g) rat succeeds in turning round, h-l) although genet is clasping rat between both forepaws, it is able to free itself, m-p) fresh attack as in a-d, q) nape bite, r-s) genet presses rat down, t) pulls it upward, u-w) clasping and repeat biting, v-y) whereby genet leans on left shoulder while keeping her hindquarters upright, x) carries helpless but not yet dead rat into her cage (drawn from film).

Fig. 3g) and bit it from below at the throat. Her teeth encircled its throat completely, so that her canines closed over the *back of its head*. The chicken was dead almost instantaneously. Netti let go, then grasped it anew and bit it hard in the breast twice. Then she began to bore her nose into the feathers in all possible places, now here, now there, as if biting tentatively, until she finally began to eat at the neck close below the head. This she did by ripping off piece after piece ("tearing action" [30]). Any feathers hanging from the torn-off scraps Netti chewed and sucked off; not once did she make a hint of plucking [23–31] any more than I was able to observe this in the Striped Genet *(Genetta abyssinica)* or the European Genet *(Genetta genetta)*. According to Dücker (1957), all viverrids she observed *pluck* "fairly large birds (jays) on the breast and back." However, both an African Mongoose *(Herpestes ichneumon)* and a Palm Civet *(Paradoxurus hermaphroditus)* [30] I observed did not pluck, nor did my two Two-spotted Palm Civets *(Nandinia binotata,* see below, p. 156).

Only once on film can Netti be seen to place a forepaw on a rat for a fraction of a second (approx. 1/30th) before biting, but otherwise—in contrast to cats [12]—she always does this simultaneously with the bite or not until after it. How subordinate the role of the paws in prey-catching still is with this species can be seen when a prey animal has hidden itself in a crevice, e.g. under a tree stump. Netti never fishes after it with her forepaws in cat fashion [12, 58], but always inserts her pointed snout into the crevice first in order to grasp the animal with her teeth and pull it out. Only if this meets with no success does she sometimes try to *push* or *drive* the animal out by *prodding* with a forepaw, when she immediately jumps to the other side of the crevice in anticipation of success.

Only when Netti is satiated can one occasionally see her *playing* with, or rather around, live prey for a short while before she kills it. Her play lacks the richness of variety which characterizes cats' play with prey [51–55]; at its climax Netti stands up at full length on her hind-legs and hops a little on them, at the same time making small sideways blows with alternate forepaws stretched out stiffly, and swinging her head sideways as she does so. The paw-blows are mostly

Fig. 4 Genet catches rat: a) Aiming for bite, b-d) bite in the shoulder, forepaw presses rear end of rat down, e-f) pulls rat upward and forepaw slides off it, g) genet gives one sideways shake, h) back to the middle, i) shakes again to the same side, j-k) swings only halfway back, l-n) tosses head with rat to the side again, opens jaws (m), adjusts grip (n), o-r) in one and the same movement pulls rat back and carries it off (drawn from film).

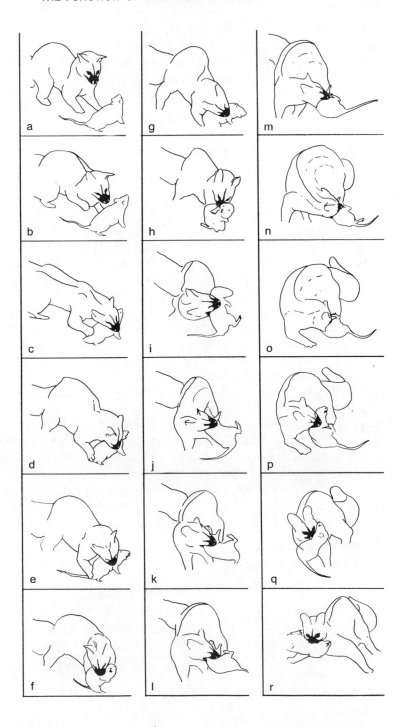

performed in the air above the prey animal; it is an exception if she touches it, and she never strikes it hard.

When grasping the prey in her teeth, making repeat snaps at it in the air, or shaking it, Netti usually squeezes her eyes half shut or closes them completely, only to open them again immediately she has a firm hold on it.

2. *Viverricula indica* Geoffroy

(Small Indian Civet; Rasse)

1♀, acquired from dealer, imported as adult animal from Siam; in Wuppertal Zoo since June 1, 1964, nothing further known.

My observations coincide completely with Dücker's (1957): Prey animals that are *sitting still* are either ignored by this animal or it fails to attack them even after sniffing them thoroughly; only a moving prey animal stimulates it to pursuit and biting. Initially the bites are mostly aimed not at the front end of the prey but at the nearest available part of the body. A fairly large Golden Hamster threw itself on its back in defense after receiving the first bite and gnashed its teeth threateningly (Eibl-Eibesfeldt 1953 b). The viverricula snapped at its flank, *shook* it twice, at the same time giving it repeat bites, and then *threw* it about 25 cm away. The hamster was left lying motionless with respiratory paralysis (Krieg 1964) but visibly beating heart, and the viverricula desisted from it at once. Only when, after some time, the hamster recovered, rolled over onto its feet and began to crawl away, did it bite it anew in the side, left off again immediately when it threw itself on its back, and only killed it with two swift bites in the neck and shoulder region when it once more attempted to run away. So far the viverricula has not used its forepaws either to catch and hold or to prod its prey; however, my observations are too few to allow of a final conclusion.

3. *Viverra zibetha* L.

(Large Indian Civet; Indische Zibethkatze)

2♀♀ brought from Calcutta in July, 1962, approximately 3 to 4 months old; probably still without any experience of prey. On arrival in Wuppertal the two animals showed marked symptoms of rickets, but after appropriate treatment these disappeared completely in an amazingly short time.

The intention was to give these animals no live prey until they were completely adult. The first live rat, however, got into their cage by accident on August 1, 1963 (when they were about 14 to 15 months old; since then they have continued to grow somewhat). The smaller of the two civets immediately *pursued* it, holding her nose close above the back of the rat, which was running around in a lively fashion. Several times she aimed at the nape, but each time the rat changed direction before the civet could strike. Eventually, however, she managed to overtake the rat and *killed* it with a loud *crunching bite,* the precise "site" of which could not be seen. Later rats were killed by her in the same manner, only the method was as a rule not single bites but series of bites.

When taking their first grasping bite the civets also snap at the *nearest available* part of the prey's body, not noticeably at the nape. As the snaps are repeated, the bites gradually move farther toward the front end, never in the reverse direction. Repeat snaps and bites are usually carried out with the head raised and without the prey touching the ground again. In the course of repeated snapping the civets often convey the head of the prey animal in one move into one corner of their mouth, and then begin to chew it off. Small rats they eat like this without setting them down: After a few chewing movements on one side, they convey the rat into the other corner of the mouth with a *swing of the head,* and so on (an eating technique practiced to perfection by Maned Wolves, as I have seen in the London Zoo).

One of the rats the civets killed was left uneaten. Dissection revealed: no external injuries; subcutaneously heavy bruising and hemorrhages on both flanks, breast, shoulders, and neck; the right parietal bone was indented, the occipital bone completely separated from the rest of the skull; nowhere had the canine teeth perforated the rat's skin; the vertebral column was intact.

A very large and *aggressive* rat was treated with much greater caution by the smaller civet. First she sniffed at the nape of its neck, withdrew a little, and then gave it a lightning bite in its back, immediately jumped back again, at the same time *flinging* the rat a little way away in the opposite direction; this she repeated five times, before retaining her grip on the rat and killing it.

If a prey animal runs toward a civet or stands up defensively before it, the civet grasps it by the neck or takes the whole head into its jaws, crushes it with one bite, and then, as already described, chews it straight off.

Like the genet, the civets never use their forepaws in cat fashion to grasp a prey animal and pull it toward them, though I should add that I have so far given them only relatively small prey animals (nothing larger than guinea pigs). However, when a rat crawled in under a leaning tree stump the small civet *prodded* at it with her paw like Netti; whereupon the rat jumped at her, but was caught in midjump by a bite in the flank and flung about two meters away. The civet approached cautiously, again the rat jumped, the civet dodged sideways, grasped the rat quickly in the back as it landed again and carried it away rapidly; as it went, it shook its prey several times extremely violently, but, unlike Netti, to both sides, let it drop, and then killed it with two crunching bites in the neck and shoulder region.

The larger of the two civets was always very interested in live prey, ran up to it and sniffed it, but never attacked; or at any rate she always hesitated so long that the smaller one had also arrived in the meantime, and she then left the rest to her. She did not kill her first prey animal until we succeeded in shutting the smaller civet away in the indoor cage. (This works only when luck is on our side; the animals panic extremely easily if one puts even the slightest pressure on them, and then any experiment is out of the question. Furthermore they are extremely sociable and stick together like burrs.) A guinea pig was placed on the gravel-covered section of the outer enclosure. The civet approached hesitantly and kept withdrawing under the nearest bush, eventually sniffed the guinea pig from all sides, but mainly on its head, withdrew again, and repeated the whole process several times. Then the guinea pig ran straight toward the bushes in which the civet took cover each time. The civet shot out suddenly, bit the guinea pig hard in its shoulders, dragged it a little way back with it and let it drop, hesitated a moment, then bit it firmly twice in the neck and at once began to eat the head off. She bit a second guinea pig in the flank first, but then killed it in precisely the same manner.

Thus, the civets catch and kill their prey just as the viverricula does, but with one exception: They also attack prey animals which are *sitting motionless*.

A chicken placed in their outer enclosure aroused great interest. They followed it everywhere at a distance and sniffed at it when they caught up with it, but time and again recoiled fearfully, especially when the chicken cackled. The experiment was broken off after half an hour. A few days later they were given another chicken in their indoor cage, and at first they behaved just as before. The chicken kept coming to the wire at the front of the cage and trying to get out and, as it did so, the two civets gave it a thorough sniffing from all sides. Eventually the larger of the two grasped it by the tail-end, pulled it out of the corner and to one side, but then let it go and the two drove it once round the cage. Then, when it was again stuck in the same corner, the larger civet rushed in and gave it a crunching bite in the back, shook it violently and flung it some meters away. The chicken lay there apparently lifeless. The smaller civet then repeated what the other had done. Subsequently they both sniffed at the dead animal, bored their noses into its feathers, bit into it here and there and threw it around, before tearing it up between them. This is their way of sharing prey and—unlike genets [47, Plate 37 loc. cit.]—contains scarcely a trace of food jealousy. Next day the smaller civet killed the next chicken after a much shorter preparatory period, but apart from this everything went as on the first occasion. The post-killing activities were also briefer. Neither of the animals attempted to *pluck*.

4. *Nandinia binotata* Gray

(African Palm-civet; Pardelroller)

♂ "Stammi" and ♀ "Slowa," both adult. Acquired from dealer December, 1963; previous history unknown.

The Two-spotted Palm Civet stands out from the other viverrid species mentioned above among other things on account of its dexterous handlike use of the forepaws, which almost reminds one of the Kinkajou (Leyhausen 1953 a, b, Poglayen-Neuwall 1962). Thus, when catching prey my animals almost always grasp first with their two forepaws, and either press the prey animal's abdomen to the ground or hold it fast between both hands and then bite *at random*, many times in quick succession, at the unprotected parts of the prey animal's body. The animal thus held has often thrown itself defensively on its back at the attack or at least turns its forequarters and teeth toward its attacker. *Nandinia* is apparently much less afraid of the teeth of a rat or a Golden Hamster than any other, even much larger carnivore is. Apparently *blindly* it bites again and again until its prey is dead. When dissected, the prey killed by my two animals revealed bite wounds almost exclusively on the underside, in belly, breast, and throat; only once had a canine tooth pierced the skull of a hamster between occipital and squamosum; in the other cases the cause of death was injury to the organs of the breast. One hamster revealed only a single bite wound: one canine tooth had penetrated the breast under the right foreleg, another had broken through the left shoulder blade; in the breast hollow I found no great injuries, only the right auricle was torn open.

Stammi also killed a small chicken by grasping and holding it down with both forepaws and then biting it many times in the breast, throat, shoulders, head, and back. The bites followed one another too fast for an observer to be able to count them, and in the freshly killed chicken the above-mentioned parts of the body were so ripped about that it was impossible to distinguish individual bite wounds.

After the investigation of the chicken, it was given to Slowa, who came too close with it, however, to a gap where the wire frame separating her from Stammi for the duration of the experiment did not quite fit against the wall of the cage. At once Stammi snapped through and had the head of the chicken in his teeth. The subsequent tug-of-war was won by the wire frame and Stammi was able to pull off only the head of the chicken and a section of its neck; Slowa kept the main body and carried it a little way away. Both of them ripped off pieces from their prey ("tearing action" [34, 35; Plate 32 l.c.]), chewed and swallowed them. They did not pluck out the feathers but chewed and sucked them off or swallowed them, too.

5. Hybrids ♂ *Prionailurus bengalensis* Kerr— ♀ *Felis catus* L.

(Indian Leopard-cat—Domestic cat; Bengalkater—Hauskatze)
3♀♀, "Natalie," "Li," and "Rani," 1♂ "Kim."

The animals were bred by a private owner: Rani and Kim were born in May, 1960, Natalie and Li in October, 1960. The father was a male Indian leopard-cat from Siam, the mother a pure black domestic cat. It is certain that none of the animals had received live prey before the experiments described here.

Natalie came into my possession in March, 1961, together with a fifth animal which died shortly after arrival. At the age of 9 months Natalie receives her first live mice. She approaches the first very hesitantly and cautiously, but follows it eagerly when it runs away from her, and jumps playfully around it when it stops. It is a long while before she at last very lightly taps at the mouse for the first time [44, 53]. It is even longer before she gently grasps the mouse in its back fur with her teeth, only to start away from it again at once. After she has repeated this a few times at fairly long intervals she takes a somewhat firmer grip for the first time and *tosses* the mouse a little way into the air. The whole is then repeated many times. Finally Natalie grasps the mouse for the first time in the nape of the neck, lets go, aims again at the nape, then *pulls* the mouse around with one forepaw until it is under her breast and parallel with her, bites more firmly into the nape and at once lets go again. The mouse is injured but still tries to run away; Natalie bites twice more into its nape, lets it fall again, and the mouse is now dead. Natalie bites it once more in the nape, then begins to eat it from the head downward [31].

With each new mouse the process is repeated without any noteworthy variations. Occasionally a mouse is not killed "properly" with a nape bite but *played to death*. Yet in the course of 14 days and many mice the number of nape bites needed for killing becomes less and less, bites in other parts of the body disappear altogether, and finally Natalie runs up to every mouse without any hesitation and kills it in the typical manner [11–16] with one single nape bite. However, when I want to film her doing this, she is so disturbed by the noise of the camera and all the unavoidable accompanying details that she relapses into a stage roughly corresponding to the middle of her period of "learning" prey-catching (as regards "learning" see p. 209). One day later (24 July 1961) I give Natalie her first live rat (approx. 300 g) (film). Everything proceeds almost exactly as just described in respect of the first mouse, but with two differences: 1. Natalie aims all her bites at the nape of the neck, not at other points. 2. The rat defends itself and jumps at Natalie several times; unlike domestic cats that are really good rat-catchers [42], she does not beat the attacking rat down with her forepaws, but adeptly side-steps the rat's lunges each time, then at once makes a fresh attack of her own. *Five nape bites* at fairly long intervals are needed to kill the rat, although it is already partially paralyzed from the first. After the third bite it can barely move any more and Natalie begins energetic *relief play* [53]; after the fifth, with the rat now dead, she changes to playing *"catch and throw"* [52], in the process of which she gives the rat two further hard bites in the nape.

In contrast to the development of mouse-killing, it took only a few more rats before Natalie was a perfect rat-killer.

The initial picture was the same when Natalie received her first two live guinea pigs (film). The new element here was cautious investigation of a so far unfamiliar prey animal: Natalie took a loose grip with her teeth in the back fur of both guinea pigs and allowed herself to be "led along" by them like this as they ran away. Similarly polecats sometimes grasp rats by the tail and partly let themselves be pulled along by them, partly try to overtake the rat as they run without letting go of the tail (Eibl-Eibesfeldt 1955 b, Wüstehube

1960 b). In both cases, however, after a very short while Natalie grasped the guinea pig in the nape of the neck in front of the shoulders (not close behind the head) and killed it, giving it many repeat bites (p. 148): 20 in the case of the first guinea pig, when she did not release her grip but, like the genet (p. 149), repeatedly raised the prey animal from the ground and pressed it down again. In the case of the second guinea pig she made 21 repeat bites, then carried it off a little way, gave it 5 more, carried it a few steps backward, gave it one more repeat bite, and then laid it down [23]. In the process of repeat biting, she worked forward along the guinea pig's nape from the shoulders somewhat toward the head. After briefly "taking a walk" [23], she grasped it in the nape again, raised it high, pressed it down, and gave it 3 more repeat bites. With both guinea pigs, killing was followed by a lengthy period of relief play [53], which later changed to "catch and throw" [52].

Li, Rani, Kim: On July 20, 1961, the three other hybrids arrive. To begin with they do not receive live prey but are fed with freshly killed mice, rats, and guinea pigs. On September 7 we put Natalie with them and now she, too, receives no more live prey.

On September 15, however, a rat which had escaped from its container climbed into the hybrids' cage and the chase began before anyone could prevent it. The three females pursued the rat immediaately while Kim was still asleep. All three very cautious, they tried to tap at the rat; they all ran eagerly after it, but at first not one of them made a serious attack. Eventually the rat found cover in a corner and now Kim joined in, too. All four now angled after the rat with their forepaws, but without success. Suddenly the rat abandoned its refuge and ran along one wall of the cage. At first the three females followed in a bunch, then Rani shot forward at lightning speed and grasped the rat in the nape of the neck; its convulsive jerking indicated that the bite was fatal [19]. It is noteworthy that Natalie's already considerable previous experience gave her *not the slightest superiority* over her sisters in this unplanned experiment, and that it was not she but Rani who killed.

Apart from this incident Rani, Li, and Kim likewise received mice as their first live prey. From the very beginning Rani killed her mice immediately with a nape bite. Kim and Li played their first mice to death, but within a week Kim was doing just like Rani. Li, however, continued to play around with her mice for a long time and then usually lost them to Natalie or Rani, who arrived like lightning from one direction or another and stole the mouse from under Li's nose.

For weeks on end each of the four animals received a freshly killed rat in the evening; the four rats were held up together by the tail, and Natalie, Li, Kim, and Rani came, one after the other, grasped their rat, always with a precise nape bite, and carried it off to their eating place. The sequence in which they came expressed not their ranking order but their varying degrees of tameness.[3] After this evening feeding had been going on for some weeks, on December 10, 1961, I held up four live rats instead of dead ones. All the hybrids took them as if they had not noticed the difference, carried them a short distance away, and killed them with one or two rapid bites. The next evening I did not hold the rats up but put them down singly in front of me on the floor of the cage. This time, too, all four came without hesitation in their habitual sequence and at once killed with a *nape bite*. After a week, first Natalie began to fall off, approached more hesitantly, and did not kill with the same speed and eagerness as before. The next day Li had difficulty with a rat which defended itself energetically, and was only able to overcome it after a long battle. From that time on Natalie and Li no longer took their rats as smoothly and unhesitatingly from my hand, nor did they kill as fast and reliably.

On December 24 the experienced Natalie killed a guinea pig immediately. Li approached the second cautiously, sniffed at the nape of its neck and laid one forepaw on its hindquarters; the guinea pig squeaked and Li drew back. This was repeated, then Kim approached. At first he did the same as Li, but then took a firm bite and carried the guinea pig into a sleeping-box. Two more guinea pigs were killed by Natalie; Li behaved just as timidly as before, and Rani was too afraid to come anywhere near.

In relation to Golden Hamsters, all four at first reacted very timidly, jumping away exaggeratedly every time one stood up or threw itself on its back in defense. Kim, initially the most timid of them all, finally killed the first hamster with a rapid nape bite. On subsequent days, too, he killed all the hamsters put in, now always doing it fast and skillfully, whereas the females merely chased around after them as usual but without grasping them. Only Li chased the hamsters energetically, and she killed her first on the third day of the experiment. Rani did likewise, killing it fast and efficiently, as she had previously done with the rat after failing to take part in the chase at first: At the time she was the lowest ranking of the four and was afraid, not of the prey animal, but of her siblings. All four accepted day-old chicks at once, though instead of killing them immediately they at first played around with them for a long while, just as they—and particularly Li— often did with mice.

Rani's social status deteriorated still further, and at feeding-time she no longer came down on the floor of the cage but stayed up on a shelf attached to one wall. We threw her mice and rats up to her there, and these she usually caught with one forepaw *in the air*, grasped with the other forepaw as well, and then without fail had the animal in her jaws with a precise nape bite. With time Natalie and Li realized that food animals were flying through the air to the shelf and tried to oust Rani there as well. As a result they eventually came, one after the other, to the end of the shelf to catch their prey as they had previously done on the ground. Rani remained the most adept, although after a little practice the other two were almost as good. Gradually I increased the distance from which I threw the food animals to four meters, intentionally threw them anything up to 50 cm to the side, and gave the mouse or rat every possible twist: Hardly ever did the cats fail to catch them, and almost always they subsequently had the animal by the nape; other grips were extremely rare and were at once corrected (Fig. 5). It should be added that, in other respects too, these hybrids are faster, more adept, acrobatic, and elegant in their movements than I have experienced with any domestic cat, although in relation to their paternal relatives, the pure Indian leopard-cats, even they look rather clumsy.

6. R₁ Hybrids ♂ Domestic cat—♀ "Rani" (see above p. 156)

♂ "Smudge" and ♀ "Pudge," born May 2-3, 1964. They, together with their mother, have the freedom of my study. Until the kittens were 5 weeks old, the mother carried all prey animals to a spot well away from the nest and not visible from it, where she then ate them. On June 11 she carried a *rat* she had just *killed* into the nest for the first time, but ate it up all by herself. Two days later she again carried a rat in, opened it up somewhat, and Smudge then ate a little of it. On June 19 Rani carried the first (dead) mouse into the nest and Smudge ate the whole of it. Pudge caught and killed her first mouse at the age of 51 days (June 23). At first she played "chase" with it for

---

Fig. 5 Rani catches rats in the air: a) One forepaw reaches out to meet rat, b) gets rat in thigh, c) second forepaw comes into action, d) both paws whirl rat around, e) Rani has rat "correctly" by the nape. (The drawings are from photos originating from more than one series. The rats were, however, thrown in practically identical manner each time, so that this reconstruction is a fundamentally accurate representation of the process and not a distortion. The photos were taken at a time when attempts to accustom this shy animal to the inevitable accompaniments of slow-motion filming had not yet met with success.)

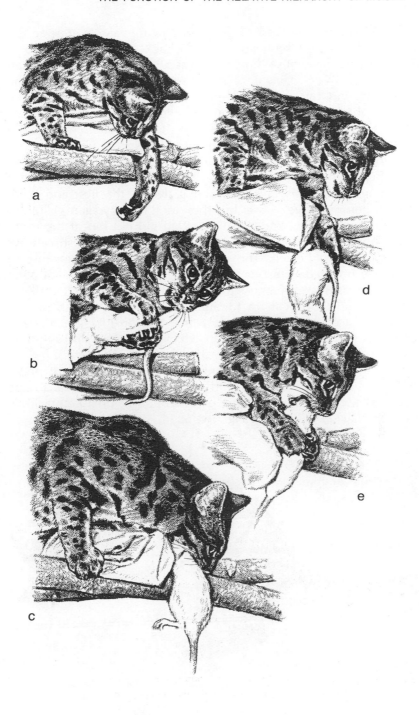

a long while, eventually tired of this, and now repeatedly grasped the mouse in the nape, by the head, or in the back and then laid it down in order to eat; the mouse, however, was still completely intact and each time ran away again. Rani made several attempts to take the mouse away, but my assistant kept her back. However, when she decided to abandon the experiment and take the mouse away herself, and Rani simultaneously approached from the other side, this was too much for Pudge: She rushed at the mouse and for the first time bit it hard in the back, paralyzed it and, the mouse now being motionless, at once began to eat it. It was June 25 before Rani failed to kill a mouse immediately herself but carried it live to the nest and there released it before Pudge's nose, but then took it away again, killed it, and only then finally let Pudge have it. Rani did not repeat the process until June 28 and then again on July 4; in the intervals she always killed all the mice herself. The development of mouse-catching in Pudge's case proceeded just as I have previously described [44-48].

At the age of 8 weeks Smudge had difficulties with his dentition; all his food had to be cut up for him. After appropriate treatment, however, he rapidly made up for lost time and on July 4, at the age of 62 days, killed his first mouse, first stalking cautiously up to it, then abruptly in one swoop grasping it with a correct nape bite.

On July 6 Smudge made the "lion attack" I have described previously [15-16] on a *dead* rat: In mid-jump he grasped the rat's nape with his teeth, clamped his two forepaws around its breast, and threw himself on his side with it (cf. Fig. 3w, 6, 14, 18).

Fig. 6   Pudge kills her second rat; the illustration shows the process shortly before the nape bite, while her forepaws are still pulling the rat backward.

Meanwhile Rani lets the kittens have almost all mice live, yet she always kills rats first (September 6, kittens 4 months old!). If one of us throws a kitten a rat, Rani rushes up and kills it, even when she has already received a rat for herself. The impression to an observer is that Rani still considers rats too dangerous for her children (but see Discussion, p. 208 et seq.). Yet, at a moment when her mother was not watching, Pudge already killed her first rat on August 24; however, the rat was rather passive and, without resisting, allowed itself to be killed by many repeated bites in the nape. It seemed as if Pudge's canine teeth were still too short for a firm bite which would penetrate the relatively thick nape musculature of the rat and into a vital center. But Rani is still unwilling to let her kittens get at rats; we repeatedly throw them rats when we believe their mother is occupied, but she is far too watchful. Without any doubt it is Rani's behavior which is responsible for the development of prey-catching by Smudge and Pudge being delayed as compared with that of normal domestic kittens [44-48].

Not until September 16 (136 days old) was Pudge at last quick enough and, lying on her side, at once bit a rat so firmly in the nape that it was dead before Rani arrived. On the next evening Pudge killed a rat almost as fast and smoothly as her mother, staying on her feet and not throwing herself onto one side with it. Smudge is shy and reserved and on such occasions allows himself to be pushed aside by Pudge, who is rather self-assured. Left alone with a rat and without the constant interference of Pudge and Rani, he would no doubt kill very quickly. However, for experimental reasons we do not intend to disturb this social situation. Thus, by the time this manuscript was completed (September 17, 1964) Smudge had so far made no serious attack on a rat.

All at once, after Pudge had killed a number of rats apparently effortlessly with a nape bite, she seemed to have difficulties: She made *"faulty bites"* at other places in the neck, had to let go again frequently, make a fresh attack, get around or (only in exceptional cases) fight down the resistance of the rat before she could grasp it in the nape and kill it (Fig. 7). Often her mother intervened, killed the rat, and then let her have it again (for fuller details see p. 210, p. 214 et seq., p. 225 et seq.).

7. *Prionailurus bengalensis* Kerr

(Indian Leopard-cat; Bengalkatze, Indische Zwergtigerkatze)
♀ "Kali," acquired September 5, 1961, approximately 7 months old.

Fig. 7   a) Pudge has grasped a rat "the wrong way round," by the throat, b) tries vainly to improve her grip, but the rat has managed to throw itself on its back again, c) this time she succeeds, d) bulging eyes, rump and limbs alternately contracting and stretching convulsively (here in contracted phase), and the stiffly stretched tail are all sure signs that the rat has suffered fatal injury to the spine.

♀ "Durga," acquired February 21, 1962, approximately 5-6 months old.
♀ ♀ "Bigger" and "Small," and ♂ "Shiva," arrived July 6, 1962; Shiva approximately 6 months old, the ♀ ♀ somewhat younger.

The age of all the animals has been estimated in accordance with the usual sequence of second dentition in the domestic cat. However, the developmental rhythm of some of the smaller cat species of domestic cat size deviates considerably from that of the domestic cat. Since nothing precise is known about the second dentition of the Indian leopard-cat, the animals could have been anything up to a month younger, but also as much as three months older than estimated. As far as could be discovered, Kali and Small came from Assam, Durga from Malaya, Bigger and Shiva from Nepal. Otherwise nothing is known of their previous history and above all about any experience with prey.

From the very beginning Kali and Durga were given live mice and from the first time onward both killed them immediately with a nape bite. Rats were given to Kali for the first time one month after her arrival, while Durga received them from the very beginning. They both killed these immediately, too, and the same applied somewhat later to live guinea pigs. Guinea pigs, especially when crouching with their limbs well drawn in, look less obviously divided up into head, neck, and rump than other prey animals, and so almost all cats take a less precise grip on them, often well back, close in front of or over the shoulders instead of in the nape.

The first live prey animals Bigger, Small, and Shiva were given were smallish rats, though on August 30 Bigger and Small escaped when their cage door was not properly closed and stumbled on a box containing guinea pigs which was standing in the neighboring room. One of the cats, probably Bigger, killed a guinea pig and carried it back to the cage; the episode was not observed. Both of them received their first rats on November 8.

Bigger killed her rat immediately, just as Kali and Durga had done before. Small first sniffed hers cautiously, ran around after it, tapped at it, tweaked it lightly in the nape and back with her teeth, but let go again immediately the rat squeaked. Bigger then rushed between them and killed this rat, too. This was repeated during the next two days in the course of three further attempts: Each time Bigger killed both rats. Then came an occasion when the first rat kept her too busy, so that Small had enough time to "warm up" and killed her first rat at last.

Shiva behaved on the first occasion (one month after arrival) just like Small. Only he was alone in the cage and killed the rat after seventy-two minutes! During this time he *worked himself up* gradually and with many relapses and rests to increasingly resolute attacks. The rat kept managing to get into a corner, where it stood up in a defensive posture and thus was almost invulnerable to the timidly indecisive cat. With one forepaw Shiva tried to press and beat the rat's head down in order to be able to seize it in the nape with his teeth. As he never struck hard enough, however, the rat was always standing and baring its teeth at him again, and each time he jumped back with a start. More often than from above onto its head, he struck from below and sideways against the rat's abdomen, trying as it were to "fell" it from its upright position. Only thus, after half an hour, did he succeed in giving it a mild bite in the nape, then he bit several times in the direction of its flanks and back, finally grasped the rat loosely by the fur and threw it around a little. The rat slowly became tired and with increasing frequency Shiva was able to grasp it in the nape; but it was only very gradually that his bites became firmer, until in the end a final bite killed the rat. After energetic "catch and throw" and relief play he ate it. The next rat Shiva already caught and killed without further ado, likewise his first guinea pig three months later.

Now, whenever possible, he normally pounces on rats and guinea pigs from the rear and takes the animal's rump between his two forepaws, seeks out its nape with his teeth, takes a bite and then raises one forepaw ready to strike, and employs this immediately if the prey animal still offers energetic resistance.

All 5 Indian leopard-cats now catch and kill in the same way as my ocelot-cat [6, 17]; above all, they have the same habit, once having taken a bite, of not releasing it again until the prey animal's terminal spasms have ceased, even when the bite has not landed precisely in the nape but less advantageously in the shoulder or throat. As a rule, *one* bite without any repeat is sufficient to kill, and only where particularly large rats and fairly large guinea pigs are concerned do they regularly make repeat bites.

The 4 females (Shiva had no opportunity) acquired the same dexterity as the *Prionailurus*—domestic cat hybrids (p. 160) in catching prey animals in the air with their forepaws and grasping them with a nape bite no matter which way around they reached them. One guinea pig was thrown too short and low for Durga; by leaning far out and down from her shelf, she caught it by the hind-quarters with her two forepaws, then "paw over paw" she adjusted her grip until she was holding the guinea pig's shoulders between her paws, raised it to her jaws, bit it in the nape, and only then pulled herself back onto the shelf by her hind paws.

All 5 animals kill rats and guinea pigs almost instantaneously. Only when the animals are dead do they perform relief play and "catch and throw" with them, often for a very long time. Mice and Golden Hamsters, however, they like to keep alive for a while to play with.

8. *Prionailurus viverrinus* Bennet

(Fishing Cat; Fischkatze, Tüpfelkatze)

♂ "Fishy," sent to us March 2, 1961, allegedly as 2-year-old ♀ ; place of origin unknown.

♀ "Laya," arrived February 21, 1962, from Kuala Lumpur, Malaya, approximately 6-8 months old.

Fishy was a perfect killer from the very beginning. With prey animals up to the size of guinea pigs he rarely uses a forepaw to hold them but simply runs quickly up to them and grasps them at once with a nape bite. If he cannot reach the nape properly because the animal is sitting the wrong way round or runs away too fast, he grips it *in the back with his teeth*, pulls it into the "correct" orientation, and then quickly bites it in the nape, as I have seen a lion do on film [15]. He then carries the animal to his eating corner, there gives it one or two repeat bites and lays it down. Where necessary, however, he knows how to use his forepaws, e.g. when catching a large guinea fowl (Fig. 8) or with particularly lively rats (see below, Laya).

For a long time Fishy disdained mice, and no matter how conspicuously they ran around under his nose he never made any attempt to catch them. But at some time or other he must have discovered that they taste good, and now he catches and eats them occasionally.

Laya, in contrast, was not quite the size of a domestic cat on arrival. She accepted mice eagerly, and still loves them even now that she is long since fully adult. From the day she arrived, she also killed rats and later guinea pigs in the same way as Fishy. Like him and the Indian leopard-cat (p. 166) she holds on to her killing bite, even when it is faulty, until the prey animal's terminal convulsions have ceased and it hangs lifeless.

As she was still so small in the beginning, she more often had difficulty with rats than Fishy did, and the technique also employed occasionally by him when overpowering *lively* rats could be observed more frequently and precisely in her case: the animals slide them-

Fig. 8 Male Fishing Cat catches guinea fowl: a-b) Cat approaches slowly with lowered head, c) guinea fowl stands up, ruffles wings intimidatingly, d-g) cat withdraws, hisses, is indecisive, h-k) moves forward again cautiously, suddenly rushes in and seizes guinea fowl under right wing, l-n) holds it down with one forepaw, reaches round to other side of fowl's body with his jaws, o-r) guinea fowl flutters wildly and cat presses it down with his forepaws and the whole weight of his body, takes firm bite under left wing, s) carries fowl thus to his eating corner, t) lays it down and, as it (u-v) again begins to flutter, w) kills it with a nape bite (drawings from film).

selves over the rat from the rear, lay the lower part of their forearms flat on the ground on either side of it, clamping it along its whole length between these, their breast, and the ground; as they do so they pull their head right back and, in this position, wait for a good moment to grasp the squirming rat in the nape. The procedure has considerable similarity to that used by *Nandinia*, described on p. 155, except that *Nandinia's* wild and repeated biting is here replaced by calm waiting and a surely aimed nape bite (cf. Fig. 15b; also Fig. 7b, though here cat and rat are "wrongly" oriented toward one another).

With her first two Golden Hamsters, Laya was able to surprise them from the rear and catch them like mice. The third, however, met her with a defensive posture and jumped at her. Laya dodged back and then employed on it the same technique as the ocelot-cat [17] used on a particularly aggressive brown rat: She dodged every attack the hamster made, and indeed avoided any frontal encounter with it, attempting time and again to jump at it from the rear or the side and quickly toss it in some direction or other; only when it was sufficiently wounded and exhausted did she again aim her bites at the nape and eventually manage to hit it. Later, however, she developed different tactics for defensive Golden Hamsters: She faces the hamster as it stands upright, gnashing its teeth, raises one forepaw to a point above the level of her ears in readiness to strike; then, after she has waited for some seconds, one single paw-blow crashes onto the hamster, knocks it down and at the same time pulls it toward her (Fig. 9). She waits for a further fraction of a second to see whether the hamster stands up again. If it does not, she bites, and if it does she repeats the blow.

9. *Profelis aurata* Temminck

(African Tiger-cat; Afrikanische Goldkatze)
♀, received August 11, 1964, said to come from the Ivory Coast.

The African Tiger-cat catches and kills rats and guinea pigs in the usual manner. Things went differently, however, when she caught a chicken: The tiger-cat was in her indoor cage, the chicken in the outer enclosure, where it ran to and fro aimlessly and in so doing came within a meter of the hatch to the indoor cage. At that instant the tiger-cat shot through the hatch with one bound, jumped over the chicken without touching it, set her forepaws down just beyond it, landed in a gentle *somersault*, rolled right over and now lay on the ground with her head nearest the chicken; in the next

a

b

Fig. 9 Female Fishing Cat catches hamster: a) Hamster in defensive posture, cat raises forepaw ready to strike, b) biting attack after the blow. For details see text.

instant she had grasped it by the shoulder, held it down with her forepaws, bit it in the neck close to its head and carried it indoors. I have described something similar [5] in the case of a domestic tom-cat when it caught a sparrow, and took this to be an accident caused by blind eagerness. In the case of the tiger-cat, however, it all looked precisely calculated and "self-explanatory"; and at this short distance she can scarcely have jumped over the chicken by accident. Instead it seems to me that this is a particular technique for making a surprise attack which no doubt many cat species possess. In effect, the roll thus performed is the only possible means for a cat to get to the back of a prey animal standing facing it, turn 180° at lightning speed immediately behind it, and catch it before it has time to react to the changed situation.

One chicken, after the tiger-cat had grasped it with a neck bite and carried it to her eating-place, hung quite limp and lifeless and she began to pluck it. As she did so, the chicken came to life again and fluttered. Thereupon the cat gripped it under the throat with a *supinated* forepaw and raised it to her mouth as if with a hand, bit into it until the chicken became still, and then went on plucking. This was repeated three times, and thus was certainly not a purely chance combination of movements (cf. Asiatic Golden Cat, p. 175). If the prey animals climb up wire-netting or a tree, the tiger-cat follows them with agility for as high as her cage permits (2.5-3 m). If she reaches the animal and is herself hanging uncomfortably and unsafely —e.g. in the wire-netting—she does not kill it up there, but pulls it away from its hold by the tail or whichever part of the body is easiest to reach with her teeth and throws it to the ground, where she first chases it anew and then kills it. This procedure is also adopted occasionally by the Indian Leopard-cats (however, cf. Asiatic Golden Cats p. 173).

10. *Profelis temmincki* Vigors and Horsfield

(Golden Cat, Temminck's Cat; Asiatische Goldkatze)

♂ "Hanno," obtained February 2, 1961. Caught young in a region 100 km west of Bangkok, said to have been reared with dogs. Age on arrival approximately 3½ years. This animal was extremely shy and is still the most reserved of the four.

♂ "Piet," obtained February 2, 1961. Previous history, age, and place of origin unknown. By comparison with museum specimens, this animal would be most likely to come from Upper Burma or Northeast Assam. On arrival he was nothing but skin and bone and incapable of standing straight or stretching his legs fully, apparently as a result of being kept for weeks, if not months, in too low a transport box. At first he was extremely shy and sometimes aggressive, but is now the most trusting of the four. He has made a good recovery, although a certain weakness of the hindquarters has remained.

♀ "Tilly," obtained February 2, 1961. Said to come from the region around Kuala Lumpur, Malaya. Nothing further known.

♀ "Nova," also said to come from Malaya and to have been about 2 years old when caught (but gave the impression of being older). Came direct from Malaya on March 24, 1961.

For roughly a year the four animals lived in separate cages, then Hanno was united with Tilly and Piet with Nova.

All four had obviously already had wide experience of live prey and from the very beginning killed rats, guinea pigs, and later also chickens and Golden Hamsters. In contrast to the Indian Leopard-cat and the Fishing Cat, they always make several repeat bites (on film between 3 and 7) when killing what is for them relatively small prey.

Hanno, Piet, and Tilly had already been in captivity a long time and had obviously not received live prey any more during that period. With their first animals they displayed *"overflow play"* [21, 53 et seq.] of an intensity more explosive than I had ever seen before. Particularly just after killing the animals they would play "catch and throw" with them, flinging them several meters away with great force, so that they struck the wall, cage wire, or ceiling with a loud bang. Unfortunately I did not foresee how quickly this mood would pass and had not immediately tried to film these still very shy animals in order not to upset them. Then it was over; even when we deprived Tilly, who had performed the most extreme overflow play, of all food animals, live or dead, for six weeks and fed her on nothing but meat, we achieved only a comparatively insignificant accumulation.

During the first months Nova was particularly shy, but at the same time very quiet and not at all aggressive. As long as she knew anyone was near she would not come out of her sleeping-box. In order to observe her catching rats I would place one on a low shelf attached to one wall of the cage and withdraw to a point where she could not see me from her box. When I had waited thus, motionless and scarcely breathing, for many minutes, there inevitably came a moment when for no more than a fraction of a second my eyes strayed from the shelf with the rat on it—and then the rat was gone. No sound could ever be heard, and Nova played this trick on me dozens of times before I at last succeeded in observing her as she did it and discovering the secret of how she was able to steal the rat so *noiselessly* and *as fast as lightning:* she moved over the rat with a snakelike movement (Fig. 10), grasped it lightly yet firmly and surely in the nape with her teeth, whereupon the rat went completely limp (*"Tragstarre"* [19]) and let itself be carried off without noise or resistance. Each time I heard the rat's limbs drumming in Nova's box minutes later, as is normal when a prey animal has been fatally bitten [19]. But to this day I still do not know how Nova knew each time just when my attention wandered briefly. However, this observation leads me to believe the reports one often reads which claim that leopards just as silently steal the dogs of African farmers literally from under their tables and feet. Since settling in, Nova has given this method up and, like the others, kills her prey wherever she happens to catch it.

Fig. 10 Golden Cat "Nova" pushes her nose over the rat so slowly and cautiously that it apparently does not notice, or at any rate does not alter its position or activity before it is too late.

If the prey animal is running away fast or facing in an "awkward" direction, all four often grasp it somewhere in the back with their teeth, pull it the right way round, and then bite it in the nape (cf. male Fishing Cat p. 167 and [15]), particularly if the animal is climbing up something (e.g. cage wire or tree stump). In the latter case, curiously enough, they do it only if the prey animal is still comfortably within reach; if it has already climbed above Golden Cat eye level (60-70 cm) before they reach it, they lose all interest, although they could quite easily stand up on their hind-legs or even climb after it. Often in such a case they will still very eagerly chase prey animals on the ground and eat them. Thus, their hunger and/or eagerness for the chase are by no means satisfied. This is not to say that gnawing and long-standing hunger could not drive Golden Cats to pursue prey animals that had climbed high as well. Yet, apparently they are so pronouncedly *ground hunters* that they do not do this if there is no real need.

The Golden Cats often restrain prey animals that are running away simply by putting one of their heavy forepaws on it. A rat thus held fast—usually squashed by the abdomen—can, of course, still turn its forequarters and go for the face of a biting cat with its teeth. So Piet and Nova very often, and obviously with conscious intent, place their paw on the tail of a running rat. A rat held fast by the tail does not usually try to turn around immediately and defend itself, but for a moment goes on running on the spot with its feet slithering help-lessly. For the cat seeking its nape it is then ideally stretched and easy to grasp.

On prey animals that are sitting still or moving only very slowly the Golden Cats more often use their *paws* than their teeth to set them to rights for the nape bite. Lightly and practically stroking it, their claws retracted, they touch the victim and push it very gradually around, leaving off immediately if it becomes restive, and when it is sitting exactly right they lower their heads just as cautiously for the bite (Fig. 11). If in the meantime the prey animal makes even the

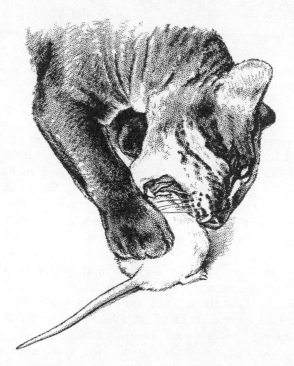

Fig. 11 Golden Cat has turned a rat the right way around with her forepaw and now bites it in the nape.

smallest alteration in its position, they do not take a bite but first set it to rights again with a forepaw; often they even go away for a while and make a fresh attempt when the prey animal has calmed down again. If an animal does not permit itself to be killed in all gentleness and calm even after repeated attempts, the Golden Cats very often give up—at least temporarily.

In each of the four animals the "gentle approach" (Fig. 12) displays its own variations; the most adroit is Piet. He not only pushes and presses the prey animals to rights on whatever they are sitting on, but I have several times observed him to insert a forepaw (pronated or supinated) cautiously under a rat's abdomen, slowly raise it from the ground and convey it to his jaws, at the same time turning it as necessary to make the nape bite easy. Up till then I might have credited a bear with something of this kind, but scarcely a cat (cf. African Tiger-cat p. 171).

In this connection I would mention briefly what an unpleasant effect the shrill *squeaks* many rodents utter when *frightened* obviously have on many cats, especially those still relatively inexperienced, or particularly sensitive ones such as the Golden Cats. If a rat or a guinea pig already starts to squeak loudly when it has only been gripped loosely or scarcely touched, an inexperienced cat will always leave it alone and an experienced one very often. The Golden Cats often abandon altogether an animal such as this which has responded every time to their repeated "gentle approaches" with shrill squeaks of fear, turning away from them with a facial expression the human equivalent of which could only be described as "disgusted." Of course, this happens only when the cats have already dulled the edge of their appetite; if this is not the case, all the squeaking in the world will not help much, and anyway there is little opportunity for it. Nevertheless, viewed statistically frightened squeaking in free-ranging conditions must offer considerable advantage in natural selection.

I should add that the animals here never have to go really hungry and thus feel no need to struggle with prey animals that resist violently or are even aggressive. In free-ranging conditions, wherever there is an abundance of prey animals which are easy to overcome things will no doubt be the same; it is a proven fact that free-ranging domestic cats specialize mainly in those rodents which are most abundant and easiest to catch (Davis 1957, Pearson 1964).

It is into this context that the following occurrences fit:—A particularly audacious rat found a niche under Nova's sleeping-box where Nova could not reach it. To this niche it withdrew each time from Nova's rather listless attacks, emerged however the instant that she turned her back, followed her, and bit her in the heels! As soon as Nova turned around, the rat hastily disappeared under the box again. This process continued for 35 minutes. The rat became increasingly bold and then eventually just that little bit too bold: A few times Nova landed some rapid paw-blows on it and then a bite in its back which partially paralyzed it. The rat did still jump away, but Nova overtook it, held it fast with one forepaw, and was able to grasp it in the nape.

A similar rat had more luck with Tilly: It managed to avoid being caught and lived for weeks under Tilly's sleeping-box. After a short time Tilly ignored it, the rat discontinued its attacks on Tilly's heels, and soon was moving around quite freely all through the cage. Tilly distinguished perfectly between it and rats which were freshly set in as food. The latter she killed immediately, whereas she now treated the "pet" rat with positive indulgence. Soon the two of them would eat in harmony from a rat which Tilly had killed, and after a month the pet rat was so insolent about it that Tilly would retire growling with her food onto a high shelf which was inaccessible to the rat. Yet, she never hit or bit at the rat, even when it pulled the meat away from under her nose. In the course of a further month the pet rat moved from its corner under Tilly's sleeping-box into the box itself, and Tilly slept there with it, holding it to her breast with her forepaws. The rat remained with Tilly for four months. The whole of this time Tilly daily received several other rats, which she always killed and ate, and not once did she confuse a food rat with her pet rat, even when the two were sitting side by side. After four months the pet rat was taken out and three months later put into Tilly's cage again. In the meantime it had become very big (600 g). The two animals gave no sign of recognition. Tilly's intentions were clearly orientated toward prey. It is true that her initial hesitation, during which the rat sat still and she sniffed it thoroughly, could be interpreted as the influence of a perhaps vague recollection, but more probably it was caused only by the unusual size of the rat. For its part the rat already attempted evasive action when it saw Tilly at a distance (something it never did during its time as a pet), nor did it run after her when she turned her back, which was perhaps for Tilly an essen-

---

Fig. 12 Golden Cat "Hanno" applies "gentle approach": a-b) He nears a guinea pig from the front, c) begins to twist his head in order to grasp it in the nape, d) but is not quick enough. Guinea pig turns and e-f) hops away a little. Hanno follows unhurriedly, g-h) opens his jaws very slowly over the guinea pig's nape and bites (drawings from film).

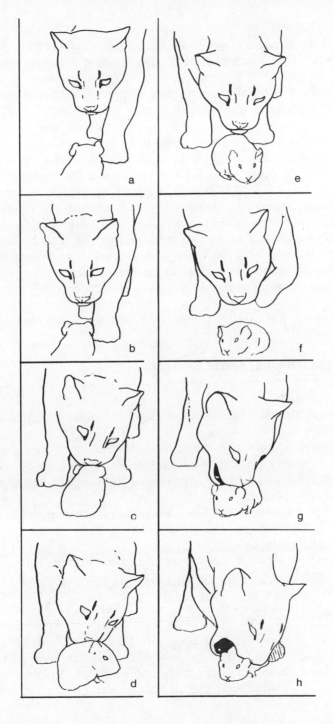

tial characteristic of "her" rat. In the cage, however, the rat proved still to be fully orientated, and promptly sought cover in Tilly's sleeping-box. There Tilly overpowered it after a short struggle, killed it, and ate it.

Naturally, there is usually a good deal of *playfulness* involved when a Golden Cat seems unable to catch a rat. This is most obvious in Hanno's case. He can often amuse himself for a very long while with chasing a "difficult" rat, angling after it under his box or behind a tree stump, and anyone watching is repeatedly deceived the first few times into thinking the rat is really too clever and the cat too clumsy. Then, after a quarter or half an hour, Hanno's attitude and expression change abruptly. He walks deliberately and unhurriedly toward the rat, there are one or two brief paw movements, and already he has the convulsively kicking rat by the neck and carries it to his habitual eating-place. No one who has once seen that happen can doubt that from one instant to the next the cat switches *from play to earnest,* and that for a Golden Cat in earnest there is no such thing as a difficult rat.

All four catch, kill, and eat mice, but without much enthusiasm.

11. *Felis (Leptailurus) serval* Schreber

(Serval)

♀ "S," arrived June 30, 1953; caught as adult animal in Kenya in the spring of 1953.

♀ "Freda," born October 27, 1961, in Basle Zoo; from there, after a brief interval with a dealer, reached the Nuremberg Zoo, and on December 4, 1962, came to me. At none of these places had she ever received live prey before.

The way "S" catches prey I have already described in detail [2, 7, 10, 13, 14, 25, 27 et seq., 31, 36, 53, 55]. Up to the beginning of 1961 I had relatively rarely been able to offer her live prey animals, and only two species—rats and chicken—in any great number. Since then, however, in addition to these she regularly receives mice, Golden Hamsters, and guinea pigs, and conditions in all other respects are also very much improved. Now this animal, which, to judge by external appearances and the state of its teeth, is already fairly senile, at times acts as *playfully* as a young cat. Whereas "S" usually kills Golden Hamsters, fairly large rats, and guinea pigs at once and then plays with them, she often keeps mice and small rats alive for a long time and plays *"angling"* with them [11, 12]: she appears to let them escape under a box, a lying tree stump or something similar, and then tries to drive or pull them out of the chink again with her fore-paw. If the prey animal does not find such a chink for itself, "S" picks it up very cautiously by its back fur with her teeth, carries it there, and then *pushes* it in with her forepaw. At first I took this to be a coincidence, as is often the case with domestic cats: They carry a prey animal around in play, then release it in order to play "chase" with it again, tap at it with a forepaw when it will not run, then it slips into a crevice which happens to be handy and in this way quite often escapes [19, 58]. However, I never saw a playing domestic cat *deliberately* and repeatedly push a mouse or a plaything into such a crevice only for the sake of being able to fish it out again. On the contrary, they hurriedly do their best to detain anything which is get-ting anywhere near a bolt-hole [19]. When "S" time and again let prey animals fall in the vicinity of a crevice, of all places, into which they promptly disappeared, I considered her stupid and only very gradually became convinced that the whole thing is intentional. How-ever, her often stubborn endeavors with her paw to maneuver into a crevice a prey animal that is doing its best to stay out rule out any other interpretation. If she is in a playful mood and has no appropri-ate prey animal, she does the same with small playthings such as bits of bark. Freda, being so much younger, plays the same game with even more eagerness and persistence (see below p. 182 et seq., p. 236).

The first Golden Hamsters elicited from "S" and later, too, from Freda behavior which resembles that of the female Fishing Cat (p. 169) but is considerably more specialized: The servals reach up very high with one forepaw (Fig. 13) and beat down one or more times with great force on the upright, defensive hamster; then, with the paw raised ready to strike, they wait to see whether it exposes its nape unprotected for a moment. Depending on what the hamster does, they then either bite or strike it anew. When striking they stretch the forepaw as *stiffly as a rod* (Fig. 13f), and in fact it sounds exactly as if someone in a rage were hitting a sack of flour with a stick. Just one such blow is capable of killing a hamster if it hits the right spot. As a rule, however, the hamsters survive even five or more blows, but can no longer summon up the strength to defend them-selves, and the servals kill them with a nape bite. Recalcitrant rats receive the same treatment. Rats, however, rarely stay so long in the upright defensive posture as hamsters do and, as a result, the servals do not wait so long with raised forepaw either. After the first blows the rat usually runs away and the chase becomes "conventional."

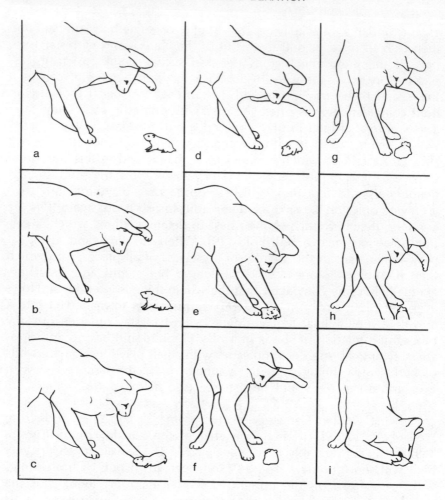

Fig. 13 "Hamster blow" of a serval: a) Serval holds forepaw high and waits, b) just before striking raises it a little higher, c-e) strikes twice, f) immediately raises forepaw into "waiting position" again, g-h) makes intention movement, but then instead of striking i) swoops in with the other forepaw and jaws and catches hamster by the nape (drawings from film).

Both their predilection for "angling" and the "hamster blow," which is conspicuously more highly developed and different in form from the way other cats beat with their paws, seem to me a strong indication that the servals have become specialized not only for catching *ground-dwelling birds* (Leyhausen 1956 b; see below p. 185) but in particular for catching *savannah rodents* which live in hamster-like burrows and have defensive behavior similar to that of the hamster. The servals also seem to be very afraid of being bitten in the paw by a resolute rodent when angling. This can be seen very clearly if for once a rat or a hamster has really escaped into a crevice and they want to get it in earnest: Whereas in such a situation the Golden Cats, particularly Hanno, for example, go about it quite brutally and ruthlessly pull or beat out even animals offering the most violent resistance and hold them fast with their forepaws until they have taken a nape bite, the servals angle extremely nervously, *pawing cautiously;* time and again, at the slightest contact with their prey, they jump back as if electrified, and it takes a long time before they hook one or two claws into the animal's fur and pull it toward them in one swift move. In their anxious haste, this hold is often released again; if they have really got their prey out, they shake it off the forepaw as rapidly as possible and some distance away, then proceed in the usual manner. It therefore seems to me that the servals have acquired their long forelegs not merely in adaptation to a life in grassland and not at all like the cheetah for peak running perform-ance over short stretches, but also and perhaps indeed mainly as a tool for fishing rodents out of earth burrows: In the foreleg of the cheetah it is the forearm which is elongated in comparison with that of other cats, in the serval, however, it is the metacarpus. For a runner, a long metacarpus, with its lack of rigidity and its many single bones bound up in an enormous tangle of connective tissue and muscles, cartilage, and tendons, would be much too prone to trouble. For an "angling" serval, the long hand with its fine mobility is ex-tremely important for groping in cavities which get larger as they go in. The "proneness to trouble" of the long metacarpus is, inci-dentally, a fact: It is not rare for servals to break this in° seemingly slight accidents. Mostly, as for example in the case of "S," the frac-tures heal without any complication and without externally visible lasting damage. But a courser such as the cheetah hobbling around on three legs is done for in the wilds; until the fracture is completely healed, it must go hungry. The serval, however, can limp to the next rodent burrow and fish into it with the forepaw that is whole.

"S" had already received live guinea pigs occasionally in earlier years. Yet she seemed to have completely forgotten this when she received her first guinea pigs here; at any rate, she treated these with the same caution and the same *mistrust* as inexperienced cats display toward *all* prey animals and *all* cats, *however experienced,* display toward prey animals of a completely *new kind* [53]. She approached the first guinea pig very hesitantly, tapped at it several times with a forepaw, sniffed at it, grasped it with her teeth by its back fur, carried

it around a little, let it fall again, and so on. Then she began to throw
it around and work herself up into a *throwing game* just as intensive
as initially displayed by the Asiatic Golden Cats with dead prey animals (p. 172). Finally she threw the guinea pig against the cage ceiling
with such force that it fell to the ground dead. She immediately began
to eat it, without once in the whole process having attempted a
nape bite. On subsequent days she flung a few more guinea pigs to
death in this way, and then the excitement of their newness and her
fear of the unusual prey animal were over. From then on she killed
all guinea pigs swiftly and undeviatingly with a nape bite.

Unlike almost all domestic cats [59], "S" is well aware that a prey
animal that has wriggled out through the cage wire is lost, and she
always hastens to prevent this. Once she just managed to grab a rat
by the tail, planted all four feet firmly on the ground, and pulled it
slowly back through the rather close mesh of the wire, carried it, still
by the tail, a safe distance from the wire netting, and there killed it.

Freda played with her first live prey animals—mice, Golden Hamsters, rats, and guinea pigs—in just the same way as Natalie (p. 156).
She did not, however, kill or even wound one of these animals, however long it remained in the cage with her. Originally there was a
solid wall between her cage and that of "S." When a section of this
was replaced by wire netting and Freda had playfully chased a hamster into the vicinity of this, "S" came to the other side of the wire
netting. For the first time Freda struck hard at the hamster, grasped
it in the back, and carried it away as far as possible in order to begin
her harmless game again. In a series of consecutive experiments, my
assistant went into Freda's cage and, by repeatedly approaching her,
tried to stimulate her so much that she would for the first time kill a
prey animal by means of a firm bite. This did not succeed, although
in her excitement Freda did once strike a hamster dead with her
forepaw, and she also struck one guinea pig and flung it around so
violently that it died. These dead animals she ate at once. Immediately afterward she received a further live guinea pig. But despite the
experience she had just had, more than two hours later she had still
not managed to kill it. When I finally killed it before her very eyes
and threw it to her, she grasped it immediately by the nape, carried
it a few steps away, and began to eat. In numerous experiments
(most of them filmed) between March 25 and April 25, 1963, we did
not succeed in bringing Freda to the point where she killed a prey
animal *lege artis* with a nape bite.

From April 25, 1963, "S" and Freda lived together in the same cage.
From the very beginning "S," being so much older but also larger and

stronger, left no room for doubt about her superiority, although we had put the two into Freda's cage. As "territory owner," therefore, Freda should have had the advantage. However, in her long captive existence "S" has lived through so many moves that she is not so easily put out any more by a slight change of surroundings. In order to give the animals time to get used to one another, Freda received no live prey for a few days, though on one occasion "S" for some reason or other showed no interest in a live guinea pig intended for her, and with this Freda played as she had done previously when alone in the cage.

On May 2 we put live rats in for the first time, and in such a way that Freda was able to seize them first; yet, it was "S" who caught the first three, though not without there being a violent exchange of blows between the two servals. Each time "S" carried the rat she had won up onto a shelf and ate it there. As she is not very fond of rats [53], she lost interest after the third and allowed Freda to play with a fourth without interfering at all. After 55 minutes we took the rat away and it was quite unharmed. Although Freda then got nothing to eat until the next day and the next experiment, the sequence of events on the previous day was repeated: In the face of Freda's timid protests, "S" collected the first rats, then lost interest, and Freda played endlessly around with the next. In so doing she often grasped it in the nape, but her bites were always too weak to wound it seriously, let alone kill it. After 65 minutes, however, the rat was completely exhausted and no longer moved. Thereupon Freda brought it to her eating-place and began to eat it, like a dead food animal, from the head, thereby naturally killing it, as it were unintentionally.

The next day "S" once more caught the first two rats under Freda's nose. But as the third rat arrived right in front of Freda and "S" again approached, Freda struck hard with both forepaws at the rat, thereby scrabbling it toward her, seized it with a nape bite, and the rat hung limply. Thereupon "S" turned away and withdrew. Freda laid the rat on the ground and gave it a repeat bite. The rat kicked convulsively. Freda gave it three more repeat bites, carried the dead rat to her eating-place, and began to eat it. With two further rats, however, Freda again played for a long time, and in the end "S" whisked both of them away. With a final rat Freda played endlessly and "S" did not interfere. Finally, when two dead chicks and two dead guinea pigs were thrown into the cage Freda ate one chick (something she disdains at other times) and both guinea pigs with obvious avidity and must, therefore, have been very hungry during the whole experiment.

Two days later Freda killed a guinea pig for the first time with a nape bite as she ran toward it almost simultaneously with "S" and reached it first. In her excitement she must have bitten harder than usual, and though the guinea pig was not quite dead when she let it fall again, it died within half a minute.

Freda killed her next rat 4 days later (May 11, 1963). "S" seized the rat thrown to her, but in her haste to get at Freda's as well she did not bite it dead; as she snapped up Freda's rat she lost her own, and Freda seized it quickly. "S" chased Freda twice round the cage to try to make her relinquish it, but then gave up. As soon as she had jumped onto her shelf, Freda killed the rat with two rapid bites; up till then she had only carried it around by its fur.

From now on the servals were always given two live guinea pigs first in the evenings. Despite her experience with the rats Freda never killed hers but played with it, mostly "angling." Every time "S" came rushing up at some moment when, in the course of her play, Freda had got too far from the guinea pig; thus up till May 28, 1963, "S" regularly caught and killed the second guinea pig as well. On that evening "S" tried to separate Freda from the second guinea pig by chasing her just as she was carrying it around, and in her postchase excitement Freda killed it as described above in the case of the rat. For a whole week the servals were given no live animals, then at the first new experiment Freda already killed her guinea pig fairly quickly, and from then on a little faster each evening until, like "S," she almost regularly killed as soon as she had grasped her prey. She could now do it as swiftly and surely as "S." This period lasted until the middle of August, in other words about nine weeks, and then Freda again began to play with live animals (Fig. 14). It should be added that by then she had usually eaten one or two prey animals already;

Fig. 14 Serval "Freda" plays with a guinea pig. It is only in play that cats employ on animals small in relation to themselves the attack intended for much larger prey, which includes rolling over on one side and clasping the prey animal tight.

she played soonest with rats which, just like "S," she valued less as food.

The forms of *play with prey* displayed by "S" and those displayed by Freda both before and after she had killed for the first time are completely identical *down to the last details of movement.* "S" can sometimes even play as extremely "inhibitedly" as Freda did when encountering her very first prey animals. This fact, which is of decisive importance to the later theoretical discussions, is supported by hundreds of meters of film of both animals.

A further serval speciality which I observed in Freda was a jump whose purpose is obviously to bring down *ground-dwelling birds as they flutter up.* Unlike the domestic cat and the ocelot-cat [5, Fig. 8 loc. cit.], she springs meter-high with her body not shooting up diagonally but held horizontally, like a *haute école* horse performing a capriole, while (unlike the horse) stretching her forepaws well out for the catch. Landing, she brings her hind-legs well forward under her body and takes the full weight of it on them alone. In this way she chases flies and butterflies—and sometimes gets them, too. Only when I had already observed this several times did I find an old piece of film cast aside as a failure, on which I had almost caught "S" performing this jump on a chicken: As I was not expecting the high jump I did not follow it with the camera, and as a result all that can be seen of "S" are a few abdominal hairs and bits of leg at the top edge of the picture; but without the slightest doubt it is this special kind of jump. In terrain covered with grass and bushes it is certainly far more advantageous than the diagonal upward jump mentioned above. Freda performs it, however, not only in the vegetation of the outer enclosure but also in the cement-floored indoor cage, and it is therefore certainly not (only) the nature of the ground which elicits it.

12. *Leopardus wiedi* Schinz

(Tree-ocelot, Margay; Baumozelot, Grosse Tigerkatze)

♂ "Bueno," received October 28, 1962, approximately 2-3 months old.

♀ "Bonita," received October 18, 1962, approximately 4 months old.

With certainty both were young animals taken from the nest when not yet fully capable of walking, and until the time of the experiments described had received no live prey. For further details see Leyhausen (1963).

Fig. 15 Tree-ocelot "Bueno"; for explanation see text.

Bueno's first "prey" was an empty *mineral water bottle* on March 27, 1963. He approached this unknown Thing inquisitively, sniffed first at the bottom half, then stood up against it in order to investigate the top part as well. As he did so the bottle fell over, and in the next instant Bueno had bitten it in the "nape," in the neck of the bottle not far below the thickened mouthpiece (Fig. 15 a), then threw his whole body over it (Fig. 15 b), just exactly as the ocelot-cat "Muschi" had done previously with the rabbit [22, Fig. 24 b and c, loc. cit.].

The first live animal the two received was a small chicken on September 3, 1964; thus they were well over two years old and fully grown. As far as was known, they had never seen a live or dead chicken before—certainly not since their arrival in the institute—though they had already been fed occasionally with day-old chicks and also with somewhat larger ones that were already fully feathered. The unfamilar animal, and in particular no doubt its cackling, sent them scuttling into the farthest corner of the room, where Bueno climbed onto a rack. After a few seconds, Bonita already started to return in the posture typical of relatives of the ocelot, a composite mixture of fear, desire to attack, and curiosity ("curiosity pendulum," Leyhausen 1953 c), in which the threat component at first clearly predominated. At a distance of about 1.5 meters she considered the chicken, which was keeping fairly quiet, for a few moments thus, then with her neck stretched well forward she came nearer and sniffed at it. Meanwhile Bueno continued to eye the situation cautiously from the rack, but when I called him he jumped down and approached to within about a meter, likewise in a mild threat posture and performing the "curiosity pendulum." Then he suddenly shot past Bonita, bit the chicken somewhere in the shoulder (the precise spot was impossible to see so fast), carried it a few meters away, and then seized it with a firm bite in the neck behind the head. Bonita had followed him and, as he let go, seized the scarcely twitching bird in the crop.

The next day we gave them their first live guinea pigs. With dead guinea pigs they had been fed regularly since they were big enough for them. Nevertheless, at first they reacted more timidly toward the live guinea pigs than they had done toward the chicken. Then Bonita very hesitantly began "inhibited play," while Bueno at first only hinted at it with intention movements, without touching the guinea pig. After only a few minutes, however, Bonita worked herself up to a game of throwing and frequently tried to bite into the guinea pig's nape, but drew back every time it squeaked. She then reverted for a few moments to inhibited play, suddenly took courage and bit into the rodent's neck and killed it, making several repeat bites (Fig. 16). Meanwhile Bueno had of his own accord fished the second guinea pig out of the tin in which it stood waiting and took a more lively part in the play with this one. However, after only about a minute Bonita killed it exactly like the first.

13.   *Oncifelis geoffroyi euxanthus* Pocock

(Geoffroy's Cat from Colombia; Kolumbianische Kleinfleck-Katze)

♂ "Ferdinand," received on December 8, 1963, as a gift from Rotterdam Zoo, where he had arrived, roughly 6 months old, on May 11,

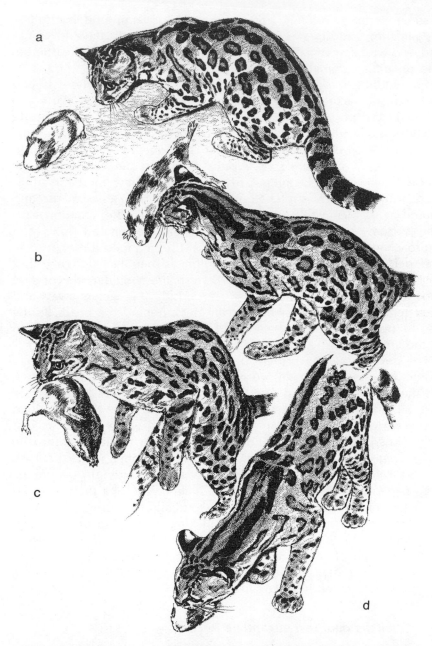

Fig. 16 Female Tree-Ocelot with first live guinea pig: a) Cautious approach, b-c) tossing game, d) intention movement of biting nape. For further details see text.

1962, by banana freighter from Santa Marta, North Colombia. Nothing is known of his previous history up to that time. Neither in Rotterdam Zoo nor with us had he ever received live prey up to the time of the event reported below.

By accident a live mouse got into Ferdinand's cage on January 3, 1965. He played "inhibited play" and "chase" [53] with it for about half an hour, but only very hesitantly and without using his claws. Then his eagerness for play waned; he began rather often to grasp the mouse in his teeth by various parts of its body, and six times he carried it onto his sleeping-box, which was his usual eating place, where he laid it down and each time made a clear intention movement to start eating. The mouse, being still quite unharmed, jumped away and he had to catch it again. Eventually the mouse squeezed itself into the gap between wall and sleeping-box and Ferdinand had to fish after it long and laboriously, in the process of which his excitement mounted visibly. When he finally got the mouse out it at once evaded him again and jumped high against the side of his box. Ferdinand lunged violently at it with his jaws and caught it in the back while it was still in the air, but let go again at once. The mouse was no longer capable of running in a coordinated manner but nevertheless hastened away. Ferdinand followed it like lightning, and now grasped it firmly in the nape. He held it up until its death convulsions ceased, then immediately ate it up.

14. *Felis s. silvestris Schreber*

(European Wild Cat; Europäische Wildkatze)

and *Felis silvestris libyca* forma *catus* L.

(Domestic Cat; Hauskatze)

♀ Wild Cat "Pola," received on February 2, 1961; already very old. ♀ ♀ Domestic cats W6, W11, W12, W13, W14; all over 6 years old. The domestic cats had all had several litters already, of Pola's previous history nothing is known. All six animals lived in the same cage. Normally W6 did not catch prey; only while she had kittens and these were at the appropriate age (approximately 6 weeks) did she catch mice, bring them to the kittens, and also eat some herself [47]. Of the six animals mentioned, only W11, W12 (rarely), and Pola normally caught mice, Pola and W13 smallish rats as well. In the spring of 1961 W11 and W12 had kittens and each was left one to rear. However, when the young were old enough *not only the two mothers* but *all the other females as well, including the wild cat,* brought them first dead and then live mice.

15. Hybrids ♂ *Felis nigripes* Burchell— ♀ *Felis catus*

(Blackfooted Cat—Tabby; Schwarzfusskatze—Hauskatze)
♂ ♂ I and II, ♀ III, born April 24, 1962.

The mother of these animals, "Blotje," was a very small blotched tabby. Although she had grown up on a farm, when she came to us she had completely lost the habit of hunting, but in a short time developed into an extremely keen rat and mouse catcher.

As with all other animals bred at the institute, the rearing of the kittens was left *completely to the mother cat.* We took particularly strict care not to induce the kittens to any particular activity ourselves, to offer them or indeed feed them prematurely with solid foods such as minced meat, eggs, or anything similar, or to "educate" them in any other way. Blotje was given only live prey animals of species which roughly corresponded to what would "naturally" be available in the wilds: mice, Golden Hamsters, and rats. The sole supplement to this diet was milk, to which vitamins and mineral salts were added. Thus, Blotje had to feed the kittens exclusively with her own milk until she herself brought them solid food. She brought the first dead mouse and a small piece of rat to the kittens when they were 23 days old. They, however, had no idea what to make of them. Yet, no more than three days later ♂ II chewed a little off the hind-leg of a mouse. Then the very next day Blotje already brought the first *live* mouse, but failed to interest the kittens in it; only when she killed the mouse and it kicked a little convulsively did ♂ II hit hesitantly at it once but then immediately got caught up again in a game with the other two kittens. Two days later Blotje brought along a whole dead rat and called to the kittens for a long while, but they did not react in the slightest. At the age of 33 days ♂ II made an earnest attempt to start eating a mouse, but without success.

At 36 days ♀ III played with a live mouse for the first time for nine minutes and in doing so bit at it time and again, mostly in the direction of the nape; a few times she also seized the tail. In the end, however, it was Blotje and not ♀ III who killed the mouse.

At 41 days all three kittens were regularly eating from rats and mice which Blotje brought them, and ♂ II became the first to make an earnestly intended attempt at prey-catching. The mouse, however, resisted strongly in defensive posture and frustrated all attempts by

♂ II to get round to the back of it. Blotje killed it eventually, but ♂ II ate it up by himself. It was, however, ♀ III who three days later was the first to kill a mouse: She had played with it for a long while, and finally several times made movements clearly indicative of an intention to start eating. However, the mouse was still very lively, and suddenly ♀ III gave it a crunching bite in the nape, then took one repeat bite, carried the dead mouse around a little, and then ate it. Not until 10 days later (54 days old) did ♂ II kill his first mouse, likewise with a nape bite and a repeat bite, as Blotje attempted to pull it away from him with one forepaw.

♂ I killed a mouse for the first time on July 7, in other words at the age of 74 days! However, this was a mouse which a firm bite from Blotje had already rendered immobile; ♂ I then simply began to eat it by the head. Not until a whole week later did he kill a mouse properly with a nape bite.

After their first, all three kittens killed several more mice in relatively swift succession, but after that almost always only played with them and left the killing to their mother again. She always watched very attentively over the kittens' play with mice, stepped in if the mouse threatened to escape, and in the end killed it if none of the kittens did so and the playing went on too long. Once having killed them she left the mice to the kittens again; only if none of them bothered about them did she eat them herself. No more than Rani (p. 163) would she tolerate her kittens anywhere near live rats.

16. *Felis nigripis* Burchell

(Blackfooted Cat; Schwarzfusskatze)

♂ "Schwarzi," bought from C. Schultz, Okahandja, on October 20, 1957. According to Schultz, caught as adult animal in stony hill country. Father of the young enumerated below and of the hybrids with domestic cat discussed on p. 190 et seq.

♀ "Braut," likewise comes from Okahandja. From June, 1960, lived at Catskill Game Farm, N.Y., together with a ♂ and another ♀, both of which died. On September 25, 1962, came on loan to me. Mother of the young enumerated below.

♀ "Buster," born May 8, 1953, at the institute.

♀ ♀ "Jake" and "Griff," born May 1, 1954, at the institute.
Schwarzi and Braut were from the very beginning *perfect killers*. Mice and small rats they kill with one nape bite which is always well aimed; they use their *forepaws* almost exclusively to pull to rights and

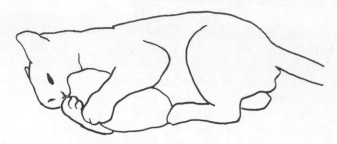

Fig. 17 On recalcitrant guinea pigs male Blackfooted Cat employs method similar to genet's (Fig. 3w): Remaining upright at the rear, he throws his forequarters onto one shoulder, clasps his prey tight with both forepaws, simultaneously biting it in the nape (nape indistinguishable in above drawing, but clearly visible in the film from which this picture comes).

hold on to prey animals that are wriggling (Fig. 17), rarely for striking. Mostly they take the bite before gripping with their forepaws. Fig. 18 shows a typical course of events with a guinea pig, which is Schwarzi's particular speciality. These, too, he usually kills with one single bite, only rarely taking one or two repeat bites, and death occurs at lightning speed. As he was so eager about it, when we had an abundance of guinea pigs we used to use him to slaughter a store for the deep freeze. In the end he was so well trained that, although he would carry a guinea pig he had just killed to his eating-place as a formality, he would bring it back again, lay it down before us, and wait for the next. After about the eighth he had to take several repeat bites before the guinea pig hung limp, and so we never gave him more than 13 in quick succession; however, his eagerness was by no means exhausted, and he always waited for more. Only his biting muscles were tired. One must bear in mind how small a Blackfooted Cat is: Schwarzi weighs 2760 g in all, Braut little more than 1500 g! Even when our food guinea pigs are young animals, they rarely weigh less than 500 g, often considerably more. The jaws of a Blackfooted Cat part just wide enough for them still to be able to grip the nape of a plump guinea pig between the canines. Unlike the premolars and molars, however, the canine teeth are situated right at the front of the jaws at the outer end of the lever, the muscles at the inner end. It is bound to require relatively great strength to penetrate the thick nape musculature of the prey animal with one bite and sever the vertebral column. This last result I found in all guinea pigs I investigated, irrespective of what other injuries were present as well. The severing always occurred between two vertebrae, but they themselves were not bitten through, nor even damaged.

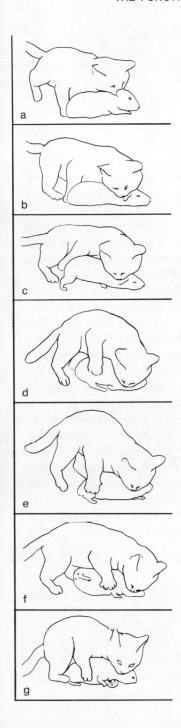

Fig. 18 Male Blackfooted Cat kills guinea pig: a-b) Approach and nape bite, c) cat raises right forepaw, d) lays it over guinea pig's flank, e) presses its hindquarters under his own, f) brings forepaw forward again and g) lays weight of his body on prey, while his left forepaw encircles victim's breast from below (drawings from film).

Braut's first guinea pig was apparently something new to her. For a long time she regarded it from a distance, then approached it from behind, sniffed at it a little, gripped it in the flanks with *both* fore-paws, drew it slowly backward under her own body until she was able to reach the nape comfortably, then bit into it.

Buster was 37 days old when we first saw her chasing a mouse which had been put in for Braut. Braut watched and made *no* attempt to catch the mouse occasionally and set it down in front of the kitten, as a domestic cat does. Only when the mouse threatened to escape did she *drive* it in the direction of the kitten again with one or two paw blows. Later, too, we observed her time and again to chase the mouse toward the kitten. Buster displayed *inhibited play* and "chase" exactly like domestic cat kittens, all very hesitant and without injuring the mouse. Braut killed it at last and Buster then ate it. Two days before she had the first time been observed to take solid food, namely the entrails of a mouse or a rat left over by Braut. At 42 days Buster for the first time *fished* a mouse very energetically out of a crevice, grasped it by the skin of its back and carried it around for a while, then let it fall, gripped it firmly in the nape, and let it fall again. The mouse was injured but defended itself as Buster tried to approach once more and apparently bit her; at any rate, Buster was unwilling to attack the mouse any more and Braut killed it. Two days later, however, Buster was again playing with a mouse in a lively manner, threatened it several times at intervals in an arched posture, then ap-proached it like this, grasped it suddenly in the nape, carried it be-hind her sleeping-box and there killed it, giving it several repeat bites.

At the age of 81 days Buster attempted to kill a rat in the same way as Braut did her first guinea pig, but the rat was able to wriggle away from her again. Not until August 22 (106 days old) did she succeed in killing a rat. Twice she abandoned her nape bite because the rat squeaked loudly, but the third time she held on and pressed the rat down with all her strength until its last twitches had ceased. On the evening of the same day she killed the next rat without delay and at the first attack.

Buster would sniff at guinea pigs but then leave them in peace. Not until she was 14½ months old did she kill a very small one. She laid one forepaw over its shoulders, made several *jerky intention movements* toward the nape with her nose, and then bit hard. The guinea pig did not utter another sound.

At 34 days of age Jake and Griff chewed for the first time at a mouse which Braut had brought into the nest. Two days later Jake stalked a mouse, seized it by the tail, and dragged it around the cage by this until Braut killed it. One week later both of them killed their first mouse, Jake with "correct" nape bite; Griff bit farther to the front: One of her canine teeth had penetrated the scalp, the second had hit the cervical spine, not severing it but dislocating two vertebrae at the joint. Despite the most careful search, the incisions made by the two other canine teeth could not be found.

On June 18, 1964, (48 days old) Jake attacked a rat which defended itself energetically. Jake tried time and again to seize it by the nape, threw herself over it with the whole length of her body and onto one side, clasped her paws around it or struck it hard with these. The rat, however, resisted and writhed so efficiently that it always succeeded in turning its teeth toward Jake and its nape away from her. Jake eventually gave up exhausted and the rat climbed a little way up the wire netting. Here Griff noticed it after a while, climbed after it, pulled it down by the fur of its nape, and went to work on it in the same way and with the same *élan* as Jake until she, too, was exhausted (Fig. 19). Braut then killed the rat and called, and the two kittens hurried to her. The rat must have weighed between 150 and 200 g and for a white laboratory rat fought unusually hard for its life. Five days later (June 23) Jake and Griff weighed just under 500 and 480 g respectively. As a comparsion one might expect an adult domestic cat to attack prey animals weighing from 2 to 3 pounds and capable of offering considerable resistance. This does, of course, happen—I have myself seen domestic cats arrive carrying stoats and polecats they have caught, and according to a report likely to be au-

Fig. 19 Blackfooted Cat "Griff" (forty-eight days old) attacks a rat for the first time. Rat resists desperately and pushes cat's face away with one forepaw (cf. Fig. 7 a, b).

thentic one even killed a Beech Marten [41]. But these are certainly tremendous rarities; normally, at any rate, in a fight between domestic cat and Beech Marten I would back the Marten. Thus, in these tiny wildcats, with their positively filigreelike little paws, hides a fighting spirit to be respected. Griff at least succeeded in landing one good nape bite in the course of the struggle; she would certainly have killed the rat, but her little canine teeth were at most 1.5–2 mm long and could scarcely penetrate the rat's skin.

For a while Braut gave the kittens no further opportunity to have a try at rats. Not until June 28 (kittens 58 days old) did she fail to kill a small rat immediately. Griff threw herself over it and bit it hard in the nape, rolled over onto one side, held on for a few seconds, and then jumped away. As she sprang at it again the rat managed to turn over a little and Griff's bite landed in the side of its neck. The rat squeaked and kicked around violently, but Griff held fast, rolled onto her side, clasped her paws around the rat and waited until it gave no further sign of life. On July 11 she killed the next rat at once with her first nape bite. Two days later Braut left a live Golden Hamster to her for the first time. She hurled herself at it as at the rat, but the hamster succeeded in half turning toward her and again her bite hit the side of the neck and not the nape. Again she held fast until the hamster was dead. The next day she received a rat which, no doubt as a result of some disorder of the labyrinth, kept turning over to one side. Griff fell on this one exactly like the others and encountered its throat. She beat off the kicking and scratching legs of the rat with her forepaws and again held fast with her bite until the end.

Jake had meanwhile been ill and had forfeited her previous developmental lead over Griff. She killed her first rat on July 21 (81 days old). The rat succeeded in beating off her first two attacks, but at the third Jake got hold of its nape and did not let go again. The next rat she killed at once with a nape bite at her first attack.

In the meantime Griff had become shyer because a rat had once *bitten* her slightly. Not until July 24 did she again attack a rat in earnest. To begin with she was very cautious, striking at the rat with her forepaws, approaching it only by making short forward thrusts with her nose and at once jumping back again. As she did so, she was now always quite clearly trying to reach the rat's nape, irrespective of how it was oriented in relation to her at that moment, and she gave up immediately and started back if the rat turned and thus withdrew its nape from her. In the end, however, the rat did lay itself open, Griff rushed in at lightning speed, had it exactly by the nape, and the rat was already dead.

17. *Panthers leo* L.

(Lion; Löwe)

Monsieur F. Edmond-Blanc approached a herd of buffalo in the savannah in order to film them. The camera was already turning when the herd suddenly stormed off and M. Edmond-Blanc caught sight of two large maned lions and two lionesses which had isolated a small buffalo cow from the herd. With presence of mind he filmed the following events, and this is probably the only film sequence in the world so far to show how lions overpower a large prey animal without the event somehow having been arranged or otherwise influenced for the purpose of filming. M. Edmond-Blanc has very kindly allowed me to make a frame-by-frame analysis of the film and publish the results. This latter seems to me to be justified even though I possess no observations of my own on prey-catching by lions.

The two lionesses are not to be seen in the film until after the males have killed the buffalo and the meal begins. Until then they watch from a distance. The two lions have got the buffalo between them and each *in turn* makes an advance toward the buffalo, thus forcing it to keep continually turning round in order to show its next oppressor its horns each time. The last of these maneuvers is shown in Fig 20 a-g. In h-j the first lion jumps at the buffalo from behind and throws its two forepaws over the buffalo's croup (k). The buffalo tries to turn toward it, but the lion holds fast and likewise springs around with its hind-legs (l-o) or is passively swung around by the buffalo, thereby losing contact with the ground with its hind-feet for an instant (p). Having landed again, it fastens its teeth into the buffalo's rump in addition, pulls it backward (q) and at the same time farther around in a circle in the old direction, pressing (r-v) and finally pulling it down (w-x) in the process. The second lion has moved around with them in a narrow circle, but so far without interfering. Only when the first lion has brought the buffalo down at the rear does it approach (y-z), grasps the buffalo in the shoulder with its teeth as it struggles to get up again (A), then, straining backward, pulls it down onto its side (B-D). The second lion lets go of the buffalo's shoulder and takes a bite somewhere behind the head, adjusting its grip twice. It is impossible to discern the exact details, however, partly because of the tall grass and partly because at the vital moment a hyena runs past between the head of the buffalo and the camera. (The whole time 5 or 6 hyenas are running around the three animals, sometimes so close that they seem almost to touch the

Fig. 20 Lions kill buffalo, 1st lion ☐, 2nd lion ▨, buffalo ■ . From film made by F. Edmond-Blanc. For explanation see text.

lions; they, however, are preoccupied with the buffalo and pay no attention whatever to the hyenas.)

IV. DISCUSSION

1. On the phylogeny of aggressive biting

Biting for the purpose of defense and attack in both intra- and inter-specific fighting occurs in all groups of vertebrates. The mammals must already have taken it over from their reptilian ancestors. Where it is missing, this is certainly a secondary loss; either the anatomical structures also disappeared (e.g., edentates, elephants), or other and more effective weapons replaced teeth which had become specialized for processing vegetable foods (e.g. many—but by no means all—horned animals and deer). Neither intra-specific fighting nor resistance to enemies of a different species will be discussed here, but only the biting attack on animals of a different species (mammals and birds) for the purpose of killing and eating them.

In an attack on prey, the *teeth* of carnivorous mammals are used for *seizing* and *killing*. The forelimbs have only secondarily acquired the function of grasping the prey, pulling it close and holding it fast. I know of no insectivore, for example, which uses its paws first and then its jaws; of the carnivores only highly developed forms do this, and not all of them by far, even when they possess the anatomical prerequisites. Originally the functions of "seizing" and "killing" do not seem to have been clearly separated: By means of repeated bites prey animals are prevented from escaping time and again, until in the end they die of the sum total of their injuries and/or loss of blood, or else one bite hits a lethal point by chance.

This seems to me to be the case with *Nandinia* and perhaps *Para-doxurus* as well [20]. It will be the same with other carnivorous mammals which are primitive in this respect, above all probably the carnivorous marsupials. The two functions separate when, after the prey has been seized and pulled close, the bites are aimed with a preference for parts of the body where injury brings rapid death. Already in the case of *Nandinia* one gains the impression that the bites are aimed at those parts of the prey animal's body which are *moving most* at the time; and when an animal resists and wriggles, it usually moves its forequarters most energetically. This factor could also, at least partly, be what makes the Large Indian Civets always snap in the direction of the front end of their prey and usually bite animals that are sitting still in the head. From this point of departure natural selection was no doubt able to breed a specific *orienting reaction* which directs the attacking bite fairly precisely toward the *most fatal spot* and thus for the first time turns it into a "killing bite"; in the "nape bite" of the *Felidae* and some *Mustelidae* it then attained its highest development. (On the question of learned orientation of the killing bite see below p. 214 et seq.) Now, the nape bite is so fatal only when it does sufficient injury to the cervical spinal cord or the medulla of the prey animal, and in the vast majority of cases investigated this is so, as I had already established earlier [20] and as many further investigations have consistently confirmed. However, when the prey animals are fairly large, genets, for example, or *Mustelidae* (polecat, Eibl-Eibesfeldt 1955 b, weasel, Goethe 1950) apparently do not easily succeed in this with one bite only; as a result these forms have the habit of frequently repeated biting described. In contrast, the *Felidae* hit the spinal cord with just one bite in a *very* high percentage of cases, although even with "good" nape bites their teeth may penetrate the prey's neck from a wide variety of directions. This cannot be explained solely by the orientation of the killing bite. My assumption is that the canine teeth of the *Felidae*—both their shape and their position in the jaws—are so well adapted to the "lie" of the muscles, tendons, and ligaments as well as to the direction of the planes of the vertebrae that with a high degree of probability these almost automatically guide at least one of the four penetrating canine teeth to an intervertebral space. The tooth then inserts itself between the vertebrae like a wedge, forces them apart and thus severs the spinal cord partially or completely. This hypothesis alone seems to me to explain why one rarely finds any damage to the vertebrae themselves. The canine teeth are exceptionally well suited to forcing things apart, but certainly not to biting firmly with their tip on something hard: As one can discover from skulls in museums as well as from badly treated zoo and circus animals, the canine teeth splinter lengthwise relatively easily.

The last "fine adjustment" is no doubt guided by the proprioceptors: When the tip of a tooth touches something hard, in other words bone, the cat could feel around a little until the point glides into a gap, and only then bite harder. The "automatic pilot" assumed above would then need to guide only as far as the vertebral bones and not so incredibly precisely as to between two vertebrae. In fact, one can sometimes see how a cat closes its jaws in two phases when it bites a completely apathetic prey animal dead relatively slowly. Only participation of this kind by the proprioceptors could also explain the startling fact that the loss of one or even more canine teeth need not affect the efficiency of the killing bite. The old female serval "S" has only one canine tooth in her upper jaw left, yet she can still kill even large guinea pigs just as quickly as before.

The correspondence between shape and position of the canine teeth of the cat and the neck anatomy of the prey animal is understandably adapted to the largest kind of prey preferred by each species of cat [20]; killing these swiftly and surely before they can resist brings the greatest adaptive advantage. Furthermore, apparently those birds which are "huntable" for the cat are relatively so defenseless that they can be "neglected" by natural selection: It is amazing how many "good" neck and nape bites a chicken can survive (p. 171). As a rule, therefore, it takes much longer and is far more a matter of chance when cats kill fairly large birds than when they kill correspondingly large mammals. With birds, a bite between the shoulder and the base of the neck is usually more deadly in effect than a nape bite. But although it is usually just there that the first bite ("seizing bite") catches a large bird [13], the cats almost always change over to a nape bite as soon as they have their prey fast (Fig. 8w, p. 168). And although some species of cats prefer birds as prey, natural selection must in the main have been played out between feline canine teeth and jaws and mammalian neck. Anyone who finds so astonishingly fine an adaptation of the shape—clumsy in appearance only—of the felid canine tooth too much to credit and therefore improbable should read Manton's papers (1953, 1958 a, b, 1959, 1960, 1964): On the basis of a mass of material on arthropods she proved down to the most incredible details that there is a close connection between shape and function, ecology and behavior.

At least some points of the above assumption are capable of being checked experimentally, and this is to be done in the near future in cooperation with an institute of anatomy.

If the felid canine tooth is not very suitable for biting on something hard with its tip, it is of even less use for opening up the great *carotid arteries* of the neck. Even the relatively sharp canine teeth of young cats are too blunt for this. Not only do the large blood vessels lie hidden deep under the thick neck muscles and the transverse processes of the cervical vertebrae, but they are also embedded in soft connective tissue in which they can be moved around easily and, thanks to their firm round walls, would be more likely to evade the thrust even of an object as sharp as an ice pick than be bored into by it. Nor do the canine teeth have an edge which would be sharp enough to cut the blood vessels. Already for these reasons I cannot credit Ullrich's (1962) report, according to which Indian lions opened up the *carotid arteries* of calves and young cattle (tied so that spectators could watch) with one single bite (*sic!* only one lioness needed to bite twice). Without changing their bite, they are then supposed to *suck out the blood* of their victims, which die from loss of blood, often not until many minutes later. Plates 2 and 5 in the paper are said to show lions in the act of sucking blood. However, the lions' jaws reach well round the neck of their prey, as Plates 1 and 4 show (in Plates 2 and 5 the rims of the lions' mouths are not visible). To be able to swallow a fluid with its jaws so wide apart and its tongue inevitably hampered in its movements by the fact that the neck of the prey animal is filling the interior of its mouth, the lion would need to raise its head above the horizontal; with its head held diagonally downward as shown in Plates 2 and 5, this is anatomically and physically impossible. Any remaining doubts are removed by Plate 8, which shows the nape of a freshly killed calf with the incisions made by two canine teeth. The holes made by the incisions have been marked by the insertion of two small sticks, so that it is quite possible to estimate where they run inside the nape musculature, and this is not where the large blood vessels of the neck lie. In other words, the Indian lions kill their prey like any other well-behaved cat. The victim's persistent kicking, misinterpreted by Ullrich, is caused by the mechanical stimulus which pressure and severing exert on the spinal cord. The larger the animal is, the longer this continues [19, 20]. In the last ten years alone (i.e. since completion of the manuscript of *Verhaltensstudien*), I have more than 20,000 times observed with the most careful attention how cats of the species enumerated here and several others as well killed prey animals of the most varying sizes. Bleeding is relatively rare, and dissection almost always shows that such bleeding as occurs comes from smaller blood vessels of the neck. On only one occasion did I find the carotid sinus ripped. Yet, in this case, too, as in the case of all observed killings where bleeding occurred, relatively so little blood had flowed out that at the latest from the moment the blood vessel was opened or immediately after the heart must have stopped beating, in other words death must already have occurred from some other cause. The myth of the blood-sucking predator is as old as (hunting?) Man. It is apparently ineradicable, and there will always be those who believe it, including some who should know better.[4]

2. The phylogeny of "shaking to death"

Formerly [29] I thought the tossing away of objects hanging from the teeth, e.g. prey animals or feathers and fur when plucking, was—just like the act of shaking to death most familiar in wild *Canidae*—to be derived from the same motor coordination as that with which, for example, any mammals shake water from their fur. This now seems to me unlikely. When they shake themselves, all mammals stretch neck and head roughly in the direction of the longitudinal axis of the body, a polar bear standing upright in the water, for example, vertically upward. As they shake, therefore, the nose is in the axis of rotation and makes only insignificant pendulous movements, if any. When tossing objects away, however, the animals pull their head in, the longitudinal axes of neck and head form almost a right angle to one another, the axis of rotation runs in the longitudinal axis of the cervical section of the spine, for of course the turn takes place around the dens epistrophei. The tip of the nose therefore describes the largest curve. Thus, the two movements are very different and the derivation of the one from the other not very probable. Tossing and shaking movements must have originated independently of one another.

All carnivores known to me grasp beetles and the like as well as larger unfamiliar prey animals rapidly, and often only loosely, with their teeth at some arbitrary point and immediately toss them away again with a sideways swinging movement of the head [29, 53 et seq.] (pp. 152, 156, 181 et seq.). This must have been the movement from which the shaking of an object originated. It is *arhythmical* and *asymmetrical:* never more than one sideways swing for an eighth to a quarter of a circle, release the object, swing back to the point of departure. As intensity increases, a second component running medially superimposes itself on the sideways movement of the head: The animals retract their chin and neck sharply and stretch them upward again with a jerk; often their entire forequarters shoot upward as well. This is how the wild games of tossing and "catch and throw" originate [53 et seq.] (Golden Cats p. 172, Servals p. 182, Figs. 16 b and c).

Throwing away to one side only develops into object-shaking when the teeth do not release their grip but take the object being held with them again as they swing back. This way of originating explains the peculiarity of the genet which at first sight seems extraordinary (p. 148): Even when shaking an object repeatedly, her head always swings out to one side only, and not back again over the median and to the other side. *Symmetrical* shaking to and fro develops first in species like the Large Indian Civets and to some extent already the Viverricula, which shake objects with far greater vehemence and frequency and are then unable to slow up their own momentum in the middle. As far as my observations show, being tossed away or shaken to one side only never breaks the neck of a prey animal, but *confuses* the normal *functions of the labyrinth* just for a few seconds. Animals thus deprived of their postural and spatial orientation are equally incapable of defense or escape movements, and the carnivore can bite again unimpeded at a more advantageous point. Cats never shake live prey animals as hard as the civets do, though occasionally some —Golden Cats and Fishing Cats, for example, do it relatively often— give a prey animal they have just seized and which is kicking violently a brief shake at low amplitude when they want to carry it to their eating-place and kill it there. After such a shake the prey animals usually hang quietly, if not always without moving altogether.

Very energetic and repeated shaking can temporarily cause *respiratory paralysis* in a prey animal (Viverricula, p. 152); Krieg (1964) has observed this frequently and is probably right in assuming that the dens epistrophei squeezes the medulla. Even harder shaking eventually causes death by "breaking the neck" ("death shake").

Since gentle shaking, with its effect of putting the prey animal's postural orientation temporarily out of action, occurs in all families of carnivores and also in insectivores (Lindemann 1952), its intensification into shaking to death could have occurred *several times convergently,* e.g. in the case of the Large Indian Civet (p. 154) and the *Canidae.* In contrast to forms such as the genet and other viverrids (Dücker 1957, 1962, Ewer 1963) and some *Mustelidae* (Goethe 1950, Eibl-Eibesfeldt 1950, 1956), the *Felidae* have neglected even gentle shaking in favor of perfecting the killing bite, and employ it only in exceptional cases. The preliminary stage, namely tossing away, however, is still fully in use by all species of cats.

3. "Generic Behavior" (A. Haas 1962) and Behavioral Norm

Haas (l.c.) has described how trifling alterations he made in the nest topography of bumblebees evoked from them changed behavior, some of which corresponded to the normal behavior of more primitive species of *Hymenoptera,* some to that of more progressive species. His tentative and, as far as I know, quite original interpretation of this was that every species presumably has the entire inventory of behavior of the whole genus at its disposal but normally "uses" or specializes in only one part of it; in exceptional situations in which this specialized behavior proves inadequate or inapplicable, however, the species "remembers" that the genus as a whole possesses a more extensive store of behavior patterns, and it now experiments until some pattern fits the unusual situation, usually with good adaptive success.

Unlike Haas who, as far as the behavior patterns he studied were concerned, investigated a species of roughly intermediate evolutionary level within its group, in the prey-killing of the *Felidae* I was dealing with what is (for the moment, at least) the group's most highly developed product. When the discharge of this behavior pattern is disturbed, therefore, only phylogenetically older ways of killing appear. The taxis guiding the killing bite to the nape of the prey animal being the phylogenetically most recent acquisition, it is also the one most prone to disturbance [48]. As emerges time and time again from the foregoing individual descriptions of the behavior of cats toward their first live prey animals (juvenile cats, adult cats without experience of live prey, and finally very experienced cats in relation to prey animals with which they were fairly or completely unfamiliar up till then), in such a situation almost all of them bite badly or without aiming, having grasped the prey animal with their teeth toss it hastily away again, and in this way often kill it (Leopard-cat—domestic cat hybrid, p. 156 et seq., Servals p. 181 et seq., Blackfoot-domestic cat hybrid p. 191) or exhaust it to the point of complete immobility, whereupon they take it for "dead" and eat it. If a prey animal defends itself with unusual or unexpected violence, the cats may even relapse into the most primitive stage of continually repeated, unaimed lunging and biting in blind rage (p. 155) [17, 43]. In an earlier paper [17, 52 et seq.] I discussed in detail all the things which may fall under the heading of *sources of disturbance*. The most important of these are *fear* of the prey animal, *unfamiliar surroundings,* and *social inferiority.* As will be obvious from the foregoing, the designation "generic behavior" (in other words behavior typical of the genus) may not be taken literally. Some of the behavior patterns which appear are phylogentically older than the genus, older in fact than the family or the order. I shall continue to apply the term, but it should always be understood in its broader sense.

Without doubt, a very effective selection pressure is necessary to breed a behavioral sequence which is so highly specialized and runs off with such positively mechanical precision as the nape bite of the cats and the method of attack necessary for its well-aimed application. But, one might ask, *what does this selection pressure consist of* if the "ideal procedure," as displayed, for instance, by the Blackfooted Cat in Fig. 17 and described by me as the "norm" [1–20], *relatively often either does not attain its goal or is not even attempted by the cat in the first place?* Now, the "norm" is quite certainly the *fastest, most effortless* and, for the cat itself, *most accident-free method of killing* that any land carnivore ever "invented"—*when* it goes smoothly! And this it does, after all, often enough to make the "investment" of developmental expenditure worthwhile. As a means of transport the automobile certainly represents technical progress; but when we get stuck in the mud we are glad to see the horse-and-cart which pulls us out again, yet this does not mean that we make the horse-and-cart the "transport norm" again.

If one asks which of the behavior patterns described for the cat are "normal," the answer can only be "All of them—depending on circumstances"! Thus, as I see it the question what the *normal behavior* of an animal species is in a particular situation that is "natural" to it may be posed in *three* ways:—

1. Which various behavior patterns occur at all in the situation? All of these must be regarded as normal provided that the situation concerned occurs often enough in the environment of the species to exert selection pressure on the development of the adaptation and adaptability (Gause 1942) of the species.

2. What can I expect with (what degree of) probability? Knowledge of the behavior which, in statistical terms, is the most frequent or average provides a "norm" against which to judge the behavior of populations. This norm makes it possible to predict with x% probability the behavior of an individual in a situation in which the variables are only partially known or controllable, and this is both important and adequate for many practical purposes. One must, however, always take into consideration that there may be a different distribution of statistical probabilities for different populations. *The "statistical norm" is, therefore, strictly valid only for the circumstances in which it was established.*

3. How does the animal behave when everything goes smoothly? In most cases this question needs to be formulated in the conditional tense: How would this process have run off if . . . the cat had not slipped on the gravel, the rat had not thrown itself on its back in time, the cat had not been too timid, and so on? This "ideal norm" of the undistorted run-off "as it was really intended" is of great significance to the qualitative analysis of behavior and thus to an understanding of the quality and structure of its internal causation. This norm is, namely, not in the least "ideal" in the sense that it represents merely an abstraction or a speculative figment of the imagination, even if in some cases it virtually never, or only rarely, occurs in its pure form but may be perceived only as something inferred through extrapolation or as a gestalt (Ley-

hausen 1961, Lorenz 1959, 1966). Quite to the contrary, it is a *highly real invariant* in the animal which is present in all variants in the perceptible run-off of behavior which may occur. It is an absolute necessity to establish such a norm *before* quantitative and statistical methods are employed. Only when this has been done can one go on to establish what the factors are which evoke the different variants and their frequency distribution. *Thus, for an investigator who wants to discover the causal interrelationships within a system of behavior the one form of run-off which occurred in only very few of the instances observed is often more important than all the rest.*

Thus, anyone wishing to discuss "normal behavior" should at the very outset state quite precisely to *which of the three norms* he is referring. The abundance of forms of a behavior modified by situation designated in (1) I would call the "behavioral range." It encompasses "generic behavior" according to Haas, regression to ontogenetically earlier stages of development, palingenetic and cenogenetic alike (e.g. the gaping of song-birds, Meyer-Holzapfel 1949), and, where appropriate, information learned by individuals. The variations of a complex behavior pattern occurring with the greatest statistical frequency (2) could be called the "behavioral median," or "average behavior"— though admittedly this latter is not quite correct. For the "ideal norm" (3) Hassenstein has suggested the term "type behavior" (1961, verbal communication). I would agree with this, though not without a stern warning that the word type here should not be confused with the quite different concept of type in systematics. "Normal" is applicable to all the manifestations designated under the three headings, and a set of complex behavior patterns modifiable by situation can pass as having been adequately investigated from an ethological point of view only if precise knowledge of all three of its "normal dimensions" has been acquired.

Certainly there are no grounds for extending the "generic behavior" discovered by Haas into a generally valid principle. There is no need to assume that every species of animal must still (or already!) be in at least latent possession of all behavior patterns occurring in related species. The "species memory" does not hold on eternally to everything in the way of behavior patterns which ever developed during the evolutionary ascent of the species, as some depth psychologists with an extreme viewpoint claim of the individual memory. A gibbon drowns helplessly even in shallow water, although its ancestors could certainly swim, just as the ancestors of the *Cercopithecidae* could and as they themselves can. But still, greater behavioral possibilities lie hidden in a species than one often believes, even after observing them intensively for many years. For safety's sake, therefore, the statement that an animal species does not possess a behavior pattern characteristic of its nearest relatives should always be interpreted as meaning "minimal frequency of occurrence in the conditions in which observations were made," as long as no completely unequivocal proof exists that, as in the above example of the gibbon, the appropriate hereditary fixed pattern is really not present in the central nervous system of the species under investigation and thus cannot possibly be elicited under any circumstances.

4. On the ontogeny of the killing bite

In the juvenile cat the killing bite, consummatory act in the sequence of actions of prey-catching, appears last [44 et seq.]. Biting, i.e. opening and closing the jaws, is, of course, something the young cat can already do much earlier; there are hints of this from its first days onward. Additional attributes of the killing bite, however, are orientation and uninhibited strength (see Section 5). By itself, the sight of the first live prey animal hardly ever excites the kitten enough to make it bite with sufficient strength to kill; usually some additional excitation is necessary, and this is elicited not by the prey animal but by stimuli from the surroundings, most frequently competition from siblings and mother. Kittens whose mother does not bring live prey to them during the decisive period between their sixth and about their twentieth week later either do not kill or else come to do so in a way which looks like slow and laborious learning. The possibility discussed earlier—that only domestic kittens as a result of weakness of reaction brought about by domestication are dependent on additional excitation for the development of the perfected killing bite— has proved incorrect, as the examples in part III no doubt prove (Leopard-cat R_1 hybrid Pudge p. 162, Serval Freda p. 182 et seq., Geoffroy's Cat Ferdinand p. 189, Blackfoot hybrids ♀ III and ♂ II p. 191). When an adequate additional stimulus takes effect, the complete killing bite usually "clicks into place" very suddenly (cf. Suricata, Ewer 1963) and subsequently is promptly employed by the kitten in other cases as well. This being so, I wondered whether we might be dealing here with a kind of motoric imprinting and whether, once a certain "sensitive period" has been missed, the motoric consummation of the killing bite cannot develop any more or only with the greatest difficulty [47]. However, it seemed that solely the beginning of this sensitive period could be fixed with any precision, whereas its end could be assumed only within broad limits. Against this interpretation Knappe (1959/60) has argued that, just as the killing bite can be lifted over the threshold by appropriate additional stimuli in the case of kittens, so it also can in the case of cats which grew up without any experience of prey animals, even when they are already quite adult.

To elucidate this question, the tests with Indian Leopard-cats, Leopard-cat—domestic cat hybrids, Tree-ocelots, and the Serval Freda described in part III were carried out. Natalie (Leopard-cat—domestic cat hybrid p. 156 et seq.), who was kept alone, produced exactly the impression of laborious learning I have described, a positively classic example of which is the lioness Elsa (Adamson 1960). With Natalie it took longest before she could kill mice, and many she played to death; with rats she "learned" faster, and with guinea pigs fastest of all. Her previous experience of mice may have had something to do with this, but without any doubt the largest part was played by the greater excitation elicited by the larger prey animals, as emerges from the numerous repeat bites, particularly when the first guinea pig was killed. The higher stimulus value of a large prey animal (provided that it is not too capable of defense and too frightening altogether) seems to me to be proved by the course taken by the tests with the Tree-ocelots (p. 186–187): Bueno killed the relatively large chicken almost at once, whereas later with the guinea pig he held back and Bonita needed much more time than he had done with the chicken.

Natalie's siblings received their first prey animals in the communal cage. Rani at once proved to be fully capable of killing. Kim needed a few days before he could do it, and with Li it took still longer. All three required less time per prey animal before they killed first, however, than Natalie did when tested in solitude. The tests in which dead and live rats were held out (p. 159) showed furthermore how easily all four could kill when they did not "know" that the animals were still alive. Thus one of the inhibitions on the killing bite in an inexperienced animal is without doubt fear of the live prey, as an earlier analysis of inhibited play and the development of prey-catching in kittens [36 et seq., 44 et seq., 51 et seq.] already showed.

A similar picture is provided by the tests with the pure-blooded Indian Leopard-cats. Kali, Durga, and Bigger had probably already got to know live prey previously. Small needed longer before she killed for the first time, but probably only because she was socially inferior [46] to Bigger, with whom she shared the cage. It was social inferiority which delayed the development of killing in Li's case, although she could do it just as well as the others when she took live rats from the hand. It was the same with the larger but shyer civet (p. 154), with Griff (Blackfooted Cat, p. 196), and with ♂ I (Blackfoot hybrid, p. 191). The cases reported by Dücker (1962) and Ewer (1963) in respect of Suricata must without any doubt be interpreted likewise and not as deficiency of instinct.

In contrast to the female Indian Leopard-cats, Shiva had quite certainly had no experience of prey. As he was alone when tested, no unspecific additional excitation came to his aid, and in a long process of play and struggle with his first rat he had to work himself up to the necessary level of excitation, just as Leopard-cat hybrid Natalie did. The Blackfooted Cat Buster (p. 194), having no siblings, had to do this too for, unlike domestic cats or, for instance, the Leopard-cat hybrid Rani, her mother never "competed," in other words never apparently or actually tried to take the mouse away from her. Comparison shows how much faster things went in the case of the young Blackfoot kittens which were in the "correct" phase of development than they did with the fully adult Leopard-cat Shiva and with Natalie. Apparently from the moment the mother cat begins to present the kitten with live prey its "sensitivity" also begins to intensify, reaching a maximum round about the 9th to 10th week of age. Thus Smudge, prevented by illness from "practicing," after recovery killed abruptly and without any playful preliminaries at nine weeks, similar to Blackfooted Cat Jake at a somewhat later point in time. Increased excitability may also have helped to elicit killing for the first time so much faster in the Tree-ocelots than in other adult animals without experience of prey. Anything new excites the Tree-ocelots even more than it does other species of cat, and in the case of our animals this peculiarity is no doubt considerably intensified by the fact that they are almost completely cut off from all external influences.

From the point of view of a fundamental evaluation of the facts, the tests with the Serval Freda seem to be of most significance, in particular because, apart from Shiva, she is the only one of our pure-blooded wild cats which with absolute certainty had no experience of prey before the first experiment.

With this animal (p. 182 et seq.) we tested as thoroughly as possible Knappe's statements about the effectiveness of additional stimuli in the case of adult animals as well, and were able to confirm them in full. However, far stronger additional stimuli were necessary than with kittens in order to achieve the same effect: Neither the sight of a competing conspecific through the cage wire nor my assistant's direct attempts to "compete"—frequently repeated and pushed to the very limit—were sufficient; only direct, positively brutal competition from the socially superior conspecific brought Freda to the point of administering a killing bite of full intensity to a guinea pig for the first time.

As the results reported all prove, there is no basic difference in the way in which the killing bite materializes for the first time whether in kittens or in adult animals which up till then had had no experience. The stimulus threshold for its elicitation the first time is, however, noticeably higher in the case of somewhat older or fully adult animals than it is with kittens in the stage of development designated above. In *this* sense, therefore, one can speak of a *sensitive period;* no irreversible behavioral deficiency results, however, if this is neglected. It is possible that with appropriate "stimulus therapy" such as was administered to Freda even the animals I have observed which never killed any prey throughout their life would have done so after all. The results of electrical brain stimulation discussed below support this opinion. Yet even so we need not perhaps abandon the assumption that we are dealing here with a motoric parallel to imprinting. As E. Hess (1959) has shown, the more muscular effort a Mallard chick needs to make initially in order to follow a particular object the faster and more lastingly it becomes imprinted to it. A causal connection of this kind between imprinting and muscular effort seems at first sight difficult to explain. The task becomes easier perhaps if one assumes a more indirect connection: It could be that the more the duckling has to *exert* itself in order to follow the constantly withdrawing imprinting object the more *excited* it might become. The experimental animals used by Klopfer and Hailman (1964)—unfortunately not ducklings of a wild species but chicks of the highly domesticated Peking duck—did, it is true, need to follow a proffered object for a while before imprinting occurred, but no quantitative correspondence could be established between muscular effort expended and imprinting success. Apart from the difference in experimental animal mentioned, the influence of which is difficult to assess, the differing results obtained by Hess on the one hand and Klopfer and Hailman on the other are no doubt due to the considerable differences in their experimental setups. On the grounds of my hypothesis I would risk the following forecast: If Klopfer and Hailman registered not only whether and for how long the experimental animal follows the imprinting object but also all externally perceptible signs of whether and to what extent it is excited as well, they would discover a quantitative relationship between degree of excitation and imprinting success similar to the one Hess found between muscular effort and imprinting success. The end of the sensitive period for both the killing bite of the cat and the following reaction of the duckling could be explained in the same way: The older a juvenile animal becomes, the more it learns about its environment and the less it gets worked up about both familiar and new objects; the threshold of excitation in relation to new stimuli rises constantly as development and experience progress. This would also explain why the beginning of the sensitive period is more sharply delineated than the end and why neglect of it need not be final. Now, the capacity of the duckling to be imprinted also disappears if it is kept in a dark incubator after hatching, in other words if it cannot become "blunted" in the manner hinted at above through broad experience in a varied environment. This, however, is not in intself an argument against the proposed hypothesis: As is the case with young dogs reared in isolation (Fuller 1964, Scott 1962), with the duckling kept too long in solitude and darkness timidity in the face of everything unfamiliar might suppress any other mode of reaction. The following reaction must, however, be aroused before imprinting can take place. Analogously, the killing bite of the cat can be lifted over the threshold only if the actions of chasing prey and seizing it with the teeth have been elicited. Overtimid cats which dare not pursue even small prey animals running away from them will never kill, and additional stimuli would at the most only intimidate them still further. If it should prove possible to verify my hypothesis with regard to ducks and other birds with a following reaction, this would simultaneously prove that there must be at least two different kinds of imprinting. For the first elicitation of the killing bite in the cat, as for the imprinting of a duckling to an object for following, the *exciting, self-intensifying performance of the associated instinctive movements is a necessary condition;* in processes such as the imprinting to a sexual object closely investigated by Schutz (1963 b) this is precisely not the case.

The interpretation of the nature of the killing bite given above, which is based on purely qualitative ethological observation and analysis, receives strong support from the results of recent neurophysiological investigations. Randall (1964) has proved the independence of the fixed pattern of the killing bite. Lesions in the caudal mid-brain of domestic cats have differential effects on two biting responses, the killing bite and the grooming bite, depending on which areas are affected. Tegmental and tectal lesions modify the killing bite so that it is readily elicited by a light touch on the cat's lip but otherwise will not appear. Ventral-lateral lesions in the same frontal plane result in spontaneous killing of prey but sensitivity to lip touch remains normal; grooming is increased and the grooming bite can be elicited by light stimulation of skin areas from which it cannot be elicited in the same way in normal cats. In both cases the response evoked is not oriented toward an object or the area stimulated.

By means of electrical stimulation in the antero-lateral hypothalamus of cats, Wasman and Flynn (1962) were able to elicit the killing bite, together with the associated appetitive behavior. Roberts and Kiess (1964) used electro-stimulation at the same point to train cats which in an unstimulated state would not attack prey to seek out a prey animal in a Y-labyrinth and bite it dead. In other words, the electrical stimulation played the part of the "additional stimulus." It was strong enough to make a cat which had been starved for 48 hours and had just been given food to interrupt its meal and go in search of the prey animal. It is interesting to note that with not one single experimental cat, even where stimulation had been repeated many times, was the effect carried over into the unstimulated state; in this they remained peaceful toward prey animals. These experiments prove unequivocally that the fixed patterns of prey-seizing and prey-killing *are present in working order in the central nervous system even when the animals do not normally use them.* If a prey animal is present, cats under stimulation perform the corresponding behavior patterns in their entirety the very first time; nothing indicates that they needed to learn anything about them, as one would have expected in accordance with Kuo's (1931) opinion. What they do, however, learn under the influence of the urge to kill elicited by electrical stimulation is to search for prey in a labyrinth when there is none in their immediate presence. In other words the urge to kill which has been activated "motivates" appetitive behavior, and of this latter the cats learn a form fitting the experimental situation.

Here the question arises why the cats in the experiments I have described went on killing after the first elicitation, whereas the cats stimulated electrically did not. For this there is one very obvious explanation. Cats which have not become accustomed to eating dead prey animals before they kill for the first time kill just as fast or as slowly as control animals whose sole solid food consists of dead animals. The latter, however, usually eat up the first prey animals they kill for themselves without much hesitation, whereas the former have no idea what to do with them; they see nothing edible in them. They must be taught this by having the dead animal cut up a little for them so that they get the direct smell and taste of the raw meat. If the cats are already rather old and not accustomed to raw meat, it is often quite impossible to persuade them to eat the prey animals intended for them by nature. Some remain eager killers nonetheless, but most do not. In other words: The cat must grasp the connection between killing and procuring food in order to keep killing in training; otherwise, without constant confirmation via the satisfaction of hunger, this may atrophy more or less completely. Analogous to the trophicity of the skeletal muscles (Heiligenberg 1963, 1964), the readiness of at least some instinctive movements to be performed is dependent on use or disuse. Everything argues in favor of the killing bite of the cat being an instinctive movement of this kind (cf. farm cat Blotje, p. 190–191). Even in the case of young cats accustomed to catching mice, "killing" is far less liable to accumulate than the other constituents of prey-catching behavior [56 et seq.] (see below p. 228 et seq.). The experimental cats of Roberts and Kiess had, however, been specially selected for the atrophy of their killing bite, and even later they did not become accustomed to eating the prey animals they had killed during the stimulation experiment. As will be discussed in greater detail on p. 224, the development of the killing bite is not simply a matter of the formation of a conditioned reaction. The "confirmation via the satisfaction of hunger" mentioned above must be interpreted as a kind of physiological "growth stimulus." Thus, hunger or desire to eat is also not sufficient on its own to lift the killing bite over the threshold for the first time (see below pp. 221, 225).

5. The orientation of the nape bite

The orientation of the killing bite of the cat to the nape of the prey animal is something I considered to be innate [14 et seq., 38, 48]. As regards the concept "innate" and its application in ethology I would refer readers to Lorenz (1961); here I would simply emphasize as strongly as possible that no ethologist has ever made the claim that innate behavior patterns have "no developmental history," as Quine and Cullen (1964) insinuate. If that were the case, concepts such as "maturation," "damage during rearing," "behavioral disturbance caused during development," etc., such as are in constant use in ethological literature, would be completely meaningless.

Eibl-Eibesfeldt (1955 b, 1956, 1958 b, 1963) denies that the polecat has an innate orientation of its killing bite toward the nape, whereas according to Wüstehube (1960 a) inexperienced animals of this species kill with a correctly oriented nape bite at the very first attempt. Eibl-Eibesfeldt's polecats (1956, 1963) without experience of prey grew up with siblings and already at least partially learned the advantages of the nape grip while playing with them. Later they were quicker in learning to apply it to prey animals as well than were polecats of the same age which had been reared in isolation.

Although circumstances could, of course, be quite different in the *Felidae* and the *Mustelidae,* the respective arguments of the two authors led me to take a fresh look at the question of the orientation of the killing bite in the *Felidae* and the ontogenesis of this orientation.

It quickly emerged that to say the orientation of the killing bite toward the nape of the prey animal's neck is innate is going rather too far. As is similar in the case of the orientation of the gaping movement of young thrushes (Tinbergen and Kuenen 1939), the directing stimuli proceed from the *indentation* in the contour of the prey animal's body between the head and the rump. Inexperienced cats do *not* at first distinguish between the upper and the lower side, in other words between nape, throat, and side of the neck. Even so, at their first attempts they almost always succeed in making good nape bites because the motor pattern guided by the orienting mechanism proceeds in stereotype fashion diagonally from above and behind onto the prey animal if it is sufficiently passive or taken by surprise not to make movements of escape or defense. If this latter is the case, the cat usually breaks off its attack; furthermore, in the early stages the mother cat lets the kittens have only very passive prey animals or ones which she herself has already damaged slightly. With its first easy successes, however, the young cat's self-confidence grows rapidly. Soon it rushes in more incautiously, more "blindly," and no longer lets itself be frightened off, or can no longer pull up, if the prey animal takes avoiding action. Thus after the first series of correct nape bites it more often hits the side of the neck or the throat (Fig. 7a, b). In this way its face comes within range of the scratching paws of the prey animal; if the cat has seized it too far to the rear, the prey animal can even wriggle free enough to bite for its own part. Wounds on the cat's nose, lips, and eye rims are quite often the consequence, and it is not until now that it *learns* that only a bite in the upper side of the neck—in the nape—offers security and kills quickly. This development could be observed time and again in the case of both kittens and adult cats without previous experience.

It made no difference whether the animals grew up with others of their kind or alone. Buster's (Blackfooted Cat, p. 194) prey-catching did not develop any differently in this respect than that of Griff and Jake (p. 195); their mother, Braut, never plays with her kittens until they are already of "mouse-catching age" anyway. Thus Buster was also unable to acquire from her any significant amount of experience about the usefulness of the nape grip. This does not, of course, mean that a kitten learns absolutely nothing in its dealings with siblings. It gains experience in movement and it gains self-confidence, the latter, however, depending on its ranking order within the litter: Animals of *high rank* develop into perfect killers *faster than solitary animals,* animals *low in rank* or somewhat retarded in their development do so *more slowly* (cf. Leopard-cat hybrids Rani and Li, p. 158, with Natalie, p. 156 et seq., Blackfooted Cats Griff and Jake with Buster, p. 194 et seq., Blackfoot hybrids I, II, and III, pp. 190–191). In kittens, loss of social rank may temporarily suppress killing which had already developed fully [46]. Other disturbances may have the same effect on both young and adult animals.

Since almost without exception the orientation of the killing bite toward the nape of the prey animal clearly develops in the two phases described, it is natural to consider the taxis of the first phase which is guided by one simple feature (indentation of the neck) as purely innate; this assumption is strengthened by the observation made with Tree-ocelot Bueno (p. 186; Fig. 15). If the orientation of the killing bite to the neck indentation were based on experience gained from siblings or mother, the eliciting stimuli would certainly be too highly differentiated for the neck of a bottle—which, after all, is shaped quite differently—to simulate them so well as to produce such a reflexlike reaction at once. It was in any case the first time I saw a cat perform the complete attack with killing bite on an object without a furlike surface [37].

Once the second phase of development of orientation is complete, however, the cat may repeatedly be observed to make a vast number and variety of movements in an attempt—often for a long time unavailing—to bring its teeth to the prey animal's nape before it bites. Often as it does so it performs the most difficult turns with its head, depending on the position and movements of the prey animal. It is impossible to doubt that it is now capable of distinguishing precisely between the underside of the neck and the nape and strives exclusively after the latter. These movements oriented toward the nape of the prey animal's neck in its narrowest sense, as well as the knowledge as to where the nape is to be found on a prey animal, even one of a kind so far unknown, are certainly all learned. In the case of disturbances or high prey-catching excitation, they are the first to be lost [Ocelot-cat Muschi, 16, 17], the "neck-shape taxis" next, and so on, as discussed in "generic behavior."

After detailed frame-by-frame analysis of the films made by Eibl-

Eibesfeldt and Wüstehube, it seems to me that conditions are somewhat different in polecats. Eibl-Eibesfeldt's inexperienced polecat
(1958, Film 14) does not only "sniff at the rat as it sits still": If one
takes into consideration the slow motion of the film (90 frames/sec.),
the polecat makes two aiming movements toward the rat's nape (i.e.
diagonally from above and behind toward the neck indentation) but,
just like an inexperienced and rather timid cat, it does not dare to
bite there and taps the rat on the back with one paw; the rat runs
away and the polecat tries to hold it back by its tail. However, one of
the polecats filmed by Wüstehube which was very experienced with
prey does *exactly* the same. *Her* objection—that Eibl-Eibesfeldt's inexperienced polecats gave the impression of being disturbed and did
not behave "normally"—is perhaps correct if she means "type behavior." But in that case the experienced polecats she herself filmed in
such detail did not behave "normally" either; for they display practically the whole "behavioral range" of the polecat, and pure "type
behavior" is hardly once to be seen! Very often, of course, the behavior of cats which have extremely great experience of prey but are
disturbed, intimidated, exhausted, or merely in a playful mood is not
in any way different from that of animals which have never yet killed
(see above, pp. 181–185, Servals "S" and Freda).

Wüstehube's view that in the polecat, too, the nape bite is fully
innate and therefore belongs to its type behavior has been criticized
in detail by Eibl-Eibesfeldt (1963). In particular Wüstehube has considerably underestimated the influence exerted by the experience
young polecats gain while playing with their siblings. Juvenile polecats grasp, hold, and pull one another by the neck far more violently
and continuously than young cats do and thus come to learn the advantages of the nape grip before their first experience of prey. The
polecat does also seem to have a neck indentation taxis (see above)
but—as far as one can judge from Eibl-Eibesfeldt's findings and from
film analysis—it is not so surely aimed as in the cat's case. It is perhaps already better aimed than in *Nandinia* (p. 155), but hardly quite
as well as in *Genetta* (p. 147). This could have some connection with
the fact that the polecat is a less optically guided animal than the
genet or the cat.

6. The relative hierarchy of moods and experience in the development of prey-catching

In the following I shall interpret the observations with the help of
Lorenz's "psychohydraulic model" (1950 c). I cannot agree with

Hinde's opinion (1956, 1960) that this model has lost its heuristic value. Nor can I see that Hinde himself has succeeded in offering in its place an overall synthesis of the dynamics and hierarchical structure of behavior. Yet such a synthesis alone can offer a framework within which it is possible to pose significant questions on which to base further detailed investigations. Above all, not only do I find the concept "action-specific energy," with its implication of accumulation, discharge, and current level (or state of the store of energy at a given moment), indispensable to an adequate description of behavior, but there are also strong reasons for assuming that it reflects a thoroughly real chemical process which is interposed between the purely neuronal activities and which in part initiates, maintains, and dominates them. This I have explained in detail in another paper (1965 b).

One objection frequently raised to establishing a model of this kind, within the framework of which the known facts can then be interpreted, is that it is scientifically inadmissible since not all parts of it can immediately be checked experimentally; that one should, indeed *must,* think only in "operational" terms. There is a methodological misunderstanding here. One must think *strictly in operational terms* when preparing and carrying out *a particular experiment. When evaluating results and fitting them into the general context of what is known so far, however, not only is there no compulsion to think operationally, but it would in fact be a serious error of method!* Thinking operationally in this case would mean enslaving oneself to known operations, letting oneself be in every sense limited by them. According to Metzger (quoted by Lorenz 1966), some philosophers are incurably impeded in the normal use of their senses by epistemological considerations. Similarly, among natural scientists there are some "experimentalists" and "operationalists" who are prevented by operational considerations, apparatus, and the blind worship of (statistical) quantity from the normal use of their faculties for speculative thought. *Only* interpretation untrammeled by preceding operations produces an overall synthesis which *opens up new perspectives* and compels one to devise new kinds of operation to test them—*as is then certainly indispensable.* With purely operational thinking, Copernicus would not have advanced beyond the Ptolemaic theory of the universe, nor would Einstein have produced the theory of relativity, to name but two examples from an infinitely long list. And we should not forget that, for a long time after Copernicus, forecasts based on Ptolemaic operations which had been refined over the course of centuries were still far the more accurate! Thus, not even the often overworked principle of the predictability of future events is in all circumstances an unequivocal measure of "correctness." Many details had to be clarified, many operations carried out before the Copernican system surpassed the Ptolemaic in this respect. And the men who carried all this out at first had little more to encourage them in their laborious detailed work than the "evidence" offered by the greater harmony of the Copernican theory of the universe. The Lorenzian model of motivation may have all or some of the shortcomings which beset the Copernican system at the beginning, but like the latter it allows a more comprehensive and therefore more satisfactory interpretation of the known facts than any other.

The first prey-catching movement—tapping—appears when the kitten is about 3 weeks old. This is the lowest level of intensity of striking with the forepaw. At roughly the same time appear the movements of grasping and pulling inward with the forepaw which, when performed as intention movements, are often difficult to distinguish from tapping. These movements are possibly a development from the "milk tread," but observations are not yet adequate to confirm this interpretation. Lying in wait, chasing, stalking, the stalking run, and the pounce onto the prey appear in rapid succession. At first they are still clumsy as a result of the immaturity of the coordination and the muscular system, but they rapidly become perfected and have all matured almost completely when the mother cat brings the first live prey animals to the kittens in about their sixth week. In the fourth week at the earliest she had already presented them with dead prey, at which the kittens soon began to suck, chew, and eat [44 et seq.]. Tossing away and jumping away also mature in this period. While playing with the mother and siblings and also with small playthings, the kittens employ all these movements, with an often exaggerated amplitude *but in quite irregular sequence.* Thus, when the mother brings the first live prey animal along, the kitten has at its disposal a whole arsenal of instinctive moments which are not yet linked up, however, in a chain of actions leading to killing. During this play, individual elements may sometimes already combine in their later form, e.g. lying in wait with stalking, the stalking run with the pounce, and so on, but at once they separate again and appear singly or in combination with other playful movements, some of which come from other functional contexts than that of prey-catching (Eibl-Eibesfeldt 1951) [51 et seq.]. It also becomes obvious that it is not without reason that the killing bite does not emerge until so late and until the kitten meets its first live prey: If it were otherwise, the kittens would often injure one another when playing at prey-catching among themselves. As they play with the first prey animals, the ordered sequence leading to the killing bite—namely lying in wait, stalking up, pouncing, and seizing—establishes itself *gradually,* though occasionally it can happen quite suddenly, and in the end the killing bite, too, is lifted over the threshold in the way I have already described several times. Once the kitten has killed just a few times, a firm chain of appetitive actions, denuded of all playful exaggeration, is welded together and without deviation or delay leads to the killing and subsequent consumption of the prey animal (p. 163, 184–185, 194 et seq.). *All* the instinctive movements contained in this sequence and enumerated above are *innate,* as is shown by the cats of Thomas and Schaller (1954) which were reared in isolation and made to wear opaque plexiglass spectacles from the time their eyes opened until they were tested at the age of 11 weeks [47 et seq.].

In spite of being connected up firmly at times into a purposive pattern of activities, the individual elements do not completely lose either their independence or their capacity for playful exuberance. *No difference* can be noticed in the kittens' play with siblings or small playthings *after* the first killing, except that they almost visibly become more agile, stronger, and rougher in their games. Before encountering live prey for the first time, the kitten already gains agility and confidence in its own motoric ability in these games; in particular when playing with objects it learns new combinations of movements, learns to manipulate the object with its paws and to move it in a desired way, to pick it up and to throw it. Curiously enough, these experiences and this ability seem *at first to be of no use* to the kitten in prey-catching, i.e. it does not seem to "remember" about them any more. Faced with a prey animal, it never produces anything but the quite *stereotyped instinctive movements.* Then, when it has killed a few times, the whole process, from first sighting the prey animal through to killing and eating, runs off as "type behavior," which I described earlier as *the* prey-catching behavior of the cat [2–20]. It is exactly the same in the case of inexperienced adult animals, except when the prey animals are relatively small: These they sometimes treat as playthings until they have worked themselves up into the necessary state of excitation or external additional stimuli elicit the killing bite. This too reaffirms the fact that fear of an unfamiliar kind of live prey makes the cat *forget* both playful exuberance and learned voluntary movements when they meet for the first time [53 et seq.]; but adult cats are not sufficiently afraid of small prey animals for this to happen. The individual instinctive movements leading up to killing (lying in wait, stalking, etc., see above) do *not* represent a fixed chain of patterns like the fighting actions of *Astatotilapia* (Seitz 1940), each step of which has a higher stimulus threshold than the last and all of which are supplied by one and the same action-specific energy. Instead, each link in the chain possesses its own endogenous rhythmicity, and its current level and thus its threshold values fluctuate largely independently of the others. Thus, when chasing has not been elicited for some time its current level rises faster than that of killing or lying in wait. Hunger and repletion have *no direct* influence on the endogenous rhythmicity of the individual prey-catching actions. All this has been proved experimentally [56 et seq.]. As described above (p. 214), when "killing" is not used for a long time it tends to atrophy, especially if the cat sees nothing edible in a killed animal. In this sense, killing is a "need-dependent behavior pattern" (Precht 1958). The desire to eat, however, is not by itself capable of lifting the killing bite over the threshold for the first time: In such a case, the animals always try to start chewing the live prey animal, usually in vain (Leopard-cat R_1 hybrid Pudge, p. 162, Serval Freda, p. 183, Geoffroy's Cat Ferdinand, p. 189 Blackfoot hybrid ♀ III, p. 191); the killing bite always requires additional excitation, as described above (p. 209 et seq.). In the case of the Blackfoot hybrid ♀ III, it could no doubt look as if the killing bite followed from the desire to eat the mouse. What finally did evoke the killing bite, however, was—expressed anthropomorphically—the cat's annoyance because the mouse would not stay still, in other words an excitation heightened by repeated lack of success. Once it has been prodded into action, however, the endogenous rhythmicity of killing keeps itself in motion independently for a certain time and no link, still less an inflexible synchronization, with the short-term rhythm of hunger and repletion is formed; even sick animals quite without appetite usually kill eagerly, sometimes right up until shortly before their death. Hunger does, however, lower the stimulus threshold for killing. These last two sentences are not mutually contradictory: A cat that is experienced with prey and enjoys killing will kill just as many mice during an experiment whether it is hungry or replete. The replete cat, however, "plays" first, works off catching movements which, as described above, have a stronger tendency to accumulate, before it kills; the hungry cat kills as fast as it can and catching becomes the briefly and purposively performed appetitive act which makes killing possible. In these two cases the "store" of action-specific energy for killing is the same, the possibility of its elicitation different. Just this example shows quite clearly that a model of the dynamics of the system of propensities constructed solely on the basis of heteronomous variations in stimulus threshold is not adequate to the facts. *The dualism existing between autonomous changes in stimulus threshold* caused by accumulation and consumption of action-specific energy and *heteronomous* changes in stimulus threshold caused by different propensities and other internal factors as well as by the external situation cannot be argued away (cf. Schleidt 1964). In extensive experiments on electrical stimulation of the brain stem of domestic chicken von Holst and Saint Paul (1960) have confirmed a dualism between "adaptation" and "central nervous switch in mood" which corresponds to this exactly. The experiments discussed on pp. 213–214 could be interpreted roughly as follows: The electrical stimulus (in the form and strength employed by the two authors) can elicit the fixed patterns of catching and killing via the points stimulated but not start the autonomous, continuous production of action-specific energy. There can be little doubt, however, that this too would be possible if the stimulus parameter and/or the loci stimulated were changed (Leyhausen 1965 b). If this succeeded, then after a short or perhaps rather longer series of stimulations the endogenous readiness to kill would obey its own autonomous rhythmicity—at least for a certain time—even if no further electrical stimulus were administered; in other words, the result originally expected by Roberts and Kiess would occur, and the cat previously incapable of killing would now be able to kill through its own propensity. However, as long as its own propensity is not aroused and its endogenous autonomous rhythm has not started up, then all the "conditioning" in the world cannot help. The propensity, the appetence must already be there, or else there *is* nothing to condition. Thus, propensities of this kind cannot be learned either. At the most, as I have already said, their "trophicity" may be influenced in the long term by use/disuse.

As I have said, the individual prey-catching actions do not depend in graduated values on the growing intensity of a unitary "prey-catching mood" to which they are all subordinate, but *all have their own rhythms* of accumulation and exhaustion of action-specific energy. Thus, each *single* action also has appetences specially directed toward it. "Appetence" is, then, the perceptible expression of the "mood" postulated from the functional properties of our model, the current level of action-specific energy surpassing the "latency mark." The "mood" which is strongest at the time prevails (wholly or partially: phenomena of superimposition and conflict!). If the external prerequisites for the immediate performance of the instinctive movements striven after are not present, the appetence appears in behavior patterns which either bring the animal into the desired preliminary situation or alter the details of the situation appropriately. Thus, each of the actions of prey-catching may become the *consummatory act striven after* if its current level is relatively high and that of the others relatively low at the time. Then within certain limits any one of them can take any other into its "service"; it activates it as "appetitive behavior" if it can be attained itself as the desired consummatory act only via this "detour." This I have called the "relative hierarchy of moods" (1955 a) [58, 109, 112]. This hierarchy does *not* arrange moods of various "orders" *linearly,* like the hierarchy models of Baerends and Tinbergen, *in which the consummatory act is not only the final link in the chain but also ranks the lowest. Instead, it is the appetence toward whichever instinctive movement is being striven after as consummatory act at the time which is the dominating factor in the momentary hierarchy.* It is this which governs and "programs" not only the motor system but also all the afferent mechanisms. Accordingly, therefore, a mouse is an object to ambush or chase, to kill, to eat, to fish after, or throw around, i.e. the stimulus quality of the mouse changes according to the hierarchical order of the appetences. This should not, however, be misinterpreted in Kortlandt's sense (1955) as a "hierarchy of goals" (see below p. 232 et seq.).

Hinde (1958) made observations in connection with the individual nest-building movements of canaries which correspond precisely to mine on the prey-catching movements of cats. He, however (1959, p. 133), shies away from the conclusions I arrived at: "Are we then to postulate a separate drive for each of these activities? If so, where is the process to stop, for each of these activities can be analyzed into constituent movements?" My reply to these two questions is that the range or complexity of the behavior patterns in question is irrelevant. If an activity can appear *alone and of its own accord,* outside the normal biological context, and develop *an appetence of its own,* if it can set in motion appetitive activities leading exclusively to itself, then there is no need to *postulate* a separate propensity for such an activity, it *has* one! In other words, if, say, a constituent movement of a particular nest-building activity could—be it only in exceptional circumstances—become a consummatory act striven after for its own sake without any connection whatever with the other constituent movements, it would in my opinion possess an action-specific energy of its own. As far as I have been able to establish, cats have action-specific energies for lying in wait, stalking, chasing, seizing, killing, eating, and a whole series of other instinctive movements within the functional system of catching and consuming prey. What they *certainly do not* have is one unitary "prey-catching drive" to which all these are subordinate. The way behavior runs off at any time must not, naturally, be regarded merely as the resultant of the current, constantly changing balance of strength of the appetences for the individual propensities, which is an opinion Hinde (1959) imputes to those who are trying to grope their way forward with the help of energy models of motivation. No one believes they can explain all observable details of instinctive movements by means of the endogenous rhythmicity of action-specific energy alone, nor does anyone imagine that the autonomy of the individual propensity is absolute. Within certain limits it is bound to be receptive to manifold influences from other propensities, from internal factors of other sorts and from external factors, as von Holst (1936 a, b, 1937, 1939 c) already proved with regard to the automatic functions of the spinal cord of a fish ("action-specific potential," Thorpe 1956). After all, observable behavior acquires its final form also as a result of internal and external influences which directly channel and regulate the functional readiness (arousal, "general drive") of the neural system prodded into action by the action-specific energy (W. R. Hess 1943 a, 1957).

Von Holst (1936 b, 1939 c) proved that the amplitude of a fin movement may be influenced in two ways: 1. by decreased or increased activity of the automatic cell group driving it, and 2. principally by reflex action increasing or decreasing the excitability (tonicity, functional readiness) of the motor neurons. The two effects overlap and cannot be identified separately in the fin movement. The constant activity of the substantia reticularis regulates and maintains the functional readiness of the neural system, but it does *not* decide *which kind* of function will be summoned up or clamor to be discharged at a given moment. Its function should not, therefore, be involved in a discussion about the nature of the individual propensities. Hinde is finally of the opinion that we could dispense with the concept of the individual propensity and action-specific energy and instead say that "changes in response strength could be regarded as changes in the probability of one pattern of neural activity rather than another, perhaps revealed by changes in sensitivity to eliciting factors." But that *is* exactly the problem and not an attempt to solve it! Why *should* the probability of one particular behavior pattern appearing *change at all,* and this not merely depending on changing external conditions but in accordance with an autonomous rhythmicity which is specific to each single one and has an associated energy which, when appropriately accumulated, forces the animal to perform, one after the other, appetitive behavior, reaction to a substitute object, and finally in many cases sheer "overflow" activity? Hinde can suggest *absolutely no reason why an instinctive movement should have a probability of occurrence at all*. As the cats of Roberts and Kiess show (1964), the "motoric template" (Kretschmer 1953) of prey-killing can reman latent for years. The *mere fact of its existence* does *not* ensure that it will be activated, even in the most adequate stimulus situation imaginable; for this, the specific propensity is necessary. The fact that the endogenous rhythmicity of the individual propensity may be influenced from without and within in a multiplicity of ways is no argument against its relative autonomy: No one doubts the automatic function of the heartbeat, although *within its functional limits* it can be influenced neurally, humorally, and medicinally in the most varied ways.

At this point we can pick up the thread broken off on p. 223. In the case of a hitherto inexperienced cat, once the killing bite has crossed the threshold for the first time, once the cat has killed *lege artis,* then for a while when prey is sighted the appetence for killing is more powerful than any other. Every prey animal is attacked at once and killed as fast as possible, and all other prey-catching actions are relegated to the role of pure appetitive behavior. In this phase, as I have explained in more detail above, the cat learns the connection between killing and procuring food. This is not immediately clear to it the first time, even if it has already eaten dead prey animals. Time and again the impression is forced on the observer that after having killed for the first time the cat is quite astonished by its achievement; it seems unable to comprehend why the dead animal no longer moves. It sometimes take a while before the cat realizes that this can now be eaten, and certainly it must kill several times before it grasps in full the connection between nape bite and transformation of a live animal into food. There is, at any rate, little room for doubt that the cat does this to a certain degree and that *only as a result and subsequently* can hunger activate the entire chain of prey-catching actions, including killing, as appetitive behavior. What now stands out as all the animals, adults as well as juveniles, continue to develop is that the period of swift, surely aimed killing by means of "type behavior" which follows the first killing (pp. 219–220) is soon succeeded by a phase which looks like a relapse into the preceding "unperfected" behavior toward prey (Leopard-cat R_1 hybrids Pudge and Smudge, p. 163, Blackfooted Cats Griff and Jake, p. 196, Leopard-cat hybrid Natalie, p. 157, Serval Freda, p. 184). In reality, however, now that the animals know "what the point of the whole thing is," they are beginning to *experiment. Not until now* do they try out on prey animals movements which they had in a certain sense already learned before killing for the first time, e.g. when manipulating inanimate playthings; *now* the "neck-shape taxis" turns into the deliberately aimed nape bite (p. 214 et seq.). Now the animals *learn* all their widely varying individual methods (Fishing Cats pp. 167–169, Golden Cats p. 169 et seq., Leopard-cat hybrids and Leopard-cats p. 156 et seq., Leopard-cat R_1 hybrid Pudge p. 163, Blackfooted Cats Buster, Griff, and Jake p. 194 et seq.) of using their teeth and paws, outflanking maneuvers and so on to bring prey animals into the most favorable position for the nape bite. In so doing they are *constantly guided* by the innate instinctive movements and taxes, but *replace these* in "earnestly intended" prey-catching *more and more with learned movements.*

Let there be no mistake about this. Constituent patterns of instinctive movements are incorporated into the learned appetitive actions, but a "transformation of an animal's instincts through experience" (Bierens de Haan 1940) is quite out of the question. *The innate fixed patterns are, namely, retained in their pure form and fully functional, alongside all learned actions.* If we ask ourselves how we can distinguish between "type behavior" and learned movements which are very similar in pattern, I should tentatively like to offer the following criterion for the prey-catching actions of the cat. When describing type behavior I have already used expressions such as "blindly" many times. I also said that some discharges of movement were "coordinated in the CNS" [13, 38]. What is at the basis of all this may be formulated roughly as follows in the language of cybernetics (Hassenstein 1960): The steering of the purely instinctive "type process," from the moment the cat stops lying in wait and pounces until the killing bite, is set *exteroceptively before* the pounce and thereafter *hardly adjusted* at all (without prejudice to proprioceptive adjustment). If the prey animal moves in a way or direction not foreseen by the cat when it pounced, the cat usually fails to reach its goal; in such cases it usually makes no attempt whatever at correction but withdraws a little and then, where possible, renews its attack. This sequence of events is the basis of Brehm's report that if a lion fails to catch its prey at the first attempt it is too "ashamed" to continue the chase. In contrast, the *learned movement* can *to a high degree* be *exteroceptively adjusted* throughout its course. Herein lies both its advantage and its disadvantage: Exteroceptive adjustment requires time (if only a fraction of a second) and constant observation—one might almost say "calm consideration." High excitation, as well as the need for lightning action, are therefore incompatible with it. For this reason, the set of purely instinctive patterns does not become superfluous with the parallel development of a set of learned behavior patterns serving the same goal. The animal could not afford a *"transformation of its instincts"* if this meant that they became lost in their original form (see above pp. 205–206). Instead, the instincts build up a system of variable behavior patterns which may be adapted to any situation experienced, *but without merging into this system completely*. They relieve themselves thus of some of the work, but retain the leadership: *Only they* engender appetences—"the consummatory act is always innate" (Craig 1918). This is not splitting hairs, for the statements are supported by neurological experience. Since the investigations of W. R. Hess (1954) we know that the coordination centers of many, perhaps all, instinctive movements in cats and many other mammals lie in the hypothalamus. For even longer it has been known that the coordination of voluntary movements takes place in the area praemotorea of the cortex. The central nervous structures which, after von Holst and Mittelstaedt (1950), in each case emit the complete impulse pattern of a motor sequence and its efferent copy, and which are the sites of the "motoric templates" of voluntary and instinctive movements, are demonstrably a long way apart, at least in the CNS of the mammals. The fact that the two have certain constituent coordinations in common is no argument against this (Leyhausen 1954 a). People have been arguing for a long time about whether particular behavior patterns of an animal are innate or learned, "rigid" or "plastic," and the protagonists of both points of view have put forward good and sometimes irrefutable reasons for their opinion. The only thing that amazes is *why it has never occurred to them that they are not dealing with alternatives but that the two functional modes might exist peacefully side by side in the organism and even in closest cooperation with one another.* At any rate, cats whose development and experiences have been normal have a complete set of pure instinctive movements for prey-catching, and *at the same time* they have a more or less rich store of learned motor patterns, varying according to the individual, which serve the same goal; some, for example the lions, can even learn to share the work out among themselves (pp. 197–198).

The individual prey-catching actions, such as stalking, lying in wait, angling, chasing, or striking, are not always *all* united in an inflexible chain, even when the appetence for killing or eating dominates; some may be missed out or they may be mutually substituted for one another, according to circumstances. Likewise later they may sometimes be exchanged for learned appetitive actions, but sometimes, too, only supported by such learned actions or brought by them into the right starting position for their own run-off. Thus, as described on pp. 216–217, an experienced cat follows every movement of the prey animal with its head in order to get its teeth into the nape, and completely substitutes this learned mode of orientation for the combination of neck-shaped taxis and the approach "diagonally from above and behind"; the cat may also, however, so pull the prey animal to rights with its teeth and paws that it is now able to employ just that combination in ideal conditions. Surprisingly enough, the latter seems harder for the cats to learn than the former. What the reason for this is in detail cannot yet be decided with certainty on the basis of the material available.

To Rempe (in correspondence, 1964) I owe the indication that there are considerable analogies between the interplay described here of the various instinctive actions of one functional system with learned appetitive actions and what is called the sub-routine technique when using electronic calculating machines:—"It is possible to construct complicated programs out of various sub-routines by jumping from the main program into the sub-routines and then, when they are completed, continuing with the main program again, whereby the sub-routines themselves may make use of various other subroutines. Important programs and sub-routines are combined in what are called 'basic programs.' In the case of the X_1 calculating machine, programs of this kind are permanently wired together, for they are in very frequent use; these could be considered as 'innate.' Users of the calculating machine can write short programs which, when they have been fed in (sc. 'acquired'), effect the interplay of various subroutines; in this way completely new calculating programs are created. By means of program sub-division, the course of events in both the permanently wired programs and those temporarily fed in can be varied still further. This interplay between permanently wired and temporarily fed in programs seems to me to be a good model of the cooperation between innate and learned behavior patterns."

7. Play and "drive surplus" ("*Antriebsüberschuss*" Gehlen 1941)

I have already dealt in detail in another paper [51 et seq.] with the particular characteristics of the cat's play with prey. These, taken together with the significance, just discussed, which the instinctive equipment of an animal has for the construction and further broadening of its perceived world, also offer new aspects for the interpretation of play.

In the play of a juvenile cat the individual instinctive movements

of prey-catching appear quite disconnectedly and in constantly varying groupings with one another and with motor patterns from other
functional systems (p. 220) [51, 52], except when the appetence for
killing temporarily welds them together into a chain of appetitive
actions (p. 225). Eibl-Eibesfeldt (1951) made corresponding observations on the play of young squirrels, but still attempted to interpret
these according to the linear hierarchical schemata of Baerends (1941)
and Tinbergen (1950) which run off only in one direction. As Kruijt
(1964) discovered, the fighting actions of young Burmese Red Junglefowl likewise develop singly and with no apparent order at first. He
therefore asks whether the concept of play in animals is not superfluous, and whether the performance of instinctive actions which is
still incomplete and immature may, or even should, be designated
thus at all. This question cannot, however, be framed or answered in
such simple terms. The authors who have dealt in any detail with the
play of animals in recent times (Bally 1945, Eibl-Eibesfeldt 1950, Inhelder 1955 a, b, Meyer-Holzapfel 1956 a, b) all agree that in a typical
case playful and earnest actions differ clearly from one another in the
way they run off (cf. Golden Cat Hanno, pp. 177–178). It proved
possible [52] to interpret one of the designating criteria in accordance
with the dualism between motoric and endogenously automatic function already mentioned on p. 224—and proven also in mammals (von
Holst 1938): Heightened reactivity of the motoric elements toward
the automatically rhythmical impulses leads to "supernormal" amplitude of movement. It is this which causes the exuberance of playful
movements. In this sense I too believe that, in accord with W. R.
Hess (1957), it is necessary to speak of an "unspecific functional readiness," not only of the motor system but of the entire neural system,
rather than of an "unspecific urge for activity" (Meyer-Holzapfel 1956
a) or general drive; this unspecific functional readiness is engendered
and regulated by constant unspecific sensory input and the activity of
the substantia reticularis. *Before readiness can turn into function,*
however, specific impulses are necessary. Heightened functional
readiness is particularly present in juvenile animals and in animals
that are thoroughly rested, well fed, healthy, not too much afflicted by
enemies, and not overstrained socially (e.g. through overpopulation
or crowding). These conditions are most likely to be met in the case
of really well-kept captive animals; and in fact all our cats, including
the obviously senile Serval "S," play with the same intensity if not
the same persistence as juveniles. This is by no means purely a
phenomenon of captivity, however, as the observations of M. Altmann
(1952) show.

It is not my intention to attempt to produce a new, comprehensive theory of play here, but only to throw a little more light on Kruijt's question quoted above. Are playful behavior and instinctive behavior really alternatives? The most blunt affirmation of this seems to come from Meyer-Holzapfel (1956 b): "Play occurs only as long as no genuine instinctive movement has been activated." Eibl-Eibesfeldt (1950) denies that it is play if a young animal produces as yet immature components of an instinctive act or when it works off an accumulated instinct on a substitute object. Bally (1945) defines play as "aimless effort expended in the appetence range" after the "instinctive compulsions have eased off." All these expressions and formulations mean basically the same: They apparently take a "genuine" instinctive act to be an innate sequence of actions which in scarcely modifiable manner serves a "biological purpose" recognizable to a human observer and which as a rule ends with the fulfilment of this purpose. In a chain of instinctive movements which succeed one another as appetitive actions leading to the consummatory act, each link is switched off as soon as the starting situation for the discharge of the next occurs; usually the consummatory act itself does not end as a result of the exhaustion of its action-specific energy but is likewise switched off by consummatory stimuli. In cases where, corresponding with Lorenz's "psychohydraulic model," the single links in such a chain of instinctive actions are all supplied from the same action-specific energy but have different thresholds of elicitation, there is in fact not much room for "play." What evokes the impression of playfulness here is either incomplete discharge (as a result of immaturity, low current level, or too slight stimulation) or the absence of a final switch-off despite the attainment of the "biological goal": Bally emphasizes the almost *infinite repeatabilty* of play actions in contrast to "earnestly intended" instinctive behavior. We come still closer to Bally's views, however, if we also take into consideration the characteristics of the relative hierarchy of appetences dealt with in the last section. Here we have exactly that "easing-off of the instinctive compulsions"! When the component links of a chain of instinctive acts (once perhaps firmly joined together earlier in phylogeny), all propelled by one single action-specific energy, set up on their own, *each* developing its *own* action-specific energy, and when the order and conditions in which they run off are determined by whichever of their single appetences is pressing most urgently at the time, then an "earnest case" can happen only when the appetence toward the act serving the biological goal is dominant. If this is not the case, component actions (if one may still call them so!) may run off independently of one another. These, of course, have no immediate consummatory purpose—they are running off "aimlessly in the appetence range," and they are repeated and persisted with until they are either exhausted or crowded out by other appetences. In other words, the common factor which seems to underlie all the statements by Bally, Eibl-Eibesfeldt, and Meyer-Holzapfel quoted above is the absence of a final switch-off: This these authors consider —in my opinion rightly—as one of the criteria of play. This, however, has nothing whatever to do with whether the play behavior in question at any time consists of instinctive movements or of something else; the two concepts are on completely different planes. An instinctive movement can run off in play and in an earnest biological context. It can be a link in a sequence of appetitive actions or a consummatory act. It can be still immature in a juvenile animal, under inhibition due to a phase of development, or available in fully functional state in the adult animal. *None of these various circumstances makes the slightest change in its character:* It is still an instinctive movement propelled by specific energy (propensity)! But now to quote, of all things, the absence of a final switch-off by consummatory stimuli as a criterion for a behavior pattern not being a "genuine instinctive act" is to stand the problem on its head. Lorenz (1937 a, b), in his new formulation of the concept of instinct, had the "ideal norm" so firmly in mind— and, in the sense of what was said on p. 206, quite rightly so—that he completely overlooked the final switch-off. For many years he and others, including myself, assumed that an instinctive act normally ends as a result of the exhaustion of its action-specific energy. Meanwhile we have become accustomed to regarding a switch-off by consummatory stimuli ("mission completed signal") in biologically earnest performance as "normal" in the sense of the frequency norm ("behavioral median," p. 206) ("attainment blots out arousal," J. von Uexküll 1909); it is in fact a *rare special case, though one of immense theoretical importance,* if the action at some time (almost) completely exhausts its action-specific energy and (mainly) for this reason simply "runs out." In play, however, this special case which, as *"ideal norm," represents a constitutional characteristic of all instinctive movements (as potential),* suddenly also becomes the rule, the frequency norm; is this supposed to be an argument against the instinctive nature of the behavior pattern concerned?!?

Kruijt's inclination (1964) to abandon the concept of play is, however, quite understandable when one follows the further development of fighting in the Burmese Red Junglefowl. Once the complete fighting behavior has appeared for the first time, the playful independence of single associated motor patterns is over and done with, and from this moment on they all behave as links in a chain of instinctive movements with threshold values of different grades, all dependent on the same reservoir of action-specific energy. With the young cat it is different. Even during the relatively short developmental period in which virtually nothing but "pure type behavior" (pp. 220–221) is discharged toward a prey animal, *in the kitten's play* with the mother cat, siblings, and objects the individual movements *retain their independence* in relation to one another, and this *remains so throughout the animal's life.*

This is "expedient," i.e. of adaptive advantage, in that most small cat species feed on relatively small prey animals and thus must hunt many times a day to satisfy their hunger. Very often they fail to catch what they are hunting, and so they must perform catching actions such as lying in wait, stalking, and chasing more frequently than the consummatory acts of killing and eating. Thus, the endogenous propensities of the catching actions must accumulate faster and to a higher level than that of killing not only because they react more easily and must run off more often: *They must develop strong appetences of their own so that even frequent lack of success cannot put the animal off ("extinguish") them.* This alone would already be sufficient reason why catching actions find their satisfaction in their own discharge rather than in the achievement of their ultimate goal. Thus, a substitute object that is anything like suitable can elicit them and keep them in motion almost equally as easily as an adequate one. Naturally it would be quite absurd to assume that a cat which in its daily existence had already killed and eaten thousands of prey animals could not recognize the difference between a mouse and a ball of paper; it knows that a ball of paper is not a mouse just as precisely as it immediately recognizes the difference between a familiar and a new prey animal or between a harmless and a potentially dangerous one. "Substitute objects" can, in fact, become supernormal objects: Sated cats can disport themselves with these in the most intensive catching games while at the same time the "adequate" mice are running around under their very noses! In other cases, for reasons described in greater detail above, the final switch-off does not function on the adequate object: When a cat has chased and seized a mouse, it now "ought" to kill; as proved many times in part III, however, it by no means always does so, but may instead release it again and chase it afresh, and this many times in succession [53]. If at intervals it catches the animal, picks it up in its teeth, and carries it around, it deliberately does this in such as way as not to injure it; it does not *want* to kill it (Leopard-cat hybrids, p. 159, Leopard-cats, p. 167). As the Golden Cat Nova proves, an experienced animal is quite capable of distinguishing precisely between a carrying grip and a killing bite in other connections as well.

All the processes discussed so far are automatically explained by the varying endogenous rhythmicity of the different prey-catching actions. There is, however, one more factor involved. As shown in section 6, when the cat is experienced learned appetitive actions may partially or wholly replace the instinctive ones when the hierarchy of the process is dominated by the appetence for killing and eating. The more successful the learned appetitive actions are and the more a cat learns of them, the more rarely will the corresponding instinctive actions be used in an earnest complete performance of the whole functional system. For the reasons just discussed, however, precisely these catching actions have particularly "intensive" endogenous rhythmicity and their action-specific energies therefore relatively quickly reach a current level which makes discharge an urgent necessity. As a result their associated appetences appear in accordance with the individual rhythm of the single action and without any concern for one another. Consequently the cat now "plays" with harmless prey animals and substitute objects in exactly the same way as a still "innocent" kitten.

In the case of the juvenile cat, the single prey-catching actions appear "aimlessly in the appetence range" because the dominant appetence toward killing in the sense of the "biological purpose" has not yet matured and so *they are not yet in its service*. In the case of a cat experienced with prey, they do likewise because they are now to a certain extent *relieved of this service* and must seek satisfaction elsewhere. In both cases it is play in the sense that it is not serving any direct "biological purpose," that the animals pursue it eagerly and persistently, expend a great deal of energy in the process and get nothing out of it except "the fun of the thing." Naturally this has a number of indirect effects such as exercising the sensomotor system, strengthening the musculature, stimulating growth of the bone structure and internal organs, and much else. This is also true of all human motoric games, but no one doubts their playful nature for that reason. It is, of course, always possible to argue over definitions, but Bally's view that inexhaustible repetition is a fundamental characteristic of play seems to me to be correct: If occasionally an immature motor pattern appears and is in reality nothing but a premature "attempt" at the earnest act, it usually gets no further than more or less recognizable intention movements; and if it is immediately repeated, then with diminishing intensity, but usually there are fairly long pauses between the single discharges. All this does not solve the dilemma in a concrete individual instance when it is necessary to decide whether it is a case of "genuine" play or how much playfulness is involved. The boundaries are not clear-cut and often—for example, in the case of the Burmese Red Junglefowl—the question will simply have to be left open. But on account of the cases where there is doubt, we should not deny those where there is none and start dispensing with the concept of play altogether.

In this connection a further misunderstanding should be clarified: According to Lorenz the final "goal" of an instinctive movement consists not so much in the attainment of consummatory stimuli as in the pleasure of being discharged for its own sake. Eibl-Eibesfeldt (1950) interprets this as meaning that "pleasure" may not be employed as a criterion of play, since basically all instinctive movements, including those performed in an earnest context, have overtones of pleasure. This is extending Lorenz's statement too far. Very often when instinctive movements run off not as consummatory acts but in the service of a dominant appetence, they are *far from having overtones of pleasure.* There is certainly no pleasure in fleeing from an attacking carnivore, but only in the "need-dependent state of rest" (Holzapfel 1940) in which successful flight ends. Of course, once flight has brought the animal out of range of the danger, it may be continued for longer than necessary out of pure enjoyment of running. As an escape game, however, it is enjoyment from the very start—and may occasionally turn into frightened, earnest flight without perceptible reason! If elicitation does not occur for a very long time, flight may even develop appetence: An animal incites its superior predator "out of sheer high spirits" just so that it can run away from it, as Spurway (1953) describes of the relationship between some cats and dogs in large cities. Likewise, earnestly intended prey-catching is often not pleasant for the carnivore; it is much too afraid of prey capable of defending itself for that to be the case. Only the consummatory act in each instance—killing or eating—has overtones of pleasure. *A strong appetence is, therefore, capable of eliciting appetitive actions which may run off only "unwillingly" against very great external and internal inhibitions.* Between a run-off which has overtones of pleasure and one which decidedly has none there are, of course, transitional stages. Thus a Golden Cat which at the moment has no desire but to eat seems to find it excessively annoying when the rat does not willingly let itself be bitten dead right away. At a different time and in a different mood, it gives it obvious pleasure to make a game of this and to delay killing for as long as possible (pp. 175, 178). Instinctive movements which run off in the appetence range may have overtones of pleasure, but must not necessarily; the more directly and powerfully the appetence toward the consummatory act controls the whole procedure and limits it to brief purposefulness, the more the pleasure is concentrated on the consummatory act and the more unpleasant the things can be that the animal will put up with on its way there. In these facts lies the oldest and no doubt also the most important evolutionary root of all work and all effort undertaken "voluntarily," in other words of "duty." Banishment from Paradise began with the development of the first central nervous system. However, instinctive movements which are performed not as appetitive actions and not with a view to attaining an object or consummatory state, but purely because their action-specific energy has accumulated to such high pressure that it "bubbles over," are always extremely enjoyable; in inexhaustibly protracted play both animals and humans extract from their effector systems heights of performance which in appetence toward a "purpose" they would be capable of executing only in an extreme emergency or under the most rigid compulsion, but never "voluntarily," let alone with pleasure as well.

Anything with such strong overtones of pleasure naturally develops powerful appetences which cause the animal actively to seek out or manufacture play situations. The latter is of particular importance. Everyone knows how cats prod small playthings into motion with a forepaw or propel them along in front of them. A small object running away, however, is the sign stimulus for chasing. A young cat soon grasps the connection, and when it feels like playing "chase" it looks for something suitable and sets it in motion. Often in the process an emotional bond is developed with particular playthings which are capable of being incentives to play far superior to the "adequate" natural objects (p. 232). For example, we gave the male Fishing Cat (p. 167) a large, yellow plastic ball, which meanwhile has become holed like a sieve from his canine teeth, has taken on an almost indescribable shape and is now quite impossible to clean and therefore horribly unhygienic. But it is quite irreplaceable. When we tried to set the female Fishing Cat with the male, he allowed her to investigate everything in his cage and walk everywhere, and he watched peacefully from a shelf as she did so, but when she dared to sniff cautiously at the "ball" she almost paid for it with her life: The male stormed down at her and bit her furiously in the nape (it was certainly no copulation grip or mating intentions!). Fortunately all this took place at the front of the cage and we had removed the cage wire in order to film them. As a result the two animals fell out into the lower lying

gangway and as they did so Fishy let go, but only this made it possible
for us to separate them again. In the case of the Servals, the dis-
integrating rags of what was once an almost football-sized red rubber
ball is held in similar, if not quite so extremely high esteem. A "beloved" plaything of this sort can be replaced by a new one only if the
old one is left there too until the new one . . . has become "old"! It
is a well-known fact that human children establish similarly strong
bonds toward favorite toys. Parents concerned about hygiene who
replace an old, three-legged, headless, scratched wooden horse with
a gleaming new one and simultaneously take "that ugly old thing"
away should not expect thanks: They are committing an act of great
cruelty. It should not be said that as regards the animals these cases
are all "products of captivity." Conditions in captivity may favor some
activities and repress still more, but with the exception of decided
stress symptoms and neuroses an animal will scarcely do something in
captivity it would not be equally capable of doing in its natural surroundings.

We are taken a step further by the angling play of the Servals described on pp. 178–197. They carry a mouse or sometimes even a
plaything to a hole or crevice and push it in, simply to be able to
"fish." Thus, the animals must be able to bring together two objects
which were not simultaneously in their field of vision at the start and
manipulate them appropriately before they can play their game. In
manufacturing such special play situations, an animal learns to perform movements and to do things which in the biologically purposive
discharge of a chain of appetitive actions would be not merely unnecessary but positively senseless—for example, having pulled the
mouse out, to push it into the hole again instead of killing and eating
it. *Here, in other words, attainment does not blot out arousal.* Thus,
in play an animal constructs for itself a far greater range of experiences with movements and objects than it would if it always acted
only under the directional compulsion of obtaining merely its basic
requirements for living. How far this can already go in the case of cats
is shown by the following observation: Smudge (Leopard-cat R_1 hybrid, p. 160) had used the sawdust-filled toilet box and was covering
in the hollow he had previously dug out. As his scraping forepaw
reached out, the back of it struck the "dune" of heaped-up sawdust,
and some of the sawdust flew up and outward in a fan shape. Smudge
at once paused, stretched his head forward and looked over the rim
of the box. Then he repeated the same movement three or four times,
setting his paw down each time and observing the effect attentively.
In other words, he was not shaking his paw but making intentional,

clearly separated single movements. Then he was satisfied and went on covering in his hollow. Never before have I seen a cat push or prod something away with the back of its paw, nor do I know of any connection or functional context in which something of this kind happens innately. The animal had noticed a chance and quite certainly unintended effect of a movement, been interested by it, and was capable of recognizing which movement produced it and then repeating this several times with conscious intent. This signifies no more and no less than that a *mammal of the developmental level of the cat already knows how to make a genuine experiment,* and so it was quite consciously that I spoke of "experimenting" on p. 225. This is not simply "trial and error" in the sense of classical behaviorism, where the first trial is blind and the probability of error therefore equal to chance. This first "trial" was already preceded by a comprehension, however limited, of the connection between events; not only did the animal *expect* a particular result, but as a consequence of its "experimental awareness" this result was *more probable than error.*

C. O. Whitman (1919) stated that the breakup of instinct, though itself not yet intelligence, opens the gate through which "that great teacher Experience enters." This has almost always been understood only in the one sense that anywhere in the sequence of actions of a functional system where a *gap* in the innate develops, a *loss* of instinct occurs, experience and learning must fill this gap so that the functional system becomes complete again. Here, however, we have a quite different way in which instincts could break up. As I have already hinted on p. 230, the individual instincts of prey-catching have probably evolved as a result of the single links of a chain of instinctive movements originally dependent on one single source of action-specific energy becoming emancipated, growing more highly differentiated in the process, and each acquiring action-specific energy of its own. What previously had been a sequence of stages of unitary appetence toward a consummatory goal now disintegrates into many individual appetences, each of which leads a (relatively) independent life of its own. The gain to the animal is that its "interests" are broadened and multiplied far beyond anything it would need to aspire to or experience if all it were striving after were the fulfilment of the "biological consummatory purpose" of the functional system as a whole. *Perhaps it is precisely this kind of "breakup of instinct" where, as with the Hydra of Lerna, seven new heads (=relatively independent instincts) grow when one is cut off, the most important factor in the whole of mammalian evolution.* It may be that invertebrates are, at least in the main, obliged to "stop gaps" with the help of experience, learning, and insight. Whereas they are all really subject (completely or largely) to the alternative "instinct *or* experience," the mammals achieved the combination "instinct *and* experience," the continuous enrichment and broadening of their perceptual world, under the direction of their propensities, the pressure of appetences from increasingly numerous individual instincts. Perhaps one of the reasons why the mammals "had" to develop such an enormous neopallium was in order to have room for the two kinds of motoric templates without having to sacrifice one or the other.

Gehlen (1941) has developed the theory of the human drive surplus. He too imagines that man is characterized by *loss* of instinct and is a deficient creature as regards his innate equipment. He considers that the drive surplus arises because the drives are no longer "tied to instincts," i.e. specific and linked to precisely defined motoric achievements; to Gehlen drive is something which creates and intensifies itself incessantly within sensomotoric cyclic processes, which becomes specific only in the course of its own activity and in this gradually changes, a kind of *perpetuum mobile*. But let us consider the question afresh in the light of what has been said here, taking into account that already in the case of higher mammals a considerable surplus of propensities can arise *not* through *loss* of instinct but *precisely through the multiplicity* of individual instincts, and that these latter do not become exhausted solely in the service of one functional system but strive after their own activation for their own sake. The conclusion now becomes obvious that the human "drive" surplus likewise owes its origin to a similar process of evolution. Thus, a study of the mammals brings our view of the propensity structure of man in a wide circle roughly back to the theoretical position of McDougall (1933, 1947), though, of course, many details have been clarified and corrected and many more must still be.

A viewpoint which comes very close to the facts portrayed here has been upheld by O. Koenig for many years: "Man is the specialist in learning and thinking on account of the large number of innate 'pre-programmed units' he possesses" (1962, p. 124). In this, however, he is referring rather more to the motoric templates in the narrow sense and scarcely at all to the special propensity functions underlying them (l.c. p. 120 et seq.); he considers that the single "units" may be combined almost at will. However, the rules governing changes in combination of units depend largely, though not exclusively, on the autonomous rhythmicity of the individual propensities and on their regulative relationships to one another, and it is *this which is the essence of the relative hierarchy of moods.*

If someone again asks, in doubt or despair, "Where is the process to stop?", the answer can only be supplied by evolution itself. There is no need to fear that in the course of further splintering the instinctive movements with a propensity energy of their own—those "component units emancipated from the whole" (Lorenz 1950 b)—might become infinitesimally small. It was not without intent that on p. 237 I compared the process of evolution in question with the mythical ability of the Hydra of Lerna to *grow* several heads in the place of one: It is not merely a question of splintering into several individual propensities, but parallel to this (in fact probably to some extent in advance) a process of growth and differentiation takes place. The primitive carnivore's act of running up and biting aimlessly first had to be broken down into lying in wait, stalking, chasing, pouncing, angling, the killing bite, etc., at the same time as or before the individual propensities began to become independent. *It is therefore extremely important that the phylogenesis of the relative hierarchy of moods dealt with here should not be confused with the evolution of the voluntary motor system,* which extends its influence to include ever finer motor elements—in the case of the mammals, parallel with the development of the pyramidal tracts. The fact that instinctive and voluntary motor systems often have common final pathways of considerable "length" is something I have already emphasized on p. 227. In the case of the highest mammals the voluntary motor system is capable of isolating small motoric elements and making new combinations of them with others in such a way that one could practically call them completely new learned movements, although strictly speaking 'new' applies only to the combination and not to the elements. In another paper (1954 a) I have dealt in detail with this developmental path taken by the voluntary motor system, its connection with the phenomena of relative coordination and especially the role of magnetic influence (von Holst, l.c.) in this, and both the common factors and the differences between learned movement sequences which have been made into automatic functions and instinctive movements with endogenous rhythmical propensities.

The evolutive differentiation described here and the consequent relativization of their hierarchical order does not necessarily affect all the instinct (=functional) systems of a mammal, and its extent in those affected is no doubt varied. Which systems are involved in each case must first be established in respect of every species. And however typical of the higher mammals these phenomena may be, it will certainly not be possible to regard them as their monopoly. A closer look will reveal something comparable in other vertebrate groups as well; Hinde's example of the nest-building of the canary will not be the only one.[5] However, the higher mammals are *the* animals for investigating and learning things, and wherever a special diversity of interests and inclinations to learn is found in them it will be necessary *not to assume, as hitherto, that there has been a loss of instinct, but to conclude that they possess a particularly finely differentiated system of instincts with relative hierarchy,* and to search for this.

It is the diversity of the propensity system which alone gives the adaptive functions experience, learning, and insight a point, *a field of application.* What should an animal do with such capacities as these if nothing "urged" it to apply them in this, that, and a score of other directions? Gehlen and others who, like him, deny the instinctive nature of the propensity system are therefore obliged to postulate that every capacity already contains the urge for activation within itself and in the state of being active creates fresh urge toward fresh activity; a propensity system of its own with a specific structure seems to them to be theoretically superfluous. This assumption is, however, inaccurate, as can be seen from the cats of Roberts and Kiess already quoted several times (pp. 213, 222, 225). If one resorts to the idea of a general reservoir of drive, the energies from which would first have to be "canalized" (i.e. rendered specific) by the constant demands of the environment, such a behavioral construction would theoretically be possible: An animal organized in this way might perhaps "function." It would, however, lack any spontaneity and autonomy in relation to the environment and to the periodically recurring internal stimuli of its elementary needs. In other words, a form of organization such as this would be as far removed from "freedom of action" as a mechanical cigarette vendor. At any rate, the propensity structure of higher animals and above all the mammals, including man, is not constructed in this way. In their case, rather, the "energy budget" of the propensity system is already divided up under "headings" according to a "plan of requirements," which was worked out during phylogeny and fixed by natural selection, *before* the detailed demands of the here and now of the external world are submitted to the individual.[6] What Gehlen (l.c.) calls "universal receptivity" arises not as a consequence of a *tabula rasa* encountering a chaotic flood of stimuli from a limitless perceptual world. It arises because in an ordered cosmos the evolutionary interaction between organism and environment has selectively bred an increasingly comprehensive, increasingly differentiated array of "implements" for mastering the environment. This alone makes the individual animal capable of investigating and comprehending the world in which it lives and finally, within the animal's limits, having it at its command. *The instinctive equipment is part of this array, and in fact the most important part because the instincts alone provide spontaneous propensities* and in this way raise the organism above the level of a stimulus-reaction-machine, making it to a certain degree autonomous in relation to the world it has to master.

Mammals, particularly the highly developed ones, learn so much and such a wide variety more than other animals because they possess so many different propensities which cannot be fully consumed in biologically earnest pursuits. And only because it is propensities that are "idle" in the sense described which cause a mammal to learn, does it learn so much that is "useless"; for what use is it to a Serval if it knows how to get a mouse it has fished out back into a hole? Would a unitary "food drive" be likely to produce such an absurdity? If it were not for the many emancipated single propensities, how should an animal ever *be able* to learn anything other than is necessary for mere self-preservation and continued existence? Biologists, doctors, psychologists, and philosophers continue to disseminate the idea that the higher mammals, and particularly the higher primates and man, are deficient in instinct. The idea owes its origin and its stubborn hold on life to the obsession with thinking in alternatives criticized on p. 227. As far as the mammals are concerned, however, evolution has done one thing *and* the other.

V. SUMMARY

1. New observations and experiments on the predatory behavior of 15 species of *Viverridae* and *Felidae* are presented as a complement to results published earlier (1956 a). The development of predation in young cats and in adults reared without relevant experience has been extensively filmed for detailed analysis, and results are compared (pp. 146–199).

2. In the course of phylogeny, aggressive biting in carnivores developed differentially into "seizing bite" and "killing bite." In the more advanced viverrids and the cats, seizing has become increasingly a function of the forelimbs, whilst biting is progressively specialized for killing. This evolutionary process is paralleled by the canine teeth

which, by their structure, shape, and position in the jaws, have become well adapted to being wedged between the vertebrae of a prey animal's neck. The vertebrae are thus disconnected and the hind brain or spinal cord is lacerated, which results in instantaneous death. Feline canine teeth are quite unsuitable for crunching hard bones or piercing large blood vessels (pp. 199–202).

3. All carnivorous and many insectivorous mammals, after seizing small prey objects with their teeth, are in the habit of throwing them away with a sideways swing of the head. If the prey is not released at the end of the swing, it is only shaken. This is the reason why genets and some *Felidae* shake their prey, if at all, asymmetrically to one side only. The function is to stun the labyrinthine reflexes of the prey and thus immobilize it momentarily; this gives the predator a chance to release and improve its grip without interference from the attacked animal. From this common root, vigorous side-to-side shaking of prey animals has probably been developed independently by several groups of carnivores, e.g. the large civets and the *Canidae*. This "death-shake" causes the dens epistrophei to injure the hind brain: Breathing stops, and if the shake is very intensive the neck is broken. No cat species has ever been known to kill in this way (pp. 202–204).

4. Haas (1962) has shown that, in certain stress situations, some species of bumblebee abandon species-specific behavior patterns in favor of others which normally occur in closely related, more primitive, or even more progressive species. In principle, he concludes, each species is in command of the behavior patterns of the whole genus, and consequently he speaks of "generic behavior" when an individual performs a pattern normally performed only by individuals of another species. The same is true of the various chains of instinctive movements a cat may employ when catching prey. The phylogenetically ancient patterns, however, have higher thresholds and occur only if the recent and more specialized patterns are obstructed by some internal or external factor(s). In this context, the question arises of what should be regarded as the normal behavior of a species in a given situation. Three parameters of "normality" are suggested: a) "Behavioral range" covers all behavior patterns an individual of a given species might perform in a set situation; b) "behavioral median" denotes those patterns of the behavioral range which are performed most frequently in that situation; c) "ideal norm" or "type behavior" is used to describe the undistorted performance of the most specialized, species-specific pattern adequate to the situation. Since a naturally occurring situation is seldom free of disturbing factors, type behavior can as a rule be observed only rarely or under exceptional

circumstances. Nevertheless it is of the utmost theoretical importance. "Type" in this context should not be confused with the concept of type in systematics (pp. 204–208).

5. Cats without previous experience are usually unable to kill when first encountering a prey animal, because they do not bite strongly enough. To achieve a bite of sufficient strength for killing, the cat has to become highly excited through prolonged and repeated play with the prey, or—as is normally the case—through additional stimulation from a source other than the prey itself. In the young cat this additional stimulation is usually provided by mother or siblings competing for the prey. If additional stimulation is lacking, the prolonged process by which the cat works itself up to a level of excitation sufficient for killing may look deceptively like a learning curve. Adult cats reared without predatory experience follow much the same pattern with the exception that their excitational threshold is higher and so they need stronger stimulation. Social ranking, among other factors, greatly influences the speed with which an individual develops into a perfect killer.—The way the killing bite "clicks into place" after only one or very few successful attempts is comparable to the imprinting process which determines the object a duckling will subsequently follow as its "mother." In both cases, the "sensitive periods" seem to be delimited in very similar ways.—Neurophysiological investigations have shown that the killing bite is mediated through other neural structures than those responsible for different types of biting.—Once established, the killing bite will continue to develop its own appetite, though this may in the long run tend to atrophy unless reinforced by the animal eating the prey it has killed. Reinforcement at long intervals is quite sufficient to keep the killing appetite functional (pp. 208–214).

6. The concept of "innate behavior patterns" as defined by Lorenz (1961) is used throughout. There is no basis for the allegation, put forward by some authors, that the use of the term "innate" implies that a behavior pattern thus designated has no developmental history (p. 214).

7. Primitive carnivores bite indiscriminately into any part of their victim's body. Some species, however, e.g. *Nandinia, Viverricula,* and *Viverra,* have a more or less pronounced tendency to bite toward the front end. Genets and cats clearly aim their bites toward the contraction formed by the neck between the head and shoulders of a mammal. This "neck-shape taxis" is innate. By means of this taxis and the preference for pouncing down on the back of the prey from behind, a young cat succeeds in biting the nape of the neck in most of its

first serious attempts at killing prey. It then quickly grasps the advantages of biting the nape rather than other parts of the neck, and soon it has learned to aim its bite purposely and exclusively at the nape. This learned orientation is an entirely new mechanism, not a modification or adaptation of the innate neck-shape taxis, which persists unaltered. The cat henceforth has the choice of either way of orientating its killing bite (pp. 210–214; pp. 227–228).

8. The instinctive movements of predation (lying in wait, crouching, stalking, pouncing, seizing, "angling") are performed independently of one another by the playing cat, in varied combination with each other and with activities derived from instinctive systems other than predation. Only when and if the appetites for killing and/or eating dominate may the other instinctive acts be linked into an appetitive sequence resembling what Tinbergen describes as a "major instinct" (1950). In fact, there is no such unitary mechanism of predation (pp. 219–220).

9. Lorenz's "psychohydraulic model" (1950 c) still seems to fit these very complicated phenomena best. Not only are his concepts of "action-specific energy," "level of specific readiness," "mood," "appetite," "accumulation," and "discharge" (sc. of action-specific energy) extremely useful for describing the observed phenomena correctly; there is also increasing evidence that their basis actually consists of specific neuro-secretive processes interposed between the purely neuronal ones (pp. 217–219).

10. It is often claimed that "operational thinking" is the only way of thinking permissible to a scientist. True as this principle is for purely experimental work, it is not at all obligatory and, indeed, often detrimental when it comes to fitting the detailed results of experiments into a wider theoretical frame. Only when the theory is put to the test—as it inevitably must be—does operational thinking come into its own again. Moreover, the scientific value of a theory depends less on the condition that it must immediately suggest viable operations for testing it, than on its power to offer a consistent explanation for a greater number of facts than the previous theory did (p. 218).

11. Each instinctive act of the predation system has its own endogenous rhythm of accumulation and discharge of action-specific energy. The action-specific energy for killing shows slower accumulation than those of the other patterns, and it is "need-dependent" (triebabhängig) in the sense in which Precht (1958) uses the term. The instinctive energy which happens to be "dammed up" most at a given moment creates the strongest appetite and tends to produce appetitive behavior toward its consummation. The appetitive behavior

may make use of any of the other instinctive patterns if this helps to bring about the desired situation for the release of the instinct which is the "goal" of the appetite. Thus the hierarchy between the instinctive acts of predation never ceases to change; it is a "relative hierarchy" only, and there is no irreversible sequence as shown in the hierarchy diagrams of Baerends (1941) and Tinbergen (1950). This, of course, does not mean that such rigid hierarchies may not be found in other animals—as in fact they can—or even in the same animal for a different system of instincts. "Relative hierarchy of moods" is a progressive feature characteristic of mammalian evolution. It may be more widespread than is suspected at present, but is almost certainly not universal (pp. 220–223; p. 229).

12. The allegation that energy models of drives and their complex interaction have ceased to be useful is ill-founded. There is no satisfactory alternative theoretical model which fits the facts so well (pp. 223–225).

13. After a cat has caught, killed, and eaten one or several prey animals and has thus experienced the causal connection between these three activities and the provision of food, it starts experimenting with the appetitive links of the chain and gradually fits learned appetitive patterns in the place of innate ones. These learned patterns vary considerably, both between species and between individuals of the same species. As with the orientation of the killing bite, it is again not a matter of modifying and adapting an instinctive pattern by grafting learned elements on to it; there is no question of "transformation of instincts through experience" (Bierens de Haan 1940). The instinctive patterns remain independent and unaffected, and the acquired patterns are "stored" in addition. The dualism of motor programming, in the area praemotorea of the cortex and in the hypothalamus respectively, is well-known to neurophysiologists. The cooperation and mutual interchangeability of innate and learned motor patterns have a precise parallel in some methods of programming electronic computers (pp. 225–228).

14. Instinctive acts may be either appetitive or consummatory, and the animal performing them may mean business or play, but none of this affects or alters the basic nature of the instinctive act. In its "proper" biological context, an instinctive act is normally switched off by "consummatory stimuli," but in play it may repeat itself until its action-specific energy is virtually exhausted. Even consummatory stimuli, although occurring repeatedly in the course of play, may fail to switch the playful act off (pp. 228–233).

15. Whether an animal is or is not capable of employing a certain

instinctive act as play, and whether the whole system of instincts to which this particular act belongs has fully matured yet or not, are two entirely separate questions, and the answer to the one has no bearing on the other. The fact that in some species play apparently comes to a stop once the instinctive systems have fully developed is no reason to conclude that this is the case in all species and that therefore the concept of play is no longer valid. There will, of course, always be cases when it is difficult or impossible to decide whether the activities observed should be classified as play or merely as immaturity of an instinct, especially as the two are not mutually exclusive (pp. 233–234).

16. The performance of an instinctive act is not self-rewarding under all circumstances. If it is serving as an appetitive act to the fulfilment of a momentarily dominant appetite, it may be carried out with indifference or even downright disgust. In play, however, the act is always performed "for its own sake," and this is a pleasure (pp. 234–235).

17. Some predatory instincts accumulate their respective action-specific energy faster than others. Accordingly they develop strong appetites after only short periods of disuse, and if not "adequately" released they tend to discharge in play. Since it is precisely these instincts which, in the "proper" biological context, are sometimes replaced by learned appetitive patterns, the animals are obliged to work them off on substitute objects. This often creates strong ties of affection toward some favorite plaything. Many individuals are very ingenious in seeking out or reproducing a particular play situation or even creating a new one. In doing so they learn far more than they ever would if they could employ their instinctive movements exclusively along the "one-way street" of an unalterable sequence rigidly confined to a "biologically relevant" situation. As it is, they enrich the scope of their experience and the range of their skills in many diverse ways (pp. 235–237).

18. The emancipation of the individual instinctive acts out of an instinctive system, the "endowment" of each with its own action-specific energy, and the ensuing ability of each, under certain conditions, to develop its own appetite regardless of the activity level of the others, seems to be an essential characteristic of mammalian evolution. Since the individual instinctive acts have no immediate biological goal—the goal, in this case provision of food, being only a factor of the system as a whole, i.e. when it is temporarily dominated by hunger—they provide the mammal with a "surplus" of undirected (though by no means unspecific!) propensities which cause it to col-

lect experiences of a far more general nature than would be necessary for mere self-preservation and the propagation of the species. This evolutionary process is paralleled by, and in part promotes, another process, in the course of which mammals gain ever better voluntary control of ever smaller motor units. The pyramidal motor system, however, derives its meaning and purpose entirely and exclusively from the relative multiplicity and diversity of mammalian instincts. There is certainly no justification for the belief that, in comparison with insects, fishes, and birds, mammals, especially the higher mammals, have fewer instincts. If anything they have more. The effects of so-called "self-domestication" apart, man himself is no exception to this general tendency of mammalian evolution (pp. 237–241).

10 *On the Natural History of Fear (1967)*

I. THE MOTIVATIONAL NATURE OF FEAR

The philosopher H. Kunz, Basle, recently (1965) attempted to interpret the phenomenon of fear roughly as follows: Admittedly there are always a number of factors, psychological as well as physiological in nature, at work in causing actual, concrete fears; the cardinal source (not the experienced but the essential one) of the phenomenon of fear as a whole, however, is man's mortality. It is by no means a matter of fear of death, of having to die; mortality is simply a constitutional characteristic of everything living and insofar the essence of fear, not however its cause or reason.

To traditional philosophical thinking as well as to a psychology and psychotherapy largely oriented toward subjective experience and life history, these words must seem irredeemably paradoxical. However, if we translate them—N.B. *without making the slightest change in content*—into the language of the biologist who thinks in terms of evolution, we come upon very revealing circumstances: Death, in the sense of being *bound* to die, threatens all multicellular organisms; in the sense of being *capable* of dying it also threatens all unicellular organisms, as well as the germ line of the multicellular organisms and thus the species. This latter, however, can survive only if either a sufficient number of individuals escapes death (in the pedigree of a paramecium living now there has never been a corpse!) or if, in the case of multicellular organisms, an adequate number of individuals lives long enough to pass on the germ line to the next generation. Thus anything which prevents dying or delays it *just a little* helps the species immensely in its struggle for existence. Many organisms simply "rely" for this on their enormous fertility: Even in the most unfavorable event the number of progeny surviving will still be enough to maintain the species and to reproduce. However, the life expectation of the individual animal is obviously far better if it can actively keep away or withdraw from sources of possible danger to life, instead of passively submitting to its statistical chance of survival. Thus, the more highly developed and smaller in numbers an animal species is and the longer its progeny takes to become capable of reproduction, the more important this becomes. However, the individual does not need to know about death in order to succeed in escaping it, at least temporarily: A mouse probably lives longer if it shies away from crossing an open space offering no cover in daylight than it would if it knew that it eventually must die. In other words: Mortality did and does offer natural selection the starting-point, i.e. the essential prerequisite, it needed in order to breed in many—but certainly not all!—organisms various forms of avoidance and escape behavior and numerous, sometimes very specialized, associated releasing mechanisms (see below). But this mortality itself does not figure in the (conscious or unconscious) "motivation" of any of these behavior patterns, at least not primarily. If the mouse feared, so to speak, in the abstract "for its life," instead of fearing specific things such as bright light, that (un-mouselike) rustling in the leaves, the shadow (of a bird of prey) sweeping toward it, the alarm sounds of other mice, lack of cover, the cat, or a stronger mouse, it would first have to have experienced each of these situations as potentially fatal before it could react appropriately to it. And since mice have no abstract language and tradition for passing on experiences to others, it would be obliged to learn its own lessons and would already be dead after the first. For human children, too, it would certainly be very dangerous if they were not afraid of many things *before* they learn from teaching and from their own observation to comprehend the connection between danger and death and then secondarily to be genuinely afraid of death. Apart from all this, in the interests of the survival of the species it is most important that an animal should be afraid, not only in situations that are genuinely a danger to life, but also and particularly in those many others which have only an indirect effect on the expectation of life or prospects of reproduction. Thus, in general in free-ranging conditions the stronger mouse does not directly threaten the life of the weaker one; the dread felt by the weaker one, however, keeps it at a distance and thus normally contributes to limiting population density. As we know from experimental investigations, the expectation of life and the reproductive capacity of the individual mouse diminish considerably when too many are obliged to live in too limited space (cf. Wynne-Edwards 1962).

Thus, between the conditions and factors which offer natural selection a starting-point and propel evolution forward and the adaptations (including specific modes of behavior and experience) to the environment (including the social environment) which organisms consequently develop there need be no *present* causal and functional connection. Kunz's statement therefore only *seems* paradoxical. Fear owes its phylogenetic origin (among other factors) to the mortality of all organisms. But its actualization in each case, its dynamics and its relationship to the environment, its entire phenomenology, reveal no trace of this. The evolution of behavior and experience connected with fear lies far back in a past which the individual can neither survey nor comprehend. It is for *this* reason that fear contains that irrational element of the a priori which time and again lures some philosophers and depth psychologists into ingenious but misguided speculations.

There are, then, functional properties of the phenomenon of fear which evolution delivers ready-made along with each individual; the individual must accept them as he must the form of his cranial bones or the hingelike function of his elbow joint, without being able to do anything to change them. These functional properties are innate in a sense which I shall define below, but before we discuss them in detail there is one more thing I should like to mention. As I have said above, actively avoiding or fleeing from dangers offers the *individual* better prospects of survival than passivity. It does, however, also contain the possibility of doing the wrong thing. A forest fire either reaches and destroys a particular oak tree or, for reasons which have nothing to do with the oak, it spares the spot where the oak stands. The oak tree cannot save itself from actual danger, but what it also cannot do as the flames approach is leave the spot which only *seems* to it to be endangered and flee to a place it *thinks* is safe but where the fire then in fact overtakes it; it is equally incapable of rushing straight into the flames in blind panic. A stag "can" do all this. In other words, to "err" (in the broadest sense) is not only human, it is quite simply animal, and is bound up with the capacity for locomotion in much the same sense as fear is bound up with mortality.

The above-mentioned functional properties of the phenomenon of fear, the dynamics of behavior and experience connected with fear, correspond to those of an instinct according to the definition given by K. Lorenz (1937 a, b), the main points of which I shall enumerate briefly; a detailed survey and literature may be found in my recent review (1965 b). An instinct consists of a motor pattern (or a sequence of these) which, like a melody, may be transposed into all possible "keys" but is always recognizable as this particular motoric discharge; like the melody, the instinctive movement is a genuine *zeitgestalt*. The readiness to perform it depends not on external stimuli, situations, or objects, but obeys an endogenous periodicity largely independent of specific external stimuli. Likewise this *readiness* is reduced again by the discharge of the motor pattern associated with it and *not* by the attainment of an external goal or object, even in cases where such consummatory stimuli may switch off the *motor pattern*. The endogenously rhythmical fluctuations in the "availability" of instinctive movements reveal dynamics similar to those of some endocrine processes. When, for example, the adrenal gland suddenly releases its store of adrenaline into the bloodstream, this initially stimulates the rapid production and release of still more adrenaline— in certain circumstances considerably more than the amount normally stored. This continuously increases the effect and then holds it at a steady level for some time. Eventually, however, production of the hormone is exhausted and the external effects gradually disappear. A purely neural occurrence displays none of these procedural characteristics. They may all, however, be observed often when instinctive movements are discharged. As has emerged from experiments by Michael (1960, 1962 a, b), the hormones themselves must not be regarded as the direct internal agents causing the instinctive movements; only in certain cases are they assigned an intermediate role (for details of the connection between the discharge of adrenaline and the phenomenon of fear see below under "fright"). Nowadays, therefore, it is concluded that there are instinct-specific excitatory substances, similar to hormones, produced by the brain; these would build up according to their own rhythm, accumulate, be released "when needed," and expended in the discharge of the associated instinctive movements, whereby in many—perhaps all—cases the discharge concerned at first intensifies considerably, like the discharge of adrenaline, as a result of positive feedback.

The biological functions of such a system of specific propensities, supplied from the rhythmic accumulation and discharge of specific excitatory substances, are as follows:—

1. Propensity reserves are created which ensure that "in case of need" the behavior pattern concerned will be persisted with even in the face of obstacles until the biologically necessary success has been attained, without the individual needing to have any subjective knowledge of this necessity or striving after this success as a goal.

2. As well as hormones, unspecific afferent impulses probably at least partially affect the production of specific excitatory substances. In relation to these and perhaps other irregular influences dependent on chance external conditions, the excitatory substances would have roughly the same function as the spring of a self-winding watch: namely, to transform the impulses arriving irregularly into an ordered, constant flow of energy.

1 and 2, then, ensure a fairly considerable constancy of the propensity potential in relation to the processes (including metabolism) which effect and guide its accumulation.

3. The urge toward activity in some particular direction which arises in conjunction with a fairly high accumulation of the specific excitatory substance "reminds" the animal in time—i.e. for example, long before a deficiency leads to physiological damage or an omission is detrimental to species survival—that the activity in question is "due": Both perception and motor system are correspondingly put and kept in a state of readiness, and appetitive behavior occurs until the adequate situation is either found or contrived.

4. Consumption of an action-specific excitatory substance temporarily weakens its influence on the system of propensities as a whole, or in an extreme case eliminates it altogether. This, together with the great differences in the speed with which the various specific excitations are recharged, brings about a rhythmical "change of leadership" in the spontaneous propensity system which by and large ensures that an animal strives after and performs any activity just as often and as long as is required for its own survival as well as for that of its social group and the species, and this largely irrespective of whether the external situation at any given time is favorable or unfavorable to a particular activity.

5. As a rule the multiplicity of specific propensities prevents the entire propensity potential from being exhausted in *one* activity, in one single endeavor, such as could not only easily happen but would in fact be inevitable if it were a case of one uniform reservoir of unspecific drive which first had to be "channeled."

The properties of this system of propensities named in 3 to 5 provide behavior with an—admittedly relative—autonomy in relation to the here and now of the external world as well as in relation to more indirect external influences such as experiences, memories, etc. It is not stimulus and reaction which represent the essential causal connection in the behavioral system of an animal, but *action and feedback* (reafference, von Holst and Mittelstaedt 1950).

But although this newly defined ethological concept of instinct diverges in many respects from older definitions of instinct, is stricter, more precise, and has better empirical backing than they, it still has one property in common with all the earlier definitions: Instincts are innate, i.e. in the course of its evolution the species has acquired them out of the constant interaction between mutation and natural selection, and in the individual they develop according to a "program" laid down in the genetic code; as far as the history of the individual is concerned, *adaptive* modification of this program is either quite impossible or possible only within very narrow limits (developmental *disturbances* are, of course, always possible). Thus, the number and kind of an animal's instincts are predetermined in a manner just as characteristic of the species as are the number and shape of its cranial bones.

With positively alarming narrow-mindedness philosophers and philosophically oriented psychologists have almost always seen in instinct only the *limitation* of individual adaptability. "The" instinct (the drive) has been positively damned and regarded as *the* enemy of human freedom, while overcoming it is looked on as one of the main goals of human development. It is also on the basis of this fundamental attitude that the instinctive nature of all man's so-called "higher emotions" is regularly disputed: Instincts are "lower-order drives." There is, of course, as little justification in fact for such a devaluation as there is for equating the area of adaptability left to the individual simply with "freedom"; for in most cases biological adaptability means *compulsion* to adapt. *Freedom from this compulsion,* our (partial) liberation from enslavement to the present physical and social environment, which makes a "may" of the "must" (E. von Holst: "A stimulus is something to which the organism can, but by no means *must,* react"; the "spontaneity of the Ego which determines its own goals," Katz 1948), all this we owe solely to the self-activating propensity system of instincts: From it springs that spontaneity which turns an organism into an acting subject instead of a stimulus-reaction machine, into a "self" instead of a mere product of its surroundings, into something which faces the situation instead of being totally imprisoned in the current "field." Our instincts are *at one and the same time* a limitation *and* a cornerstone of our freedom. Just as the bone structure in many respects limits our possibilities of movement, prescribes to the last detail those left to us, and yet at the same time are what makes it at all possible to stand on top of the earth, to walk "freely" about on it and to conquer it, so the pre-adaptation of our propensity system which occurred during evolution guarantees our (relative) autonomy in relation to our environment.

The individual instincts of the autonomous propensity system do not simply co-exist without any relation to one another. An animal is not, as a well-known biologist once thought, the equivalent of a ship with several captains (= instincts), with the one on duty always stepping down when another comes onto the bridge. In fact, it is positively an exception if a higher animal is controlled by no more than *one* instinct for a time; if this is a frequent occurrence in one individual, then, as with humans, it is sure to be pathological. Instead the individual instincts form a self-regulating system which *over a period of time* keeps itself in a state of equilibrium (principle of imbalances compensating each other in sequence; von Holst 1937, 1939 a, Leyhausen 1954 a). Within the framework of this overall regulation the relationship between any two instincts—in some cases, at any rate (Heiligenberg 1963)—consists now of mutual facilitation, now inhibition, and between them prevails relative, not absolute hierarchy (Leyhausen 1965 a).

In our view "fear" is one such instinct whose propensity is rhythmically and automatically produced. It is safe to assume that evolution has bred into the members of every animal species a rate of production of fear which corresponds to the average degree of endangerment in which the species must live and survive. Since most species are exposed to many dangers of very varied kinds, they are more or less timid, and it is positively striking when one species, or even a whole fauna such as that of the Galapagos Islands, apparently possesses no corresponding reactions. In many species the instinct of "fear" is so incessantly in a high state of tension that the motoric expression of it forms a more or less clear part of almost all actions (Hediger 1959). An animal of this kind can better afford to go without food or sleep for a whole day or even longer, or to miss a mating, than to relax its constant alertness even for five minutes. And constant alertness of just this kind can be supplied only by an automatically generated propensity which does not have to rely on being elicited time and again at short intervals by adequate external stimuli. As long as the endogenous production of fear roughly matches actual endangerment and the overall harmony of the instinct system which has been won in the process of evolution is maintained, then for the organism concerned this is only "right."

The instinctive movements associated with the excitation of fear are those of alarm, avoidance, hiding, and escape; the associated appetitive activities consist of what I hinted at with expressions such as "alertness" and "watchfulness," in other words specific sensitivity of the sensory organs and centers toward all danger signals, and thus the motor patterns of wary scanning, alarm calls, and finally even cautious investigation of "uncanny" objects and processes. Many animals have specifically different escape patterns for specifically different danger situations. *Tetraonidae,* for example, take to the trees if a ground enemy (cat, fox) approaches, but run into cover on the ground when a bird of prey appears in the sky; and for both cases they have different alarm calls. Thus, it is probably wrong to speak of *an* instinct of fear; there are no doubt several. Above all, fear of a conspecific which is in some form or other threatening and dominant seems always to be specifically different from other instincts of fear. Thus, it is no doubt correct to assume at least two different instincts of fear in man, too. This idea is quite compatible with the fact that certain constituent mechanisms such as the ergotropic autonomous functions and those of the substantia reticularis, which regulate tension and govern readiness to act, are more or less extensively involved in every form of behavior associated with fear. The principle of the "common final pathway" discovered by Sherrington is in no way limited to the purely peripheral nerve and muscle units but is to be found at all levels of integration of nervous functions.

Up to now I have consciously used the word "fear" in a purely physiological sense as a designation for particular instinctive forms of propensity. About subjective emotional experiences and the content of consciousness in animals we cannot, of course, say anything concrete, only conclude their existence with a probability which does, however, border on certainty and regard them as homologous, homeologous, or analogous to our own depending on the position the animal concerned occupies in the zoological system. If, however, the following is to make any contribution at all to the subject, a few remarks about the relationship between the propensities or instincts of fear and the experience of fear as seen from the point of view of the ethologist are unavoidable. True, these remarks are necessarily in part still hypothetical and insofar represent an appeal for the development of a research program designed to test them rather than proven fact. They do, however, seem to me to take us further than any hypotheses I know of so far.

Although we must assume the existence of two or even more instincts of fear, it does seem to me that the emotion of fear, the basic experience of fear, when not yet specified by *external* situations and objects, is uniform in quality: " 'Free fear' is one-dimensional" (Cohen 1965). The qualitative differentiation occurring at the propensity level is obviously unnecessary at the level of consciousness and would perhaps even be troublesome: The subsumption of technical details is, of course, in other respects too the *prerequisite* for many "higher functions," and not only in the nervous system! Insofar, therefore, the register of our qualitatively distinguishable emotions and feelings is "poorer" than that of the system of propensities; for the principle seems to me to be valid not only for the propensities of fear, but practically in general. Since, then, our experience "abstracts" uniform emotions from whole groups of propensities, concepts such as "fear drive," "sexual drive," "food drive," or even "self-preservation drive" and "species survival drive" are even more of an abstraction, for which no corresponding functional *units* in the organism exist, but instead functional *systems* which *in themselves* are both genetically and causally very heterogeneous. This does not, however, mean that experiences of fear in the broader sense are not differentiated in quality: Diffidence, shyness, watchfulness, uneasiness, anxiety, panic certainly represent forms of experience which are also distinct in quality. On the propensity side, however, they are matched not by qualities but by *levels of intensity!* The principle of breaking up continuities into groups or classes, as a statistician does, and then "processing" them further as qualitatively separate is quite obviously characteristic of a fairly large number of higher nervous organizing functions. For example, we are familiar with this in connection with the color spectrum, where perception quite arbitrarily picks out "typical" ranges of wavelengths, calls these "primary colors" and degrades intermediate colors to mixtures of the two adjacent "primary" ones, although seen from the point of view of physics they are equally simple (5800 A = yellow, 5300 A = green, 5750 A = greenish yellow); just this latter phenomenon is something we also meet quite typically in connection with the qualities of experience enumerated above. In the motor field we find a corresponding phenomenon in the "typical intensity" of some expressive movements which have been ritualized as signals (Morris 1957), and in the stability of whole number phase ratios between various automatic rhythms of the spinal cord (von Holst 1937, 1939 a). I have already spoken above of the various motor patterns associated with the instincts of fear. Here we must distinguish between those which correspond to qualitatively different propensities, such as the ways in which *Tetraonidae* flee from ground enemies and from birds of prey, and those which correspond to different intensities of the same form of propensity: Within the range of *one* propensity of fear lie, for instance, the motor patterns of being briefly attentive when a (distant) danger is first perceived, pausing in the movements being performed, staying still, through crouching, hiding, evasive action, and running away, right up to paniclike flight. It seems quite easy to draw parallels between such qualitatively different motor patterns ("motoric templates," Kretschmer 1953) available to one and the same propensity of fear as intensity rises, and their equivalents in the emotional sphere of fear. Whether this is more than an analogy, whether the emotions have really been molded into a form qualitatively "fitting" the motoric phenomena, or whether here language is perhaps "talking us into" a correspondence, must for the moment remain an open question.

For clarity, the ideas developed in the two previous sections may be summarized as follows: The "spectrum" of one group of qualitatively different propensities and the "spectrum" of the associated group of qualitatively different emotional experiences are on two planes set at right angles to one another. In this fact I see one of the main reasons why a psychological theory of motivation based merely on phenomenology (for a summary concerning anxiety and fear see Fröhlich 1965) is bound to produce systematics that are qualitatively as well as quantitatively different from those produced by a theory based on studies of behavior, physiological methods of investigation such as those of W. R. Hess and E. von Holst, and observations made in neurological and psychiatric clinics. Likewise, in spite of the grain of truth in them, attempts such as McDougall's (1933) to define the type and number of human instincts from the type and number of "basic" emotions and feelings which can be qualitatively distinguished were bound to founder on the facts I have described. So far it has proved impossible to combine the different systems harmoniously with one another, because no one has succeeded in relating the different datum levels *to one another*. Perhaps the above statement may be regarded as a contribution in this direction.

A propensity mechanism of the kind described here is, therefore, primarily dependent on the production of a specific excitatory substance reacted to selectively by special neural structures which in some cases, however, are situated far apart. This, of course, is just as impossible to "learn" as it would be for an organism to "learn," say, to acquire a functional pituitary or adrenal gland; something of this nature an organism either has or has not. In this sense, therefore, there is also no such thing as learned fear. Just as with the incretory glands, however, insufficiencies and hyperfunctions, both endogenously hereditary and exogenous, exist. Now, evolution has adapted the speed of production and rate of accumulation of an excitatory substance specific to an instinct to meet "requirements," as has already been said on p. 252 of the excitation of fear. In the case of instincts which have to be activated either only once in a lifetime (e.g. egg-laying by many insects) or very regularly (e.g. seasonally governed activities such as the nest-building of many birds) the production requirements of specific energy are not subject to large fluctuations governed by situation, and so they may be, and often are, hereditarily fixed within very narrow limits. In other cases, however, the "requirements" can be forecast only within sometimes very wide minimum-maximum limits. It would, for example, be very unpractical if a stag in a biotope free of large predators took to flight just as often as one in an area thickly populated with them. For this latter stag, however, it would be extremely dangerous if it were simply incapable of summoning up enough watchfulness and readiness to escape in order to evade the constant threat of danger. Thus, such propensities are adaptable within the given limits for each animal species. This adaptation in an upward or downward direction, however, happens gradually, not abruptly. As I mentioned on p. 251 some instincts at first reinforce themselves when they begin to discharge. Similarly, over longer periods of time the constant endogenous production of excitation of some instincts reinforces itself when these are discharged very frequently and diminishes when they are only seldom activated: They are strengthened through use and weakened through disuse. Heiligenberg (1963) has proved this in the case of the fighting instincts of a fish, and I (1965 a) was able to demonstrate it myself in the case of one of the prey-catching instincts of cats, namely killing. Although unfortunately not one single special investigation has so far been made, there is reason to assume that the instincts of fear of many animals and of man are also dependent on being frequently exercised. Quite certainly, however, it is not a question of a learning process but of a mechanism of adaption comparable to muscle trophicity; the biceps also does not learn to become thick and strong when its owner frequently does pull-ups, nor is it forgetting something it had learned when it atrophies for lack of exercise. Nevertheless, under experimental conditions of an appropriate kind such adaptations of the trophicity of an instinct can produce data which may be presented in "learning curves." And this has quite certainly happened frequently in the works of very many learning psychologists, particularly in America, without the authors becoming conscious of the basic difference in the nature of the processes they describe under headings such as "learning" and "conditioning." As I shall show, the differentiation is not only of academic interest but also has practical consequences.

II. ELICITATION AND APPETENCE

The foregoing has intentionally dealt only with the internal autonomous side of the dynamics of instincts and thus also of fear. But I have emphasized time and again that the autonomy of the propensity system is, indeed can be, only relative: An absolute autonomy would allow the organism to act with complete disregard for its environment and the current situation and would, therefore, be bound to lead to the elimination of the species within a very short time. Phylogenetic adaptation can breed the specific excitatory substances and associated systems which allow these substances to be stored in large or small amounts and for short or long periods, so that adequate reserves are available in case of need; it is able to develop neural structures, each of which is particularly sensitive to one specific excitatory substance and is thus capable of reacting selectively even when it is so tightly matted together with other neural systems less sensitive or completely insensitive to the same excitatory substance that the histologist or neurologist cannot disentangle them; but the effect of all this can further the survival of the individual and of the species, in other words be an advantage in natural selection, only if the instinctive movements set and kept in motion by this excitatory substance are discharged in the biologically "correct" situation and on the "correct" object, at least with statistically adequate frequency. Thus, it must be possible within certain limits to synchronize internal rhythmicity and external event with one another. This is the function of what are known as releasing mechanisms. These consist of a receptor constituent, which is tuned to specific eliciting stimuli in the environment, and another constituent which actually does the releasing and "activates" the excitation specific to the instinct. Many releasing mechanisms are innate in their entirety. In that case a "sensory correlate" (Lorenz 1935) to particular external conditions, to which it reacts "correctly" the very first time they come together and without any previous experience, lies ready in the animal. Most instincts are equipped with corresponding innate releasing mechanisms. For all instinctive acts which it performs only once or seldom in its lifetime an animal must have an innate releasing mechanism, for it has, of course, no time or opportunity to learn anything about them. As regards instinctive acts which may be frequently repeated, however, the *innate* releasing mechanism very often only serves the purpose of letting the animal get to know the adequate situations or objects. A young jackpaw's reaction of fleeing from predators, for example, can in the first instance be elicited only via the alarm call of the parent birds; only through association with this call does the young bird get to know the predators to be found in the area. Prey-catching is initially elicited in young cats by all small objects which run away from them, and thus also by the first live mice which the mother cat brings them. In this way, with time the kitten gets to know all species of prey animals occurring in the area. Only after that does it also know what to make of prey that sits still. The relationship between the innate and the acquired sensory correlates can be very varied (Schleidt 1962), but we need not go into this in greater detail in our present context. Finally, it seems that there are also instinctive acts for the elicitation of which no innate sensory correlate exists whatever. The animal must learn in full the situations best suited to their performance. According to Eibl-Eibesfeldt (1955 a) an inexperienced rat at first performs the "wall-papering movement" in the air without fitting it into its "correct" place in the sequence of all the other nest-building movements; only gradually does it realize that the movement (patting with alternate forepaws) "feels nicest" against the elastically resisting softness of heaped-up nest material. In this way, the movement at last finds its function in the building of the nest, namely to make the rim of the nest firm. As we shall shortly see, this case is of particular theoretical importance.

Certainly as far as man is concerned there is also a whole series of situations and objects which he fears innately or which elicit an escape reaction without his having previously experienced them; e.g. darkness, sudden loss of static orientation, the threatening expression of a dominant conspecific, any large object approaching fast (especially if it is dark in color). Man must certainly "learn" the vast majority of eliciting situations and objects somehow or other. It is, however, important to retain the fact that it is never "a" fear which is learned but only a new way of eliciting it; the instinct must be there already, otherwise it could never be elicited.

Whether innate or acquired, the receptor constituents of the releasing mechanisms have two characteristics in common: (1) They all have a tendency to "decline in stimulus-specific sensitivity" (Schleidt 1962, "adaptation" Prechtl 1953) when the same combination of eliciting stimuli occurs too often and in too quick succession; (2) if the stimuli are continuous or regular in rhythm, habituation sets in. Decline in stimulus-specific sensitivity affects the sensory organs themselves and the primary sensory centers; once stimulation is discontinued sensitivity re-establishes itself rapidly. Habituation to stimulus, however, affects the higher sensory centers which continue the processing of data, and it usually lasts longer than a decline in stimulus-specific sensitivity.

In order to "activate" an instinct, a releasing mechanism must overcome a kind of internal resistance which, adopting the concept of the stimulus threshold originating in sensory physiology, we call the threshold of elicitation. This threshold is dependent on the level of instinct-specific readiness: If this is exhausted, not even the strongest "stimulus" can coax out a "reaction," but if it is high even the weakest stimulation can elicit the most intensive activity. In order to arrive at quantitatively consistent results when experimenting, it is therefore necessary to measure stimulus strength and internal readiness *independently* of one another and, in addition, to take into consideration any decline in stimulus-specific sensitivity or habituation to stimulus which may occur in the course of the experiment (principle of dual quantification of external stimuli and internal excitability, Seitz 1940). As if this were not enough, internal readiness also influences the selectivity of perception: The less readiness there is, the more precisely the eliciting situation must "fit" the releasing mechanism—the more adequate it must be; the higher readiness mounts, the less the situation needs to resemble the adequate one, until finally even quite inadequate situations and objects may persuade an instinctive act that is dammed up to bursting point to discharge itself ("reaction to a substitute object," Lorenz 1937 b). In other words, the increasing endogenous readiness "sensitizes" the receptor constituent of the releasing mechanisms, sharpens the senses for anything which *might* render the situation of use to the accumulated urge toward a specific activity. The pressure exerted on perception by the propensity finally becomes so powerful that perception is positively "forced" to falsify the situation to fit these "wishes." In such cases animals very probably also have illusions or even hallucinations. Finally, if neither adequate objects nor ones suitable as substitutes appear for a long time, in certain circumstances complete "overflow instinct activity" may occur for which no specific external cause can be identified. Only a propensity to which the possibility of setting a specific activity in motion "spontaneously" without any external cause and purely on the basis of an increase in internal readiness is inherent can, like the wall-papering movement of the rat, make do without an IRM and yet via overflow activation rapidly find the adequate situation and use for which it was bred during evolution.

As described above, the propensity pressing to be activated can influence perception to such an extent that it adapts its interpretation of the objectively given situation accordingly. In this fact there already lies an impetus to *search* for possibilities for appropriate activity. Before the point of complete overflow discharge is reached, this searching usually infects the motor system as well. The animal begins to move restlessly around and—once it has had appropriate experience—to search for or manufacture the adequate eliciting situation with a positive aim in view. Precisely this often very prolonged and complex searching behavior ("appetitive behavior," W. Craig 1918, Lorenz 1937 a, b) by both animal and man conveys time and again an immediate impression of spontaneity: "I speak of an incipient action rather than 'reaction' because it seems clearly wrong to speak of a reaction to a stimulus which has not yet been received." (W. Craig, l.c.). The objection that at least in the case of aimed searching for a known object the mental picture of the goal must be regarded as the eliciting stimulus is certainly not sound: What else but the spontaneous propensity allows this mental picture of the goal to form and gives it "power" over the motor system and the sensorium?

Now, a part of appetitive behavior consists, to a degree which varies according to the animal species, of learned, conditioned, habit-formed behavior patterns, as well as others newly formed in immediate insight into the situation. All acquired motor activity not merely develops "in the service" of appetitive behavior for an instinctive act but can be spontaneously activated exclusively via such behavior; it possesses no propensity potential of its own. The other part of appetitive behavior consists of instinctive acts which become activated by the mounting urge of the instinct forming the appetite.

It may seem extraordinary that an animal should also have appetence for situations which elicit fear; yet, in fact it is possible to quote many examples of this for both animals and humans. Let it suffice if I mention only the games involving running away played by animal and human young, the habit some cats in big cities have of deliberately inciting dogs to chase them (Spurway 1953) and the passion for positively dangerous kinds of sport which many people who are healthy and full of vitality have. I am not saying, particularly in respect of the last-named example, that appetence for situations eliciting fear is the only motive for practicing such sport, but it is quite certainly *one* of the motives involved!

An animal that is ready to perform a particular instinctive act and, in this mood, also meets with the adequate eliciting situation may nevertheless be prevented from performing it. For example, a cat trapped by the farm dog in a corner with no way out cannot run away. Not only external circumstances but also internal factors are capable of blocking escape: A mother cat "cannot" run away because she is unwilling to abandon her kittens. In such a situation, too, the instinct that has been activated but is either wholly or partially blocked in its own specific motoric pathways is capable of directly or indirectly stimulating other motoric systems. When its specific reaction—escape—is blocked, fear has a strong tendency to activate another very specific instinct: aggression. This mechanism is so common and so stereotyped that some authors have already put forward the view that aggression possesses absolutely no specific propensity of its own but is simply *learned in fear*. This hypothesis is quite untenable: There are demonstrable cases of fearless aggression which also develops its own appetence (Leyhausen 1956 a, Heiligenberg 1963, Lorenz 1966).[2]

In situations where there is no way out, such as in the example of the cat, attack is initially only an appetitive act: By feigning attack the cat attempts to "bluff" its enemy, to cause it to withdraw and thus to drive it away altogether, or to open up an escape route for itself. If this does not succeed, it is at first followed by "limited" fighting in defense against the attacking enemy; and finally in an extreme case "genuine" attacking behavior can also be elicited, followed, if successful, by the pursuit of the opponent. After one or more experiences of this kind, just the sight of the dog—even if at that moment it is not aggressive—suffices to elicit the cat's attack. The corresponding situations vary from species to species, but the dynamic interrelationships between fear and aggression are basically identical in all vertebrates, and particularly all mammals.

However, as I have already demonstrated above, both fear and aggression are among the instincts whose condition may be affected by use or disuse. This being so, someone who frequently gets into a situation from which there is (actually or only supposedly) no escape may, as time goes by, become increasingly aggressive; and since exaggerated and unnecessary aggressiveness lands him with increasing frequency in (really or apparently) dangerous situations, this again increases his endogenous production of fear and a classic vicious circle is in motion. This is possible not only in the case of individual people, but also with whole groups and nations. The Franco-German relationship offers an impressive, but certainly not isolated, historical example of this.

Finally I should like to mention briefly that almost all situations met with, and particularly social situations, contain eliciting factors for more than the releasing mechanisms of only one instinct. Accordingly the behavior of the animal in this situation often reveals a varied mixture, represents compromises of varying degrees, or falls into conflict. If we take all that has been said about the endogenous rhythmicity of the individual instincts and its dynamics which fluctuate in the same rhythm, about the possible ways in which the various instincts mutually influence one another and the appetitive compromise or conflict behavior which results, about the role of acquired behavior patterns, and about the functional characteristics of the innate and acquired releasing mechanisms, and combine it into a functional model of the propensity system, it should become clear how extraordinarily complex and how individually variable the behavior caused must necessarily be. And even so for reasons of space the details have had to be represented in a very simplified form for the present purpose. Even if we ignore the learned components of the behavior as a whole, merely the various possible combinations of the innate components in their varying conditions result in immeasurable variability in the actual behavior performed. This is absolutely no argument against the instinctive nature of the individual propensity, or against the idea that the individual elements of behavior are genetically determined. Instead it is what one would expect from a theoretical point of view on account of their functional characteristics. The opinion that instinctive behavior must always be as inflexible as a slot machine, which is based on old viewpoints such as Ziegler's chain reflex theory of the instinct (1920), refers to borderline cases but is not the rule, particularly with higher animals.

Rather than complicate matters more than necessary, I have made no distinction in this article between fear and anxiety. Various attempts have been made to define fear and anxiety separately: For example, anxiety as an unspecific mood not clearly connected with an object, fear as something concrete—"fear of . . ."; or anxiety as "possibility," say in the sense of a potential but not yet activated motivational energy, and fear as "reality," a system of behavior and experience activated in a concrete situation. Yet, the attempt to separate the concepts sharply looks artificial and in the end founders on the imprecision of everyday language, which, of course, the scientist also has to use. Considered from the point of view of the theory of propensities outlined here, there also seems little point in giving the *same* propensity different names depending on whether it appears as potential or kinetic energy. I have therefore preferred to use qualifying words—propensity of fear, emotion of fear, fearful behavior, motoric reaction of fear, activated and latent fear, etc.—to indicate clearly which particular form or effect of fear is meant.

It is different with fright. Many people connect fright closely with fear; the fact that being profoundly startled often elicits fear was also one of the main arguments in favor of the James-Lange theory, according to which all emotions and feelings were said to be peripherally induced. Fright and fear are, however, by no means so inseparable. I would rather say that fright is a neutral feeling: It seems to me to originate primarily when at one stroke all ergotropic mechanisms are aroused by a strong stimulus, the nature of which cannot, however, be "classified" so quickly. This, as far as I know, is the only case in which the central nervous state of excitation and tonicity in a *healthy* organism comes anywhere near what is known as "general excitation." And the consequences are precisely those which a state of "general excitation" would be bound to have if it ever existed apart from this: For the duration of this "fright paralysis" the organism is incapable of action, since agonist and antagonist muscles are equally tense. Fright paralysis normally lasts for only a short while, and is of practical value in that it prevents mistaken behavior and gives perception time to recognize the nature of the stimulus and "what lies behind it" and to activate specific releasing mechanisms. The propensities activated by these are then adequate to the situation and correct the distribution of excitation and tonus in the direction of their specific pathways, just as always happens quite normally when a behavior pattern is elicited adequately: Before the motoric impulses reach the musculature, the distribution of tonus necessary for the "intended" motor sequence is prepared via the substantia reticularis. Thus, in principle fright can dissolve into anything requiring energetic action: escape, attack, . . . or dancing for joy! In keeping with what was said earlier on, however, the reaction following fright is not dependent solely on what perception "establishes" about what stimulated it, but also on the differing level of readiness of the individual propensities. This can be regularly observed when a number of people are severely startled without any specialized behavior being subsequently elicited *by the situation,* for example, after a loud explosive noise whose source remains unidentified. Shortly afterward the majority of those present more or less show signs of having overcome fear, but there are always some who react with rage (=aggression) and others who react by brimming over with jollity which is often also motorically uninhibited, either because they are permanently more disposed in these directions, or because the momentary state of their propensities favors these modes of reaction.

Fearful reactions predominate because the instincts of fear are constantly kept at a particularly high level of readiness and are, therefore, most likely to be more ready for action than any other instincts: Being afraid, being ready to run away, particularly in unclear situations, is so extraordinarily important for survival, for "dying a little later."

Although, as I have described above, the production of fear can within broad limits be "trained," i.e. adapted to the actual danger content of an individual environment, in the case of modern man in many respects not even the constantly produced minimum of fear left over after he has been completely disaccustomed to it gets "used up." We simply live such protected lives that in general for weeks, months, even years we have no need to fear a genuine, present threat and run away from it. As a result many people live constantly in a basic mood that is more or less anxious without having any real cause for it. Of course, we all fear the atomic bomb, another war, communism, or whatever else it may be; but we cannot run away from any of these things, we cannot work off our instinct of fear in successful escape, and so, whether we like to admit it or not, habituation to stimulus sets in with all of us. Otherwise it would be impossible for the whole of humanity to look on—I would even say with complete composure—as new atomic bombs are constantly being produced, stockpiled, and brought into position, as slowly but surely more and more states produce their own and not one of the governments concerned makes even the slightest attempt to deny that "in case of emergency" these bombs would also be used. We have all long since grown accustomed to "living with The Bomb," and even those who still give the matter some thought scarcely become excited about it any more. Whatever else one may think about this, it is a thoroughly natural and necessary form of self-protection for the organism; but it does not help either to get rid of the danger of the atomic bomb or to work off the individual's instincts of fear. Some people choose the outlet I have already mentioned of engaging in a dangerous, or dangerous-looking, sport. Others find a kind of substitute satisfaction in detective novels and horror films. Incidentally, one should not imagine that a vivid emotional experience *must always* accompany the adequate discharge of an instinctive propensity and thus also of fear. Much remains below the "threshold of consciousness," or is only a fleeting, indefinable impulse: Here we dodge an approaching car, there we disappear quickly into a side street to avoid meeting someone, and another time we withdraw a hand from a strange dog . . . all little things. But even the tiniest hint of an escape movement consumes some specific propensity of fear, even when what is involved are things we regard as natural which do not seem like fear to our conscious experience. Viewed along a longitudinal section of a lifetime, a person in fact probably consumes by far the largest part of his propensity energies in this way and only a relatively small part of them in fully intensive discharge of the entire motor patterns of the instinct and all associated emotions. Since, furthermore, in the course of man's so-called self-domestication many instincts with strong emotional content are obviously atrophying, i.e. going through a hereditary diminution of the production of specific excitation, one might hope that in this way humanity would one day be freed from its automatic fear, which is a nuisance because it has in the meantime become superfluous. But it is not as simple as that, and furthermore, for reasons which will shortly become obvious, it would also be quite undesirable.

III. THE SOCIAL FUNCTION OF THE ANTAGONISM BETWEEN FEAR AND AGGRESSION

First, in the self-domestication of man there is no selective breeding as is the case with our domestic animals. Human genes mutate at random, like those of all other living creatures, and since no selective elimination is made we find not only people with atrophy of instinct but also people with hypertrophy of instinct. If hypertrophy has affected the production of fear, we get the whole range from the overfearful to the serious case of anxiety neurosis, where the minimum level of the automatic production of fear has shifted considerably farther "upward" and thus does not fall a victim to atrophy from disuse even when there is a complete lack of adequate releasing situations. The person affected is therefore constantly under pressure from the strongest appetences for fear, looks for and finds a "substitute object," and since this is, of course, not the real cause of his fear, in this instance no habituation to stimulus or decline in stimulus-specific sensitivity can set in. As various authors (Bilz 1965, H. Schulz 1965) agree, such neurotics were free of symptoms in conditions which allowed these to be worked off in genuine behavior connected with fear (during wartime, in heavy fighting at the front, or in concentration camps). They did not, however, remain so as soon as they were again living in fairly normal conditions. A "normal" person with an endogenous production of fear which under "normal" conditions is only moderate very frequently reacts in precisely the opposite way when subjected to a rapid succession of powerfully fear-eliciting situations over a long period of time: He becomes more and more anxious, for his production of fear gets into training, provided that the fear-eliciting factors are not always the same and so no habituation to stimulus occurs. Nothing shows more clearly than these two examples to what extent the stimulus quality perceived *and* the stimulus effect are dependent on the level of readiness of the propensity elicited: The same stimulus sources which provide the anxiety neurotic with a safety valve for the adequate discharge of fear, thus leading to a decrease rather than an increase in his endogenous production of fear, may train the production of fear of a normal person up to a level which, under certain circumstances, makes him seem like an anxiety neurotic for quite a long time if the training situations abruptly cease. This is a phenomenon directly to be expected from the trophicity and dynamics of use-dependent instincts. For the moment it still seems questionable whether intensive and continuous exercise can achieve a permanent increase in the endogenous production of specific instinct excitation so that atrophy from disuse does not occur. It does, however, seem quite certain that this cannot be caused by a single traumatic experience.

In a detailed study, Lorenz (1966) has investigated the instinctive nature and functions of intra-specific aggression. The result may come as a surprise to some: In man's case, too, intra-specific aggression has not only regrettable consequences but also quite positive social functions which make it seem inadvisable to try to dispense with it completely. It is just the same with intra-specific fear. As the counterpart of intra-specific aggression this is totally indispensable. The two propensities make "sense" only in conjunction with one another. Why should one fear a conspecific if he were never aggressive? And conversely, if the one attacked were not afraid aggression would either be quite unsuccessful or would lead to uninhibited self-extermination of the species. Indeed, in very many animal species intra-specific aggression is also "limited"; usually its aim is not to destroy the animal attacked but only to drive it away. The differences may be particularly clearly observed in carnivores: A cat pursues a prey animal until it has caught and killed it, but it pursues a strange cat only as far as the boundary of its territory or not far beyond. The counteraction between intra-specific fear and aggression is the foundation of all—all!—social hierarchy, whether absolute or relative (Leyhausen 1965 c), and thus of all social order whatsoever; for without the individual being prepared to accept a higher or lower social position according to circumstances, no vertebrate, and certainly no human, social community is possible: No family, no village, no club, no school, no firm, no state, no church, nothing of the kind could exist and function without this counteraction. The fact that in all these we are dealing with institutions and traditions which are largely based on rational mutual consent in no way contradicts the above claim. That it is at all possible to institutionalize these organizations, to assist them to more or less general recognition and to persuade the individual members to adapt their behavior in the long term to the framework of the institutions, is so *only because* an instinctive basis exists for them, because the institution *guarantees* each individual the satisfaction of these instincts in a socially acceptable framework to an appropriate extent. When institutions embark on a development of their own and depart too far from their instinctive foundations, complaints about the worthlessness of human nature and demands that it be changed are regularly to be heard. However, what in the end either changes and approaches the natural state again or disintegrates is the institution concerned; for making basic changes in human nature in what, seen from a phylogenetic viewpoint, is the tiny space of time we call "world history" is something which as yet nothing and no one has succeeded in doing. Certainly in all periods there have been maniacal "institutionalists" who preferred to destroy mankind along with its intractable nature rather than admit that the institution represented by them was bad or at least in need of reform. Thus, toward the end of the war Hitler commanded the German people to abandon itself to destruction since it had proved unworthy of his party and state institution. If institutions are to fulfil their purpose and be viable, if among other things they also hope to regulate the various instinctive activities in a form which largely prevents them from having harmful effects on people in general, then they cannot allow themselves to depart too far from these very instincts—they must stay *close to the instinctive*. For we have already seen that exogenous regulation of instincts is possible only within certain species-specific limits—and only to this extent it is necessary or even desirable in the interests of the community.

When I said that the counteraction between fear and aggression is indispensable to all human social communities, this naturally does not mean that it is their sole basis, nor even their sole instinctive one. It also does not mean that fear and rage are the dominating social emotions. As I have already described above in another connection, in social intercourse, too, we mostly dispense our specific propensities in "small change" without getting as far as strong emotions; and lower levels of the propensities are often accompanied by qualitatively different emotions, if by any at all, as I have likewise already described.

Apart from that discussed, however, the counteraction between fear and aggression has a further biological function in the case of all animal species having a social form of life: The balance between the two establishes itself only when any two individuals keep a particular, species-specific distance between them. In this way, the number of individuals which can inhabit a particular area is automatically limited. This, in conjunction with other internal and external factors, regulates the individuals' rate of reproduction and population density remains constant over long periods of time (Wynne-Edwards 1962). In man's case this regulation of the reproduction rate has been upset, and meanwhile the concept of the "population explosion" has become common knowledge. People live increasingly close to one another, but their intra-specific counteraction between fear and aggression is fundamentally the same as it was at the time of Neanderthal Man. High density multiplies the areas of friction, the vicious circle already mentioned causes the two instincts to inflame one another mutually, and people simultaneously become increasingly irritable and increasingly anxious. Against open indulgence in aggression and escape, however, the community, the law-givers, the keepers of order proclaim increasingly severe sanctions—necessarily, for otherwise utter chaos would be unavoidable—but unfortunately often in vain, for this does not, of course, remove the cause of the tensions. Thus, people lose more and more of their inner harmony, become increasingly discontented, and riotous outbursts among the young, brutal acts of violence by individuals, and the exogenous neuroses become predominant. It is precisely this mechanism which hinders social contacts in the mass community, which makes the individual in the mass solitary. Genuine social contact requires distance, and not only in a metaphorical sense. One can without exaggeration say that the majority of the world's political and social problems, whether of the individual or of people as a whole, would at one stroke—no, not be solved—they would simply cease to exist, if we could ensure that there were nowhere more than five to at the most twenty people per square kilometer. In this connection, too, it is again not the large outbreaks which are the most important. The constant small annoyances of everyday life, with one's neighbor, one's superior at work, the small worry whether one will be caught parking in a prohibited area (often simply unavoidable), the frustration and envy when another gets the job one thinks should by right have been given to oneself, the small triumph when one wins some dispute with officialdom and thus annoys someone else, all this adds up and, slowly but surely, ruins the mental and finally also the physical health of the individual. It is no different in public life, for politicians are also human: The small annoyance here, the great ambition there, the desire to get on and up and to acquire as much power and influence as possible, and the fear of having to admit a mistake openly and publicly, all this and much more, in big things as well as little, "makes" more politics than any ideals. Here it must also be said that in this lie not only dangers but also the impetus which keeps the whole business in motion at all. Thus, one cannot and must not simply lump together under one heading the much maligned habit of the parliamentarian of keeping one eye on the voter, the official's ambition, the civil servant's unwillingness to take decisions, or his struggle for promotion, and condemn them all. All this is thoroughly necessary—to a certain degree. Yet the dangers must not be underestimated, particularly those inherent in the "small" fears and aggressions, for they are the least controllable. If one day the world perishes in atomic fire, it will in all probabliity not be because Kosygin or Johnson, seized by a titanic rage, "presses the button," or, in the guise of an "institution fanatic," tries to destroy a humanity that is "unfit to live" and refuses to see that its sole salvation lies in communism or western democracy as a form of life. No, the disaster is much more likely to happen because, say, a ministry official has an argument with his neighbor in the morning, this makes him forget to pass on a vital piece of information, he is later afraid to admit the omission to his superior, and so, at the end of a perhaps even longer chain of trivial motivations and their effects, someone makes a slight but fatal mistake in assessing the situation.

11 The Biology of Expression and Impression (1967)

I. INTRODUCTION

All organisms are the products of a historical process. Their present-day forms and functions can, therefore, never be understood solely from a consideration of their fitness and adaptedness to the environment. In each individual case a large number of equally good or even better solutions to a particular problem of adaptation could be found. The phrase "survival of the fittest" never means that it would be impossible to imagine something fitter.

Historical developments do not always obey the laws of logic. If only for this reason, it is futile to try to contain phenomena produced by a historical process in a conceptual system construed by way of logical deduction. A purpose-tailored conceptual garment of this kind will always be too tight here and too loose there; it often reveals more about the specific qualities of human deductive thinking than about the natural order inherent in the phenomena to be investigated, their historical and causal connections. Purely by deduction it is not even possible to infer the existence of a particular group of phenomena, let alone justify a special discipline for their investigation, and that applies just as much to a science of expression as to any other biological and psychological discipline. Yet, precisely this is unfortunately being attempted in recent times with respect to the psychology of

272

expression. Not merely is thinking in prefabricated containers being elevated to a principle, but it is even claimed that only this makes expression psychology into a legitimized, independent discipline within psychology (Kirchhoff 1962 a). Quite to the contrary, however, *absolutely nothing* makes a branch of research legitimate except the existence of an initially perhaps only vaguely definable group of *phenomena* which it seems possible to investigate with the help of scientific methods. Whether this branch of research then develops into an independent discipline is a question of the results obtained and what specialized methods become necessary in its course, but from the point of view of scientific theory this is of minor importance.

The basis of all such attempts to insist that in science at least the world begins with logical concepts is to be found in the claim, tirelessly repeated for centuries, that science has "philosophical foundations," a theory which B. Blumenberg (1952), for example, once more tries to validate scientifically. It is for this reason that Kirchhoff (1965 a) repeatedly emphasizes "... that only the technique of logical constructs can provide the foundation stones" (sc. of a science). Of course, it is possible to philosophize *about* the foundations of science, but this does not make philosophy the first prerequisite of science. As Topitsch (1962, 1963) has shown, such a claim can be justified neither from phylogenetic history nor by epistemological reasoning: Experience, indeed in principle the entire arsenal of the empirical, is there in phylogeny and ontogeny *before* thought; thought develops *after and out of* experience. Even the "a priori" categories of reason and intuition are comprehensible only as phylogenetic a posteriori, as outcome of the struggle between organism and environment (Lorenz 1941, 1959), and they are therefore no more than approximation formulae with limited validity, a fact of which microphysics has emphatically made us conscious. Even when theory to a certain extent determines the course taken, as it nowadays does in "established sciences" (Kirchhoff 1962 a) such as physics, this is not to say that the theory in these sciences is the "foundation stone"; Planck's quantum theory was given its first impulse by experimental results which did not accord with the ideas of "classical" physics. Planck, Einstein, and the other founders of modern theoretical physics owe their theories not to the exclusive pursuit of pure mathematics and logic—they had studied physics, and classical physics at that, for there was no other. And without the whole experiential content of classical physics their theories could never have been conceived. Precisely the example of microphysics makes it plain that basically pure logic and mathematics are not independent sciences but codes of procedure: In any given case the method must adapt to the phenomena being handled. Thus originated Reichenbach's (1944) "three-valued" logics (true, false, uncertain) and the matrix method of calculation used in atomic physics, where, unlike other forms of mathematical calculation, it is no longer immaterial in which order the factors of a product are stated.

It is, of course, possible to abstract progressively from concrete experiences until one has finally constructed a system of "pure" mathematics and "pure" logic that is absolutely true because it is now absolutely devoid of any content capable of being experienced through the senses. But quite apart from the fact that this is still not the first but decidedly the second, third, or even more remote link in the process, the applicability of these systems to concrete reality is subject to the limitations demonstrated by Lorenz (1941): 2 equals 2, certainly! But do 2 apples equal 2 apples? No, for no two apples are exactly alike. Yet, as the numbers increase so the statement becomes increasingly accurate, for only a finite number of variants exists. "Concepts are what they are decreed to mean and nothing more" (Kirchhoff 1965 b), certainly, in pure *l'art pour l'art* logic. Concepts of that sort, however, can be applied to the empirical content of a science only *tentatively*, with a measure of caution and at best within limits. To regard them as the founding legitimation of a field of empirical knowledge or, worse still, of the phenomena to which such knowledge refers is an example of such unadorned, utterly naive Cartesianism that it should be unthinkable more than eighty years after Wundt's drastic and definitive criticism (1882); basically the circumstances have not changed since then (Metzger 1952). The formulation of concepts in any and every science proceeds, one way or another, from a comprehension of the matter; as our comprehension progresses, so the conceptual content must evolve accordingly. Thus, too, a science of expression can proceed only from the *phenomena* of expression and of the apperception of expression, and *not* from a system of prefabricated, purely logically deduced, inflexibly constricting definitions.

Rejection of a conceptual logic of preordained harmony, existing before experience as an indispensable prerequisite to the experience of phenomena, has incidentally nothing to do with naive realism—although as point of departure for a new science that is far sounder and more harmless than "the carefree confidence only the exclusive pursuit of speculation bestows" (Wundt 1882)—or with the shallow operationalism so often prized nowadays, as will be obvious from the ensuing text.

Admittedly, a conceptual system shaped after the phenomena and the results obtained from investigating them is neither inclusive nor final. Essentially it consists of *injunctive* concepts (Hassenstein 1954). With luck, it will provide the best possible résumé of what is known and clear indications as to the next steps necessary in research, the results of which then determine whether the system can still be considered adequate or needs modifications, additions, or complete reconstruction.

II. THE ORIGIN OF EXPRESSIVE PHENOMENA

1. Reasons for introducing phylogenetic considerations

For a long time now the psychology of expression has been in a precarious situation, as Kirchhoff (1962 a) has also emphasized. Certainly the blame for this does not lie with the lack of an unconditionally valid delimitation of the area of investigation by means of preconceived "airtight" definitions. Rohracher's plain speaking (1961) is probably more to the point: "The main reason why science has as yet been able to contribute so little to the study of expression is probably due to the fact that we do not know how expression achieves its effect." Apart from much else, some of which will be dealt with later, human psychology is, so to speak, constitutionally impeded when it comes to investigating this and similar questions: It confines its investigations almost exclusively to *one* species; yet much of what interests it in this species is very much older than the species itself, and the specifically human manifestations are therefore simply incapable of providing an answer to questions formulated correspondingly. Ewert too (1965 a) has noted this fact, but he himself does not draw the obvious conclusion in detail. Human expression and human comprehension of expression both have roots which are much, much older than man. It is therefore useless for anyone wishing to know where they came from and how they function to question man (or at least man alone) about it. The attitude of many European psychologists, mostly educated in the humanities, to the general problems of human psychology coincides surprisingly enough with that of their American colleagues working experimentally—often *with* animals but not *on* animals—in that by implication they proclaim this procedure to be the only appropriate one. The dilemma of expression psychology can, like much else, be overcome only if it ceases to limit itself to investigations of the one species and probes in at least equal measure into evolutionary history using comparative methods.

As most readers will be aware, every single organism has two histories: a very ancient one which it shares with all other organisms of the same species (phylogeny) and a very brief one purely its own, which begins the moment its zygote is formed and ends with its death (ontogeny). The phylogeny of an individual comes to an end in the very instant that its zygote is formed. Thereafter it can carry on phylogeny through its progeny but is not itself affected by any change it may transmit. It follows that ontogeny can work only within the framework of possibilities which phylogeny has created—and not eliminated. Applied to the phenomena of expression this means that what an organism is at all capable of expressing and how it does so has on the whole already been laid down by the phylogeny of the species, and individual modifications are possible only within the given range of modifiability. Thus, individual variants of expression may be explained in terms of ontogeny, but for the origin of expression itself we have to search far back in phylogeny. This paper therefore deals only with the phylogenetic and ontogenetic aspects of expression and its communicative functions. The process of actualization will not be discussed.

But are we in a position to shed light far enough back into the darkness of phylogeny? The development of preservable structures such as teeth and bones, calcareous, silicious, or chitinous carapaces, and much else is certainly more or less well documented by fossils, but how does one proceed with functions such as behavior patterns?

We are, of course, denied a direct approach. Even with structures, however, research cannot rely exclusively on paleontological material. Tissue and internal organs are rarely preserved and, even when this does happen, they are always incomplete. In such cases phylogenetics has long used the comparative method. In related groups of animals an organ does not evolve at the same rate. For example, the circulatory system from fishes, amphibians, and reptiles to birds and mammals gives a fair and detailed representation of the various stages through which the circulatory system of mammals has passed during its phylogenetic development. The comparative method has been extraordinarily well worked out and its conclusions, though indirect, are often more reliable than those obtained by setting up morphological series of fossils. This is because, when correctly used, the comparative method almost always makes it possible to distinguish with certainty between homologies on the one hand and convergencies and analogies on the other, which is often impossible with fossil material (Kühn 1949, Remane 1952). Lorenz (1943 b) and Wickler (1961) have shown how the method may be applied to ethological

research. I will confine myself to drawing attention to the basic significance of the concepts homology, analogy, and convergence in
every kind of comparative research on organisms: *Homologous* refers
to organs and systems of organs which demonstrably have the same
phylogenetic origin, such as the skeletal elements in the arm and
hand of a man, in the foreleg of a horse, and in the wing of a bird;
in short, in all forelimbs of all vertebrates. The limb's functions may
be the same, as it is in horse and deer, or as different as it is in bird
and horse. *Analogous* refers to organs and systems of organs which
have a similar function but different phylogenetic origins, such as the
compound eye of an insect and the camera-type eye of a vertebrate;
or the horns of an antelope and the antlers of a stag. The concepts of
analogy and homology, and in particular the criteria for the definition
of homology, were originally developed in the service of comparative anatomy. How they may be applied to functions and behavior
patterns has been amply described by Remane (1952) and Wickler
1961). From the point of view of psychology, H. D. Schmidt (1958)
has emphasized the importance of making a distinction between
behavioral homologies and behavioral analogies. He is, however,
mistaken in his assumption that ethologists believe the criteria of
homology may be applied only to instinctive movements—although
it is certainly less difficult to determine whether instincts are homologous than it is with other behavioral elements (cf. Wickler 1961). We
cannot, however, agree with what Schmidt calls "environmentally
conditioned behavioral homologies." Identity or similarity of structure
and/or function which has been caused by external conditions should
correctly be called *convergence* if the original material consisted of
analogous structures and functions, or *homeology* if they were homologous. Familiar examples of convergence are the body shape of
fishes, whales, and ichthyosaurians, or the camera-type eyes of vertebrates and cephalopods; examples of homeology are the predatory
death-shake, which has developed from the same root but independently in canines, martens, civets, and opossums (Leyhausen 1965 a),
and rumination, which has developed separately at least four times
in the course of phylogeny—in kangaroos, hares, cattle, and hyrax
(Hendrichs 1965). As far as Schmidt's so-called "environmentally conditioned behavioral homologies" are concerned, therefore, it is essential to check first what the circumstances are in every individual case.

There is no hope for a comparative psychology which attaches
insufficient importance to phenomena classifiable according to the
concepts I have outlined above, which accepts as a basis for comparative research only the conclusions arrived at through *logical*

analogy and, following on from this, indiscriminately labels all similarities of form and function as analogies (although the logical and biological concepts of analogy do not even coincide). Despite Schmidt's endeavors this procedure is still customary, particularly among German-speaking psychologists (cf. for example Holzkamp 1965). This method precludes from the very start any deeper insight into phylogenetic connections and, through them, into the natural relationships between phenomena. Relationship comes, after all, from having the same ancestors, not from attending the same school. In the latter case identical or similar-looking external modifications may result, but these can and will largely disappear by the next generation. This has no effect whatever on the genetic code.

Only by viewing the question from a phylogenetic point of view do we find the key to the fact that a kind of expressive Esperanto runs through the whole range of vertebrates. Certain homologous forms of expression used by vertebrates in homologous circumstances are similar to one another and have remained comprehensible beyond the boundaries of species, genus, family, even order and class. Misunderstandings and misconstructions do, however, continue to occur, and the reasons for these are to be found in convergencies and analogies (see pp. 325 et seq., 364 et seq.).

2. The problem of differentiation

In a comparative investigation of expression the very first question to arise is: "What is the minimum level of development or organization, the minimum degree of functional differentiation which a living organism has attained when manifestations of expression become observable?"

The unicellular alga *Chlamydomonas eugametos* normally swims free in the water by means of its flagella. From time to time, however, a certain number of individual *Chlamydomonas* shed their flagella, settle on the bottom, and excrete a substance (gamone) which is attractive to the free-swimming specimens. One immobile ("female") and one mobile ("male") individual then fuse to form a zygote (Hartmann 1939, Moewus 1938). Should we in this case count loss of motility and excretion of gamone as "expression" of female readiness to copulate?

In a school of minnows *(Phoxinus laevis)* one is bitten by a pike. The minnow's wounded skin excretes a substance which causes the rest of the school to flee in panic (K. von Frisch 1939). Is this fright-inducing substance "expression" of the fish's fear of death?

A human being is suddenly confronted by some apparently ineluctable, deadly danger. Sweat breaks out on his forehead, on the palms of his hands, in his armpits and eventually over his whole body. Is this "expression" of fear?

Without stopping to consider the criteria, the answer in the first two cases would be "no" but in the last "yes." The question "why?" can most easily be answered in the second case: Excreting a fright-inducing substance is purely the reaction of the fish's skin to being wounded, and the skin of recently dead or anesthetized minnows also reacts in this way.

In the first case one might initially be inclined to answer, "Yes, this is expression"; the alga is ready for copulation and "expresses" this by immobility and excretion of gamone. Why should this not be called expression? Let us consider another example. A paramecium is swimming in a straight line through the water. This it does by means of the well-coordinated rhythmical beating of the cilia distributed all over its body. Now it encounters some small obstacle and the beat of the cilia nearest this obstacle is reversed. Suddenly we have two groups of cilia working in opposite directions. The majority prevails, and accordingly the paramecium either moves on in the same direction only more slowly, or at least strains against the obstruction, or else it moves backward. In both cases the minority of cilia betrays the presence of a tendency which nevertheless fails to predominate in the ensuing behavior of the animal as a whole. It is immediately obvious in what way the paramecium in this situation differs from the "female" *Chlamydomonas* which is ready for copulation. The *Chlamydomonas* has no other behavioral possibilities. It is exclusively female egg-cell, and apart from this there *is* nothing else to express. The behavior of the minority of the paramecium's cilia is certainly not expression in the full sense of the word, yet it does demonstrate for us two conditions which are essential if expressive phenomena are to materialize at all:

1. The organism in question must have a central nervous system which is sufficiently differentiated to be able to activate at least two different behavioral tendencies simultaneously; and

2. its effector system must likewise be sufficiently differentiated to allow both tendencies peripheral effect without thereby totally disorganizing the behavior of the organism as a whole. As a first approach, then, one could define expression as being the changes in the effector system of an organism which are brought about by the tendencies currently in a minority. This establishes two points:

1. "Expression" is *something happening*—to be precise, something

happening physically in effectors, in glands, and in muscles. Even someone who, as opposed to the behavioral physiologists, believes in the existence of psychical phenomena, independent of all physical processes and limitations, must admit that there can be no such thing as a purely psychical expression. A knowledge of its physiological bases is, therefore, even more essential to an understanding of the processes of expression than in other areas of psychology.

2. Effectors—at any rate in multicellular animals, including humans —can be activated only by nervous and/or humoral impulses, i.e. by drives in the broadest sense of the word. It follows inescapably that any psychology of expression can only be as good or as bad as the motivational theory on which it is based.

Gottschaldt (1958) takes a view similar to my own of the connection between motivation and the expressive occurrence. According to him "motivational structure" and "expressive structure" are not different in essence but merely methodologically different aspects of the dynamic bases of behavior. However, by "motivation" he understands something quite different, above all something very much less differentiated, than do the ethologists. Also, in accordance with the interpretation presented here, only part of the whole motivational state is reflected in expression; thus investigating expression is not solely a way of approaching motivational problems but also pertains to a specific class of phenomena.

In other papers (Leyhausen 1952, 1954, 1965 a, b, 1967) I have dealt in detail with the processes of motivation presented in model form, based largely on the works of Lorenz (1935, 1937 a, b, 1939, 1940, 1953, 1966) and von Holst (1936, 1937, 1939), and the possibility of applying them to human situations as well. Familiarity with these works must be assumed hereafter. I should, however, like to point out three frequent misunderstandings: 1. Instincts are not necessarily simple and primitive; 2. A motivational system built up of instincts is not inflexible like a machine; it does not force the organism endowed with it into a sequence of compulsory activities (although that can happen under certain conditions), but instead permits the organism precisely that degree of autonomy in relation to the external conditions of its existence and that diversity of internal possibilities for decision which in human beings we call "freedom of will." 3. Motivational system and emotional qualities do not correspond—at least not completely—in the sense of a psychophysical parallelism.

On point 1: It is just as possible to list a whole series of general characteristics of "the" instinct as it is of "the" automobile. But there are "Beetles" and Mercedes 600s, coaches, towing cabs, and forty-ton lorries, and the instincts of an animal as well as those of different animal species are at least as varied. As soon as one proceeds from general characteristics to individual properties—the "details of design"—one must specify which instinct of which animal. Instincts are "inflexible" only in that they are apparently slow to change during phylogeny, in that the instinctive movements toward which they strive retain their identity, as a melody does, through all changes of tempo, intensity, and transposition, and in that they can neither be learned nor modified by learning. This does not, however, preclude adaptive methods of regulation of some other sort, or malfunctions.

On point 2: The instincts of an animal form a very largely self-regulating system; within this each instinct is involved with every other in a vast multiplicity of inter-relationships which vary according to the current state of activity of the individual instincts. In this way, hierarchically organized systems are formed which in individual cases may run off in a predetermined direction (Baerends 1941, Tinbergen 1951) but in others may reorganize themselves smoothly in accordance with changes in external and internal conditions (Leyhausen 1965 a). A motivational system with such a structure is capable of coping with even the most complicated and sophisticated tasks. In this respect it is in no way inferior to the motivational models offered at present by human psychology. Versions of the ethological theory of motivation such as that offered by M. Koch (1959) or Cofer and Appley (1964), some of which oversimplify its findings and conceptual formulation while others reproduce them with slight or even total inaccuracy, are unfortunately not a suitable means of conveying an adequate idea of matters to the human psychologist. Under the influence of traditional ways of thinking which have been molded by scholasticism, Cartesianism, and similar philosophical theories, it has become usual to oversimplify animals, particularly the higher mammals, only to add hastily that, of course, in humans everything is much more complicated and anyway quite different. What real knowledge we have so far gained about the higher mammals, however, leaves such notions without support.

On point 3: It seems that the number of individual propensities vastly exceeds that of the qualitatively distinguishable emotions and that whole groups of propensities are therefore represented by the same quality of feeling or emotion. On the other hand, at least in some cases, emotional impulses and states of mind (e.g. disquiet, fear, panic) which, though related, are yet clearly different in quality seem only to correspond to different levels of intensity of the same propensities (Leyhausen 1967). This explains why attempts such as McDougall's (1933) to ascertain the human instincts simply from the number of emotions which could be qualitatively disinguished have proved unsatisfactory despite the grain of truth in them. According to these, "emotions" would only represent the motivational state rather summarily and, in part at least, would not run parallel to it. In fact, however, many a motivational process appears in expression which has not (yet) stirred the emotions and has not even clearly entered consciousness.

For identical reasons any theory of motivation which is content merely with phenomenological analysis remains a prisoner of what superficially appears in the phenomena (of consciousness) and furthermore is all too prone to yield time and again to the temptation of interpreting a *post hoc* as a *propter hoc*. In addition to this the propensities are partly not capable of being consciously experienced at all, partly they are represented in consciousness in only a vaguely emotional manner and furthermore not "in parallel" (see above, comment on point 3). For this reason the phenomenology of experience constantly tends to take the motives—in other words *the eliciting factors*—for the propensities themselves. This misinterpretation explains, for example, the theory of Gehlen (1941) according to which man spontaneously develops his own propensities to meet his needs and these propensities then bring new needs in their train. It cannot be emphasized too often or too strongly that with Lorenz's works of 1937 both the eliciting factors and the subjective goals of activity were definitively excluded from the definition of instinctual propensity, and any attempt to reinstate them would have to be paid for by the loss of the analytical progress won by Lorenz. The "pull of the pictures" (Klages 1936) is after all an illusion created by the phenomenological "viewfinder"; by themselves and without the endogenous pressure exerted by the propensities on which they have a releasing effect, the "pictures" (stimuli) would have absolutely no power to set behavior in motion. A conscious act (or whatever one may call a hypothetical "smallest unit of consciousness") is no more a direct consequence of the preceding one and direct cause of the one that follows than would be true of the single picture dots on a television screen: The machinery which effects the apparently simultaneous as well as successive coherence of the pictures is not sited in the television screen and remains invisible. The consequences of these facts to psychology as regards the delineation of problems, methods of investigation, and continual overstepping of bounds in both directions, from conscious to physiological experience and vice versa, I have discussed in detail in another paper (Leyhausen 1954).

For three reasons the "minority" definition of expression proposed above can be considered only as a first approach: 1. It applies only to the "raw material" of expressive behavior before this becomes involved, *together with* the capacity to form an impression, in the formative interplay between mutation and natural selection. 2. It should not be understood as implying that expression contains information *only* about the motivational minority; it is only through conflict with the "epiphenomenon," in contrast to it as well as by fusing to various degrees with it, that the central phenomenon acquires any distinctive meaning. 3. Theoretically two borderline cases could be postulated in which it is no longer possible to speak of a motivational majority or minority: a) The minority gains strength until it balances with the former majority. This case can not only be postulated in theory, but is also of great practical significance, since most manifestations of so-called pure expression owe their origin to it (see p. 301 et seq.). b) The minority could shrink until it disappeared altogether and the organism fall completely under the domination of one single, super-powerful propensity. It is questionable, and would no doubt be difficult to prove, whether this case ever quite occurs in higher animals and particularly in man. In those instances in which this appears to be the case an external inhibition must usually take the place of an internal one in order that the propensity concerned can produce an expressive phenomenon corresponding to its own strength. If there is no inhibition whatsoever, the animal concerned often proceeds to act as motivated with no expression at all. Even then the expressive minority plays an important part in determining the character of the expression simply by contrast: Unusually and surprisingly it is missing altogether. It is for this reason that expressive character could be denied as far as the behavior of the *Chlamydomonas* ready for copulation was concerned: There *was* nothing missing.

Both the peripheral and central nervous systems of higher organisms are so far differentiated that more than two propensities may (but not necessarily must) take effect simultaneously. Just as in a parliament neither those supporting a particular decision nor those opposing it need be absolutely homogeneous among themselves, so in each individual case the propensities which strive to make a particular form of behavior prevail and those which strive to inhibit it may be of quite heterogeneous nature. This creates extremely manifold possibilities of superimposition and combination of expressions.

3. Impression and the capacity to form an impression

The example of the paramecium wavering between swimming forward and swimming backward shows that it is possible to tell in more or less full detail what the state of propensities of an organism is at any given time from what is happening in the sphere of expression. Only the paramecia cannot do this themselves; they are not equipped for the purpose. The entire life cycle of some animals which live in isolation or in "anonymous bond communities" (Kramer 1950), where their behavior never has any direct reference to conspecifics, is controlled exclusively by stimuli from the physical and chemical environment. Here expression is indeed merely an external phenomenon, the resultant of various activated tendencies. But when the individuals of an animal species abandon their anonymity and make contact with other individual conspecifics (individualization, Kramer l.c.), this renders some form of response behavior necessary. It becomes important to gather information about how a conspecific is prepared to act or react at any given moment. Quite in keeping with this Haecker established as far back as 1900, in his detailed investigation of the evolution of birdsong, that vocalization was *primarily* "purely an expression of feeling" and only *secondarily* was firmly integrated "into the instinctive life of the species through natural selection" because of its usefulness as a method of species recognition; differentiation into sounds with different communicative functions then followed as a third stage. It remains uncertain to what extent, if at all, the second and third stages of differentiation are to be understood as successive or as developments starting more or less simultaneously. We have no idea when or how in phylogeny an animal first achieved the particular cognitive faculty which would enable it to "interpret," i.e. to react specifically to, a particular mode of expression by a conspecific.

An animal possessing the minimum level of organization outlined on p. 279 cannot at any moment of its life be "absolutely expressionless," just as there can never be "absolutely no weather," and for precisely the same reason. Weather occurs incessantly, even in places where no one records whether the sun is shining or a blizzard is raging. For countless millions of years fishes, amphibians, reptiles, and birds have yawned (for a review see Hediger 1961), but only in mammals—and only in some groups of these—did the yawn become "infectious." They were the first to pay conscious attention to it, to be affected by it, although the whole series of vertebrates preceding them had constantly seen conspecifics doing it! If a carp sees another carp yawning, this does not cause it to alter its behavior. If a man sees another man yawning lustily and he is himself be it ever so slightly weary or tired, he is practically compelled to yawn, too. Is yawning, then, expression in humans but not in carps? After a long walk through the zoo, a man steps into the semi-darkness of the aquarium. If a carp yawns at him, he yawns, too, at least often, or he feels the urge to do so. Is the carp's yawning expression *now*? Finally, if the man is very exhausted by then, the fish need not actually yawn. Just the sight of its great jaws opening and closing rhythmically as it breathes is enough to make the man yawn. Here there can be no more talk of expression, but an *im*pression has been produced and stimulates a reaction corresponding to itself and not to the external situation! Rohracher (1961) quotes examples such as these, only to generalize them then in a way which categorically denies the existence of expression as a separate phenomenon quite independent of any impression which may be created: "Expression is that part *of the perceptible* which elicits the impression, the subjective attitude" (my italics).

It will be obvious that any attempt to define expression from impression or to include the capacity to form an impression in the definition of expression is an *a posteriori* misconception which must sooner or later lead to theoretical and practical difficulties. Astonishingly enough this misconception has not only survived from the psychology of expression of Klages ("Polarity of expression and impression," 1936) right through to Kirchhoff (all expression is "another person's so-being made evident *for someone*," 1962 a; my italics), but even the ethologists have almost without exception fallen a prey to it. Schenkel (1947) designates expression as "the function of behavior and structures whose biological purpose it is to cooperate in regulating social life by influencing mood or eliciting reactions." Lorenz (1951) narrows this definition still further: He will speak of expression only if some form of behavior became more elaborate in the interests of coordinating social life. As Ewert (1965 a) has shown, this linguistically narrow concept of expression is philologically speaking the earlier; which does not alter the fact that it by no means describes the *phylogenetically* original circumstances. Eibl-Eibesfeldt (1957) does indeed view this specialized expressive behavior against a background of "epiphenomenal, undifferentiated modes of expression," which animals and humans may understand in the light of individual experience. However, he deals in detail only with expressive behavior in particular and seems furthermore to assume there are no innate cognitive faculties for recognizing purely epiphenomenal, "undifferentiated" expression.

In contrast to the above authors, Hediger (1961) regards as expression "all identifiable, changeable, non-pathological phenomena in an animal which may help one to understand its situation," but freely admits that this is a definition untrammeled by theoretical pretensions and intended purely for practical use in zoo circles. Certainly the definition is rather too broad. R. Lorenz (1966), for example, observed face-washing activity in langurs and discovered that the monkeys perform these activities only when they feel absolutely safe and undisturbed. If, then, one observes these animals washing, it certainly helps one to understand their situation; we may even go so far as to say that their feeling of security is expressed thereby. But we still cannot regard the washing activities as "expression," and obviously for the same reasons as made it impossible in the case of the receptive *Chlamydomonas* (p. 279). Apart from this, however, Hediger with his definition is saying, as I do, that expression is *not primarily or exclusively a matter of intra-specific communication.* Hediger alone refers to "internal" expressive phenomena which can be recognized only indirectly, e.g. if an animal urinates or defecates out of fear. Here let us recall the "minority of motivational tendencies," whose effect is not limited solely to what the partner or observer can directly perceive. The use of the word expression, however, already implies perceptibility and therefore already contains the seeds of a—philologically inevitable (Ewert 1965 a)—misinterpretation, namely that expressive phenomena originated *from the very first* as agents of intra-specific understanding or because of the possibility of using them to this end. However, think of the changes in electrical resistance of the skin, which are certainly "internal expressive phenomena" in Hediger's sense but are not perceptible to the senses.

Stamm (in his collective review 1965) and others have failed to recognize the deeper theoretical significance of the difference between Hediger's interpretation and that of the other ethologists quoted. It is, however, easily explained by their different points of view: The ethologists have so far scarcely ever investigated the expressive phenomena of animals for their own sake but almost exclusively on account of their function in social behavior; for zoo staff the problem is how to put an accurate interpretation on the expression of a different species from oneself, and here it is of no immediate relevance whether the phenomena observed and requiring interpretation are a means of inter-specific communication or not. Even so, the perceptibility of expression or of its immediate effect is central to Hediger's definition. However, it should be adequately clear by now that, when the organizational complexity mentioned above started to evolve, in the struggle between the motivational minority and the motivational majority it did not at first matter whether a conspecific could perceive the effects or not. But natural selection toward intra-specific communication could work only on the perceptible, and so it is only natural if all expressive phenomena in the service of this function, and particularly all those specially developed and differentiated for this purpose, occur predominantly "on the surface," as Fiedler (1964) demonstrates in detail in his study, "The mammalian skin as expressive organ."

Much more difficult to understand than the case of the ethologists is why human psychologists investigating the problem of expression cling so stubbornly to the conviction that a primary and complete polarity exists between expression and impression. Psychological diagnosticians have been obliged to realize that working purely on the impression created one cannot be sure of establishing personality and character with statistical accuracy greater than chance. Since then the effort has been directed toward establishing, describing, classifying, and interpreting by rational means those expressive signs in particular which are not involved in the immediate impression formed, and to employ these for the diagnosis. Almost all these signs are unobtrusive; it requires special training to find and pay attention to them. Furthermore the interpretation of all of them is not straightforward but requires long practice and often the use of auxiliary apparatus (think of the "lie detector") whose express purpose it is to eliminate as far as possible the diagnostician's immediate impression or "personal equation." It is therefore perfectly clear to any psychologist working in diagnostic practice just how much expression there is, even in one and the same species, for which absolutely no corresponding immediate impression exists, and that over and above this the capacity to form an impression has a tendency to certain typical malfunctions, with which I shall deal more fully later. However, expression theory has partly ignored these facts and partly been incapable of drawing any conclusions from them. It goes on as ever mixing up the definitions of expression and impression, and always holds the one as the prerequisite for the other, thereby rendering it impossible to see the origins of either. Thus it can happen that, for example, in a work called "The dimensions of facial expression" (Hofstätter 1956) there is absolutely no mention of expression but only of impression (in the broadest sense and not the narrower one I have defined here). With a similarly unlovely confusion of language and concept Holzkamp (1965) continually speaks of "the origin of expression" when he means the ontogeny of the apperception of expression.

As far back as 1938 Brunswik and Reiter already made a sharp distinction between expression and impression, though purely for reasons of method. Phylogenetic considerations were obviously far from their thoughts, and so the theoretical consequences of the fact that such a distinction is at all possible escaped them. Similarly Lersch (1943) drew no conclusions from the fact that it was possible to test the upper and the lower face separately for expressive content. Brunswik and Reiter demanded a "consideration of the functional mechanism of social perception (what is meant is 'perception of social "stimuli" ') . . . without reference to the mediating external event." ". . . The concern here is not factual correlations between certain occurrences and the personal domain of another, but mere laws of *reaction*." . . . "We are concerned here only with questions connected with the analysis of an objective stimulus situation from the point of view of the person reacting, *without anchoring this consideration in the subjective reality of the other person* (my italics). If such a reality is in fact the basis of any particular case, then the problem, expressed at its briefest, becomes the question what impression expression produces." To which we need only add "and *what* expression produces any impression at all"! It is therefore both linguistically and factually incorrect to speak of a receiver of *expression*. The impressive mechanisms never evaluate more than some of the stimulus data transmitted as expression, and they evaluate these only according to the laws of *impression,* often without concern for the objective content of a given stimulus situation. This is *one* of the reasons for the ambiguity of many expressive signs emphasized by Ewert (1965 a).

Expression in its original form simply occurs, like the weather. It is absolutely essential to understand that the capacity to be impressed by expression did not automatically accompany the emergence of expression itself, but is a separate function which evolved later. The polarity of expression and impression has come into being gradually and bit by bit over a long period of time and it is never and in no case complete. On the contrary, it has never appeared except where it made "biological sense," i.e. somewhere which offered natural selection a starting-point. Klages (1936) is fundamentally mistaken in the assumption that the basic prerequisite for comprehending expression is an ability to mimic the expressive process.

In the following text I shall use the word "impression" exclusively to signify *innate* apperception of expression, and "capacity to form an impression" to signify the perceptual processes mediating this apperception. This is not to claim that *all* apperception of expression is impression, and so innate. Individually acquired comprehension of expression exists in at least two more or less sharply distinct forms, whose peculiarities in connection with the different modes of evaluating sensory data will be dealt with later (see Section V.,4). In this paper, however, impression and the faculties of impression are of foremost concern because these have so far not been investigated by human psychology either with sufficient precision in formulating the problems or with really adequate methods, and because they form the basis, partly direct, partly indirect, of all other forms of apperception of expression. I am quite conscious how difficult it is to try to narrow down in this way the concept of impression, which is usually employed in a broader, indistinctly defined sense; this can easily and repeatedly lead to misunderstandings. On the other hand, we need a short and pertinent designation for this particular perceptual function and for its distinctive functional characteristics. For this reason I hope that I may with time succeed in establishing the use in the behavioral sciences of as narrow and precise a concept of impression as Lorenz did with the concept of instinct.

The capacity to form an impression stems from other roots than expression and its paths of evolution were therefore necessarily different. The correspondence between the two is purely functional. In every animal species there are broad areas of expression which are not grasped by its faculties for impression. It is, on the other hand, perceptual processes quite similar in principle to these faculties which cause an animal to react adequately to "signals" from its environment which are quite different from expressive phenomena in its conspecifics. The corresponding perceptual processes existed for this function long before the above-mentioned point in phylogenetic history when they also "interpreted" expression for the first time; and in their simplest form they are probably even much older phylogenetically than "genuine" expressive phenomena. On the other hand expressive behavior often provides the conspecific with more information than is contained in the actual expression itself (Marler 1961): The song of a male bird tells a female in the vicinity not only of its "matrimonial intentions"—in other words, the motivational state of the male—but also what sex the singer is, where its permanent habitat is, and that it possesses a suitable territory. Analytically, therefore, it is perfectly possible to extract expression and impression separately from the process as a whole, but in the natural situation things are, as a rule, much more complex. This paper cannot, however, set out to investigate all modes of conveying and comprehending information which occur in animals. On the other hand, conveying information is only *one* function of the expressive processes. It is, indeed, an important function and one so striking that so far it has attracted the almost exclusive attention of researchers into expression, but it *was* developed only secondarily. It can in fact be shown that true expressive character is lost to the same extent as the communicative function of a particular expressive behavior becomes enhanced by natural selection during phylogeny (see pp. 329, 342, et seq., 369, 378).

It follows from the above that it is not only legitimate but indeed essential to pursue the study of expression and impression separately and independently up to a certain point, just as Brunswik and Reiter suggested (1938). The two are totally different in origin and are capable of being studied independently. It was only under the later functional pressure to cooperate that selection toward a certain degree of accommodation between their respective functional characteristics occurred.

4. The element of the future in expression

The remaining question to be answered is, "What advantage in natural selection does a species gain from possessing the capacity to form an impression?" One needs only read the textbooks and handbooks of biology and zoology to learn what advantages in the struggle for existence are won when an animal species reaches the stage of bisexual reproduction with a choice of partner, internal impregnation, long or even permanent cohabitation of the sexual partners, care of the young and life in an ordered society (not an anonymous mass community). It should, however, be immediately clear how essential it is in all these cases for the individual to have information about what its partner(s) will do in the next instant or what may be expected of the partner(s) if it behaves in a certain manner itself. An impression can, at least within certain limits, supply just this information because expression, being as it were the resultant of the current motivational state as a whole, contains an indication as to which propensities will, or at least could, gain the upper hand in the next instant. The paramecium which approaches an obstacle and changes the direction of the beat of a section of its cilia no doubt reveals to a practiced observer when, for instance, it will alter the direction in which it moves or even turn right round, or when its forward movement will come to a standstill. But another paramecium which might be following is not capable of forming an impression from the expression of the one swimming ahead of it. It will not on this account change its direction earlier or stop until it reaches the obstacle itself. In contrast to this, it is enough for the foremost fishes in a swarm of herrings to see an obstacle and hesitate. The reaction time of the following fishes is so brief that to our eyes it looks as if the whole swarm turns simultaneously and swims away, and only with the aid of slow-motion film can one see that the turn in fact runs from front to back through the swarm (Leyhausen 1960). In this sense expression is an image of the (future) action, but certainly not in the sense that Klages meant (see p. 326–327).

This element of the future in expression and the possibility, inherent in its interpretation, of adjusting oneself to a partner's future behavior, indeed of inciting or inhibiting it, is what constitutes the advantage in natural selection which in the course of phylogeny compelled the capacity for expression and the capacity to form an impression to become linked and in very many cases even adapted them functionally to one another.

Does the definition just given also fit the example, quoted earlier, of a man who breaks out in sweat from fear at the threat of danger? First I should add that in the case described a whole series of other expressive symptoms also appear, such as wide-opened eyes, extremely distended pupils, spasmodic trembling in all limbs, and so on. All this together indicates complete paralysis. At that moment no action of any sort, in particular no resistance, is to be expected from this man. During fighting it is most important to be able to make such a forecast.

In many cases at least, the forecast is not only qualitatively but also quantitatively very precise. Hediger (1961) quotes an impressive example of this: Every tiger or lion has what is known as a critical distance. If it is approached (be it by a conspecific or by a human) the animal first tries to withdraw. If it is prevented from this and the approacher comes within the critical distance, the animal will attack. Animal trainers exploit this situation by constantly moving on the border of the critical distance, thus compelling the animal to withdraw or to jump forward accordingly. By swinging to and fro between these two reactions, a trainer can direct the animal to almost any point in the ring he likes. Where he is at any time in relation to the critical distance he can tell only from the animal's expression. There is no hard and fast rule for it, because the distance varies from individual to individual as well as according to circumstances. A trainer's life therefore depends, quite literally, and particularly at the beginning of training, on his ability to form a quantitatively correct judgment of his pupil's expression.

III. THE DEVELOPMENT OF THE CAPACITY TO FORM AN IMPRESSION

1. The innate releasing mechanism (IRM)

As the level of organization of an organism rises, not only does its internal functional apparatus become more complicated, but it also becomes dependent on ever more specialized conditions in its environment. Parallel with the internal profusion of functions, therefore, it is compelled to develop a correspondingly differentiated capacity for reaction to ever finer factors in its surroundings. The general sensitivity of "living matter," as enumerated in every textbook of biology among the most important characteristics of life, differentiates and divides itself out among the various sensory modalities. Organs (or, in the case of unicellular organisms, organelles) come into being which produce only one kind of sensation in response to any kind of stimulus; the retina produces only light sensations whether it is stimulated by electromagnetic waves, by shock, by temperature, or otherwise (Law of specific sensory energies, Johannes Müller). They become specialized, however, for certain "adequate" types of stimulus (for example, the eye becomes specialized for light waves) and for these they have an extremely low stimulus threshold, whereas "inadequate" stimuli need to be unusually strong before they can excite the sensory cells. Out of a simple sensitivity to light develop directional vision and movement vision, visual perception of pictures, objects, and spatial relations, color vision, etc., and the systems of organs necessary for these capacities. The organism must receive information about the occurrence of conditions specific to special functions so that the two can be synchronized. In many cases the necessary information is extremely complex and makes demands not only on the various capacities of one sensory facility—for instance color, shape, and movement vision simultaneously—but also on the capacities of various modalities, for example taste and hearing, or sight and smell, and so on. A good example of this kind is the behavior of the tick, analyzed by von Uexküll (1909). The creature sits near the tip of a blade of grass or thin twig and lets itself drop when this look-out is shaken. If it falls on something which has a temperature of approximately 37°C and smells of butyric acid, it pricks and sucks. If both of these conditions are not met, it climbs up to a look-out again. The perceptual apparatus of a tick must, therefore, contain devices which distinguish 37°C and butyric acid from all other temperatures and chemical stimuli, and there must be one further stage which releases the act of pricking when the two stimuli occur simultaneously. All so-called "unconditioned reactions" are released by arrangements of this sort, some simpler, some more complicated, but all similar in principle. In the environment of the tick the simultaneous action of both the stimuli mentioned can in practice happen only when the tick touches the skin of a mammal. Everything else which characterizes a mammal, as well as what constitutes the differences between the various species of mammal, is ignored. On the other hand, it is scarcely possible to think of two other perceptually as simple stipulations which would distinguish a mammal so unmistakably from all other objects occurring in the tick's environment. The perceptual apparatus of the tick, therefore, makes a very simplified, abstract, schematic, and yet sure definition of *"the"* mammal, or perhaps one should rather say it recognizes, practically without error, when the event "contact with skin of mammal" occurs and sets the (from the point of view of the tick) "right" responses in motion.

The information as to which combination of stimuli designates the correct situation for a certain behavior pattern may have entered an organism in two ways: through individual experience, or through mutation and natural selection in the course of phylogeny. In the latter case the information is stored in the genetic code of the species and is transmitted from generation to generation; from the point of view of the individual it represents an *a priori*. A third way which the information could take does not exist (Lorenz 1961).

In the case of the tick, we know for certain that learning and experience play no part in releasing the act of pricking. It works the very first time. It is true that the larval stages also prick and suck, but these attach themselves to other vertebrates as well, such as reptiles and birds, and only in the fully developed female does this specialization of the sensorium occur irrespective of what it sucked from as a larva. However, the mature female has no opportunity to "make improvements" in its behavior, for it pricks only once in its life, sucks itself full of blood, falls to the ground, ripens its eggs, and then dies. The perceptual capacity which enables the tick to pick out the two stimuli distinguishing the skin of a mammal with certainty from all other stimuli and to respond to their simultaneous occurrence with the act of pricking has been called an "innate releasing schema" by Lorenz (1935), in elaboration of the terminology employed by von Uexküll.

"Schema" is the name Lorenz gave to the sensory correlate in an animal to the "adequate" situation, because it is always tuned to only a few relatively simple but very distinctive characteristics of the situation as a whole or of the relevant object but is for practical purposes blind to all other accompanying phenomena in these, at least in the case of an animal without specific experience in the sense I have just defined. As Schleidt (1962) explained in detail, the term "innate releasing schema" constantly led to misunderstandings and even misuse, so that nowadays the term "innate releasing mechanism" (IRM) introduced by Tinbergen (1948) has taken its place. But as Schleidt rightly emphasizes, Lorenz's idea of a schema highlights more the afferent functions, the recognition of the adequate situation or the adequate object, whereas Tinbergen's releasing mechanism lays greater stress on the efferent mechanisms activated. Schleidt seems to assume with certainty that both functions must be bound up inseparably with one homogeneous physiological mechanism, however complicated such a mechanism might be. As long as we know so little, however, about the physiology of the process as a whole, we are equally justified in leaving the other possibility open, namely that we could be dealing not only with mentally separable functions but even with clearly distinguishable physiological mechanisms which are indeed connected up in a relay system but by no means fully integrated with one another (cf. Baerends 1956, 1957). This assumption offers at least theoretical and didactic advantages, for it facilitates the understanding of sometimes extremely complicated situations. Furthermore it is the perceptual and not the releasing function which is of interest in connection with this paper.

In their simplest form mechanisms of perception of the kind described are certainly phylogenetically very old, possibly as old as the very first forms of life and therefore older than the beginnings of expressive phenomena. As I have already emphasized, we can scarcely hope to establish when it was in the course of phylogeny that such a perceptual mechanism became sensitive to expressive characteristics in a conspecific for the first time with the result that the capacity to form an impression was created. We do know, however, that the elicitation of suitable response activity independent of any experience —i.e. innate recognition—of biologically relevant situations or objects, whether it be inanimate matter (e.g. building material for the larva cases of caddis flies), creatures of a different species (food, prey, predators) or conspecifics and their expressive phenomena, is effected by perceptual mechanisms which are all similar in principle. In gaining control, as it were, of the phenomena of expression, this function becomes innate apperception of expression or, as I would prefer to say, the capacity to form an impression. To avoid misunderstandings I would emphasize yet again that acquired or acquirable apperception of expression also exists, only this I would call *comprehension* of expression.

"Innate" here means that the relevant information is not acquired by the individual but transmitted along with the hereditary characteristics. What it specifically does not mean is that the function serviced by it must be available from birth onward, but merely that this appears or can appear during the pre- or post-natal development of the individual *without* any help from the stimuli which characterize the *adequate* situation for any particular behavior.

We must, however, first deal with the phylogenetic information and the functional characteristics and limitations of the mechanisms processing it, for without them the individually acquirable functions cannot be properly understood, whereas the converse is possible. There are indeed functions—e.g. the instinctive movements designated by Lorenz as "fixed action patterns" and the innate releasing mechanisms just discussed—which are fully adapted on the basis of phylogenetic information alone, but there are none which require only individually acquired information. Functions needing individually acquired information still require at least a basis of phylogenetic information (Lorenz 1961). It would be a retrograde step, and one which the psychology of expression least of all can permit itself, if we were to blur or ignore the dividing lines between these groups simply because analysis has (so far) proved impossible or unsuccessful in a particular case, or even to regard them as irksome handed-down theses which ought to be cast aside once and for all (Kirchhoff 1962 a). It is true that Gottschaldt (1960, p. 225) says "that hereditary effects and environmental effects do not summate but combine; they are also not to be regarded as complexes of factors in psychophysical development which work independently of one another and thus can each be investigated by itself. The question, then, is not whether hereditary effects or environmental effects are demonstrable and what proportion one factor has in relation to the other. The question is *how* heredity and environment *combine* their effects during development." However, misunderstandings such as Kirchhoff's cannot be justified in this way. They are instead the result of misinterpretation of actually perfectly correct statements such as Gottschaldt's, misinterpretations due to inadequate knowledge of the object, method, and language of genetics! To one gene the nearest genes lined up next to it on the same chromosome are already "milieu" on which its specific effect in the organism as a whole *may*, but not necessarily must, depend. To the milieu of genes is added the plasmatic "environment" of the living cell, to the single cell the surrounding tissues, organs, organism, to the latter the inanimate and animate environment. Even a chemically isolated gene would not be without milieu; genetic *effects*, however, can be observed only in living cells, in other words in connection with "environmental factors." Insofar, therefore, it is true that hereditary and environmental effects cannot be separated and investigated by themselves, isolated from their connection in the living organism. But it *is* possible to establish what proportion of the individual variations in any given phenotype is due to heredity and what to environment. Classical genetics has been doing nothing else since Mendel. Concepts such as mutation and modification would otherwise be quite pointless, for they would not be based on any observable facts which may be checked at any time. The vital point of the whole problem is indeed the question "*how* heredity and environment combine their effects during development." A great number of environmental conditions must always be available or appear at the right time if a gene is to be able to manifest itself in a phenotype (structural or functional), and specific changes in the environment or the specific relationship between certain environmental conditions governs type and degree of modification of a feature. This modifiability, however, does not possess adaptive value right from the start. Natural selection takes direct effect only on features and not on genes. It can then work in two directions: With some features it is obviously an advantage in selection if they develop in practically the same version in all individuals of a species without concern for differences or periodic variations in developmental conditions; they become peristostable. Many environmental conditions must, it is true, be fulfilled if an organism is to develop with all its features, but peristostable features do not alter as a result of changes in environmental conditions; in contrast to this, with other features it is precisely toward individual adaptability to the periodic variations and peculiarities of some of the environmental conditions in an individual case that natural selection works. In these cases, however, both the type and the degree of modifiability of a feature are just as genetically fixed as are the specific few out of the countless total of environmental conditions to which the feature adapts. It is continually overlooked, although it should be self-evident, that these two ways in which the genotype effects the adaptation of the phenotype—namely on the one hand a guarantee of a stable version of features *in the face of* changing environmental influences, and, on the other, adaptive modifiability *in correlation with* individually varying developmental and living conditions—can be viewed only against a background of those environmental situations which were present during the phylogeny of the species *and* have remained fairly constant. As far as these are concerned natural selection had no starting point for breeding stability of features or adaptive modifiability; the same is correspondingly true of environmental influences which never appeared in the environment of the species concerned, e.g. extremely low temperatures in connection with an animal of the tropical rain forests. If one changes such conditions or provides them for the first time, for example in laboratory, acclimatization, or introduction experiments, it is useless to expect the safety measures of feature stability and adaptive modifiability bred by natural selection under other conditions still to be adequate. And yet they sometimes prove to be more resistant than one could in fairness expect. The concepts of feature stability and adaptive modifiability are therefore both dependent on the environmental background which prevailed during the evolutionary history of the species, and only in this qualified sense do we speak in ethology of innate, i.e. peristostable, behavior patterns.

In the case of stable features furthermore it is not always a question of very small or "simple" units, but often even of highly complex ones. It is true that cases have become known (Bastock 1956, Russell 1963) in which innate behavior patterns depend on single genes, but this is hardly likely to be the rule. Genetic investigation of populations has shown instead that populations of wild animals may be far more uniform in phenotype than they are in genetic make-up! In other words, natural selection guards stability of features not only against the influence of changing environmental conditions but also against diversity in the allele pool of the species. This whole complex question may be studied in more detail in Bresch (1964), Dobzhansky (1939), and Kühn (1965).

Nor can it be claimed that separating innate and "acquired" (i.e. adaptively modified) elements of behavior has no prospect from the point of view of method. The ethologist can make use here of the method of analysis of hybridization (e.g. von Hörmann 1955) and of rearing without specific experience (deprivation experiment, Lorenz 1961). If the use of these methods in human ethology meets with some difficulties for ethical reasons, it should be the task of human psychology to develop suitable methods. It is, of course, up to every investigator to decide for himself whether he will tackle a certain problem or not; but no one has the right simply to deny the existence of a problem or to pronounce it intractable merely because evolving a method is difficult.

2. How expression and impression came to match

In a strict sense the innate capacity to form an impression alone conveys the immediate and intuitive awareness of what is going on in another person (*Originäres Innewerden im Modus der Begegnung,* Lersch 1940) which is referred to time and again and in all possible formulations in the literature of expression psychology. It alone releases the instantaneous, unreflected reaction of which Rothacker says: "The Id has a different (i.e. faster) reaction time than the Ego" (1941). Direct identical experience of another person's emotional state is naturally an illusion, for only the personal emotions of the receiver can ever be stimulated by an expression. These match the expressed emotions of another only in so far as like (i.e. homologous) facilities for emotional experience exist in individuals of the same species as a result of their common phylogeny. For the normal requirements of social life, incidentally, a correspondence on broad lines is quite sufficient; identity down to the last detail is not necessary and scarcely ever occurs, except possibly in identical twins (cf. Spindler 1955). Where there is considerable individual diversity "misunderstandings" accordingly occur, and frequently the observer projects his own emotions into the partner. For the same reason genuine, naive, and unreflected apperception of expression between individuals of different species is possible only if, and to the degree that, homology exists between what is expressed and what impression is received (see p. 326 et seq.).

An IRM does not always "fit" so precisely as that of the tick for "contact with skin of mammal." It is often sufficient if the IRM ensures synchronization between environmental event and response behavior with statistically adequate frequency. This is quite unavoidable where one and the same releasing mechanism can elicit very different modes of response behavior, which is particularly often the case with the kind of IRM which reacts to expressive phenomena. The preliminary display of the fish *Hemichromis bimaculatus,* for example, although considered objectively the expressive *content* remains the same, can, depending on the mood *of the partner,* stimulate the latter to fighting, escape, or courtship. From the point of view of the ethological model, therefore, the "ambiguity" of an individual expressive sign stimulus (Ewert 1965 a) is also a theoretical necessity (but see p. 338). Since the perceptual function of IRMs was by no means specially "invented" for the purpose of interpreting expressive phenomena, the same releasing mechanism may often add together not only expressive data but also other features into a subjectively "whole" impression. Herein, and in the naive assumption that expression and impression must match completely, lie what are probably the most important, because largely unconscious, reasons why even up to this very day no one can agree as to what should be included in the range of expressive phenomena and what not. If one tries to define from the point of view of impression, one's analysis soon stumbles on phenomena whose expressive character seems at least dubious (e.g. facial architecture, Lersch 1943); if one tries to start from the expressive phenomena, one frequently ends up, like Klages (1936), with an extravagant overestimation of the capacity to form an impression. But if one will only realize that expression and impression are very different functional activities of an organism, whose ranges coincide only partially and which can exert a certain amount of influence on one another only within the area in which they coincide, then the claim I have already made—that the two should first be investigated separately from one another—follows automatically; but it follows still more that, in every species of animal investigated, for every single correspondence discovered between expressive phenomena and specific impression mechanisms the "range of coincidence," the degree of their mutual influence in phylogeny, and the particular form and extent of the correspondence must be established. Up to the present time, at any rate, general functional principles for all this can no doubt be stated, but certainly no definitive definition of expression or impression or, say, of any integrated functional whole covering both in all individual cases. The latter is particularly impossible for the simple reason that scarcely two identical examples of this functional interplay exist.

IV. BASIC PROCESSES OF EXPRESSION

The effector systems in and through which expression takes place in all multicellular animals consist of muscles, glands, and the chromatophore systems (which in many lower orders of vertebrates and nonvertebrates help bring about a rapid change of color), together with the connecting nerves and in some cases certain ancillary systems which will be dealt with later. Nothing else is involved—even vocalization is, from the point of view of the effectors, the result of muscular contractions.

The neural supplies of the effectors belong partly to the autonomic, partly to the motor system. The latter are, so to speak, under the direct control of the propensities; the former have a relative amount of autonomy which is, however, within certain limits governed by the demands of the motor system. Any particular expression is usually a mixture of both effects. The motivational minority achieving expression has various possibilities for exerting influence on the effectors:

1. It can "take over" the ones not, or not fully, claimed by the motivational combination currently dominant. This is above all true in the case of autonomic functions, such as pupil reactions, blushing, and perspiring, which betray so much that is not in keeping with the rest of the behavior of the individual concerned. Often, therefore, they are particularly good indicators of an imminent change of mood; for example, a sudden narrowing of pupils, which announces imminent attack, and dilation of pupils which indicates a readiness for escape or for defense, depending on the situation, while all other behavior still simulates complete composure.

2. The motivational group striving for expression can force a direct influence on the effectors already claimed by the majority, and it can do this in three ways:

a. by changes of tonus. Every posture and movement requires for its unimpeded and harmonious performance an appropriate distribution of tonus in the musculature involved. In the case of what are called "voluntary" movements, simultaneously with the movement impulses to the motoneurons corresponding impulses reach autonomic ganglia, which regulate muscle tonus, by way of extrapyramidal tracts. As the speed of conductivity of the extrapyramidal tracts is greater than that of the pyramidal tract, the motor impulses find the correct distribution of "readiness" awaiting them in the musculature when they arrive. "Expression," i.e. the tendencies not gaining the upper hand in the motor sphere, can strengthen muscle tonus, weaken it and/or distribute it differently, in a manner from scarcely noticeable to extreme, and this brings about a very characteristic change in the flow of the movement being performed, although the motor impulses themselves remain unchanged (de Crinis 1943, W. R. Hess 1943).

b. by changes in threshold of the motoneurons in the spinal cord. As von Holst has shown (1936–1939, Hugger 1941), all rhythmical and complicated movements originate from the interplay of groups of automatically and rhythmically active neurons and groups of moto-neurons in the spinal cord. Rhythm and form of the movement are influenced solely by the automatic elements, the amplitude of move-ment, however, by both kinds. Without affecting the activity of the automatic elements, the amplitude of movement can, therefore, be changed by reflex alterations in the threshold of the motor cells. The expression of playfulness in many kinds of motor play is produced in this way (Leyhausen 1954, 1956).

c. by motor superimposition. Through the superimposition of the motor systems of two or more conflicting propensities, mixed motor patterns occur from which it is possible to tell the relative strength of the propensities involved with quantitative precision. An early example of this, provided by Lorenz (1952), was the facial expression of the dog torn between escape and attack. It can be shown in even greater detail in the facial expression and body posture and movement of the cat (Leyhausen 1956) (Fig. 1). The arched back of a cat pro-duced by this process appears phenomenologically to be a thoroughly uniform expressive (threatening) posture, but experiment and analysis reveal that it consists of several movement patterns superimposed on each other. Tembrock (1963) analyzed corresponding superimpositions in "mixed calls" by the fox. The principle has been found in practically all vertebrates investigated in this connection (Eibl-Eibesfeldt 1957, 1967, Ewer 1963, Morris 1956 a, b, 1958, Moynihan 1962, Tembrock 1957, 1959, 1961). Leonhard (1949) has described it in detail in con-nection with the "social miens" of humans.

The expressive phenomena contained in this group are primarily responsible for the opinion that expression is to be found only in the particular way in which a behavior pattern is performed (the "how") but not in the pattern itself, in fact that no behavior patterns exist which *are* largely or even completely expression. To this way of thinking, only so to speak the overtones, the timbre could be ex-pression but never the melody itself. Klages already wrote in this sense in 1936, although he did not adhere to it consistently; and recently Kirchhoff (1962 a) has done so most emphatically. The working hypoth-esis proposed here—that expression is the effect produced by the current motivational minority on the effectors—is, as I have frequently emphasized, only a first approach and can in no way be employed in support of a rigorous limitation of the definition of expression to the "how." In Fig. 1 the "how" hypothesis can be used only in con-nection with the products of superimposition in which one of the two components is relatively weak; if one looks at square 4D the super-imposition of maximum readiness for defense on maximum readiness

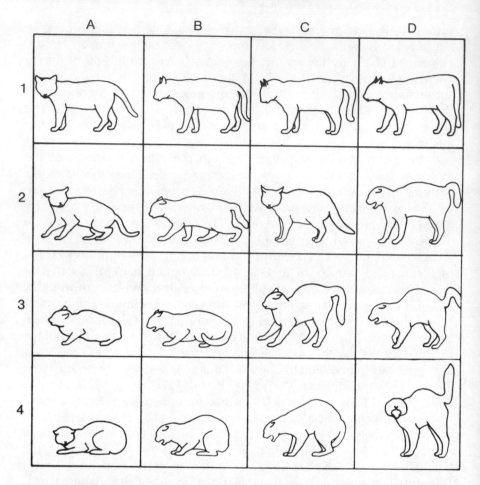

Fig. 1 Expression of readiness for defense or attack in the cat. 1 A-D horizontal: from "neutral" to maximally aggressive; A 1-4 vertical: from "neutral" to maximally defensive. The other squares show corresponding superimpositions. No posture has been interpolated, all are drawn from photographs or film. Under suitable conditions every stage may be experimentally elicited in the same animal (cf. Film E 27, Leyhausen 1955 b).

for attack impresses one not only as a quite new, unique expressive gestalt, it *is* in fact for practical purposes nothing more: Any real action, any other kind of behavior is totally blocked for as long as this posture lasts; it is—in this sense—"pure" expression of rage. And between the extremes there is an unbroken continuum of transitions (diagonals 1A–4D). Where would one draw the line in order to satisfy the "how" designation of expression? The "how" designation characterizes a great number of expressive phenomena, but nothing like all of them.

3. Intention movements are beginnings of behavior patterns which, as a result of only slight motivation or simultaneous, strong inhibition exerted by conflicting tendencies, cannot (yet) be completed (for further details see p. 317). Various simultaneous intentions alternate rhythmically or are superimposed on one another (ambivalent movements; Bastock, Morris, and Moynihan 1953). This, however, represents only a special case in connection with 2c (say 2B in Fig. 1).

4. Displacement movements. In situations which stimulate conflicting propensities, or in which one propensity is prevented by external circumstances from being transformed into activity, behavior patterns often appear which have no obvious connection with the situation and the propensities activated by it. A stickleback wavering between attack and escape digs in the sand; an avocet in the same situation adopts the sleeping posture; a cat which would like to get up but is too lazy to do so licks its shoulder; a father, in two minds whether he should give his child a kiss or a slap for a pertinent but untimely remark in the presence of relatives, scratches himself behind the ear. The nature of displacement movements and the hypotheses as to their cause which are available at present cannot be dealt with here (see chap. 4). For our purposes two points are of significance: a) Displacement movements are very characteristic of certain internal and external conflict and inhibition situations, b) in the circumstances concerned they are very conspicuous because they do not seem to fit into the framework of the situation. It was principally expressive movements derived from displacement movements, such as laughing, which defied Darwin's efforts to derive them from a "serviceable movement" in accordance with his First Principle of Expression (The Principle of Serviceable Associated Habits, 1872). in the framework of the situation at any given time displacement movements have never had a purpose, but some have acquired one secondarily in the service of social communication. At this point in the performance of behavior, they have no further function *except* expression; they represent the second category of "pure" expressive movements.

5. Partial anticipation of an action. When, for example, cats are sitting close to desirable prey without being able to reach it (perhaps because there is a fence between them), one may observe that in expectation or anticipation of eating they not only salivate and lick their lips but often open and close their jaws spasmodically as well ("teeth-chattering"); this is nothing more nor less than the rhythmic, mimically exaggerated anticipation of predatory biting. Köhler (1921 a)

describes the "sympathetic movements" which a chimpanzee performed as it watched another piling boxes under bananas which had been hung up in the neighboring cage. Similar sympathetic movements can easily be observed in sportsmen or in children watching a Punch and Judy show. With all these movements it is not a matter of imitation, but quite simply of an often exaggerated performance, in facial mime and pantomime, of movements or parts of movements which one would perform if one were in that situation oneself or could only get at the object. Closely related with these phenomena are

6. Actions using an alternative object (redirected activities; Bastock, Morris, and Moynihan 1953), some of which can become expressive movements: the fist which dares not hit the opponent pounds the table top and so becomes an expression of violent but helpless or barely controlled rage.

7. Severing contact. Chance (1962) was the first to point out how noticeably often an animal breaks off agonistic encounters with a conspecific by means of movements and postures which render it impossible for it to see its opponent any longer. Mostly these are escape intentions such as closing the eyes or turning the head, or displacement movements; many birds preen the underside of their wings ("displacement preening"); the avocet, as already mentioned, uses the sleeping posture as a threatening gesture. Intention movements of escape are perfectly understandable in such a situation, but the curious fact that displacement movements of the kind mentioned are so frequent when the animal actually ought to be keeping a careful watch on its opponent led Chance to the following conclusion: The sight of the opponent acts as a stimulus on the animal which through stimulus summation would eventually be bound to arouse either its escape or its fighting behavior if the stimulus flow were not interrupted. By turning away from the opponent in intention movements of escape or in displacement movements and thus severing contact with the stimulus ("Cut-off acts," Chance), the animal gives itself, so to speak, a respite in which to await developments, or a pause in fighting, and thus often the possibility of avoiding a fight or further fighting without leaving the scene or stimulating the opponent to a chase by running away. Chance quotes examples of this from his own observation of rats and from ornithological literature. In cats I described this "cut-off" as "looking around" (1956); this is of practical use to an inferior animal in strained social situations, precisely as Chance assumed, and also, above all, when the partners approach one another in courtship and mating. Such behavior, how-

ever, indicates that, on the one hand, an animal is not prepared to yield but also that, on the other, it is not for its part in an aggressive mood. Such a gesture of severing contact contains an offer of peace as well as a warning to the other not to push matters to the limit, and this is the effect it often produces, i.e. in many animals there are appropriate receptive IRMs. According to the case, one aspect or another may be emphasized; the sleeping posture of the avocet became a pure gesture of threat, "looking around" by the cat a gesture of inferiority to inhibit attack—but without being a "submissive gesture," for if the cat is nonetheless attacked it defends itself energetically. In at least partial accord with Darwin's Second Principle of Expression (The Principle of Antithesis, 1872), failure to look away, that is express staring, comes to mean an active challenge to the opponent, as Schenkel (1947) discovered in wolves, and as is likewise true in the case of cats and quite certainly a large number of other mammals as well, including man.

In other sensory areas severing contact is less obvious. Slower, shallower, or interrupted breathing occurs in many situations; whether or how far one may interpret this as "cut-off" from olfactory stimuli is still an open question. It is equally unclear with the sense of hearing; perhaps one may assume that threatening sounds and calls often serve not only to intimidate an opponent but also to deafen the caller to the other's threats.

V. THE FUNCTIONAL PECULIARITIES OF THE INNATE RELEASING MECHANISMS

1. Filtering of stimuli

Innate releasing mechanisms do not always react to so few and so simple environmental features as in the case of the tick. However, in all cases which have been analyzed with any precision it was found to be relatively few and mostly simple features to which the mechanism reacts. With an inexperienced animal at least, all other features, conditions, etc. which constitute the biological situation concerned are of no account for the purpose of arousing a reaction. In individual cases, such as that of the tick, the sensory organs of the animal concerned may indeed, like a specially adjusted antenna, transform only these signals and no others into excitation and pass them on to the central nervous system. This is naturally not so in the case of higher animals with sensory organs capable of greater performance. Such animals, however, make use of only a fraction of what their senses perceive in any situation while, as it were, "ignoring" the rest. The female grayling butterfly (Tinbergen et al. 1942) reacts to the courtship flight of a male without regard to its color characteristics and thus behaves as if it were color-blind. The butterflies are, however, eager flower-visitors, and when searching for food can—like other diurnal moths and butterflies (Ilse 1929) and bees (von Frisch 1914)—differentiate remarkably well between colors. The IRM reacts, it is true, to only few and often qualitatively very varied features of the situation as a whole, yet only seldom—and in the case of higher animals certainly never—is such selectivity due to a limited performance capacity of the sensory organs. From the study of human perception we have adequate knowledge of the extent to which our expectations, wishes, and fears sharpen our senses to appropriate impressions but more or less dull them to all else (Drever 1961, Graumann 1966, von Holst 1957, Metzger 1953, 1954, Witte 1965). Under the general heading of "social perception" (cf. collective review by Graumann 1956) American research workers in particular have carried out thorough investigations of these correlations and demonstrated the decisive influence the current motivational state has on perception. Anything "irrelevant" finds it difficult to attract attention. The whole of perception is therefore by no means merely a passively receptive process, but a highly active one largely governed by the current motivational state. There is no reason to assume that the perceptual processes we have designated as innate releasing mechanisms are an exception to this rule. On the contrary, it may even be presumed that they and their functional peculiarities provide the main basis for the entire phenomenon.

2. The law of stimulus summation

The first releasing mechanism reacting to expressive phenomena in a conspecific to be subjected to strict experimental analysis provided a considerable surprise: The features by which a male fish of the species *Astatotilapia strigigena* recognizes the readiness of another to fight, so that it can prepare either for battle or for escape, are apparently processed by the releasing mechanism not into a complex or gestalt, but only into a sum. Coloring of body and fins, spreading of fins and lower jaw, beating of tail, and ramming all possess their own separate stimulus value. Single features may be missing or be replaced by others; this changes the stimulus effect not qualitatively—as might be expected according to the theories of gestalt perception—but only quantitatively. In his experiment Seitz (1940) was able to make a quantitatively precise forecast of the stimulus strength of a dummy from the type and number of features assembled in it. It is not possible to deal here with the methods employed. I would, however, emphasize that the strength of effect of a stimulus may be determined only in relation to the readiness to react of the tested fish. This must, therefore, be established in every single experiment. The procedure is known in ethology as the method of dual quantification of external stimulus strength and internal excitation (Seitz 1940, Lorenz 1943 a).

The "law of summation of heterogeneous stimuli" has so far been confirmed in every releasing mechanism closely investigated in this respect (Ahrens 1953, Andrew 1956 a, b, c, Baerends 1941, 1956–1958, Drees 1952, Fisher and Hale 1957, Heinemann 1958, Lorenz 1950 b, M. Schleidt 1955, Tinbergen 1948, 1951, 1962, Tinbergen et al. 1939, 1942).

3. The supernormal object

The stimulus value of individual features is not constant. The individual features may be quantitatively changed within broad limits, and the stimulus value or success rises and falls parallel with these changes. If one invests a dummy with brighter colors, larger contours, more emphatic movements than ever appear in a genuine *Astatotilapia* male, its effect is correspondingly quantitatively stronger than that produced by the living fish ("supernormal object"). This principle— that individual features may be quantitatively modified *independently of one another* (and not somehow correlatively!)—was first discovered by Koehler and Zagarus in the ringed plover (1937). Since then it has likewise been confirmed without exception, if we ignore features (such as 37°C in the case of the tick) in relation to which the IRM leaves no scope for quantitative modifiability.

Wörner (1940), on the basis of his film analyses of the expressive behavior of some rhesus monkeys, describes how individual features vary without reference to the whole, or may indeed be omitted altogether, without influencing the effect of the remaining features. He continues literally: "The extent to which one is inclined to designate such formations as wholes or gestalts depends on how these are defined and will not be investigated further here." Had he investigated further there is no doubt that the principle of independent quantitative modifiability of individual features, discovered three years before by Koehler and Zagarus (l.c.), would have become clear to him and he would have been obliged to realize that it was incompatible with even the most generous interpretation of the gestalt criteria. From the broader context of his work, however, it is obvious that he is completely captive to the theoretical opinion that *all* perception must be of an integrated whole or gestalt, and this prevented him from recognizing that a mode of perception of a completely different kind also exists.

Ahrens (1953) found independent quantification of individual features and the effect of stimulus summation in the course of an experimental investigation of the individual stimuli which arouse smiling in babies; in the case of older babies, however, gestalt features were necessary in addition (see p. 357 et seq.). Peters (1937) had found that the stimulus combination "hole between eyes" causes the young of a mouth-brooding fish to swim back into the mother's jaws in the event of danger or at dusk. Here a dummy with four eyes made out of plasticine was greatly superior to the normal state. I therefore persuaded Ahrens to use dummies with four and six eyes in his experiments as well, and during a certain phase of the baby's development the six-eyed dummy in particular proved to be a classic supernormal object.

According to Wolfgang Schmidt (1957) even in the case of older children the impression "laughing face" is still conveyed by individual features whose combined effect obeys the above two rules applying to IRMs. Schmidt was able to make a supernormal dummy whose extreme characteristics of laughing the receiver of the impression can, for anatomical reasons, never see simultaneously when looking at another human laughing, but only separately from various points of view. This dummy achieved precisely the result forecast: It beat even the strongest "normal dummy" by a long way. Gardner (1965) and Hückstedt (1965) investigated what Lorenz (1943 a) called the *Kindchenschema* and here too found the law of independent quantifiability of individual features confirmed. They did not check the law of stimulus summation.

Proving beyond all doubt that an IRM exists is possible only in an animal reared without specific experience. If, however, the releasing effect of a complex situation is demonstrably based on only a few features which, singly and independently of one another, may be quantitatively modified and presented in every possible combination, and if in experiment the effect of each combination can be calculated in advance as the sum of the stimuli, then the presence of an innate releasing mechanism may be presumed with a fair degree of certainty. Furthermore, no case has so far become known in which learned or otherwise acquired eliciting mechanisms possessed *all* these properties *simultaneously*.

Grzimek (1943, 1944), supported by his own observations and those of Spindler and Bluhm (1934), has already drawn attention to the fact that complexes of conditioned stimuli can also produce a kind of summative effect. Sea lions observed by Spindler and Bluhm in the Koenigsberg Zoo recognized their keeper equally well by his face and keeper's uniform as by his face and keeper's cap, but not by only one of these three "features." But this particular point contradicts the law of summation of heterogeneous stimuli. According to that law, even the individual feature taken out of its context should have been able to elicit a reaction, even if one of lower intensity; male sticklebacks ready for reproduction, whose red-colored belly is a warning and a threat signal, reacted with threat to a red post van driving past the laboratory window (Tinbergen 1951), and a few rust-red feathers fixed to a branch in the territory of a robin were sufficient to stimulate the territory owner to attack (Lack 1939). Most important of all, however, in the cases quoted by Grzimek the individual features cannot be quantitatively modified independently of the rest of the configuration as a whole, e.g. by covering the keeper's face and making the cap twice as large or more brightly colored. The apparent accordance of these cases with the law of stimulus summation does not stand up to closer examination.

Whereas Grzimek based his argument on chance observations, Baerends, Bril, and Bult (1965) recently attempted to check experimentally whether a summative effect could be proved in the case of the individual components of a complex stimulus pattern which before the experiment was quite certainly unknown to the experimental animal, a pigtailed macaque, and which plainly has gestalt character. The three authors do indeed arrive at the conclusion that they had, if not proved the effect of stimulus summation with certainty, at least made it extremely probable.

The monkey was tested in the choice experiment. The standard stimulus was a gray circular disc with a concentric ring of dark dots and dark spikes set in star formation on the periphery, in other words a geometrically regular figure, a "distinguished configuration" (ausgezeichnete Gestalt). (As far as I can see, however, it never happens in nature that the IRM-effective individual features of a situation or a partner can be combined in a genuine gestalt, not to mention a distinguished one.) In preliminary experiments the monkey had not spontaneously preferred any of the individual elements used to any of the others. Now it learned to prefer the standard drawing to a series of "negative" figures; these were all without exception irregular in outline and/or patterning. When this training was complete, a series of further figures was prepared of which the standard drawing was a basic element, but disc size, number, size, and shading of dots and spikes, and all independently of one another, were largely altered or omitted altogether. *But in no case was the regularity of the figure destroyed; the "basic gestalt" of the standard drawing was always preserved!* Out of each pair of test figures set out for its choice the monkey now showed statistically significant preference for the "stronger" in terms of number and execution of the "individual features." This result, however, need not indicate stimulus summation. It can be interpreted just as well, if not better, if one assumes that the monkey was guided by the degree of similarity of the configuration as a whole to the standard drawing. The control—namely setting up a new test series on the basis of calculated relative eliciting values of the individual features (see W. Schmidt 1957), the result of which would have to be quantitatively forecast, and testing this forecast experimentally—was omitted. Characteristically, it was furthermore impossible to construct a permanently effective, "supernormal" test figure by exaggerating the given elements of the standard figure. This attempt by the three authors to prove the effect of stimulus summation also in the case of "acquired" perceptual configurations must for the moment be regarded as a failure. A repetition, in which the complication bound up with the use of distinguished configurations would have to be avoided and the necessary controls carried out, is urgently desirable. For if the findings were to be confirmed, then not only would the theory of the general validity of the gestalt principle ("Gestalt is not the sum . . .") in the case of all individually acquired perceptual functions (at least in the optical field) have to be revised, but we should simultaneously lose what was so far the only experimental aid which we could hope would help us prove and investigate IRMs in humans as well, the "deprivation experiment" (rearing in isolation) being, of course, denied us here.

Man very probably has IRMs, i.e. therefore innate apperception of expression (Lorenz 1943 a), for a great many more expressive phenomena. Quite obviously innate elements independent of specific experience play a far greater and profounder role in man's expressive behavior as well as his comprehension of expression than has hitherto been assumed in human psychology (Koehler 1951, 1954, 1955). As already mentioned, W. Schmidt (1957) found an incontestable effect of stimulus summation in the case of the five features making up the impression "laughing human" which he investigated. Using a similar method, I was able to confirm this fully in extensive, so far unpublished experiments concerning human display behavior. As Lorenz

(1943 a) shows, it is most probably also the effects of stimulus summation which enable the fashion in clothes to emphasize now this, now that feature of the female or male body far beyond its natural size, only to neglect it again completely and display another instead, without thereby lessening the stimulus effect—on the contrary, constantly amplifying it or at least keeping it alive in this way. The available characteristics are, however, restricted in number, and so fashion is obliged to repeat itself. It cannot simply choose or invent characteristics as it likes, but must confine itself to "IRM-effective" ones! If it were a question only of the principle of maximum variety, the basic themes of fashion would certainly have become much more numerous in the course of time, just as in fact the small accessories are very much more diverse. But if a fashion designer does at some time dare to break out of this "monotony," his creations never enjoy very long-lived success. Thus, in the IRMs of men and women which react to the other sex there are probably two "proportion features" (Lorenz 1943 a), one of which emphasizes the narrowness of the waist and the other the length of the legs. And since IRMs react not negatively but positively to exaggerations, the women's fashion of Biedermeier (Empire to early Victorian), for example, with its extreme over-accentuation of leg length (though hidden by skirt), was able to last a long time while diametrically opposed more modern creations, which filled out the waist and moved the belt deep down onto the hips, were adopted by only few women and died again soon after their creation. The same is correspondingly true of fashions in make-up, which are meant to overemphasize attractive expressive characteristics of the face to varying degrees and retain them as in a mask, or to give appropriate assistance to expressive movements; it is also true of a large number of time, group, culture, and race dependent mannerisms of style in movement, language, and so on. I shall return to these relationships later in connection with the question where and how learning intervenes in the history of expression and impression.

4.   Level-dependent evaluation of sensory data

Here I should like to guard against a possible misunderstanding. The fact that an IRM "calculates" the sensory data affecting it purely summatively and that in this particular case, in contrast to Klages' opinion, the "summative nature of perception" (*Addierbarkeit der Anschauungswelt*) is proven beyond doubt does not mean that *these same* sensory data could not simultaneously and together with a quantity of other data to which the releasing mechanism is "indifferent" be processed to complex, gestalt, background, or other forms of perception. On the contrary, in the case of all higher animals sensory data are quite certainly evaluated simultaneously by at least two different filtering, sorting, and integrating central nervous mechanisms working at different levels and on different principles. In the case of the sense of vision, for example, three such "levels" may even be discerned anatomically: a) Before the optic nerve passes into the lateral geniculate body, it establishes connections with practically all parts of the brain stem from the hypothalamus to the substantia grisea in the medulla. From the nature of these connections with nuclei of nerves serving the eye musculature and the extrapyramidal motor system (nucleus ruber), it can be concluded that here mainly the attention and the directing, spatially orienting mechanisms (taxes; for concept of taxis see Kühn 1919, Koehler 1950) of the sense of vision are supplied and activated. b) From the lateral geniculate body, that great switching station of the optic tracts, relatively unobtrusive nerve tracts stretch directly to the interbrain. Largely ignored so far by neuroanatomists and neurophysiologists, they are not even mentioned in most textbooks and anatomical atlases, and their function has scarcely been investigated. Only Clara (1942) mentions briefly that they are probably responsible for the "emotional tone" of optical perception. That, however, is roughly how we can expect an IRM to affect subjective experience: It does not produce a differential, detailed picture, but directly stimulates specific feelings, bearings, attitudes, or actions in response. The suspicion that these nerve tracts exist in the service of IRMs would therefore certainly deserve closer investigation. c) Finally, the main projection tract goes from the lateral geniculate body to the optical cortex of the cerebrum via which the "normal" functions of gestalt, color, movement and distance vision, etc., are mediated. Naturally the hypothesis postulating a load-sharing according to b) and c) is not to be interpreted as meaning that emotional reactions cannot be released via the optical cortex—for example by association. The functional differences between the two kinds of "apparatus for evaluating sensory data" described in b) and c) may perhaps be illustrated by the following model: As is well-known, the sequence, range of frequency, and (by means of differences in shading) also the volume of sounds recorded on tape can be portrayed in what is known as a "sound spectrogram." This would correspond to total evaluation of all sensory messages arriving at any given time at mechanism c). The impulses from the tape can, however, be fed into a sound level recorder instead of a sound spectrograph; the curve obtained in this way merely reflects summatively the total volume of sound, its total energy. If between tape recorder and sound level recorder we now interposed a battery of band-pass filters in parallel, each of which would let only one particular frequency band through, the sound level recorder would reproduce in *one* curve the summation of the sound energy supplied by the frequency bands selected, and something corresponding to this apparently happens in the IRM. The model possesses one further interesting property which cannot, however, be dealt with in greater detail here: It explains automatically why the selectivity of an IRM increases when the releasing threshold rises and decreases when it falls. Naturally this is not to say that the model is anything more than an illustration of one functional property of the IRM. The "detector theory of optical releasing mechanisms" (Jander 1964), for example, provides a model for another functional property of IRMs, the task of which is to stimulate directional mechanisms (taxes) and not to release instinctive movements. This distinction is perfectly possible, as Tinbergen and Kuenen (1939) have shown. The concept of the IRM is built up on the basis of its functional peculiarities, but of course functions of the same kind must not necessarily come about in the same way (Lorenz 1943 a). Certainly *an* IRM is not an anatomical unit but already a functional apparatus with a varying degree of complication in each case. (p. 322 et seq.).

The inevitable question now is what point there is in an organism "going to the expense" of developing at least two systems so different in function for the evaluation of sensory data, what advantage in natural selection it had during evolution and of course still has and will continue to have. We find one possible answer to this in the results and considerations of Kohler (1955): In the field of optical perception "ordered and therefore stable relationships between changing stimuli . . . themselves act as permanent stimuli, but of a 'higher order'." Adaptation mechanisms[1] adjust themselves to these in such a way that in the process of structuring perception and in the resulting structures themselves the covariance of the individual stimuli, the accustomed stimulus context or complex, represents the "zero state" to which the details of the whole perceptual field are related. If the covariance changes, the mechanisms of adaptation follow with a certain amount of delay, for example in an experiment with Stratton-type lenses. These mechanisms, the functional apparatus of which Kohler was able to represent in a relatively simple model, thus determine the precise correspondence between perceptual norms and normal environmental conditions. According to investigations carried out on young cats by Held and Hein (1963), these mechanisms of adaptation seem to coordinate only when the organism performs actions in its momentary perceptual situation. Corresponding experiments on human ESS (for example with Stratton-type lenses) have, as far as I know, not yet been carried out. Patients with severe paralysis resulting from spinal lesion, injuries to the cervical vertebrae or similar illnesses who are, or must be kept, immobile for a considerable time might well be persuaded to cooperate in such experiments, for these would very probably provide them with a highly welcome distraction from their condition. The observations of Freedman on congenitally blind children, described in detail on p. 332, furthermore encourage the assumption that the hand and its use at first play a leading role in the ontogeny of perceptual organization. This is a further and important indication of the extent to which motivation has a hand in building up and determining the perceptual world, not only during actualization but also during ontogeny (see p. 306).

The IRMs, on the other hand, do not take their norm from the current perceptual situation but *set the norm themselves*. Being independent of the stimulus situation as a whole, the effect of an individual feature pays no heed to covariances, and the independent quantifiability of the individual feature leaves the norm, so to speak, open at the top end. These properties of the IRMs have without doubt developed during phylogeny primarily because in many cases, but particularly in the case of short-lived lower animals, the response to a stimulus must "go right" from the first and there is no opportunity whatever for the adaptive adjustment of a "norm" of covariants. Secondarily, however, just because the IRMs do not seek but set the norm (and indeed a norm open-ended in one direction) for the individual, they assume an extremely strong influence on breeding, particularly so the IRMs relating to conspecifics, as Lorenz has frequently emphasized (1940, 1943 a, b, 1951, 1966). The principle or orthogenesis certainly has no such universal validity in evolution as its discoverer Eimer and others after him assumed. Yet, there were constantly factors which compelled, if not whole organisms, at least certain of their organs and functions to take a particular evolutionary direction and held them fast in it for considerable periods of time. IRMs coined for conspecifics, particularly those of the higher animals, are quite certainly factors of this kind which have influenced and still influence structures as well as functions (and therefore also behavior patterns) in the sense of orthogenesis and have thus caused them to differentiate more and more. This is without doubt a powerful advantage in natural selection, even when one allows for the fact that the process occasionally went too far. The two systems for the evaluation of sensory data are, therefore, quite classic examples of the two evolutionary directions noted on p. 295 et seq., toward maximum adaptability on the one side (perception in the narrowest sense) and maximum preadaptation on the other (IRMs). As I shall show, the products of these two functions can blend together in experience to such an extent that the contribution made by each cannot be distinguished from that point of view, a fact eminently suited to throwing light on some otherwise incomprehensible results and conclusions drawn from experimental research on expression in humans.

5. Afferent throttling

One very important functional characteristic of the IRM is its exhaustibility in relation to specific features (adaptation, Prechtl 1953; afferent throttling, M. Schleidt 1955). Young song-birds in the nest stretch their gaping beaks toward an approaching parent bird for feeding. Three stimuli release gaping in an inexperienced nestling: a slight jarring of the nest, sounds more or less similar to bird twittering (whistling, cheeping, clicking the tongue and so on suffice), and a dark body at the rim of the nest above the level of the young bird's eyes (Tinbergen and Kuenen 1939). As Prechtl found, each of these stimuli alone is fully effective. If, however, he presented the same stimulus many times in succession and at short intervals the young birds eventually stopped gaping, but immediately gaped with full intensity again in response to one of the other two stimuli. The gaping movement itself, therefore, is not exhausted. After a pause for recuperation sensitivity toward the stimulus that had been presented too often returns. Presenting two or all three stimuli simultaneously led to adaptation only after a far greater number of single tests than did the use of one stimulus only. The exhaustibility of the IRM in relation to specific features represents only a special instance of the adaptation to constantly or repeatedly effective stimuli well-known in sensory physiology. It is a factor which must additionally be taken into account when using the method of dual quantification (p. 306/7).

VI.   THE MATCHING OF EXPRESSION AND IMPRESSION DURING PHYLOGENY

1.   The "phylogenetic plasticity" of expression and impression

As will be obvious from the two preceding sections, expression has a great choice of means and combinations of means at its disposal.

Compared with this, the IRMs, various in type as they may be from what little we know so far of their physiological nature, display certain matching and very particular functional characteristics which likewise impose particular conditions on expression if it is to become impression. Expression, being the more "plastic" partner in phylogenetic development, has therefore adapted itself far more and more obviously to the functional conditions set by the IRM than vice versa. Indeed, it almost seems as if it was only in the case of animals with the highest forms of social life that selection pressure insisted so strongly on differentiated means of communication that the capacity to form an impression became considerably more refined than it was in its primitive state.

As a result the literature of animal psychology and ethology is full of examples of the first-mentioned adaptive direction (see section VI., 2), but scarcely one example of the other is to be found. Furthermore, when anyone has discovered fairly complex and refined functions of the capacity to form an impression, he has been all too ready to regard the familiar limitations of the IRM as something given once and for all and to impute anything going beyond this to experience and learning (Schenkel 1947, Ahrens 1953, Gwinner 1962). Naturally this may be correct in an individual case, but it does not have to be, and the question still remains what is experienced or learned, when and how. At the present moment, therefore, we can establish *that* numerous IRMs reacting to expressive features originated during phylogeny. To my knowledge, however, we so far possess not one single special investigation as to the manner in which a particular expressive event has had an effect on the breeding not only of specific sensitivity to features but also of functional peculiarities of the specific capacity to form an impression. Therefore, when I attempt in the following text to demonstrate appropriate evolutionary processes, this is based on a series of observations and indications, but is nonetheless very speculative.

2. Impression-dependent breeding of expressive phenomena

The primary breeding influence which the functional peculiarities of the IRM described in V. exerted on the history of expression (and, of course, still do exert in the case of all free-ranging animal species) may be discussed under four main headings:—

a. *Concentration.* Apparently it is difficult for an IRM to become receptive to a large number of features, and so it tries to reduce complex expressive phenomena to just a few elements and instead to make these few particularly impressive. In the case of mammals and birds, for example, an excretion of adrenaline, such as always accompanies the elicitation of escape and defense, leads among other things to the excitation of the smooth muscles which cause hairs or feathers to stand erect; as a result, in animal forms which are in this respect primitive, such as rats and many other rodents, the hairs stand on end over the whole body. In many species, however, the effect of the adrenaline is concentrated in narrowly restricted sections of plumage or fur, mainly on the head and back (Morris 1956 a). Finally, as a result of a further step, differentiation can occur; in the case of the cat it is possible to determine the relative mixture of propensities for defense and attack at any given moment from which particular sections of hair have been erected and how these change the body contour (Leyhausen 1956).

In the case of many gregarious animals there are IRMs which react to particular behavior patterns performed by conspecifics—especially those of locomotion, lying down to rest and feeding, often too of defense—and elicit the same kind of movement in the "receiver." In ethology this is known as "sympathetic induction of mood by an IRM" and, it may be mentioned in passing, forms the biological basis of what in human psychology is commonly called "the immediate experiencing and understanding of the reality of another person's mind" (see also p. 298). If a cow in a resting herd stands up and begins to graze slowly away, all the others soon follow suit. On the basis of such and similar observations Klages (1936), like many others before and since, concluded that *any* perceived "self-driven movement" stimulates imitation. This is out of the question. Instead, a mood-inducing IRM specially sensitive to the movement in question is necessary in every case, and this IRM naturally originates only as a result of correspondingly directed selection pressure. In the above example, sympathetic induction of mood ensures the cohesion of the herd, which would otherwise be lost sooner or later. Where, once begun, a change of location could take one member of the herd or swarm too quickly out of the perceptual field of the others, the sensitivity of the IRM is tuned above all to preparatory movements (e.g. before flying), "intention movements." Once again the IRM is a force for concentration; it becomes particularly sensitive toward only certain constituent parts of the intention movements, in general those which already attract the most attention anyway, and the effect of selection is obviously that these become more and more strongly emphasized, more and more conspicuously performed. In the case of the Graylag Goose, for example, there are two such elements—the sideways shaking of the beak and particular calls—to which the mood-inducing IRM reacts and which are therefore exaggerated in a conspicuous manner (Lorenz 1935).

b. *Typification.* In general expression reflects the degree of excitation of an animal and its current "motivational balance" fairly precisely. Differences in intensity of expressive phenomena can go from "just implied" to "maximum possible." This fits well with the "independent quantifiability of individual characteristics" and the law of summation of heterogeneous stimuli, and in general ensures that the relationship between expressive phenomena and response behavior is a balanced one. There are, however, circumstances in which it seems important that a particular expressive movement should not be overlooked or too weakly answered on account of its slight intensity. Morris (1957) provides various examples of this from tropical finches. Irrespective of their degree of excitation, the male birds always display the most intensive form of certain body and feather postures when courting; the degree of excitation is expressed only in the frequency with which these are repeated. Morris considers that in such cases refinements of expression have been sacrificed to the need always to produce a clear signal, just as the telephone bell always makes the same amount of noise whether the call is urgent or merely the result of the caller's whim. This interpretation will often be accurate; however, M. Schleidt (1955) indicates a further possible explanation: the IRM adapts more slowly to high stimulus intensity than to low; presenting as intensive a display of a characteristic as possible protects expressive movements which are performed frequently or in fast rhythm from becoming ineffective all too soon.

c. *Symbolization.* In a fairly long sequence of instinctive movements, component actions or the intention movements of these frequently occur earlier than they would really have a right to in accordance with the biological function of the behavior as a whole. They have expressive value, for they are *de facto* an anticipation or hint of what is to follow later—often many days and several links in the chain of action later. Many species of cichlids, a family of teleost fishes, form pairs which stay together at least for a reproductive period until the young become independent. They lay their eggs on smooth stones and similar objects, guard them, and fan them constantly with fresh breathing water until the larvae are ready to hatch. They then pick the spawn up in their mouth and bring the larvae into a nest-hollow prepared in readiness on the sandy bed. Both partners dig out this hollow together: They dive steeply or at right angles into the sand with their head, bore and bite into it, push the material along before them and heap it up into a wall, spitting material which has got into their mouth out over the rim. In the male of *Geophagus brasiliensis* nest-digging awakens early, at the same time as the male adopts a territory; he digs particularly intensively, however, when a female approaches. If the female is ready for mating, she digs likewise. When both dig together on the site of the same nest, the marriage is arranged for that season. In the case of this fish, therefore, nest-digging plays a role in courtship, long before a nest is needed in the process of rearing young. Males of *Herichthys cyanoguttatus* rarely perform the digging movement completely during courtship; usually they only dive head downward, often without quite reaching the bottom. This "symbolic" nest-digging is also not bound up with a real nest-hollow, and the female performs the movement only seldom. *Tilapia mossambica* males pose roughly upright before the courted female in open water and without relation to the bottom. They fold their tail fin tightly, so that only the flame-red fringes can still be seen. These they quiver and flick in a unique manner (Leyhausen 1949, Baerends and Baerends-van Roon 1950). Out of this posture they proceed to "lead swimming"; they swim ahead of the female to the spawning hollow. Only the male of this species digs a hollow, and this is used for the act of spawning only and no longer for rearing the young, for these fishes are what are called "mouth-brooders": After spawning, the female takes the fertilized eggs into her mouth and keeps them there until the young hatch complete with the ability to swim. As a movement, the "headstand" of the *Tilapia mossambica* male has scarcely any similarity with the original movement at the beginning of digging; its origin could be deduced only through a knowledge of the intervening forms occurring in the case of *Herichthys* and a few other species. Recently Baerends and Blokzijl (1963) discovered that a closely related species, *T. melanopleura,* occasionally dives from its headstand right to the bottom and performs digging movements, thus proving the old interpretation of the headstand to be correct. Such movements are designated "symbolic movements" because they stand in very abbreviated and modified form so to speak "symbolically" for the invitation "Come, let us dig a nest together and rear young"—and this in a species in which the females no longer dig nests (except when they play the role of a male in what are called "female pairs") and the males no longer participate in rearing the young. As a means of expression the mode of movement has taken on a new meaning completely different from its original purpose: Like a genuine symbol, it scarcely has any similarity with its origin and to a certain extent stands as *pars pro toto*. Yet, that same animal, as I have described, has at its disposal the complete coordinated pattern of digging, for it prepares the spawning hollow. However, symbolization not only endows behavior patterns, which in their original purposive connection remain thoroughly intact, with expressive and communicative function, but it also leads to the preservation of rudiments of behavior the original purpose, indeed the original "working structure," of which has been wholly or partially lost. Primitive species of deer such as the musk deer have no antlers as weapons, but instead upper canine teeth which project daggerlike beyond the lower jaw. Even the muntjak deer, which has small antlers, still uses its canine teeth and also threatens an opponent not with its antlers but by raising its head to an oblique angle, drawing the upper lip back from the canine teeth and parading to and fro in this posture, grinding its teeth and rolling its eyes. The deer of the Rusa group, on the other hand, fight with their antlers and their upper canines have shriveled almost to nothing; yet, they threaten, not as our red deer and fallow deer do, with their antlers, but still in exactly the same way as the muntjak. Thus, the threatening movement and the conspecific capacity to form an impression reacting to it have outlived a whole range of fighting behavior and the organ serving it by countless generations! Yet, one may not assume that the fighting behavior itself would automatically disappear with the loss of the organ. As Krummbiegel (1941) has shown, behavior patterns are perfectly capable of surviving the loss of an organ: Hornless races of cattle and goats, for example, still butt exactly like their horned relations—which is even more noteworthy since artificially dehorned cattle of horned races very quickly learn that this is now pointless! Analogous with the Rusa deer, a ragingly aggressive man—as Darwin already pointed out—still bares his teeth, although humans no longer bite, at least in attack; in a case requiring extreme self-defense, however, women and children still do so frequently. Expressive movements which, like those named, "symbolically" threaten the use of a no longer existent weapon are the most typical examples of Darwin's First Principle of Expression (The Principle of Serviceable Associated Habits, 1872).

The "mimic exaggeration" (Lorenz 1951) so characteristic of the expressive movements falling under (a) and (c) in particular is probably facilitated in many—if not all—cases by the neurophysiological mechanism described in IV. 2a and b. Wörner (1940) made corresponding observations and formulated a kind of "amplifier theory" of expression, since ". . . facial expression represents the small fluctuations in the emotional process on an enlarged scale." This is not, however, valid for *all* expressive processes.

d. *Variation.* As described, an IRM adapts to characteristics presented too frequently in too rapid succession. One way to counter this we already found in typification. If, however, a particular expressive behavior (e.g. the song of many birds) is repeated practically unremittingly, typification is no longer sufficient to compensate for the loss of sensitivity in the mechanisms of impression reacting to it. As birds reared in soundproof chambers have shown (Sauer 1954, Messmer 1956), only certain basic elements of the species song are innate, while further elements are more or less uniformly learned, although in different populations of the same species the traditions may vary from place to place. In addition there are individual variants, the range of variability of which differs in size according to heredity and species. The IRM reacting to species song has one ingredient which, in the sense of independent quantifiability of individual characteristics, reacts quantitatively to "richness of variety," and in some species this has bred an extraordinary capacity for song-learning.

3. Releasers and ritualization

Building up on the basis of the primary processes just described, two further developments occur which come into action partly simultaneously with these primary processes and partly not until later: the evolution of releasers and ritualization.

a. "Releaser" is the name Lorenz (1935) gave to any expressive movement whose form has changed as a direct result of the influence of IRMs on breeding, in a way frequently hinted at already in VI. 2a-c. In addition, however, he also gave the name "releaser" to *structures* which quite clearly developed, or were perfected, only because they contributed toward making some expressive phenomena particularly conspicuous and thus easy for the IRM to recognize. A further step is signified by specially modified movements which present the structures mentioned in a particularly advantageous way to the partner; some movements—such as the folding and the twitching movement of the tail fin of *Tilapia mossambica* described on p. 319—were perhaps bred solely and expressly for this purpose ("display movements," Tinbergen 1948). I would stress with all possible emphasis:

1. *Only* those behavior patterns and structures which *emerged or were perfected through mutual effect between them and an IRM* are "releasers," not, as many authors (e.g. Frijda 1965, Kiener 1965) assume, any "unconditioned" stimulus complex, i.e. one which has effect on an IRM in an innate manner but has not been special-

ized just for that purpose. Extending the concept of releasers in this way would render it completely superfluous, for it would then be merely a synonym for "unconditioned stimulus."

2. Some authors (e.g. Kiener again) interpret Lorenz's model of the lock-key relationship as meaning that as a basic rule an inflexible compulsory mechanism exists between IRMs, the sign stimuli (in particular social releasers) acting in a releasing manner on them, and the instinctive actions. This is a misunderstanding, and in the whole of ethological literature I do not know of anything which would justify it.

To begin with there are structures which are affected by the concentration of autonomic expressive phenomena described in VI. 2a. Frequently feathers or hairs in the regions in which the pilomotor activity is concentrated become elongated. In this way conspicuous crests, beards, and feather or hair combs are formed which are frequently endowed with striking, often dazzlingly bright color markings as well. Finally, many animals can control the pilomotor activity of these areas voluntarily. They can suddenly erect and flatten the structures concerned, which naturally increases their effect considerably (Morris 1956 a). The voluntary motor systems for such display movements can, of course, be evolved by natural selection only when the necessary structures are available.

The structural releasers provide a graphic example of how homologies, analogies, and convergencies can be amalgamated with one another in the process of evolution. In all groups of vertebrates a homologous IRM exists which, among other things, reacts to the feature "(sudden) enlargement of contour" in a conspecific; to be precise, in the sense that it intimidates the receiver of the impression. Almost all vertebrates in "display" or aggressive mood therefore make themselves as large as possible by drawing themselves up tall. Most fishes cannot do this, but instead spread all their fins wide. In addition, however, under the selection pressure of their homologous IRMs numerous species in all groups have developed *analogous* structures and sometimes even accompanying analogous display movements. Some fishes can spread the radii branchiostegi of the lower half of the mouth extremely wide, and the branchiostegal membrane stretched between these considerably enlarges the outline of the head. Sometimes, as in the case of *Cichlasoma meeki*, the membrane is brilliantly colored. The tailed amphibians develop median skin combs on the tail and the back which may likewise be brightly colored (crested newt *Triturus cristatus!*). In the case of some lizards, skins have developed at the throat which, with the help of a specially differentiated hyoid apparatus, can be spread like the branchiostegal membrane of fishes and are often likewise brilliantly colored. The analogous formations in the plumage of birds and the hairy coat of mammals have already been mentioned. Thus: for homologous moods homologous IRMs induce analogous expressive movements and structures which lead to numerous convergencies (branchiostegal apparatus in fishes and hyoid throat skin apparatus in lizards; skin crests in salamanders and dorsal crests in other saurians). A particularly curious convergency of this kind in the same organ can be found in two representatives of the heron family, *Nycticorax nycticorax* (night heron) and *Cochlearius cochlearius* (boat bill heron). The males of the two species perform a nest-greeting ceremony, the movements of which are completely identical in both cases. As it performs the ceremony *Nycticorax* closes its iris suddenly so that the whole eye flashes bright red-yellow. *Cochlearius* has a black iris; it achieves a similar effect by just as suddenly pulling the lower, snow-white nictitating membrane across (Lorenz, personal information 1964). Ravens, carrion crows, and jackdaws when displaying likewise pull the snow-white nictitating membrane with lightning speed over the eye; the magpie, which also belongs to the crow family, has in addition a bright yellow spot in the middle of the nictitating membrane, and in the shape of a ring around its eye are small white-tipped feathers which it erects when excited, thus positively compelling the observer's gaze toward the bird's eye (Gwinner, in correspondence). A further instructive example of such an evolutionary process is offered by the mechanism effecting sympathetic induction of mood, already mentioned briefly, which governs the cohesion of herds and flocks on the move. In simple cases such as a herd of cows, this is probably basically a menotaxis (Kühn 1919), which endeavors to keep the retinal picture of the neighboring animal, and especially that of the leader, constantly the same size (the "set size" may vary within broad limits according to circumstances and the individual). If the leading animal approaches another, the latter withdraws; if the leading animal moves away, it follows it, wherever possible always at the same distance. As most hoofed animals, like many birds, have eyes set at the side of the head (hoofed animals having a horizontally almond-shaped pupil), with relatively little movement of the eyes they have an almost 360° field of vision. As a result, the leading animal does not always need to be at the front of the herd; it can equally well draw the members of its herd along behind it by means of "menotactic pull" or compel them along in front of it by means of "menotactic push."[2] However, if the whole herd needs to be conveyed suddenly in one direction, for instance in the event of danger, menotactic pull is apparently inadequate and might be liable, as it were, to "snap." Thus, in the case of almost all animals living in communities, social releasers have developed. These are mostly pale to white color signals, often with dark edges for contrast, and together with these particular display movements often occur, along with arrangements which make the signal inconspicuous or quite invisible when the animal is at rest (the white areas under the tails of deer, hares, etc.). The sudden presentation of these in the moment of danger increases the stimulus effect. The best-known and most extreme example of such an adaptation is probably the springbok. It could be that the extremely conspicuous facial masks of some animals (e.g. bar-headed goose and gemsbok), for which no other satisfactory functional interpretation could so far be found, in fact came into being as auxiliary signals reinforcing menotactic push, just as rear signal apparatus reinforces menotactic pull. Most observers were no doubt so preoccupied up to now by the (anthropomorphic) opinion that a leading animal must always be at the front that this interpretation simply did not occur to anyone. Here it is possible only to indicate briefly that the basic mechanism of menotaxis I have described recurs as a component part of many other releasing mechanisms, in some cases highly specialized and reacting to numerous single characteristics. In conjunction with sensitivity toward the characteristics of size of object and speed and direction of movements, IRMs evolve which stimulate the chasing of prey or of a beaten opponent and likewise, in the opposite direction of movement, escape, and defense. It is very probably the same mechanism and a thoroughly familiar optical illusion to which the auxiliary apparatus bringing about the sudden enlargement of the body outline owes its existence: particularly in the case of animals without a horopter—in other words, without any real criteria of depth in their optical perception—a sudden enlargement of outline must have the same effect as an equally sudden, fear-inducing approach. In a tachistoscopic experiment with human ESS, if a smaller and a larger dark circular shape are shown successively against a light background, the ESS are subject to the same illusion. Not only that, but if the second shape is large enough, distinct alarm can be induced.

As all this no doubt adequately shows, the individual constructional elements of even highly differentiated IRMs can retain a certain independence, belong to a wide variety of "levels" of the CNS, and some of them be summatively involved in a wide variety of releaser processes. For this reason, if for no other, it is imperative not to think in terms of "an" IRM, and certainly not of that particular function of

IRMs, the capacity to form an impression, as being localized in one particular spot in the CNS. Furthermore, the facts described are a further reason why certain "expressive signs" can be ambiguous (see pp. 298/9, 333, 338, Ewert 1965 a), and in cases such as that of the menotaxis which is "built into" many different IRMs, this certainly has nothing whatever to do with embedding or integrating the sign into a gestalt or apperceptual whole. This menotaxis is integrated into the mechanisms of impression that cause an animal, confronted by a partner which is either approaching or withdrawing, a) to attack, b) to run away, c) to give chase or d) merely to walk or run with it (see also p. 317). This encourages the assumption that menotaxis was primarily concerned only with the release of the locomotion involved in all these behavior patterns. There is room for speculation here as to whether more complex IRMs did not grow together at the same time and at the same rate as animals progressed in evolution from being organized according to the principle of "a reflex republic" (von Uexküll 1909) to having controlling centers of coordination in the CNS. As far as I know, no investigations in this direction have so far been made, but they could perhaps yield information about the phylogenetic development of quite complicated IRMs and thus, too, about the human capacity to form an impression.

Homologous mechanisms of impression can not only influence the breeding of analogous modes of expression with analogous ancillary apparatus, but homologous expressive processes can also come to express very different things; they can, so to speak, undergo a change of meaning, analogous to what happens to concepts in language, and evoke the development of corresponding impression mechanisms. As I have already mentioned (p. 284), yawning occurs as an expressive movement in almost all vertebrates. Considered from a physiological point of view, it characterizes a transitional state of the sleep center which is passed through both before falling asleep and when waking, only in opposite directions. Man possesses a mood-inducing IRM which, provided that he is already somewhat tired, makes him sleepy if he sees another yawn. In the case of the *Canidae* it is just the opposite: They infect each other mutually with yawning when they wake, and this signifies a kind of mutual preparation for communal departure. Yawning occurs frequently, however, for reasons which cannot be discussed here, as a displacement (alternative) movement in the course of agonistic disputes between conspecifics. Thus, apparently convergently, it became a threat movement in baboons and hippopotamuses (!); yawning at an old male baboon at close quarters is not, therefore, to be recommended. Faced with a defensively inclined lion or tiger, however, it is very appropriate, for yawning is a gesture of appeasement in the *Felidae*.

All old world monkeys use a friendly grin as greeting. The *Cercopithecidae*, however, do not draw their lips back from the teeth a little as we do, but around the teeth and inward (Andrew 1963). We, therefore, do not gain an immediately correct impression of the friendly greeting directed at us by one of these monkeys, and it for its part misconstrues our greeting smile as a threatening baring of the teeth, and it either withdraws screaming or bites suddenly! In contrast, the Black Ape, alread quoted by Darwin (1874), grins as we do with slightly raised lips, but on account of its rather different anatomy our impression is that it is baring its teeth in threat. For similar anatomical reasons, some of the facial expressive movements of chimpanzees which are completely homologous with those of humans (laughing, crying, rage) are not very similar to ours. It is not, therefore, astonishing if Foley's ESS (1935), who expressly had no knowledge of chimpanzees, did not recognize the expressive content of chimpanzee photographs with more accuracy than corresponded to chance; furthermore the method of allowing them to judge static photographs is largely inadequate (Wörner 1940); for it is expressive *movements* which have to be judged, and so the appropriate IRMs are at least partly dependent on characteristics of movement for their ability to convey an adequate impression. A *human* must therefore know chimpanzees well to interpret their expression correctly. He can learn this; then, although he receives no immediate impression from the expressive movements of the chimpanzee in question, he *knows* whether the chimpanzee is in a good or a bad mood. From these circumstances Klineberg (1954) draws the premature conclusion that no "real similarity" exists between the expressive movements of the chimpanzee and those of man, and that one must therefore assume that expression is culturally and socially conditioned. The external difference between the facial expressive movements of chimpanzee and human exists, however, in respect of the three movements named only to the extent that no impression or a false one is created. As far as others such as sadness, excitement, and curiosity are concerned, this is not true to the same extent. While, as I have mentioned, the chimpanzee's mime of rage does not immediately impress us "correctly," its pantomime certainly does, and so on.

Even if Klineberg were right and no expressive movement whatever in the chimpanzee directly became impression for a human, that is still far from saying that either chimpanzees among chimpanzees or humans among humans had to learn anything in the process. As I have frequently emphasized, the ethologist does not, as he is often accused of doing, make the reciprocal mistake: He does not assume that because, say, the biologically necessary "basic and minimum equipment" of behavior patterns of an animal for a certain functional context is completely innate, that animal cannot learn additional things within this context and interlock them functionally with the innate elements (Lorenz 1937 a, Leyhausen 1965 a). Thus, some parts of expressive behavior are certainly *also* governed socially and culturally, and this will be discussed in more detail in section VIII. Here, however, I should like to point to another aspect of the facts discussed above: The appropriate movements expressive of feeling in chimpanzee and human are without any doubt quite as homologous as the neural patterns of impulses which bring about the corresponding expressive movements of the effectors. Only because of varying differentiation in the effectors does this lead to externally different expressive pictures. In evolution, however, it is necessarily to these pictures that the receptivity, the specifically analytical sensitivity of the mechanisms of impression adapts; thus it became correspondingly different in chimpanzee and human, and this to a degree which, at least from a static picture, can convey to us an immediate impression of laughing from the mien of an enraged chimpanzee. This demonstrates better than anything could that the facilities for impression evaluate external features and not "the reality of another's mind" or "another person's so-being," and that they therefore necessarily and in predictable manner make "false reports" when the subjective state expressed, the expressive feature, and the capacity to form an impression do not specifically correspond with one another. It is characteristic of such impression illusions that they cannot be influenced by teaching, and the fact that the "correspondence" was created by natural selection and not by learning is proved all the more unequivocally when it comes into conflict with knowledge born of experience (see Section VIII., 2, IX.).

The last two sections should suffice to counter the two theses of Klages—that expression is a likeness of the action, and that the prerequisite for "impression" is the possibility of imitating the expressive movement.

Man, too, possesses structural social releasers. Lorenz (1943 a) has explained in detail the releasing function of lips, eyebrows, beard, the hair on head and shoulders of adults, and the head form of a baby (*Kindchenschema*). Many facial and body movements and some autonomic expressive phenomena (blushing) are also without doubt social releasers, i.e. under the selection pressure exerted by the communicative function of expression they have been bred into their present-day form or, as in some cases, have evolved for the first time. This much can be said with certainty, even though for the moment, apart from the work of Ahrens and W. Schmidt on smiling and laughing already mentioned, we unfortunately possess no special investigations on this subject (cf. also Eibl-Eibesfeldt 1957, 1966, 1967).

The objection will be raised that, in discussing structural social releasers and the display movements accompanying them, we have moved rather far from the field of expression theory as it could be of interest to psychologists. However, as I have already emphasized on p. 298 et seq., impression makes no distinction between "genuine" expression and its ancillary apparatus. It all goes with equal right into the summation of impression. Without warning and experience, man is as susceptible to dummies—including supernormal ones—as any animal. Lorenz (1943 a) likewise offers an extensive collection of examples of this.

b. Ritualization is the name J. Huxley, in his work on the Great Crested Grebe, first gave to the complicated interplay between highly differentiated social releasers and corresponding IRMs which in an enormously large number of vertebrates is, as it were, firmly built into the process of courtship and mating, territorial and rival fighting, and which cannot be omitted without disrupting or even completely blocking the whole process. In the case of very aggressive animals, e.g. herons and some cichlids such as *Herichthys,* a partner returning to the nest must exchange with the one sitting there a specific greeting ceremony derived from threat display. This gives the animals time to recognize one another, which in its turn inhibits the attack which the partner guarding the nest makes on any strange conspecific daring to come close. As H. Fischer (1965) has proved with the triumph ceremony of the Graylag Goose, in the course of further phylogenesis —but not ontogenetically!—a ritualized expressive movement of this kind which originally developed through superimposition out of various constituent parts, each with its own "motivation," can develop (it is not yet known how) a specific propensity of its own—in other words become a "genuine" homogeneous, independent instinct. Some human expressive movements, too, such as smiling, laughing, the intimidation and threat gestures so impressively described by Lorenz (1943 a), and much else, are in all probability specially differentiated instinctive movements. As yet, however, this has been proved beyond doubt only in the case of smiling (Koehler 1954 a).

Strictly speaking, the ritualization process begins the instant that aiming and steering mechanisms, in other words taxes, become involved. In this way an "expressive front" is created which is turned toward or even emphatically away from a partner (peacock), or one or more recipients. As soon as expression ceases to "occur like the weather," as soon as it becomes expression "for someone," it loses its innocence and takes the first step toward the subsequent "fall from grace," namely toward dissociation of expression from expressed content, the step which makes expression first ritual, formality, convention, then a means to an end and finally a lie. Then, where it is possible to create impression by means of sham expression, comes "exploitation." And because impression cannot be influenced by teaching, for this reason (or if not for this reason alone, at least to a considerable extent *also* for this reason) they are all repeatedly and continually successful: the small and the great flatterers, legacy-hunters, career men, marriage swindlers and confidence tricksters, demagogues, and whatever else one may call them. This is no audacious collection of analogies, it was and is quite simply the path evolution takes.

This brief look at the undesirable products of ritualization should not obscure how enormously valuable it is to the development of community life. Something which has forced itself forward in a process of constant interplay, from the first attempts at developing social releasers, typification and symbolization of the signal and corresponding differentiation of IRMs to peak performances such as the courtship of the birds of paradise, has not only esthetic but also very practical effect. In the same measure as "genuine" expression disappears from social releasers and is replaced by ritual, ceremony, convention, these latter facilitate and guarantee the formation and preservation of a stable, spontaneous social order which is not disturbed or even destroyed at every instant by the variations in mood of single individuals. The *contrat social,* a social order deliberately based on reason, would not have been possible even as a mental exercise without the tacit, perhaps unconscious prerequisite of a basic order of this kind which existed before reason.

4. The gradual differentiation of the capacity to form an impression

On the basis of his studies of the expression of wolves kept in narrowly confined captivity, Schenkel (1947) came to the conclusion that most of the variants of expression he noted obeyed no rule and could therefore not be attributed to the interplay of a limited number of innate expressive movements. Lorenz (1952) was able to refute this, and many later works have repeatedly shown what an incredible diversity of expressive pictures can present themselves out of the superimposition of relatively few "simple" expressive phenomena in their various degrees of intensity. Gwinner (1962, 1964) observed not only an extraordinary richness of nuances in the expressive behavior of the raven, but also that these animals have an amazing capacity to react to all these nuances which are often scarcely perceptible to the human observer. He deduces that a very highly developed sense of vision makes this possible, which is certainly correct, and furthermore that the capacity for reaction to so many expressive variants cannot be innate but must be learned. Similar conclusions concerning the human capacity to form an impression are quite familiar. Without prejudice to the role played by the learning processes (to be discussed later) I would emphasize that the innate norms of expression and impression are far from being as inflexible as slot machines, that they seldom have a strict and exclusive relationship to one another and that the products of their superimposition ("mixed forms") can therefore be very diverse since the intensities of the various propensities can fluctuate quite independently of one another. Thus, it is also possible to see good reasons why the increasing demands made by expression on the capacity to form an impression and the finer direction of social life which became necessary succeeded in exerting sufficient selection pressure to cause the IRMs on which the capacity to form an impression was founded to be differentiated beyond their original limits. It would have been necessary to learn a very great number of variants in an incredibly short space of time in order to provide an adequate background of experience against which variants and combinations *being met for the first time* could be classified with certainty. In the case of young ravens, anthropoid apes and humans, misunderstandings of expression would then be bound to be more frequent than they in fact are. Even adult humans, suddenly arriving in a world with strange traditions and customs, may perhaps make the odd blunder in other respects, but as far as the immediate understanding of the expression of general human emotions in humans of different race, attitudes, and cultures is concerned, mistakes are not much more frequent than at home in intercourse with strangers in one's own familiar surroundings: the correspondence between the qualitative estimation of expression by people with the most widely varying cultural backgrounds is very great (Davitz 1964), only the *quantitative* relationships seem to be more strongly governed by culture (see below p. 340, 344). Leonhard (1949), to whom we are indebted for what is so far probably the most painstaking and comprehensive description in detail of the facial expressions of humans, indicates for example that vertical folds in the forehead occur in many "composite expressions" and in all these retain the same basic significance (pp. 324–325). Kohts (1935, quoted from Marler 1961) has proved that the same is true of the expressions of a chimpanzee. The facial expressions concerned, however, are experienced and responded to as a unit; their composition, i.e. the superimposition consisting of two or more "simple expressions," can indeed be analytically separated secondarily, but in the moment of primary experience of impression this is certainly not obvious (l.c., p. 143). Indeed, as Rothacker has so accurately described (1941), the facial reaction to an expressive movement of a partner is faster still than the experience of an impression. In fact, in many cases it is highly questionable whether an *experience* of impression in semi- or wholly conscious form occurs at all. It is true that learned reactions can also switch themselves on as automatically as the unconscious and as fast as lightning, but in every case this requires much practice. Certainly individual and group-specific forms of intercourse develop in humans living for a long time in constant mutual contact, no one denies that. But this cannot be applied to the human modes of expression in general, their variants and mixed forms, or to their combination with releasers; and that is already a tremendous amount. We may assume, therefore, that man possesses a far greater number of highly specific and highly differentiated innate mechanisms of impression than is generally supposed (Koehler 1954, 1955).

Lersch, in his well-known investigation "Face and mind" (1943), refers to observations by Piderit (1925) on blind people: People blind from birth onward, as well as those blinded shortly afterward, do not display any expressive movements of the musculature of the forehead, whereas those becoming blind later as well as those *"who still possess a certain, if incomplete,* optic function" (my italics) display normal forehead mime. Lersch considers that this shows that a person who can see *learns* the expressive movements of the area around the eyes, and further even *all* expression. He forgets, however, to explain how those blind from birth still have normal mouth mime, although they have not been able to copy it from anyone. It is essential to make a sharp distinction between unspecific developmental stimuli and their effect, and specific stimulus situations which evoke adaptive modification of behavior through experience and learning. Light stimuli are necessary for the normal growth processes of the optic tracts and of all motor tracts connected with them, including the musculature served by the latter. These light stimuli can quite well be diffuse and without configuration, and for this reason normal forehead mime develops even in children "with incomplete optic function." Had Piderit investigated those blind from birth in this connection, he would in all probability have discovered an extensive or even complete atrophy of the forehead muscles. One cannot, naturally, conclude from such results that facial mime must be learned. Freedman (1964) has indirectly confirmed the above assumptions: According to his observations, congenitally blind infants smile just as sighted ones do, the searching nystagmus of their eyes halts in response to sounds, the eyes turn toward the source of the sound; at the same age as sighted infants they move their hands before their eyes and the eyes follow the hand movement as if they could see. This hand-eye coordination, however, disintegrates only a few weeks after its first appearance, probably because the eyes cannot, as in the normal process of development, take over control from the hand. Koehler's detailed investigations (1954 a) show furthermore that normal newborn babies, as well as those born prematurely, also smile *long before* they are physiologically capable of picture vision. Van Iersel (1953), incidentally, has proved experimentally that in some cases one and the same stimulus situation effects and continuously directs an adaptive modification of behavior, and at the same time sets in motion a long-term physiological process of development which then proceeds autonomously and neither needs any further action from the stimulus situation concerned nor, if this occurs, is influenced by it.

To sum up one may say that, in the case of humans, too, what we may here call the "basic equipment" of capacities for expression and impression follows the same functional principles as is the case with all other vertebrates and therefore is no doubt likewise completely innate. Man, however, as well as some other animals with an extremely efficient sense of vision, was able to develop very refined optical mechanisms of impression. This brought with it the result that, in the case of man and of these animals, many (though by no means all!) releasers developed on the basis of optical perception are less spectacular and more inconspicuous than is the case with creatures that are optically less well endowed. This has obsolutely nothing to do with the developmental level of the animals concerned in other respects. One need only compare Koehler's (1943) training results from ravens with those of Rensch (1953/55) from elephants to establish the incomparably higher "intelligence" of the elephant. Yet the expressive movements of the elephant (Kühme 1961, 1963) are far more dramatic than much that Gwinner (l.c.) observed in the raven. The raven simply has by far the better eyes.

VII. HOW IMPRESSION IS MODIFIED BY SITUATION

Let us assume that an enormous heavyweight boxer storms up to me with every expressive sign of primitive human aggressiveness. I should have the choice of either running away or taking on a fight. In the first event what I experience is fear, in the second rage, or in case of doubt a more or less balanced mixture of the two. Which course of action is in fact adopted is decided by my own internal situation, my natural disposition to escape or attack, and the experience I have already had of these, and also earlier personal experiences, if any, with this particular attacker. In an experiment with animals the experience factor can be eliminated and then reintroduced in controlled amount and form (Diebschlag 1941, among others). As a result we know that the ambivalence of a situation functions to some extent independently of experience and also fluctuates in accordance with endogenous rhythms independent of external stimuli. In the case of animals with a fixed territory, readiness for attack or escape, and with it the animal's reaction to an attacking conspecific, varies with the distance from the action center of its territory (first-order home). Admittedly the animal must learn *where* it is at home; but "being at home" increases its readiness for attack and "being away from home" its readiness for escape. This the animal does not learn; it is innate. Cover is likewise a factor which considerably influences an animal's readiness to react. Whether a male cat is taken by surprise by a stronger rival on a completely open stretch of ground, or somewhere where a hedge or something similar offers protection from the rear, greatly influences its reaction to the threatening behavior of the opponent. In the former case it will run away, in the latter it adopts a defensive posture or even tries to open up an escape route for itself by feinting attack (Leyhausen 1956). In this case, too, an animal must admittedly learn *where* in its environment cover is to be found, but it does not learn *what* represents cover, nor does it learn the change in threshold brought about in the releasing mechanism by its presence or absence. A further situational factor independent of experience which helps considerably to govern impression and reaction is the directedness of expression, as discussed in detail on p. 342/3.

The dependence of the impression on situation *cannot* therefore be ascribed *in every case* to experience and learning. Instead it is governed to a considerable extent by the mood of the receiver of the impression. According to this expression and impression can be assimilative (sympathetic induction of mood; not only in the sense of social coordination but also: threat elicits threat, and so on), complementary (courtship and mating) or antithetical (threat of attack → escape). Researchers in "social perception," as mentioned on p. 306, were able to show experimentally (quoted from Graumann 1956) that in a social situation the motivational state of the receiver of impression interprets identical expressive pictures at any given moment according to its own tendency. Since this motivational state may be influenced via social experience and since the researchers of "social perception" are all adherents of the learning theory and do not know, or will not accept, that there is, as I have already emphasized several times, a difference between motives and motivation, they quite simply consider both the motivational state itself and the receptivity toward impression resulting from it to be "learned." This tendency to global judgments as to whether something is learned or not learned confronts one time and again in the literature of human psychological research into expression—and not only in papers on learning theory. In reality, however, things are a great deal more complicated (cf. p. 338, Klineberg). In experiments of the kind named, all that is really learned are the factors releasing certain propensities and constellations of propensities; and this, too, succeeds only if prior to the experiment the ESS are in a really balanced mood and have not already been motivationally activated in a biased direction by internal and/or external causes having nothing to do with the experiment. The "coloration" of perception or the shifts in threshold brought about by the activated propensities themselves within the various IRMs sensitive to expression are based not on a learning process but on the regulating mechanisms already discussed on p. 305 which are there before any experience—social or otherwise. In addition to these, processes of adaptation may then also occur in the "afferent system" (see VIII., 2).

It would seem appropriate to draw particular attention at this point to the following historical facts: At the sight and smell of food held before it ("unconditioned stimulus") a dog begins to salivate ("unconditioned response to stimulus").[3] If in spatial and/or temporal combination with the appearance of the food a lamp lights up ("conditioned stimulus"), after a few repetitions the lamp alone is sufficient to elicit salivation, even without food. It became customary as a shortened form to speak of "a conditioned response" instead of "a response to a conditioned stimulus." Soon people began to take this literally, *and that is simply false!* The alteration has taken place *exclusively* in the afferent system, whereas the response—the efferent side—has not changed in the least. *It is still as "unconditioned" as ever!* In the case of comparatively simple, "purely reflex" responses to stimulus, this is relatively harmless if, as was usual in the old psychophysics, one takes the stimulus to be *the* cause of the response. But as soon as one approaches more complicated, and furthermore largely autonomous, behavioral systems with this attitude and promptly categorizes the whole as "learned" if at some point in the proceedings a learning process is discovered, then it is quite easy to see how the imprecision of language leads to imprecision about facts, and there is no need to be surprised if this has an enormously inhibitive effect on analytical progress. The early carelessness with language which we are still dragging around uncorrected with us today is responsible for nine tenths of the internal contradictions and absurdities of the theories of learning based on the principle of "conditioning," in which the process of reduction explains something learned by something learned *ad infinitum,* in which one eventually has the chicken embryo already learning to peck in the egg (Kuo 1932, Lehrman 1953), without noticing that one is only going around in circles the whole time like a cat chasing its own tail. It is a wonder that no one has yet traced the links of the chain of learning back beyond the zygote to ovum and semen and thus brought the whole theory to the point where, logically, it cannot help but end if thought through consequentially to the finish: namely in unadulterated psycho-Lamarckism! This is naturally not meant as an attack on *all* learning theory but only on attempts to introduce a monism of explanation by learning theory into all behavioral science and psychology. No one disputes that in the behavioral development of higher animals learning is among the things which play a not unimportant role. Holzkamp's assertion (1965) that "organization theory" and learning theory are not mutually exclusive is indisputable, but the two are still not merely "methodic aspects" of one and the same thing. What is much more important is to discover the role of learning within the general organization of behavior and subjective experience, and to discover this separately for every individual functional context. Premature generalizations are a greater evil here than anywhere. When Holzkamp demands that in connection with the problem of the origin of expression (by which, as I have already said, he really means the origin of the apperception of expression) learning theory must be given a chance if for no other reason than that the sole alternative would be the assumption that expression is a "last, irreducible fact," I certainly will not refuse learning theory its chance. I must, however, decisively point out that the methods of learning theory do not represent the only "reducing agents" when investigating ontogenetic processes, not even in behavior and the psychic field. Embryology knows of many other possibilities (Kühn 1965). Furthermore individual development is by no means the only temporal dimension to be considered. It is as unnecessary as it is senseless to hope to find the answer to all "reductionist questions" in and from individual development. For the purpose of reducing what cannot be reduced within the ontogenetic dimension, we have at our disposal the phylogenetic dimension, the geological periods and the processes of speciation. We should really not start bothering about last, irreducible facts and "Ur-phenomena" yet.

VIII. EXPERIENCE AND LEARNING

1. Changes in expressive behavior

It would seem questionable whether expression as such can be learned at all. Habituation and upbringing, as well as positive and negative experiences with other people, may suppress some expressive phenomena and encourage others, but they will not create completely new ones. Astonishingly enough—and leaving aside vague theories of imitation—since Darwin's work (1872) there have been no fundamentally new attempts, not even in the field of learning theory, to investigate and explain the origin of expressive phenomena. The opinion voiced by Lersch—that expressive movements have to be learned—I have already discussed on p. 331. Frijda (1965) has produced an admirably concise and clear review of the available evidence. There is nothing to add to his conclusion that no single explanatory principle can do justice to the entire range of expressive phenomena, as long as one gives "expression" as broad a meaning as is still usual in human psychology and takes it to mean all communicative functions, including language. Holzkamp (1965) does postulate that the apperception of expression be ontogenetically traced back to "non-expressive elements," but completely overlooks the fact that the same problems exist in connection with expression itself, so that he speaks of "the origin of expression" instead of "the origin of the *apperception* of expression (p. 288). Incidentally, it is scarcely appropriate to label Darwin's theory of expression simply as learning theory, as Holzkamp does. In accordance with his First Principle Darwin does, it is true, attribute the majority of expressive movements to association and habit formation. One should not, however, overlook the fact that in the English language the word "habit" had, and to some extent still has, a much broader meaning than the German equivalent used by Holzkamp *(Gewohnheit)*. Particularly before the appearance of the theory of heredity, all behavior patterns of an animal which occurred fairly frequently, including, and above all, the instinctive actions, were, and to some extent still are, known as "habits." In Darwin's time, however, the only way in which one could imagine how complex behavior patterns could become instinctive was to assume that individually acquired habits became hereditary. Darwin himself was known to be a convinced Lamarckist, and from his whole presentation it is clear beyond doubt that he saw the "association" of the enormous number of "serviceable habits" as being acquired during phylogeny, and that in the case of recent animals and humans he therefore held them to be instincts. He expressly uses the word "innate" in this connection. If we rid Darwin's statements of the inaccurate Lamarckist assumptions, we are left with a picture matching present-day ethology to such an extent that it amounts to prophesy. Above all, however, it must meanwhile have become clear that Darwin's Third Principle of Expression (The Principle of Actions due to the Constitution of the Nervous System, independently from the first of the Will, and independently to a certain extent of Habit), which until now has led a fairly neglected and disregarded existence and was considered at best as a makeshift and clumsy attempt on Darwin's part to explain vegetative expressive phenomena, if viewed in conjunction with the hypothesis put forward here concerning the role of the motivational minority in the expressive occurrence, takes on a positively universal significance, whereas his two other Principles of Expression become relegated to secondary roles.

We may safely say, then, that research since Darwin has seriously neglected the question of the origin of expression both in phylogeny and ontogeny. Probability is still on the side of a largely nativist assumption, as long as one is considering "genuine" expression as yet unadulterated by communicative *intention* of any kind. An exception to this are certain stereotyped movements which, as such, are certainly wholly or partly learned, and which in particular situations and in individually modified forms can become expressive movements, as described below. As opposed to this, however, it seems to be impossible voluntarily—e.g. via training, education, or force—to turn some chosen behavior pattern or other into the "expression" of particular motivational states and emotional dispositions. No one will succeed in training a child in an appropriate case to suppress all other innate expressive phenomena of pain and grief completely and instead to recite the multiplication tables. Even if, by some means or other, I could bring the child to do this in my presence, the expression of grief would still return the moment the child believed himself to be unobserved. The multiplication tables will not become the expression of grief.

It is different with the stereotyped movements just mentioned, which first develop in a particular situation, for example scribbling on a piece of paper during a conference when one is afraid of missing the train. Through frequent repetition such behavior can become habit and then, in persons who are compelled or accustomed to keep their expression under control, the sole expressive sign in certain tense situations. Fundamental to such individually acquired expressive behavior is a) that it originates from genuine epiphenomenal expression in that the expression takes over, so to speak, not only the manner of the movement performed but also the movement itself; b) that releasers, in other words means of expression which have occurred as a result of adaptation to innate mechanisms of impression, are never involved; c) that for this reason they also cannot be understood from the direct impression they create but can be fully interpreted only on a basis of personal acquaintance. And since these are individual habits, their type and mode of performance do not make it possible to recognize from the very first and without additional criteria what they are expressing; they are therefore not only ambiguous from the point of view of the receiver of an impression but also primarily indeterminate from the point of view of expression: If, during a conversation, someone repeatedly winds his watch, this can signify shyness in one person, boredom in a second, in a third aggressive irritability, in a fourth extreme interest disguised as indifference, in a fifth impatient expectation, in a sixth fear, and so on. Indeed, some individuals have such a tendency to unvarying stereotypes that it could signify all these things in the same individual. If in many cases a more general interpretation not arising out of intimate personal knowledge is nonetheless possible, this is apparently due to the fact that the possibilities for epiphenomenal expression are also relatively limited in number and in comparable circumstances regularly lead to the same or at least very similar stereotypes. Holzapfel has demonstrated numerous occurrences of comparable stereotypes in animals (1938, 1939 a, 1939 b).

Certainly there are gestures which differ according to convention, culture, and race, and are comprehensible to an outsider only with the help of experience or instruction. This, however, is by no means an adequate reason for regarding *all* expressive occurrences or behavior as being conditioned by social culture, as Klineberg does (1954). In the first place, such gestures of greeting, affirmation, negation, and many others are actually predominantly *intentional* communication and thus not expressive movements in the narrower sense. In the second place, however, one must beware of overlooking the inbuilt, innate elements in such gestures. The extent to which one can be misled by regarding apparently purely conventional gestures and attitudes as completely and absolutely learned is demonstrated particularly impressively by the following example. Desmond Morris, widely known for his investigation of chimpanzees "painting" (1963) and certainly a distinguished connoisseur of chimpanzee behavior, reports (1962) on a meeting with two trained chimpanzees which were being taken for a walk by their trainer. Morris tried to greet them with chimpanzee calls which he had practiced to perfection. The chimpanzees, however, only looked at him with astonishment and offered a hand in greeting. Morris proceeds from this incident to meditate on how far such an intelligent animal as the chimpanzee can already be "culturally influenced" so that, instead of the innate greeting ceremony appropriate to its species, it uses the handshake it has learned from man even when greeted "in chimpanzee language." Meanwhile Jane Goodall (Baroness van Lawick) has spent practically two years observing wild chimpanzees and was able to attach herself so closely to a group that the animals treated her almost as belonging to it (1962–1964). At the International Ethological Conference in Zurich in September, 1965, we were able to see a film made by her husband, and in this the handshake occurs frequently among the wild chimpanzees, although it is true that it does look a little different from our human handshake. Goodall explained it to us as follows: When a higher-ranking chimpanzee approaches one lower in rank and the latter is not quite clear about the superior chimpanzee's intentions, it stretches its hand out with the palm opened upward. If the superior animal is in a peaceful mood, it lays the outstretched fingers of one hand on the fingers the other has stretched toward it, and with their hands in contact the two move them up and down simultaneously a few times. This reassures the inferior animal, and it now tolerates the continued approach of the other without fear. It is an assurance of good will and friendly intention and its significance thus coincides largely with that of our handshake. Convinced though I am that very much more of human behavior is innate than most contemporary human psychologists are prepared to admit, if anyone had said to me before that September that the handshake is actually phylogenetically a very old instinctive movement, I should probably at first have assumed that the person concerned was merely joking. This is, however, only half the historical origin of the handshake. As we have known since Köhler's chimpanzee studies (1921 b), chimpanzees beg food from one another, but only an inferior animal begs from a superior one. The chimpanzee handshake described above, varying slightly from the conventional human version, is a symbolic handing-over of food and thus not only in man's case but already in the chimpanzee's a genuine symbolic act (see above p. 318). We should therefore be far, far more cautious than hitherto about designating such gestures as conditioned "purely" by convention, culture, or other social circumstances.

That such gestures can to a varying degree be quantitatively favored or suppressed in their external appearance by social influences in the broadest sense is no argument whatever against the idea that innate components cooperate to a considerable extent in them. Even if we consider only expressive movements, such as smiling, which may be regarded as pure instinctive movements without any additional ingredient, we already find four different possible ways of quantitatively modifying the frequency of the movement in the individual and in the population:

a. As far back as 1941 Lorenz expressed the opinion in conversation that in the case of some instincts the endogenous production of action-specific energy is subject to a use/non-use trophicity in much the same way as musculature is. This was first proved with certainty by Heiligenberg (1963, 1964) in connection with the fighting and escape instincts of a fish, and by myself (1965 a) in connection with predatory killing by cats. The findings of Diebschlag (1941) concerning the ranking order and display and fighting behavior of the domestic pigeon may probably also be interpreted in this sense and not only in that of learning theory; given the rather complex phenomena appearing in these cases, both processes are bound to interact variously with one another, and an interpretation *solely* in one or the other direction would certainly be inappropriate (see below, b–d). Many instincts which are frequently "called upon" during the life of an animal probably adapt themselves in this way to the average long-term requirement of the individual life situation, as some innate expressive movements probably do also (for greater detail see Leyhausen 1967). If, like the triumph ceremony of the Graylag Goose analyzed by H. Fischer (1965), they have become independent instinctive movements—in other words, have been perfected or have appeared for the first time under the selection pressure of the connection between expression and impression—the "regulator" of this regulating mechanism is to be found in the relevant social situation itself. In the case of pure, originally epiphenomenal expression, however, frequency and intensity are dependent on the propensities of the motivational minority causing it. The situational regulator of any of these which are subject to the use/non-use trophicity may lie quite outside the social sphere. All this is admittedly pure hypothesis as far as human beings are concerned, for no appropriately oriented investigations have so far been made. It does, however, conform very well with the experience that people who live for a long time with no, or very little, social contact are noticeably impoverished in their facial and other expressive movements. Trophic instinctual adaptations of this kind have as little to do with learning as muscular trophicity has.

b. Other propensities inhibiting or favoring the intensity of expression—whether in general or, specifically, only certain modes of expression—may be released socially or culturally and be linked by "conditioning" with the releasing situation for expressive behavior: In other words, an individual learns as far as possible to repress expression or to give it free rein. If the appropriate social situation lasts long enough, then under the influence of mechanism (b) the trophic adaptation of mechanism (a) sets in and the socially fixed norm of expressive intensity becomes "natural" to the individual.

c. The individual adaptation of instincts which can be trophically influenced is not unlimited, but can vary only within a certain range of modification above or below a standard line which is genetically fixed. To the same extent as genetic differences in this respect exist between individuals as well as whole populations, the "normal standard level" of intensity and frequency of expression, and with this also the range for learned as well as trophic adaptation, can fluctuate likewise. The relevant "frequency norm" within a tradition group, population, or even race can for its part also carry some of the responsibility for the level at which the social norm is set by mechanism (b), and this norm for its part also does not come into being exclusively as a result of "pure" tradition and convention.

d. Finally, convention can single out particular components of innate expressive movements and make these into vehicles of intentional communication, as would seem to be the case with at least some of the gestures quoted by Klineberg (1954). To the Greeks of the classical age, for example, the *Ananouein,* a jerky upward and backward pull of the head, served as a gesture of negation or refusal, whereas we today shake our heads for the same purpose. Both gestures, however, contain—indeed, for practical purposes still *are*— ancient expressive movements to be found throughout the whole range of vertebrates, whereby drawing the head up and back expresses predominantly the rejection of an optically and/or olfactorily perceived situation, while shaking the head expresses the rejection of one perceived through smell and taste. In some populations mechanism (b) can likewise permit or make fashionable certain expressive movements for one situation but "forbid" them for another. The kiss developed in all probability out of an instinctive act already present in the anthropoid apes, whereby babies are fed from mouth to mouth with pre-chewed food during weaning. This is still quite usual in all primitive tribes, and eyewitness reports repeatedly tell of how even young mothers belonging to highly civilized peoples resort to this method quite instinctively and without any guidance in extreme situations (such as refugee treks) in which they are deprived of the paraphernalia of advanced baby culture. Out of this instinctive ("serviceable") act, the kiss first developed as an expression of tenderness from mother to child and was later adopted into the love-play between the sexes and even into purely social intercourse—even chimpanzees and orang-utans kiss! Now, the kiss is quite unknown in some cultures, in others it is exchanged only between mother and child, in yet others it is quite usual between lovers but frowned on between adult men, while in still others it is practically obligatory in connection with almost every kind of social greeting. Yet, all this in no way denies the original and still-existent instinctive nature of kissing, but is solely the result of the extremely complicated interplay of the four causal connections I have described.

An animal with a fair amount of learning ability and a fixed set of innate mechanisms for expression and impression, with the help of which it stimulates specific behavior in a conspecific and reacts itself to the other's expressive behavior, naturally cannot with time help noticing that this is so. From this point it is but a small though very significant step to producing expressive movements with the object of attaining a desired reaction from the conspecific, in other words to attaching a *communicative intention* to the expressive movement. Strictly speaking, only from this moment on should one speak of "transmitting" an expression, but up till then of "wearing" an expression, this being more neutral and lacking the implied assumption of a receiver. Here begins a development which is the introductory stage of a dissociation of expressive behavior from what is to be expressed. Already in the cat one can observe how animals which know each other well as individuals "voluntarily" employ single components of the mime and gestures of threat and defense without the firm correlation with intensity of excitation which is always the case during an encounter between strange animals. Ranking order and external circumstances play a more decisive role in the choice of means of expression, whether it be hissing, growling, flattening of ears, paw-blow, etc., than the degree of excitation of the animal performing it (Leyhausen 1956). Cat A, for example, knows precisely that it had better not walk past B when B pulls back only *one* ear (namely, the one turned toward A), but that it can still step over C with impunity even when C is growling. Precisely this development of one-sided mime, whereby only the ear turned toward the partner is flattened, only one eye squeezed shut, only one lip raised in the merest suggestion of baring the teeth and growling, while the rest of the animal looks quite uninvolved, shows clearly that the cat *intends* a warning without yet having become particularly aroused. Reynolds (quoted from Chance 1963) observed something very similar in apes, and makes a distinction between "operative threat" and "symbolic threat." The symbol concept, however, is both linguistically out of place, since the warning is not symbolically but quite earnestly meant, and also terminologically, since it is already in use in ethology but with a different meaning (see p. 318). What is in reality going on here is the development of expressive behavior away from "expression" in the narrower sense into an aimed and finally consciously employed "means of impressing." As the cat example clearly shows, this transition does not take place abruptly and in the sense of an either/or, but quite gradually and with a considerable amount of overlapping.

At first the *qualitative* correspondence between expression and expressed content (judged from the point of view of impression) continues to exist. But animals too can already "lie" by means of expression, i.e. produce expressive movements deliberately with the aim of extracting a particular reaction from the partner, without themselves being in a mood corresponding to the expressive behavior. This is revealed most forcibly in intercourse between animals of different species, or in intercourse between human and animal; Lorenz (1950 a) and Hediger (1961) cite examples of this that are as amusing as they are instructive. An example of my own may illustrate and prove what is meant. Some of the 35 or so wild cats and viverrids at our institute know very well how to ask for food. If they have already received their ration for the day, they can distinguish precisely between the member of staff who fed them and the others. In particular a genet, a male Blackfooted Cat, a hybrid of Indian Leopard-cat and domestic cat, and a Golden Cat are then capable of looking at and begging from the latter so piteously that dialogues such as the following are far from seldom: "Nova (the Golden Cat) says she has had nothing to eat all day."—"She's lying! I just gave her a guinea pig and two rats." It is noteworthy how naturally and automatically the word "lie" found its way into the jargon of the human keepers. We do not, of course, mean that we are talking of lies in the full human sense of the word. But there can equally be no doubt that a certain *intent* to deceive is there, particularly as we "fell for it" often enough, especially in the early days. Winkelsträter (1960) has shown, from the way zoo animals beg, that many animals learn to use expressive movements voluntarily in order to achieve an effect completely different from the original one. The most grotesque example is perhaps the threat yawn of the hippopotamus which in the zoo becomes a begging gesture of proven efficacy. The transition from unconscious and innocent expression to semi- or fully-conscious use of expressive behavior as a means to impress a partner is particularly easy to observe in children and is often perfected with unbelievable speed. Two- to three-year-old girls, for example, at first in all innocence and certainly without intent, are capable of smiling at men they find pleasant with extremely coquettish glances. At some time or other they notice the friendly attention this provokes in men who like children, mostly men in their family circle of relations or acquaintances, and—sometimes first in shyly tentative transition, but often quite abruptly—they loose an aimed and consciously produced pyrotechnic display of female coquetry on the partner. If he enters into the spirit of things, this can very quickly develop into a delightful game, one in which scarcely anything of the original expressive content of flirting can be found and which eventually degenerates into a wild romp. In this way children can learn at a very early age to act "expression" under compulsion or with intent, in all gradations from harmless high spirits to cunningly planned deception, as enumerated on p. 329.

2. The habituation of impression

It is not known whether or to what extent the receptor aspect of an impression mechanism can be modified under the influence of experience. Much argues against this. Processes of habituation such as "afferent throttling" may well often produce a simulance of this. Lersch (1943), for example, points out how important it is when analyzing expression to distinguish between expression simulated by the facial architecture and genuine expression.[4] Curiously enough it does not occur to him to wonder how, then, such a misunderstanding is at all possible if, as he considers, all comprehension of expression is learned! Our relevant IRMs, however, cannot be taught, and they react to *features,* irrespective of whether these result from the facial architecture or the physiognomy, or are the symptoms of current expression. From the point of view of our impression, a round face with small eyes is primarily a friendly face, regardless of whether these features are the result of a friendly broad smile or of the basic facial architecture. After being acquainted with the owner of the face for some time, however, one will gain the "correct" impression from its expression. No precise research has been done on this question, and the possibility that one has learned to judge the expression correctly cannot, therefore, be ruled out. However, an afferent throttling which reduces sensitivity toward the unchanging feature is much more probable. If one does not see the person concerned for some time, namely, at the next meeting the original impression recurs at first. Possibly both processes interplay, in that on the basis of previous experience afferent throttling occurs faster when the parties meet again for the first time later. Afferent throttling also effects a separation of physiognomic features from those resulting from current expression: In the impression produced at the first meeting both kinds of features produce an equally strong effect side by side; in daily intercourse, however, the physiognomic features become rapidly less effective and only the constantly changing current expression retains full effect. The opposite of afferent throttling also occurs. In countries and social circles where it is an offense against prevailing custom to allow free rein to the expressive processes, and where children are therefore trained from earliest youth onward not to do so, sensitivity to impression is correspondingly increased. This too can look very like learning, but the process is probably better comparable to the eye's adaptation to darkness. As is well-known, the light sensitivity of the retina can increase as darkness falls to eight thousand times its sensitivity in daylight. The extent to which the sensitivity to impression can fluctuate has not yet been quantitatively investigated. To achieve the effect described here, certainly far smaller fluctuations than those in the sensitivity of the retina are sufficient. Thus, an Englishman among English people picks up thoroughly adequate impressions, whereas someone belonging to a more temperamental people, suddenly set down in the atmosphere of a refined London club, would pick up virtually none. All he would see would be almost immobile masks. In contrast, a North Friesian fisherman who suddenly found himself amid the din of a south Italian marketplace would feel as if surrounded by madmen. In both cases the mechanisms of impression largely adapt if the persons concerned remain in the strange surroundings for some time. The modes of expression, however, assimilate only to a certain extent after long years, and hardly ever completely, while the autonomously controlled phenomena of expression barely adapt at all. At this point one is tempted to recall Helson's concept (1964) of the level of adaptation. Helson, however, just like Kohler (1955; see p. 313), seems to me to be dealing with much more complicated modes of perceptual adaptation. In the interest of future analysis, as well as of conceptual clarity, it would perhaps be better not to include them in the concept of adaptation, but rather to keep this limited to the original meaning it was given in sensory physiology.

3. The integrated action of IRMs and acquired information

The releasing effect of an impression mechanism often becomes limited, in that its effectiveness becomes dependent on additional conditions first being fulfilled *before* the features affecting the IRM can arouse a reaction via it. A prime example of this is imprinting (Lorenz 1935). A male Mallard, for example, directs its sexual reactions only toward birds of the species with which it lived during a particular period of its youth, what is called the sensitive period. In a normal case, these are its mother and siblings and all is in order. If, however, it is reared with chicks of another species, it later directs its courtship —exclusively and irreversibly (Schutz 1963)—toward birds of this species. A male Mallard, therefore, has no innate knowledge of what its female should look like, but "learns" this only via the process of imprinting. The female Mallard, however, possesses social releasers, ritualized expressive movements, which are essential to the release of specific constituent parts of the male's mating behavior. To these releasers the male reacts innately, in other words it possesses corresponding IRMs. It can react, however, only when the releasers in question are present in a bird of the species to which it was imprinted. Imprinting seems to operate a kind of censorship which decides whether or not features shall be allowed through to the impression mechanism. Occasionally supernormal objects (p. 307 et seq.) may, however, override this censorship. The female Mallard invites the male to copulate by making herself as flat as possible in the water and stretching her neck far out to the front. "Flat" and "stretched long" are, then, the main features to which the male Mallard's IRM for the release of copulation reacts. Even quite normally imprinted male Mallards, which under other conditions never waste sexual impulses on humans, attempt to mate familiar humans *swimming* with them (Lorenz, verbal information 1964); for no Mallard can ever be as flat and long as a human swimming, and such a super-object is simply irresistible.

The object of the imprinting need not have any great similarity with the natural object. Birds of the most widely differing species, from canary to crane, can be sexually imprinted to humans. In the case of mammals, imprinting mechanisms are probably more widespread than we have so far been aware. Cats of either sex which have been reared by humans and isolated at a very early stage from all conspecifics later direct their sexual impulses irreversibly toward humans (Thomas, verbal communication; own observations). Whether in the case of humans imprinting processes occur in the field of expression and impression is unknown; not even assumptions are possible at the moment.

One limitation of the conditions for effectiveness which, though different in origin, is similar in result to imprinting, exists in the case of the mechanisms effecting the sympathetic induction of mood, which function—or function fully—only within a group, family, herd, in short a closed social unit. Examples of this in civilized as well as degenerate form can be experienced at any football ground. McDougall (1939) describes another impressive example: Communal fighting mood spread in a matter of seconds through a crowd of five thousand natives assembled in Sarawak, although not one had been able to see the original cause of the tumult.

Seitz (1940), in his dummy experiments with *Astatotilapia strigigena,* found that experimental fishes which had grown up normally not only failed to react to some dummies in the expected manner, but even became panic-stricken. In contrast, a fish reared in isolation from the egg onward behaved according to expectation. The reason proved to be that the lacquerlike sheen which a colorless covering of slime gives to the skin of a healthy fish was lacking in the dummy. The fishes which had grown up among their own kind were already familiar with it and felt afraid of a fish which was, so to speak, "not a proper fish." Seitz gave this the highly appropriate name of "ghost reaction."

Apart from this, "familiarity values" have an important role to play in that they limit the effectiveness of some IRMs to situations in which the animal is familiar with the conditions. For example, cats at first abstain from any social intercourse whatsoever with strange conspecifics if they are brought together in a completely unfamiliar setting (Leyhausen 1956 a). An investigation of the strange surroundings has absolute priority.

All the innate components of behavior discussed in the foregoing are "unconditioned reflexes" as Pavlov understood it and may naturally be "retrained" more or less easily to conditioned stimuli and then elicited by these, whereby the familiar rules for the formation, maintenance, and extinction of so-called conditioned reactions apply unchanged. In many cases, this is in fact "provided for" and the uncon-ditioned stimulus, or the IRM reacting to it, plays the part of the "innate schoolmaster" which under normal living conditions ensures that the right thing is learned at the right time. Some birds do not know innately which are their enemies. What needs to be feared they learn by association with the alarm call of their parents, and for this alarm call there exists an escape-releasing IRM. Conversely other birds have IRMs for winged enemies and must learn to associate the alarm call of their conspecifics with these (Lorenz, verbal information 1964). Whether such processes play any part in human expression-impression behavior is so far totally unknown. Children probably learn to grasp the sense of conventional attitudes (injunctions and prohibitions) through the fact that in the beginning the adults ac-company these with expressive movements and sounds, sometimes purposefully exaggerated, which are directly comprehensible to the child because it has IRMs for them. Research in this field, employing suitable methods, would certainly be worthwhile, for the results which could be expected would no doubt be of the highest significance not only for expression theory but, far beyond and above this, also for developmental psychology and all disciplines connected with it.

Heiss (1956) differentiates between direct and indirect comprehen-sion of expression, whereby the latter is meant as consciously inter-pretative understanding "with the aid of explanations." It cannot, however, be unqualifiedly correct to equate direct comprehension simply with innate comprehension, in other words with impression. If, as described above, the mechanisms of impression function as "innate schoolmasters," the subject receiving the teaching is no doubt conscious of it only in the rarest of cases. The "knowledge" concern-ing the significance of certain social gestures is simply there all of a sudden, and as far as subjective experience is concerned may per-haps not seem so different from impression, insofar as impression becomes an experience at all; for the direct function of impression is the release not of an experience but of a *response action,* even if this consists only of responding expressive movements. If ever im-pression does become conscious experience, it still does not encom-pass the realization "That man there is angry" but, if it may be put (inadequately) into words, "He *makes me* angry" or "He *makes me* frightened," etc., according to one's own state of mood and the situation, as discussed on p. 333. In other words, the impression brings about a change of disposition, mood, emotional balance, or whatever one likes to call it, in the *receiver of the impression,* and he can only directly experience something like the motivational state of the one transmitting the expression if it is a case of sympathetic induction of mood (see above p. 317). Thus, whenever subjective experience obtains concrete "evidence" as to the state or personality of the wearer or transmitter of expression, it seems safe to assume that this knowledge has been gained as a result of a learning process, even though this may have been largely unconscious. Well in keeping with this is the observation by Ahrens (1953) and Kiener (1965) that a child does not begin to *comprehend* the expressive content of a stranger's smile until the second half of its third year, although by way of *impression* the child starts reacting to it from the time that it is five months old (Ewert 1965 b). It is therefore quite inadmissible to speak of impression as being "innate comprehension of expression" in the strict sense of the word "comprehension." Nor does such genuine comprehension normally occur in the direct social interplay between expression and impression, for example during a lively conversation between two acquaintances meeting by chance! Almost always it occurs later as subsequent rationalization, or perhaps only as subsequent astonishment at one's own reaction; such as when, after a conversational exchange of this kind, one asks oneself later "Why on earth was I so nice to him, he doesn't really mean it?", or conversely, "Actually he was quite friendly and cooperative, why was I so cross the whole time?" Reactions of this and similar kind can, in my opinion, be explained only if one takes into consideration the various independent "methods," discussed in detail on p. 311 et seq., by which the organism simultaneously processes sensory data: The mechanisms of impression work incredibly fast and count only relatively simple features, are however very precise in their quantitative evaluation of these; perception (in its narrowest sense) requires (somewhat) more time but processes a far greater number of single data and their complex relationship to one another. Accordingly these two types of evaluation are also subject to characteristically different forms of error: The mechanisms of impression do not differentiate between a feature containing expression and one empty of expression as long as it is the *same* feature; perception can be induced, by means of complex similarities, to "conclude" that things are identical, often ignoring gross differences in individual features in the process.

As will be discussed in greater detail later, even an adult human is thoroughly subject to both forms of error, and the idea that in the process of ontogeny the function of the impression capacities becomes gradually transformed and finally usurped altogether by "higher" perceptual functions, as Ahrens (1953) seems to conclude, is therefore quite out of the question. Kiener's statement (1965), that comprehension of expression (in the broadest sense) is "not a particular mode of experience . . . . but only a subsidiary problem of perception theory," is therefore also acceptable only if "perception theory" is understood to mean the theory of all possible modes of sensory data processing existing in an organism; the apperception of expression as a whole, however, makes use of modes of experiencing which differ widely from one another in origin, organization, and function (see Fig. 2).

In addition to innate impression, and the comprehension of expression which in part or even in full is unconsciously acquired, there is also the indirect understanding of expression acquired by means of conscious observation and experience, as understood by Heiss (1956). This always remains interpretative understanding, devoid of the immediacy of impression, and only via association evoking reactions rather like the subjective experiencing of impression, but practically always in a very jaded form. If this kind of understanding did not exist, we should never be able to learn anything about expression and impression in animals whose modes of expression are not identical to ours. Nor would the diagnosis of character by a trained psychologist be superior to the simple impression of an unschooled observer. Only rational analysis can succeed in separating expression which is of significance in judging character from the effects of social releasers and thus correcting "misunderstandings" arising from impression. And only through observation, experience, and finally comparison and experiment can those still numerous expressive phenomena which have not resulted in the breeding of corresponding mechanisms of impression and which are still nothing more than "epiphenomena" be successfully interpreted and rendered usable for diagnosis. Yet without a set of innate mechanisms of impression, without the "innate schoolmaster," even the best diagnostician would be helpless, for he would have nothing against which to relate and classify his experiences.

Finally there is the question how all the acquired "accessorial criteria" link up with the IRMs. Are they totally integrated, or only interposed just before or after, or what other relationship could be imagined? Unfortunately, nothing is known about this with certainty, and the opinions of the ethologists and behavioral physiologists vary widely. Koehler (verbal information) says information is "learned into" the IRM. If, like Schleidt (1962), one assumes that the IRM is a completely integrated system, it is possible to accept Koehler's formulation. If, however, one inclines to the hypothesis, described on p. 294,

Apperception of Expression

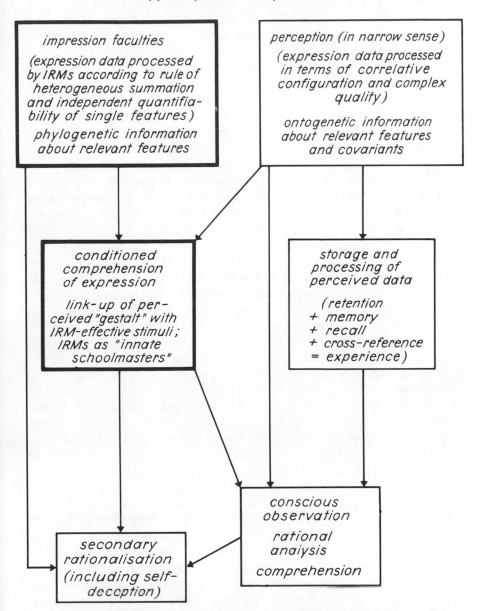

Fig. 2 Tentative diagram of the functional relationships between the mechanisms of impression and "true" perception in the apperception of expression. The blocks with heavy frames correspond roughly with what Heiss (1956) has called "immediate understanding," the others with what he called "interpretative understanding" of expression.

of two stages connected in relay fashion, the statement could be taken to refer only to the second stage, that setting the reaction directly in motion. Lorenz's "sensory correlate" remains unaffected. So far there is no basis for supposing that sensitivity toward an *a priori* feature, effective before any experience can be gained (sign stimulus, Lorenz), could be specifically and quantitatively changed. The sensory correlate in the IRM is dovetailed together with acquired information —analogous to the interweaving of instinct and training (Lorenz 1939)—as far as the elicitation of a reaction is concerned. The two do not, however, melt into a single unit defying analysis, but instead the sensory correlate most probably retains its functional individuality unchanged. W. Schleidt (1962) believes that in the later life of the individual the function of an original IRM and that of constituents acquired later are no longer distinguishable. From a purely phenomenological point of view this may in many cases be correct; Schleidt considers his statement so obvious that he does not attempt to prove it in detail. However, if one considers the differences in type of error to which the innate and acquired mechanisms of the apperception of expression are subject (see section IX.), it would no longer seem so pointless to play them off adeptly against one another in experiment. In this way, even with mature and experienced humans, it is possible to break open the "totality of experience" of expression, to pursue the individual constituents further and thus gain insight into the complexity of interaction between the functions which bring about the wholeness of the phenomena, just as, in other branches of perception research, optical illusions have been used with great success experimentally in order to acquire information of this kind. When acquired mechanisms degenerate (e.g. in sickness or old age), the innate function sometimes reappears clearly without inhibition or limitation. A tomcat with brain damage of this kind could be stimulated to full rival fighting many times in succession by a simple dummy; no normal tomcat reacted to the dummy at all (Leyhausen 1956 a). In the field of the motor system, corresponding signs of degeneration have long been known as a "regression" to the behavior of juvenile stages (cf. Wieser 1957).

The foregoing sections will no doubt have shown clearly enough that a "biology of expression" in the broadest sense is far from leading to biased, nativist theory. The sole reason for the rather strong emphasis placed at the beginning on the innate functions and capacities is the neglect with which they have so far been treated in more recent psychology. How innate and acquired cooperate, how uniform functional systems, experienced as a whole though made up of single functions of different phylogenetic age, varyingly adaptable in ontogency, heterogenous in structure, different in receptiveness to the process of actualization, and running off at different frequency, tempo, and intensity, are switched together, guided, and regulated—all this can be grasped only if the nature and history of the individual functions have first been discerned and investigated, both in isolation *as well as united* in the system as a whole. This analytical viewpoint does not ignore the fact that a "part" can function differently and sometimes achieve other functions within the framework of the whole than in isolation; that it needs to be integrated into the system if it is to manifest certain of its functional characteristics (v. Bertalanffy 1933). But "wholeness" and "gestalt" explain nothing—they are problems themselves (Lorenz 1950 c). And so we shall also be unable to assign the part played by experience and learning in the process of expression and the apperception of expression its correct place in the picture as a whole until we regard all the other factors involved, some of which are phylogentically much older, in the right perspective and in the light of a precise knowledge of the extent of their functional contribution.

4.   Investigations into the comprehension of expression in humans

Readers will perhaps wonder why I have so far made only passing mention of experimental investigations into the question of the comprehension of expression in human psychology, and why the examples from the human sphere cited to illustrate my theories seem almost exclusively to stem from a pre-scientific homespun psychology. There are several reasons for this. First, like Frijda (1965), one is bound to discover how extremely meager the harvest of recent investigations on this subject is, though somewhat richer than that resulting from investigations of the phylogenetic and ontogenetic origin of expression and the adequate cataloguing and description of expressive phenomena [though it must be added that Frijda fails to mention the work of Leonhard (1949)]. Next, such investigations as are available are, however, either in their statement of the problems, or their method, or both, far too generalized, too seldom planned with the aim of detailed analysis and far too global in their conclusions to get a firm grasp on the multiplicity of individual functions and factors involved. What then emerges as a result melts in the hand when one tries to evaluate it for the questions—of primary importance to us here—of the phylogenetic and ontogenetic origin of expression and impression as well as of secondary comprehension of expression.

Recourse (call it regression if you will) to homespun psychology is, then, not a virtue but dire necessity. A few examples will prove the point:

a. As examples of globally biased conclusions, Klineberg (1954) and Foley (1935) have already been quoted. A similar kind of approach which fails to make any distinctions is frequently met with in relation to all changes occurring during juvenile development: These are all unceremoniously interpreted as the results of learning, and maturation processes quite independent of experience are not even considered.

b. One vital flaw in almost all investigations lies in the use of the verbal method, which is something Kiener (1965) also criticizes. Furthermore, since the ESS are almost always allowed a relatively long time in which to arrange and formulate their impression, the result is mostly a mixture of all the functions which have been reviewed here. Often enough rational considerations outweigh the immediacy of the impression, because the ESS take pains "to do as well as possible." Brunswik and Reiter (1938) showed their ESS faces sketched in black lines on a white background and asked them, among other things, about particular color impressions. They received answers to these questions, too, but there is room for grave doubt whether illusions of color or synesthesia of this kind would have occurred *spontaneously* in normal ESS; and even if they did, this would have no relevance whatsoever to problems of expression. The verbal method not only has the disadvantage that the experimenter can have a suggestive effect without being aware of this, it is also often dependent on the ES's ability to express himself rather than on his capacity to form an impression and his comprehension of expression. Thus, Davitz (1964) finds there is a weakly positive correlation between "verbal intelligence," the capacity to formulate and use abstract symbols and the knowledge of vocal characteristics, and "emotional sensitivity"; he claims that taken together they are responsible for approximately 40% of differences in performances. Davitz makes no attempt to analyze the other 60%. Above all, however, the psychology of expression is still far from having reached a scientific stage in which the use of quantitative methods in this form would be meaningful. The first requirement is not percentages but insight into the quality of structural and functional elements, into extremely complicated functional networks consisting of components that are extremely heterogeneous in structure, capacity, adaptation, and adaptability. As in chemistry, so in *all* other sciences qualitative analysis is the prerequisite for quantitative, *and not vice versa*.

An extremely instructive example of this is provided by Hofstätter (1956): He instructed his ESS to establish so-called "polarity profiles" in relation to eight expressive photographs under a series of stimulus headings such as "life," "love," "hate," "dictator." With a vast expenditure of mathematical calculation, he then counted and factor-analyzed these profiles. According to this 74% of the variability was attributable to two factors: positive and negative orientation. Hofstätter concludes from this that "the process of being impressed by facial expressions contains an act of categorization which makes use of a very simple, in the main only two-dimensional system of connotation." But if one employs stimulus words heavily loaded with emotion and attitudes and has the photographs judged according to the degree to which they appear to show corresponding expression, one is oneself introducing the two-dimensional valuation into the experiment as a dominating factor, and need hardly be surprised when it emerges again from the calculations of the mathematical machinery. Quite apart from this, it is scarcely possible to imagine any somatic or emotional behavior which does not involve facing toward or away in some form or other. Facing toward and facing away are, however, only the generalized results of the factors effecting them and not the factors themselves. Applied to the example quoted here, this means that in the apperception of expression (an apperception not guided by stimulus words or influenced by suggestion) "facing toward" and "facing away" are not the "connotations" with the instrumental help of which expression is comprehended; instead they are the more or less compulsory accompaniments of the behavior elicited by the expression. I have chosen this example here precisely because it might at first sight seem as though Hofstätter's two-dimensionality of the apperception of expression fitted well with the "one-dimensionality" of the stimulus summation phenomenon.

c. Wörner (1940) is particularly critical of the older expression psychology because it looks for more or less static "fruitful moments" in the course of the expressive process, whereas he considers that only the temporal sequence of movements actually makes reliable interpretations possible. This is true of very many expressive movements, but is not universally valid. Many expressive movements, particularly the display movements (p. 321), frequently culminate in a static mien or posture which is held for a varying amount of time, e.g. the arched back of a cat as illustrated in Fig. 1. If static features were quite ineffective, then features of the physiognomy as well as of the facial architecture could have no effect. However, where static and dynamic features work together on the same IRM, the dynamic ones are almost always by far the stronger (see p. 326).

d. A further difficulty in evaluating almost all investigations lies in the fact that the data they present for assessment in one and the same experiment consist of an uncontrolled mixture compounded from the current expression, the physiognomy, and the facial architecture. Thus, the result offers no opportunity for discovering whether, for instance, the respective stimulus data have been evaluated predominantly via innate or acquired mechanisms. One exception, at least to a certain degree, is the investigation carried out by Brunswik and Reiter (1938), which will be reviewed separately below. The greater part of current expression is evaluated primarily via the impression-forming capacities; features of facial architecture are certainly evaluated mainly via IRMs of the kind which Lorenz (1943 a) has described as "schemata for esthetic proportions." Nothing certain can yet be said about the evaluation of lasting traces of expression in the physiognomy, insofar as these are not "misinterpreted" on the impression side as current expression. My assumption would be that one must learn how to recognize and assess these correctly. To the subject, the content of his experience may quite well seem primarily unitary even though it stems from so widely differing "suppliers." However, this fact may not be used, as Kiener (1965) does, as "proof" that features of the facial architecture *must* also have expressive content. For one thing they may, as Lersch (1943) quite rightly states, be "misunderstood" by impression as features of the current expression and/or physiognomy; for another, however, they may have lost the information value they once had at an earlier time in phylogeny (see section IX.). In either case they are not expression in the narrowest sense, unless one is willing to extend the concept of expression so far that expression = biological information. For it is no more true to say that all expression creates an immediate emotional effect than that whenever a human is so affected this may be equated with innate apperception of *expression*. As well as IRMs reacting to expressive features in conspecifics, humans also have IRMs specially intended for other features in the same conspecific which have no expressive content. And finally they have IRMs which do not react to conspecifics at all. All these IRMs should also create an emotional effect if, in the process of reacting, they release any subjective experience at all. Thunder is, after all, not the expressive behavior of some being, even if a primitive human "emotionally affected" by it primarily experiences and secondarily interprets it as such. One is constantly struck by the pernicious confusion and the hindrances to analytical research and functional resynthesis created by taking as one's point of departure an ontological, irreducible, primordial interdependence between expressive phenomena, impression-forming capacities, and secondary comprehension of expression, and then constantly trying to "explain" the one by means of the other and deducing the one from the other.

e. In their work (1938) which I have already quoted so often, Brunswik and Reiter confined the questions they posed to the rules according to which the perceiver reacts, without regard to whether what is perceived really or only apparently has expressive content. Although their methods were rather clumsy, they do provide information, or rather indications, about the various types of "rules" operating. As "stimulus material" they used line drawings of faces with quantitatively controlled variations in the length of the lines and the position of the lines in relation to one another. But what is the use of this precise stimulus quantification if one allows the ESS enough time for comparison, thought, and rationalization and then asks them for such general overall judgments as whether a face looks jolly or sad, young or old, good or evil, etc.? The disadvantages of the verbal method used have already been mentioned. Yet, in spite of these deficiencies the work does yield some interesting points. For example, it is the same features which make a face appear benevolent, likable, or beautiful, and likewise the features for cheerful and young and those for sad and old coincide. One must, of course, bear the abstraction of the line faces in mind. But in addition to the properties mentioned, the ESS were also asked about intelligence and willpower, and now something extraordinary emerged. The features by which the first-named groups of properties were recognized could apparently produce their effect whether or not they were combined into a complex with all the other features—in other words more or less summatively. However, for a judgment of the line faces with regard to intelligence and willpower the total configuration of all features present was decisive; here the effect produced by an individual feature changed quantitatively and qualitatively depending on how it was combined with the others. Thus, two years before Seitz (1940) the law of summation of heterogeneous stimuli had already been discovered in the case of humans, if not recognized in its more profound significance, and in one and the same experimental setup the two so different types of apperception of expression had appeared, each in a specifically different connection, though analytically so far incompletely separated. Eventually (1957) W. Schmidt,[5] also using line faces but with a method more precisely adjusted to the problems involved, found the effect of stimulus summation in pure form.

f. The work of Ahrens (1953) is to my knowledge still the only one which undertakes the attempt to investigate the ontogenesis of a relationship between expression and impression and in which the experimental planning takes into consideration the results and indications from ethological investigations of animals. The psychological basis of the work is the earlier findings of Bühler (1928, 1934), Kaila (1932), and Spitz (1946). As I have already mentioned, Ahrens succeeded in proving that smiling is a genuine instinctive movement and appears spontaneously much earlier than the IRM belonging to it matures (cf. also Koehler 1954 a, 1955 a). As far back as this he recognized that the "sensory correlates" of the various effective features combined in one IRM may quite well become functional at very different times and have a very different rate of maturation. It is with this in mind that he interprets the shifting of the stimulus "center of gravity" (if one may call it that) from the ocula (the eyes and their immediate surroundings) to the mouth region which occurs about the end of the fourth to the beginning of the fifth month of age. Likewise he recognizes quite rightly that experience poses new conditions which must be fulfilled *before* the sign stimuli can impress the IRM, but that the effectiveness of these stimuli continues unchanged. He overlooks, however, one very important factor in this development: Namely that here again an "innate schoolmaster" is fundamentally involved in shaping this experience. As I described in 1956, for example, a young cat without experience initially regards any other mammal, perhaps even vertebrate, as a "fellow cat," most probably on account of precisely this age-old influence of the ocula, assumed by Ahrens, which releases the first moves toward social contact. That mice, rats, and other small animals are not conspecifics but prey is something the young cat must learn, and this it does mainly under the influence of another maturing IRM which causes it to chase and catch small objects running away from it. My own observations show correspondingly that maturing components of an IRM for a further "ancient social mien," the threat expression, compel a baby's attention to additional parts of the face and thus "teach" the child to see them as well. This development begins, mostly unnoticed, rather earlier than the familiar "shyness toward strangers," with some children as early as toward the end of the fifth month. A person can elicit reactions of intense fear in babies of this age by holding black objects of sufficient size near his own face; the object having the most fearful effect is a black hat, whereas a pale-colored hat worn by the same person receives no attention. On the basis of my own experiments, so far unpublished, it may be taken as certain that this at first glance surprising effect of apparently artificial properties is due to the fact that an IRM in babies has remained "conservative" and continues to react to a releaser which modern man has largely lost: It may be safely assumed that primitive man could still erect the very dark hairs of his head and beard and in this way accentuate the threat mime. This ancient IRM, which has outlived its own releaser, is probably also the main reason for the subconscious sense of menace which the color black is capable of evoking. A second reason is no doubt to be found in the fact that an animal so dependent on vision as man is afraid of the dark (Lorenz 1940). All such "primordial relationships" to colors, sounds, spatial coordinates such as "above" and "below" can with certainty be explained in the same way. Klages (1936) is surely turning things upside down when he claims that man has a primordial relationship to "above" and "below" and that, for this reason, a joyfully excited face displays ascending lines and a sad face descending ones! If one takes the foregoing facts and considerations into account one can no longer concur unconditionally with Frijda (1965) when he calls the fact that, according to Ahrens, recognition and comprehension of laughter and threat mime become ever surer and more detailed up to the sixth year of age "an extremely unlikely finding." If recognition and comprehension in the narrowest sense are meant, Ahrens could quite well be correct. Frijda is, however, right in saying that the facts should be checked by other methods than verbal.

A further observation by Ahrens provokes interesting questions. In its first months a baby reacts to dummies composed of lines and dots which do not even need to represent complete faces. Thereafter, as the baby or small child grows older, the stimulus situation must be increasingly differentiated and complete in the way already described if it is to elicit smiling, and not until about the age of six years are the children again capable of apperceiving the expression on line faces adequately (or merely of giving them the correct linguistic designation?). Ahrens considers that the line drawings seemed strange to the children, and the younger children are not capable of overcoming this impression of strangeness and breaking through to an interpretation of the drawings. This phenomenon can, however, be interpreted in another way: In the process of youthful development newly acquired facilities often tend to be particularly tyrannical. The acquired capacity to apperceive and interpret total facial mime more or less consciously may at first impose and exercise a particularly strict "censorship," later however relax this and thus permit the IRMs a broader field of reaction once more. Ahrens's interpretation and mine can be brought under a common denominator if one regards this "censorship by acquired information" as a mild form of the ghost reaction. No special investigations have yet been made on the subject, but from my observations on fish and on cats it would seem that it is precisely the freshly experienced animals which are scarcely prepared to react to rough dummies, whereas animals of long-standing experience often do. Possibly, indeed very probably, the "censorship by acquired information" is subject to some form or other of afferent throttling and habituation to stimulus. Furthermore the phenomenon may also be connected with the fact that the acquired prerequisites and supplementary conditions under which an IRM becomes effective are at first complex qualities in which each of numerous details is equally important; when later gestalts emerge from them, many details lose their significance and the importance of the rest becomes unequal. It must be, however, that this moderates the "censorship," since to a certain degree it allows for deception through similarity. Finally, in the individual case under review one should remember that Ahrens confronted the babies with dot and line dummies of roughly natural size, the older children, however, with line drawings of greatly reduced size. Quite apart from difficulties the latter may perhaps have had in transposing the sizes, we must above all recall here the independent quantifiability of the single feature: On account of their smallness, the features of the drawings already possess only minimal releaser value; in addition the characteristics of movement are missing and these, as we know from all the investigations on the subject of the stimulus summation phenomenon quoted above (p. 307), always have greater— mostly many times greater—effectiveness than static characteristics. W. Schmidt (1957) has shown how, by adopting a suitable procedure which, except for the meticulously formulated experimental directions, eschews the verbal method, stimulus summation phenomena can also be proved by means of small line drawings.

It will, then, be seen how the most varied factors dependent on experience can participate to different degrees, sometimes varying according to the life phase, in the total process of the apperception of expression, while the capacity to form an impression is always present as a constant support function and, once maturation is complete, itself remains unchanged.

From the work of Ahrens and to a lesser degree also from that of W. Schmidt, it becomes very clear how fruitful it can be for research into expression in human psychology if those involved are not only aware of the results of ethology but also take these into consideration when formulating their problems and planning and laying-out their experiments; how incomparably more differentiated and precise the questions and answers then become, and how many new questions the results pose which must then be considered just as precisely. But despite the brave and encouraging start made by these two authors, no one has so far followed their example.

IX. CHANGES IN THE EXPRESSION-IMPRESSION RELATIONSHIP DUE TO DOMESTICATION

Lorenz (1940, 1943 a) and many others have pointed out the striking fact that man has many biological peculiarities in common with his domestic animals and have indicated numerous details in support of this statement. I would mention in particular the most important of these, namely that the variability in phenotype of a population of domestic animals which has not been subjected to strict selective breeding for particular characteristics is many times greater than is usual in wild populations, as the allele pool of a wild population is largely restricted to recessive mutants; the picture presented by the wild population is therefore even more uniform than the genetic pool. This is not so in the case of domestic animals and man. Individually, therefore, human beings are extraordinarily different, not merely in somatic and physiological phenotype, but also in their modes of behavior. This is *not only* due to a broad range of modifiability in some characteristics; innate human behavior, too—that part which can scarcely, if at all, be modified by experience and learning—*varies extraordinarily from individual to individual*. This in no way alters the fact that the ontogenetic development of these individual components is based purely on phylogenetic information. It has, however, led to a constant failure to make a distinction between this form of *variability* and genuine *modifiability*. The resultant conceptual confusion defies analysis and is the basis for the axiom that human beings possess absolutely no innate modes of behavior or, if so, only a few base ones of no significance to all problems of higher intellectual life.

Theories such as these are disproved by disturbances in the sphere of both expression and impression, disturbances in which all the eagerness to learn and all the teaching in the world are of no avail because the "innate schoolmaster" has failed to function. The dissociation between what is to be expressed and adequate means of expression can progress so far that a person may be incapable of matching the two up, however hard he tries. And he cannot try until the fact has been pointed out to him, since he cannot notice it for himself. Furthermore, there are people whose faces are so unfortunately shaped that, for example, a friendly smile always takes on the form of a spiteful grin, and they are not aware of it either if no one tells them; but that is the impression they produce, and even their closest acquaintances have difficulty in resisting the impression. In the face of all knowledge to the contrary it persists in obtruding; for the mechanisms of impression evaluate features and not "the reality of another's mind." Where increasing heterozygosis has caused the original harmony—i.e. the harmony between the reality of the mind and the feature, bred during a long phylogenesis—to disintegrate, the mechanisms of impression are helpless. Finally there are also people with localized weaknesses in their impression faculties which may go as far as complete "impression blindness." From childhood onward these people have difficulties in social intercourse, and in extreme cases become neurotics with paranoid symptoms, or at least eccentrics and often misanthropists. Usually neither they not those around them can guess where the cause of their lack of capacity for contact lies. The phenomenon is not restricted to introverts, nor can it be explained by introversion. In serious cases extroverts, by their very nature, suffer more from it than introverts, to whom contact with numerous people does not mean (almost) their whole life. Impression blindness is the special effect of a process which, being a result of domestication, is very common among our domestic animals, and which Lorenz (1940, 1943 a) has described as "a coarsening of innate releasing mechanisms." A very complicated and therefore highly selective releasing mechanism possessed by the wild ancestor of the domestic animal concerned loses its sensitivity in the first instance toward finer features. Its selectivity diminishes and as a result the animal becomes less "choosy," e.g. when selecting a mate. Where the breeding of domestic animals is concerned, this is an advantage, for it enables the breeder to pair animals off as he chooses. Where there is loss of selectivity in the mechanisms of impression, the finely tuned interplay between expression and impression in humans must naturally at once be upset and the whole reaction to it go awry. Then, if the component mechanisms of the relevant capacity for impression reacting to the more obvious features are also caught up in the "coarsening process," a more or less expression-specific impression blindness occurs, bringing with it the consequences just described. These consequences vary according to which special mechanism of impression is affected, and their effect on the person's social adjustment and adaptation also varies accordingly. Partial compensation is possible, but only provided that the person concerned learns to suppress all immediate reactions of the Id and in this way gain time for deliberate response behavior.

It is precisely these largely incurable disturbances in the relationship between expression and impression which show more than clearly that the phrase "direct experience of the reality of another's mind" is merely a metaphor. Expression and impression do not form a system of communicating pipes in which some identical fluid rises and falls according to the distribution of pressure. The correspondence between expression and impression, between what is expressed and what is received as an impression, is due solely to the correspondence between phylogenetic information and adaptedness in organisms with an identical phylogeny—in other words to homology. If the genetic differences between individuals become too great, the phylogenetic information in the transmitter of expression no longer matches that in the receiver of impression; if their respective scales are not only differently calibrated but even already differently labeled, then it is no longer possible to reach agreement over the readings.

As I have already mentioned above, it is true that in human psychological research into expression a distinction, varying in sharpness from author to author, is drawn between the symptoms of current expression, the physiognomic traces left by a particular, very frequently performed expressive occurrence, and purely anatomically and physiologically determined facial architecture. Yet, the question how these various "modes of expression" (in the broadest sense of "expression") are apperceived, or whether, for example, different modes of apperception also belong exclusively or largely to them, is hardly ever raised. Now, the capacities for impression—in other words the IRMs reacting to expressive phenomena in a conspecific—are quite clearly geared primarily to the symptoms of current expression, and with good reason. Since they are mechanisms which release reaction, it is in the first instance a matter of indifference as far as their function is concerned whether, for example, when two conspecifics meet the threat mime displayed by one is a result of permanent disposition or momentarily provoked rage; in either case the other will be well advised to construe the expression as current threat and react accordingly. Thus, natural selection had little or no foothold on which to build into the mechanisms of impression an information register which alone would have made it possible to evaluate according to frequency of occurrence and thus to differentiate between the symptoms of current expression and physiognomic traces left by expression. The capacity to distinguish between the two and to react specifically to each is of advantage only when individuals who know each other personally form stable societies—in other words, not until a very differentiated level of phylogenetic development has been reached. But in that case the animals must learn to recognize each other individually anyway, and so it is highly probable that in the process they also learn the various individual permanent dispositions to particular moods, indeed that such permanent dispositions in fact mediate, or at least greatly facilitate, individual recognition.

Facial architecture has a quite different position in relation to the symptoms of current expression from that of physiognomic traces left by expression. Traces of expression merely assist an otherwise transient feature to make a lasting mark; what is expressed in them both is identical in quality. Due to the range of variation brought about by domestication I have mentioned, however, the facial architecture often "copies" expressive features (see p. 345) without processes corresponding to the expressive occurrence being involved. Lersch's warning (1943) that such copies should not be interpreted as expression is, therefore, fully justified; Kiener's objection (1965), that an impression is nevertheless created and that therefore expression in some form or other must be involved, is a *non sequitur,* as I have already shown abundantly. Lorenz (1943 a) has explained the age-old physiognomic interpretations of animal faces in this way. For example, the facial architecture of the camel "copies" human expressive features which *in man* indicate arrogance. This is not true in the case of the camel, but the impression we receive nonetheless ascribes this trait of character to it.

Portmann (1948) has emphasized that, over and above functional usefulness and the direct announcement of fluctuations in mood, the gestalt of an animal's body and the perceptible changes in it also possess a value in themselves and for their own sake, and that this is particularly true of the secondary sexual characteristics. Portmann's linguistic style sometimes gives the non-biologist the impression that a kind of "gestalt mystique" is under discussion, which was far from Portmann's intention—at least I like to think so. In fact, however, he is talking not of a metaphysical question of "purpose," scientifically out of the question because fundamentally impossible to verify, but merely of the adaptive value possessed by even the apparently use-lessly esthetic, which Darwin (1871) dealt with in detail in his theory of sexual selection—a theory which for so long has been erroneously regarded as inaccurate or applicable in only a few special cases, and which ethology has confirmed to a far greater extent than even Darwin himself could have suspected (Lorenz 1943 a, b, 1965; Eibl-Eibesfeldt 1960). As Lorenz (1943 a) shows, within wild popula-tions particular anatomical features and functions are correlated to a statistically significant degree with capabilities and the readiness to use these which have positive social value, so that selection of the anatomical features simultaneously effects the selection of these capabilities. The correlation mentioned above is in no way fortuitous but, at least in many cases, is itself the result of natural selection aimed in this direction, and the reason—or at any rate one of the main reasons—for this seems to me to lie in the original functional limitations of IRMs described in greater detail on p. 305. The func-tions and capabilities in question—for instance the ability of a male to acquire and defend a good territory, its readiness to protect a female and brood, and similar "qualities of character"—are in fact mostly very complex and cannot themselves be recognized from simple, at all times perceivable features. Anatomical features, on the other hand, can easily possess the simplicity which already comes partway to meet the "keyboard" of an IRM. For the reasons given, it was not possible for natural selection to "construct" an IRM for "benevolence," "bravery," or similar lasting traits of character, but it *was possible* to create one for broad shoulders and slender hips, and to correlate these anatomical features with those qualities of character. In the case of wild animals, the male that is largest, strong-est, and endowed with the most well-developed secondary sexual characteristics is usually (i.e. with sufficient statistical frequency to ensure success in natural selection) also the most self-sacrificing, the bravest fighter, etc. However, this correlation is often rather unstable and breaks down as soon as selection pressure is relaxed, as is the case in domestication, including what is called the self-domestication of man. The IRMs reacting to anatomical features, however, are often more stable and remain in existence. Thus, the anatomical features themselves lose their information value, but the IRMs evaluating the information continue to react to them. Thus, an impression is indeed created, but Kiener (1965) is doubly mistaken when, as mentioned, he concludes from this that facial architecture must therefore also have expressive content. In the first place, information corresponding to the impression need not in fact be present; in the second place, where the correlation has not (or not yet) been upset, what we have is still not expression in the strict sense, for the "features" evaluated by the mechanisms of impression are not causally determined, not even partially, by the qualities of character "deduced" from them in terms of the impression created. What Lorenz (1943 a) called the "schemata for esthetic proportions" and the famous *Kindchenschema* are IRMs of the sort which play an important part in the mutual attraction of the sexes and in releasing parental tenderness and care. The list composed by Lorenz is far from complete. For example, we are indebted to Wynne-Edwards (1962) for the indication, certainly accurate, that white hair can be counted not only as a sign of deteriorating bodily functions and approaching death, but also quite positively as a releaser which, via an IRM, persistently influences the attitude toward an old, experienced, wise conspecific. Such respect for the old, incidentally, is not confined to humans. Old chimpanzees also become gray-headed, and Kortlandt (1962) observed that in a free-ranging horde of chimpanzees one old male, which physically had long since ceased to be capable of competing with the others, enjoyed certain privileges of old age: Not one of the younger, stronger males attacked it, and any member of the herd would readily give it fruit that had just been picked if it as much as stretched out its hand. Washburn and DeVore (1961) report comparable experiences with baboons; in the case of this species, a group of "wise elders" in fact rules the herd.

We are aware *that* the correlation between qualities of character and physical features has been upset in man and particularly in civilized man. The pretty, charming do-no-good and people who are ugly but noble-minded are part of our everyday experience, just as they may be found in inexhaustible variations in the world's great as well as less great literature. Already for the Greeks of the classical age to be at once beautiful and good was apparently a desire, an almost unattainable ideal, rather than something customary and automatically expected. However, *to what extent* this correlation has in fact been upset, how different peoples, races, groups within a population (e.g. city-dwellers in comparison to country-dwellers), etc., behave in this respect—on this question no research at all has, as far as I know, yet been made. Research into constitutional biology and psychology is without interest here, for not once in all of it has the question ever been raised whether the physical and constitutional features investigated, and in some cases correlated with particular qualities of character and psychic disposition, are of a kind reacted to by an IRM, which for its part then furnishes an immediate impression of the mental qualities correlated according to the actual state. As far as most of the physical features listed in the various typologies are concerned, this possibility can in fact be ruled out with certainty.

Impression on the other hand behaves just as if nothing in the correlation had changed. It is, therefore, not in the least surprising, but rather to be expected, when for example in the experiments by Brunswik and Reiter (1938) already referred to the impressions "benevolent," "likable," and "beautiful" are governed by the same features in the line faces.

When we speak of the "unteachability" of impression in this context, this certainly does not mean that an impression created in this way exercises a compulsion on the individual from which he cannot break free. For example, the releaser effect some secondary sexual features exert on relevant IRMs does not *necessarily* force partners otherwise unsuited to fall in love and be unhappy afterward; yet this does happen often enough, and offers strong evidence of the "unreasonable" power exercised by the mechanisms of impression. In a normal case, however, they provide no more than the first incentive for two people to get to know one another better, and many other— and certainly *not only* innate—conditions must be fulfilled before love develops out of the first falling in love. None of these impression mechanisms exerts such an inescapable and final coercion as is assumed by some authors (e.g. Schlegel 1960); they cannot, if for no other reason than that the propensities and actions released by them are largely self-regulating and independent of stimulation (see above, p. 280 et seq.).

On account of its close connection with characterology and psychological diagnostics, the psychology of expression has always occupied itself more intensively with the question how, and how dependably, the apperception of expression provides information about the more or less permanent traits and qualities of "the reality of another's mind" than with the functions of expression and impression in the service of current communication, functions which guide and regulate social behavior not in an indirect and underground fashion but directly while it is happening. Furthermore a distinction has not always, and not precisely enough, been made between these various functions—a criticism I have already made before. The works of Brunswik and Reiter, Davitz, Hofstätter, and Klineberg quoted in section VIII. are only a few examples, which could be added to at will, of how uncritically the various different functions on both the expression and the impression side get jumbled together. Here again is conclusive evidence of how unhomogeneous is the field of traditional research into expression as a whole and how dangerous it is to formulate premature, abstract superconcepts if we are to hope to disentangle all the heterogeneous phenomena to be found therein. Not everything which creates an impression is expression; not all expression becomes impression; the apperception of expression is a function with many strata, even if the experience is unitary; the various functions of the apperception of expression and the different phenomena which evoke impression are not primarily related to one another and do not mutually define one another.

Lorenz attributes man's capacity for projecting expression into the inanimate environment, thus populating it with demons and ghosts, to the law of stimulus summation: Even when presented in isolation without their accustomed background, expressive features prove to have a releasing effect, if often only a weak one. In the case of individuals with specific experience, however (see p. 346), we must always reckon with a "censorship by acquired information"; the gestalt of a typical situation or known object must be there before the IRM is allowed to react to the releasing features. However, as I mentioned already when reviewing the work of Ahrens (p. 359), this censorship apparently begins to relax again gradually soon after it is first imposed. It seems that in domestication this limitation diminishes still further or is absent altogether. In this way mechanisms of the sympathetic induction of mood, which normally remain confined to one's own social community, are thrown open to all humans. This naturally renders the projection of one's own emotions into inanimate matter very much easier. If in its beginnings—for instance in the case of primitive peoples—this process is combined with the other which Seitz (1940) so accurately designated the ghost reaction, then it is perfectly "natural" if projected emotions are fed back as "ghost," "demon," etc.

X. SECONDARY EXPRESSIVE FORMS AND RELATED PHENOMENA

1. Traces of expression

Many mammals mark their own body and/or particular places and pathways within their habitat with scents. In relatively simple cases they use normal body excreta such as feces and urine for the purpose. But marking behavior obviously has enormous selection value.

It is the origin of the glands which mammals of the most widely differing groups have on the cheeks, lower jaw, nape of the neck, upper arm, flanks, back, soles of the feet, and anal region. There is scarcely a single part of the body on which a scent gland has not developed in some mammal or other (Hediger 1949, Eibl-Eibesfeldt 1957). Special movements serve to extrude the secretion from the glands and apply it to the animal's own body, to its female or—most frequently—to some object or other such as stones, branches, tree roots, etc. (Fiedler 1964). This is without any doubt expressive behavior, functionally analogous to a symbolic act of taking possession. The animal subsequently goes away, but the scent mark remains. Later a conspecific comes along. It has not experienced the expressive behavior of its predecessor, but it sniffs the scent mark and receives an impression. In fact this impression is probably often a very detailed one; in the case of some species—indeed perhaps always—it may be assumed that the state of excitation of the animal making the mark has a specific influence on the composition of the secretion. The animal smelling it later therefore learns from it not only "a conspecific was here already," but "a conspecific was here which was angry, ready for mating" or whatever, an impression such as is otherwise created in the course of a personal meeting via the perception of expressive phenomena. Furthermore the mark may also contain other information, for it may be assumed that neighbors in a fairly large habitat recognize each other individually not only directly when meeting but also from their scent marks (Hediger 1946, 1961, Ortmann 1956, Schaffer 1940, Wynne-Edwards 1962). If during an actual meeting animals secrete scent substances specific to their state of excitation and mutually react just as specifically to these, then this is without doubt an expressive phenomenon. Already when they transfer the scent of the secreting gland to another part of the body (as, for example, the Ring-tailed Lemur draws its tail over the glands on its upper foreleg), and then carry it around with them constantly like a scented flag, it becomes doubtful. Finally, when they separate themselves completely from the scent substance and deposit it somewhere "to whom it may concern," the doubts become even stronger.

In the case of at least some American species of deer, the stags do not rub their antlers only in order to remove the velvet; they rub them particularly vigorously, slashing and whipping shrubs or saplings, if a rival is watching. This has become display behavior and impresses accordingly (Graf 1956). The sight of the destruction caused, however, can also evoke the same impression, if in attenuated form, in a rival which was not able to watch the activity itself. In this case, then, the stags do not even physically leave anything of themselves behind. Where does expression end here? Analogous instances can be found in human behavior. As only one of many possible examples, I would mention handwriting. This is, after all, also a product separated from its originator, in the production of which expressive processes are involved. It is true that intended communication is foremost here and the expressive occurrence only epiphenomenal, not the prime object as in the two animal examples I have quoted. But this is, as it were, a difference of degree and can be overlooked in this connection. Not only can the traces of expression in the handwriting be elucidated by rational methodology for the purpose of diagnosis, but a genuine physiognomic impression may even be gained from it, though admittedly within narrower limits than is often claimed. The piece of writing itself is certainly not expression; but it bears traces of expression. It is difficult to see why a trace of an indubitably genuine expressive occurrence should be a legitimate object of expression research only if it is fixed in the physiognomy but not if it appears on a piece of paper. Kirchhoff (1962 b) would like to separate the two distinctly and to exclude graphology completely from expression theory (even applied) as not being pertinent. Yet, expression and impression theory cannot afford to ignore handwriting and similar material. Here, too, we cannot fix a boundary for all time, but only one which corresponds to the particular purpose and scope of an investigation and/or the presentation of results.

2. "Uniform variability"

In addition to those listed in section VIII. 1, there is a further exception to the rule that expressive behavior is not learned. In some cases the IRM reacts not to behavior patterns or structures but to a particular effect; the way in which this effect is produced is, within broad limits, often immaterial.

At the beginning of such a development we have, for example, song-birds in whose case within genetically determined limits (see section VI. 2 d) variety of song *as such* possesses releasing quality. There is, however, apparently another factor in the selecting IRM which works in the opposite direction, namely toward uniformity within a population. This results in dialects which vary from place to place, and these each bird must learn as well as its own individual variations (Isaac and Marler 1963, Marler 1960, Marler and Isaac 1960 a, b, c, 1961, Marler and Tamura 1962, 1964, Marler, Kreith, and Tamura 1962, Thielcke 1964, 1965, Thielcke and Linsenmair 1963). The antithetical action of the two factors leads to a result which may be somewhat anthropomorphically expressed in the following rule: "Sing similar to your neighbor but never quite the same." In the case of the chaffinch, for instance, this could be ascribed less to a "uniformity factor" than to the generally rather limited breadth of variation in its singing ability. In the case of the shama, the males of which species can easily master thirty and more quite different song sequences and in addition exchange these from year to year for new ones, this no longer explains the fact that, however great the richness of variation, neighboring birds have a repertoire which coincides in many details. What I have considered here as a component mechanism of an IRM which reacts to uniform vocalization and thus "teaches" this may seem to some merely a not particularly fortunate choice of a new name for the old familiar "imitative instinct." Certainly it is a form of imitation, but a very special one which, in combination with the counteracting factor "teaching" richness of variation, strives toward imperfect copies of the original. In the case of birds like the shama which are *capable* of reproducing absolutely faithful copies of virtually all sound sequences they hear, something must ensure that within a population a certain basic stock of vocalizations remains sufficiently uniform to make species recognition possible. A mechanism of fundamentally quite the same sort is also responsible for the fact that, in spite of any amount of variability in detail, the fashion of a season or an epoch remains clearly recognizable as such.

Just like traces of expression left in the physiognomy, individual variants within the uniform vocalization of a population contribute to mutual recognition among individuals. With time, of course, stimulus habituation sets in, but there are two sides to that, too: Habituation creates intimacy, and this can develop into a firm and lasting bond between partners. The individuals of many animal species have a comparably strong need for both familiar conspecifics—and not only their sexual partner—and familar surroundings, above all their home; Holzapfel (1940) therefore speaks expressly of "the individual with the home character." How far such personal intimacy can go, how far a partner can be identified by means, for example, of a vocalization peculiar to it alone, will be discussed in (5). Relationships of familiarity similar to those between individuals of the same species can, however, occur between individuals of different species which breed in mixed colonies. Bergman (1964) recently proved that these relationships do not develop between any and every kind of species, but that an innate inclination and a capacity for learning to understand the calls of a different species are necessary in addition.

3. Acquired means of expression

In the IRM of many monkeys, the anthropoid apes, and man which reacts to the threat display of a conspecific there is a constituent mechanism for a "feature" which could perhaps most correctly be described as "rhythmical noise." The original instrument for producing noise was, without doubt, the vocal apparatus. This is still so today with many species and has been brought to enormous heights of performance by the South American howler monkeys and gibbons. In the case of some old world monkeys noise production did not stay limited to the voice, and any kind of noise has full releasing value as long as it is loud and can be subjected to rhythm. One might assume that one of the IRM's stipulations, which in the other species mentioned lays down the "species-specific vocal register," has been lost or at least become less selective as a consequence of a coarsening of the IRM. Then, in accordance with the law of summation of heterogeneous stimuli and individual quantifiability of features, the greater amplification which can be achieved in some other way could in the truest sense of the word drown the no doubt still existent selectivity toward the species-specific voice—in other words, a supernormal "din" would have a similar effect on the IRM constituent concerned as the super-flat, super-long object "swimming human" on the copulation reaction of the Mallard drake. Male rhesus monkeys climb onto a sturdy, well-projecting branch and shake it with all their might. As they do so they often scream in the same rhythm. The noise produced by the branch is usually not very great and the whole thing still looks rather stereotyped and is certainly still largely pure instinctive action. Chimpanzees perform similar shaking movements on the ground, clap the naked soles of their feet on a hard, smooth surface, clap their hands, beat, and jump on fallen hollow trees, and in the process of these so much more manifold sequences of movement very quickly learn how they can best produce the most noise. In captivity, for example, cage wire and iron doors are supernormal instruments for the production of din. Here, then, an IRM having a particular requirement encounters an already very highly developed voluntary motor system which it can "teach" how to find or create the most effective "feature" capable of being produced with the means available in the area at any given time. The production of warlike din by humans certainly has a quite homologous history. The youth showing off by revving his stationary motorbike hard and rhythmically is incited to his nerve-racking activity by the same mechanism of impression. Is noise such as this, produced with the help of instruments other than one's own body, "still" expression?

4. Expression, impression, and the reafference principle

Different as they may seem, the cases listed in section X. 1-3, all have one common factor: The manifestations concerned find their confirmation not only—and in the cases described last certainly least of all—in the reaction of the conspecific to which they are addressed, but also in the reaction of the animal's own IRM to them. When an animal deposes a scent mark, it almost always turns around and sniffs at it; often it repeats the marking process and sniffs at it again before going away. The regulation and direction of the sensomotor system serving vocalizations are already familiar, and the reafference on which they are based was discovered, described, and analyzed by von Holst and Mittelstaedt (1950). If the effectiveness of a form of expressive behavior needs to be measured by its success with a con-specific, this necessitates a number of "individual tests" on the principle of trial and error, and for this there is no opportunity, particularly in situations of the kind which occur only rarely in the normal life cycle of an animal species. "Testing" can, therefore, only be carried out on a phylogenetic time scale, and the resulting information can only be stored in the "species memory," in other words the genetic pool. In all these cases, therefore, the IRM is helpless to do anything but exert selection pressure aimed at the creation of adequate *innate* expressive phenomena. If, however, the emphasis of testing for success is shifted onto the IRM of the individual producing the expressive behavior, this individual can carry out almost continuous tests on itself if only it can find effective methods of counteracting the afferent throttling of its own IRM. In this way the strongest selection pressure will probably be exerted in the direction of variability, of having the motor system as freely available as possible. And with the IRM and its feature requirements as "teacher," this "free" motor system will then learn the best methods of producing highly effective features in any given situation. The significance of reafference to the development of the vocalizations of birds has already been experimentally investigated in various species (Messmer and Messmer 1956, Konishi 1963, 1964, Sauer 1954, W. Schleidt 1961 b, 1964). The importance of acoustic feedback in the development of speech in humans is well-known from experiences with the deaf and dumb. Gehlen (1941) has attributed to sensomotor feedback a fundamental significance in the development of the entire human motor system and motivational structure. As far as I know, however, there has not so far been any detailed investigation of its influence on the development of expressive behavior in the narrowest sense.

Man—perhaps man alone, though perhaps other highly developed animals have at least modest beginnings of it, too—possesses yet another capacity which goes even farther than anything described so far. He can *imagine* how a genuine expressive picture, produced by him and based on unreflected, innate reactions, looks to a partner, provided that he is at least subsequently conscious of his behavior. In accordance with this imagined idea, he can then remodel his expressive behavior under the control of his IRM (a control of which he is largely unaware). What he imagines need naturally not coincide with the impression another gains from the expression which actually emerges; yet, via his imagination a human being can to a certain extent become his own "you," the impression partner of his own (imagined) expression. In this way and above all, of course, in front of the mirror, the pose originates. Now, on account of the self-domestication discussed on p. 361 et seq. and its consequences, there is no guarantee that the expression he is capable of producing is up to the standards set by his own mechanisms of impression. Consequently in the pose a projection of the individual's own capacity to form an impression *can* take the place of genuine expression. The tendency to exaggeration so frequently inherent in pose is explained, at least in part, by the afferent throttling to which a person frequently posing before himself is subject: He does not notice it any longer, but everyone else does, for they, of course, see him less often than he sees himself. This has an embarrassing effect on those around him for two reasons: The poseur rarely succeeds in having equal command of all expressive phenomena, and the incongruity exposes the fake; very pronounced exaggerations cause a mild "ghost reaction." In the complicated conditions I have only lightly touched on here lies a considerable potential for stress and conflict.

From the foregoing it should have become clear that the mechanisms of impression—without prejudice to the phenomena of coarsening and dissociation—have shown themselves to be both phylogenetically as well as ontogenetically more stable than the modes of expression. One should not, however, make the mistake of thinking that the innate modes of expression become completely ousted or permanently changed in form through the superimposition of acting and pose and other processes of learning and habituation. In a moment of surprise or great stress they cast off all acquired accessories and break through in unadulterated form—i.e. provided, however, that there has not already been loss of phylogenetic information as a consequence of domestication.

One further example may show how tremendous the pressure can be with which one special mechanism of impression forces the creation of a feature toward which it is sensitive. As I have already described on p. 321 et seq., erectile crowns of feathers, crests of hair, etc. belong to the releasers which have been bred as attributes of the threat and display behavior of many vertebrates in response to a corresponding mechanism of impression. Animals which erect the hair on their heads in display include the chimpanzee and the gorilla, the nearest relatives of man; as Lorenz (1940, 1943) has pointed out, the—macroscopically ineffective—diminished remains of the corresponding pilomotor system demonstrably still exist in man, too, but the releaser itself has been lost. The IRM, however, has remained highly sensitive toward it, and in literally every age and culture has caused men to set crowns of feathers, tufts of grass, tall hats, and helmets on their heads, or to pile their hair up in a tall artificial construction by sometimes extremely laborious and even painful means; our impression still reacts to them in thoroughly unenlightened fashion. Nor does the head decoration serve merely to simulate higher growth: even someone standing on stilts for that purpose usually puts on exaggerated headgear as well. It is the adornment of the head as substitute for hair that can no longer stand on end which lends the wearer greater "impressive value" and gains him more respect, if only for the first instant. Only a factor remaining common beyond the boundaries of all ages, races, peoples, and cultures can explain the basic uniformity of such head decorations. All humans possess a mechanism of impression sensitive to this feature, just as they all have noses, *and for the same reason*. Thus, it was and still is possible for the mechanisms of impression to evoke the most absurd dummies, such as the secondary wing feathers of the Argus pheasant and the top hat, in such different ways as through natural selection in phylogeny or through fashions and traditions which themselves do not know how far down their roots go. Qua expression the function of the dummies is *analogous,* but the impressions they elicit are homologous!

5. How individual traits in expression serve as "names"

I have already quoted the work of Gwinner and Kneutgen several times. In this they report that ravens, like the shamas mentioned on p. 371, learn numerous and sometimes very complicated sequences. In a pair each partner has certain sound patterns which are peculiar to it, and which the other never utters as long as the two are together. If one partner disappears from view completely for rather a long time, the remaining partner begins to call after a while and what it calls are the sequences otherwise uttered only by the one which has disappeared. If the latter hears and it is physically possible, it returns immediately. Shama pairs do the same, and now that the possibility has been pointed out one may safely prophesy that soon a large number of corresponding observations will be made in other species as well. Finding out in detail what is behind this faculty must be the task of further investigations. But consider the fact itself as one will, in *effect* the birds are calling each other by name.

Expressive behavior has been named as a root of speech and language by Gehlen (1941; work also lists specialized literature), as well as by Koehler in his publications on animal pre-forms of human language (1949 a, b, 1951, 1952, 1953, 1954 b, c, 1955). The case of "name-giving" in birds just described indicates a way in which *one* very particular function of speech possibly originated. In the examples discovered so far, however, the recognition of such "names" is restricted to two individuals; perhaps cases will emerge in which more are involved. But this is no argument against the phenomenon. One need only think of the fact, quoted by Gehlen, that with some South American aborigine Indians the possibilities of making oneself understood in language are restricted to the smallest possible group; practically every family speaks its own language, or at least a dialect of its own. One need only think of the case, described in the same book, of the highly neglected children who grew up in the company of a deaf woman and developed a language of their own which no one else could understand.

A further function of language which can probably be traced back to expressive behavior is the designation of objects. This assumption is based on the following observations. When cats bring live prey animals to their growing kittens for the first time, they utter particular calls to attract the kittens. Even to the human ear there is a distinct qualitative difference in the calls, depending on whether the prey animal is small and harmless (mouse) or something larger and potentially dangerous (rat). In the one case the kittens approach without anxiety, in the other they come hesitantly and crouched. In fact, however, the two calls are only different levels of intensity of the same call, as we discovered purely by chance when we wanted to make sound recordings of them. We used a mouse to coax a cat which was particularly good at carrying prey to her young into the next room, shut the door and then gave her the mouse. She picked it up, immediately began to call "mouse" and hastened in the direction of her kittens, but was prevented by the closed door. She began to run to and fro excitedly at the door and, as she did so, the "mouse" call intensified in a process of gradual transition into her "rat" call. Later we happened to observe the same thing when the kittens were somewhat older and did not want to come out in response to her "mouse" call from their hiding-place, inaccessible to their mother, behind the woodwork disguising a radiator. Normally however—at least according to our observations so far—it does not happen that a cat with a mouse in its jaws calls "rat" or vice versa. This example is so particularly instructive because the process of differentiation between qualitatively different designations is still incomplete. On the other hand it is definitely not a case of a "hangover" from the different intensities of excitation connected with catching a rat or catching a mouse; for even when the cat first eats part of the rat herself, she still calls "rat" when she brings the kittens the remaining third or quarter, although such a piece of rat is no larger than a fat mouse and the excitement of the kill has certainly long since died down. It is scarcely possible to interpret this in any other way than that the cat herself somehow already makes a *qualitative* and not merely quantitative distinction between rat and mouse and the corresponding calls. It seems perfectly clear how the complete separation of two (or more) "typical intensities" (Morris 1957) out of a series of intensities which was originally continuous can lead to qualitatively different "conceptual designations" and above all to qualitatively different response behavior by a conspecific or conspecifics. On p. 281 I have already described briefly how different intensities can be "translated" into qualities in other areas of behavior and experience as well, and this I have discussed at greater length in another paper (1967; p. 256–257).

At a conference in Birmingham, England, the Director of the Chester Zoo, Dr. Mottershead, made the following report (published in shortened version 1959): The new, large outdoor enclosures for chimpanzees at Chester Zoo were at first separated from one another and from the public only by shallow water ditches. However, this method of enclosure proved inadequate and an electric wire was installed in the middle of each ditch about 20 cm above the water. On the largest of the islands was a group of chimpanzees comprising several adult males and females and a few juveniles. The most active of the males promptly waded into the water to inspect the new electric wire and just as promptly received a shock. He sprang away, but after a while tried again, naturally with the same result. Thereupon he went in turn to every member of the group, scattered as they were over the whole island, put an arm around each and "it looked as though he whispered something into its ear." The one thus "spoken to" immediately went to the point in the ditch where the male had had his experience. When they had all gathered there, another male chimpanzee—the largest and strongest—picked up a twig, waded a little way into the ditch, stretched out the twig, and touched the electric wire. Unluckily for him he had taken one which lay in the water, and so he likewise received a shock. Since then not one member of this group has ever made an attempt to approach the electric wire.

What is, of course, incredible about this story is that, contrary to everything anyone thought they knew so far about the ability of chimpanzees to communicate among themselves, one chimpanzee should be able to send another to a particular spot without somehow leading it there. In reply to questions as to how the animal had done this, Mottershead could say nothing certain and was also unwilling to speculate. I repeated Mottershead's report to Hugo and Jane van Lawick (p. 339) and asked them for their opinion. They too could say nothing definite, but did not think it was done by sounds. From their observations, however, they considered it possible that one chimpanzee could send another in a particular direction by means of its eyes. If this interpretation were correct, we should be dealing with a method similar to speech by which information is conveyed through gestures of the eyes, perhaps reinforced by sounds of excitation. Köhler (1921 b) observed that in another, i.e. sexual, connection chimpanzees are capable of making themselves understood simply by means of glances.

These three examples from such different spheres naturally do not prove that something similar *must* have been involved in the first beginnings of the development of human speech. But whatever one's opinion may be as to how probable this is, these examples do at any rate open the way to much more highly differentiated questions for investigation in connection with the origin of language. They give an idea of how much more numerous and specialized the roots of language could have been and almost certainly were than the five Gehlen has listed, and they show once again quite clearly how little service is done to research into expression if it is hemmed in too narrowly and above all too inflexibly by abstract definitions, whereas the living processes themselves recognize no limits or definitions. It is still a thoroughly open question how far expression and impression, together with all their basic etho-biological processes, reach into the field of actual language, even if one does not consider specifically informative functions such as description, communication, and conveying of messages as expression in the narrowest sense. The analysis of the various communicative functions of language (e.g. Kirchhoff 1960) proceeds from the *status quo* and allows itself at best mere glances into ontogeny. It is perfectly legitimate to restrict one's sphere of investigation in this way as long as one remains conscious of this self-imposed restriction; facts thus determined are indisputable and in general I agree here with Kirchhoff's interpretations. But considered from the point of view of phylogeny much that can be functionally separated today probably goes back to the same roots, and much that now appears a uniform function both in ontogeny and in actualization can probably be traced back to quite different phylogenetic roots. Subjects which, viewed from the standpoint of the *status quo,* seem with justification to have ceased to belong to the sphere of expression research would have to be included once more —wholly or partially, depending on the case—if phylogenetic standards were applied.

XI. CONCLUSION

Expression began as an insignificant epiphenomenon of the differentiation of behavior. In impression it found a counterpart which helped it develop into a "serviceable habit" in its own rights. It became signal, ritual, convention, fashion, intentional communication, name and designation, and thus one of the main roots of language. In the very instant, however, that the original phenomena of expression begin, as it were, to "lose their soul," i.e. become mechanical devices of intentional communication, epiphenomenal expression is again superimposed on them.

Impression intervened in the protean multiplicity of phenomena of the expressive processes and out of them bred the most inflexible and complicated systems of signals, the most ruthless synchronizers, highly differentiated learning capacities with amazing plasticity and yet at the same time extremely specialized adaptation, the most absurd dummies (many, however, possessing boundless esthetic attraction) and yet finally became capable of conveying to us the tenderest and most beautiful phenomena of our existence.

All this is something which must be viewed as a historical process *within which* the appearance and disappearance of a species may be compared with a non-perennial plant, the ontogeny of an individual with an ephemeral flower. We may concentrate our interest on the flower, but we shall understand nothing—absolutely nothing—about it if we do not view every detail constantly in relation to the one, in the truest sense of the word perennial process of evolution. Phylogeny is not something which once (perhaps) happened somewhere but from which man has in the meantime been emancipated by his intellect. This intellect in particular, with its quite specific functions as well as its equally specific malfunctions, cannot explain itself, but we *can* try to understand it to a certain extent by tracing its evolution. Evolution is a current process, so current that, considered precisely, the actualization of every single, fleeting thought the reader has literally began a billion years ago in a Precambrian sea. Phylogeny is, therefore, not a word that can be more or less adroitly inserted here and there as a sop to the zeitgeist and apart from that safely forgotten. We must learn to think in terms of phylogenetic inter-relationships, or else be prepared to believe in a pre-established harmony, a harmony incidentally—and that is what is most difficult to believe about it—with a positively human tendency to occasional disharmony. But if we could finally take seriously the investigation of phylogenetic adaptation in man also and stop confusing phenomenological similarity with relationship, logical deducibility with descent, then there is no reason why this should not prove just as profitable to the psychology of expression or to psychology as a whole as it already has been without exception to all other branches of the life sciences.

Notes

The comparative study of behavior
First appeared in: Verhandlungen der Deutschen Zoologischen Gesellschaft, Rostock 1939.

1. The fertility of hybrids cannot, however, be taken as a general measure of the degree of relationship between species. When geographically isolated, separate species may evolve from a common primitive form and a reproductive barrier develop sooner or later. But this is not necessarily so, for of course the danger of hybridization does not exist. Thus, even animals belonging to different genera may be mutually fertile; in contrast, sympatric animals—in other words, those occurring side by side in the same area—*must* develop a reproductive barrier, even, or rather particularly, when they are very closely related; otherwise they can neither evolve nor continue as separate species.

2. In his earlier writings, Lorenz still spoke of "reaction-specific energy": Such is the power of a traditional manner of speaking that, while arguing against the theoretical concept that all overt behavior observed is nothing but reaction, and while clearly stating the case for action independent of present stimulation, he still used the conventional terminology. This is a phenomenon which, in this case as in many others, befogs discussions about new findings and concepts consequent upon them. Although we have on the whole adhered to the principle of not altering the style and terminology of the articles in order to demonstrate through their sequence the progress of research and the development—often not along a straight line—of concepts and theoretical ideas, in this one case we thought it better to change to the later term "action-specific energy" for the sake of clarity.

3. *Naturwissenschaften*, 1937; English version in *Studies in Animal and Human Behaviour*, Vol. 1, Methuen, London 1970, p. 259 et seq.

4. But see p. 226 et seq., p. 237 et seq.

5. Meanwhile W. Schleidt (1961 a, 1962) has discovered from birds reared in isolation that the innate releasing mechanism of the turkeys is not essentially different from that of the Graylag Geese: In the normal biotope of both turkey and

Graylag Goose short-necked, slow-flying, large birds are much rarer than long-necked ones; thus they become habituated to the latter, whereas the former retain their fear-inducing, "frightful" effect. The naive turkey without experience reacts equally strongly to both, and, in experiments on turkeys reared and kept in isolation, if short-necked dummies are presented very frequently but long-necked ones only rarely, the "fright value" of the two is reversed as compared with "normal" conditions.

Introduction to the study of impression
First appeared in: Schola 6, 1951.
    1. For a more detailed explanation of this assumption see p. 311 et seq.

The relationship between drive and will in its significance to educational theory
First appeared in: Lebendige Schule (Schola) 7, 1952.
    1. The word "drive" *(Trieb)* has an extraordinarily manifold and usually vaguely defined meaning—almost every philosopher, psychologist, and biologist employs it in a different sense. In his article printed at the beginning of this volume (page 1), Lorenz uses the term to define more or less clearly directed appetitive behavior serving an activated instinct. In this article I use it as synonymous with "propensity" *(Einzelantrieb)*. For reasons very similar to W. McDougall's when he reintroduced the word into psychological terminology, I have always used "propensity" in the later articles, thus avoiding the many-faceted concept of drive completely. There is, of course, no question of adopting the whole of McDougall's theoretical position along with the term.
    2. The German term *Leerlauf-Reaktion* originally used by Lorenz (1937 a) is self-contradictory, since there cannot be *reaction* when there is no stimulus. In his later publications Lorenz therefore used *Instinktleerlauf* or *Leerlauf*. This has been translated into English as "vacuum activity," in my opinion a most unfortunate choice, though prompted by Lorenz's discussion of Tolman's (1932) contention that behavior "cannot go off *in vacuo.*" The two authors are, of course, not using "vacuum" in its precise physical meaning, but trying to describe a situation devoid of any eliciting or "supporting" stimuli *specific* to the behavior in question. In German, however, the term *"Leerlauf"* is in no way connected with a vacuum, but describes something running off while not serving its normal function; more specifically it denotes idling in an automobile engine. Lorenz used the term to emphasize this "idling" aspect when an instinct becomes active in the complete absence of its adequate eliciting stimuli, goal, object, etc. Thus, "vacuum activity" is both misleading and imprecise. Armstrong (1950) chose "overflow activity," a term which well describes a specific internal propensity surmounting its releasing threshold without the aid of specific sensory impulses, and which fits in with Lorenz's often misinterpreted and therefore much maligned but still—if properly understood—heuristically valuable "psychohydraulic" model (cf. pp. 217–218). For accuracy's sake it must be added that Armstrong doubted the existence of true overflow activity on the grounds that in each case claimed the possibility that there was some minute stimulus imperceptible to the observer could not be ruled out with absolute certainty. However, this is just splitting hairs: If the releasing threshold can lower itself far enough to allow an imperceptible stimulus to release an instinct movement in full, why should one rule out the possibility that the threshold becomes surmounted entirely from within and without any external stimulus? I am, therefore, using "overflow activity" here in the sense the words convey directly, without in any way sharing Armstrong's theoretical views.
    3. In its present form this sentence is no longer quite correct, for some—though not all!—propensities, while inaccessible to learning and insight, can be influenced like a muscle by use and disuse. For details see pp. 257–259.
    4. Spranger speaks of "ethical guarantors."
    5. Naturally it is neither anatomical nor behavioral characters which are *directly* determined by heredity, but rather the developmental processes, from the fertilized

egg onward, which produce them and the degree to which these developmental processes can be influenced by environmental factors. "Hereditary" are those characters whose development shows only a very slight tendency to environmentally governed changes (modifications).

6. The concept of "stabilizing systems" is most nearly comparable to McDougall's concept of the "sentiment" (1947). Motivational theories centered around the method of "operant" or "instrumental" conditioning mean basically much the same. In any event, what welds the stabilizing systems together is their—innate or partly or completely acquired—*releasing mechanisms.*

Theoretical considerations in criticism of the concept of the "displacement movement"
Paper read at the II. International Ethological Conference in Buldern/Westphalia, September 1952.

1. This earlier assumption is not quite correct: learned stereotyped movements (for example, winding a watch) may also occur in "displacement"; usually, if not always, it is a matter of strictly rhythmical motor patterns, in other words the activation of central nervous automatic functions (see p. 73 et seq.), which, of course, are not of a purely reflex nature either.

2. The hypothesis of "disinhibition" of displacement movements, which was already expressed by Lorenz (1939, see p. 25) and later expanded and experimentally developed by van Iersel and Bol (1958) and Sevenster (1961), overlooks this dualism. Fentress has been able to prove, also experimentally, that disinhibition alone does not answer the purpose, if it is taken to mean only the influencing of the stimulus threshold (paper read at the IX. International Ethological Conference, Zurich 1965).

The discovery of relative coordination: a contribution toward bridging the gap between physiology and psychology
First appeared in: Studium Generale 7, 1954.

1. Nowadays some ethologists and neurophysiologists consider von Holst's methods, results, and conclusions to have been overtaken by more recent research, such as that of Eccles (1964). This is out of the question. Von Holst's investigations covered far more complex functional relationships than it has so far proved possible to reach or analyze with methods such as recording monocellular action potentials and similar approaches. Far from the two types of method and their results canceling each other out or rendering each other superfluous, they are rather a necessary complement to one another.

A comparison between territoriality in animals and the need for space in humans
First appeared in: Homo 5, 1954

1. For the purposes of this article territory, home range, range, etc. are treated as more or less synonymous. A more specific discussion of these terms may be found on p. 121.

2. The case assumed here is purely theoretical and does not occur in natural conditions (see p. 122); it can occur, however, with animal species which man has decimated almost to extinction, so that the last surviving animals live vast distances apart, then, being bound to their territory, never find one another and thus fail to reproduce, although the number of specimens left would in itself have permitted the species to recover. This is possibly the case, for example, with the Lesser Indian Rhino on the Malayan Peninsula.

On the choice of a sexual partner by animals
First appeared in: Zeitschrift für Sexualforschung 6, 1955

Social organization and density tolerance in mammals
This article is a combination of two papers:—
a) The communal organization of solitary mammals; first appeared in Symposia of the Zoological Society of London *14*, 1965.
b) The sane community—a density problem?; first appeared in Discovery *26*, 1965.

1. Mammals, especially the highly developed ones, are long-lived and capable of

learning. That they develop traditions, including the handing down of social status from parents to progeny, has actually been proved in some cases and is probably far more prevalent than we assume at present. Thus, the social structure of such a mammalian population can be adequately investigated and correctly evaluated only if the investigation covers at least several generations.

2. I am grateful to Dr. Rosemarie Wolff for generously allowing me to use her invaluable records.

On the function of the relative hierarchy of moods (as exemplified by the phylogenetic and ontogenetic development of prey-catching in carnivores)
First appeared in: Zeitschrift für Tierpsychologie 22, 1965.

1. Dedicated to Professor Otto Koehler with heartfelt wishes on the occasion of his seventy-fifth birthday.—Supported by the Deutsche Forschungsgemeinschaft.

2. I should like to renew my thanks here to the following for their support in the form of material, animals, or advice, or for discussing specific problems:—
Animal Supply, Guayacil; Farbenfabriken Bayer, Wuppertal; Behring-Werke, Marburg/Lahn; Dr. A. C. V. van Bemmel, Rotterdam Zoo; Dr. Maria v. Brodorotti; the Deutsche Forschungsgemeinschaft; Monsieur F. Edmond-Blanc; Dr. I. Eibl-Eibesfeldt; Dr. R. F. Ewer; Dr. Fritz Frank; Dr. Lutz Heck Jr.; Dr. med. vet. F. Henning; Dr. H. Knappe; Prof. Dr. Otto Koehler; Dr. Lilli Koenig; Prof. Otto Koenig; Dr. H. Kreiskott; Mr. R. Lindemann and Dr. Heinz Heck, Catskill Game Farm, N. Y.; Prof. Dr. Konrad Lorenz; Dr. D. Morris; Dr. R. Müller and Dr. G. Haas, Wuppertal Zoo; Mr. G. Munro, Calcutta; Herr U. Rempe; Prof. W. W. Roberts; Herr F. Roth; Herr W. Scheffel; Dr. A. Seitz, Nuremberg Zoo; Dr. H. G. Thienemann, Duisburg Zoo; Prof. Dr.-Ing. G. Wolf, Institut für den Wissenschaftlichen Film, Göttingen; Dr. Cosima Wüstehube.

Thanks are above all due to my assistant B. A. Tonkin for her tireless help and critical understanding during the preparation of this paper.

3. Although these animals were reared by a private owner and grew up mainly in his house, they stayed very shy all their lives. Rani, the sole survivor, has lived in my study for six months, where she has complete freedom of movement and has reared her kittens. She will come to me and take something from my hand as long as I sit still, but as soon as I move she runs away. If a stranger can so much as be heard, not to speak of entering the room, she disappears from view. I have hardly ever known an adult caught wild cat which took so long to become trusting as these domestic cat hybrids!

4. G. Schaller (1967) and other field workers (verbal communication) have assured me that tigers, lions, leopards, and cheetahs very often seize large prey animals (e.g. buffalo in the case of lions and tigers) by the throat and kill them by strangulation. In the present paper, too, several examples can be found of prey animals dying of something other than a nape bite. This does not affect the innate behavioral equipment of the carnivore: In a wonderful series of photographs of "Schaller's" tigers in the Kanha Park in India (*Life,* 25 February 1965) it can be seen that the very same tigress which in one picture is pulling a buffalo down by the throat in the next picture is biting the already dead animal in the nape while her almost adult young have already begun to eat. Time and again I have made corresponding observations: If cats use some other method to kill their prey, they usually still give it a "pro forma nape bite" subsequently before beginning to eat, and sometimes not until shortly afterward, during the first pause in eating. The same often happens with prey animals which are given to them freshly killed.

Apart from this, however, all these observers have never dissected the killed animals, and only that can tell anyone where the incision wounds left by the cat's canine teeth in the throat of its prey really run. Probes help little, and in any case only if the prey animal was not moved after the cat released its grip: Otherwise the neck musculature, being very mobile and lying in several layers which are not parallel to one another, closes the incision again or turns the probe in quite an incorrect direction. Many observers, including zoologists, apparently do not realize that in most mammals the cervical section of the spine runs more or less down the middle of the neck and that the carnivore thus hardly needs to reach farther around it from below than from above in order to land between the vertebrae. This whole discussion can, therefore, reach a satisfactory conclusion only if dissections are made properly and with the necessary experience.

5. Gwinner's paper on the raven (1964) did not appear until after this manuscript was completed. It is, therefore, impossible to go into detail, but a compelling impression emerges that in the case of the raven instinct and learning interact in a very similar way to what has been described here.

6. This is not the place to enlarge further on the simile. Let me just say this much: The "budget economy" in the propensity system can work with relatively little friction because no "budget total" is laid down; when its energy requirements increase, the animal can eat more. Furthermore, the turnover of energy in the propensity system is infinitely small in relation to the total energy turnover of the organism. For in no case does the propensity system provide the working energy for the effectors, but only, as it were, completes a "working current relay." Thus the simile may not, for example, be regarded as "biological justification" for the budget system in public finance administration. But the simile does fit in one further respect: The more headings the budget of a service has, the more diverse its range of activities obviously is!

On the natural history of fear
First appeared in: Politische Psychologie 6, 1967
1. Dedicated to Dr. Margarete Lorenz, who gave me the idea for the hypotheses discussed on p. 256 et seq.

2. Recently Wuttke and Hoffmeister (1967) have produced elegant proof of this: Tomcats treated with high doses of Megaphen lose not only all fear but also any desire to attack. This is not so if instead of Megaphen another tranquilizer, Librium, is used: In that case the animals likewise lose all anxiety and very high doses of the medicament upset muscle tonus and coordination, particularly of the hind-limbs; this does not, however, prevent the animals from indulging in energetic rival fighting or, when necessary, from pulling themselves toward the rival (not visible in the experimental setup) by their forepaws, dragging their hind legs after them, in appetence for the agonistic situation.

The biology of expression and impression
First appeared in: Psychologische Forschung 31, 1967.
1. Here Kohler extends the concept of adaptation considerably. In the *principle on which they function* the mechanisms described by him resemble a mnemo-menotaxis (A. Kühn 1919) rather than the familiar adaptation mechanisms of sensory physiology.

2. Meanwhile E. Shaw (1965) has also been able to prove this experimentally in the case of schooling fishes. My pupil, I. Heinemann, tested the hypothesis assumed here on a small herd of free-grazing cows and found it to be confirmed in full (in press).

3. Although on the whole in ethological terminology an unconditioned reflex could be defined as an innate behavior pattern elicited via an innate releasing mechanism, this is not quite correct: Pavlov and his followers, namely, never bothered to investigate whether the unconditioned reflexes of their experimental animals were truly innate. Unconditioned reflex is what the animal shows on arrival at the laboratory!

At this point one might speculate what the learning theories derived from the principle of conditioning would look like today if their terminology were not based on errors in translation. Pavlov wrote his first papers on the subject in German, and for what made the conditioned stimulus a more and more reliable eliciting agent he used the word *Bekräftigung*. This was later translated into English as "reinforcement" but really means "confirmation." What Pavlov meant to convey is that the animals in his experiments behaved as if they had formed a hypothesis about the connection between the original stimulus and the experimentally concurrent one which he then called *bedingt,* meaning not "conditioned" but "conditional": the conditional stimulus works only *on condition* that this connection is fairly reliable. After a few such experiences the animal takes the conditional stimulus to be a reliable indicator of the incidence of the unconditional one; if the coincidence continues the hypothesis is *confirmed,* if not it is rejected and the animal adjusts or readjusts its subsequent behavior accordingly. The magnitude of the difference becomes immediately clear if one realizes that such terminology suggests not that the process of conditioning could in any way create new motivations but that it is entirely dependent on motivation already existent before conditioning starts, and I hope it is also apparent how much more suitable such concepts are for coping with the complexities of, say, instrumental conditioning.

4. Traditionally the term "physiognomic features" is taken to include both features of the anatomy in its broadest sense as well as the traces and permanent traits brought about by the frequent occurrence of certain current processes of expression. As the two types of feature are fundamentally different in origin, I should like to suggest that they should also be separated terminologically: Lasting traces of expression should be classified as physiognomy in the narrowest sense, features characteristic of the form and structure of the anatomy as facial architecture. It is in this sense that I employ the terms in the following text.

5. Schmidt's work had already been completed in 1942, and it was only due to the war that publication was delayed.

References

Abderhalden, E. 1941: Lehrbuch der Physiologie. 3rd Ed., Berlin-Vienna.

Adamson, J. 1960: Born Free. London.

Adrian, E. D. 1950: The control of nerve-cell activity. Symposia of the Society for Experimental Biology 4, Cambridge.

Ahlquist, H. 1937: Psychologische Beobachtungen an einigen Jungvögeln der Gattungen *Stercorarius, Larus* und *Sterna*. Acta Soc. F. Fl. Fenn. *60*, 162–178.

Ahrens, R. 1953: Beitrag zur Entwicklung des Physiognomie- and Mimikerkennens. Zeitschrift für experimentelle und angewandte Psychologie 2, 412–454, 599–633.

Altmann, M. 1952: Social behavior of Elk, *Cervus canadensis nelsoni,* in the Jackson-Hole area of Wyoming. Behaviour *4*, 116–143.

Altum, B. 1868: Der Vogel und sein Leben. Münster.

Alverdes, F. 1937: Die Wirksamkeit von Archetypen in den Instinkthandlungen der Tiere. Zoologischer Anzeiger *119*.

Andrew, R. J. 1956 a: Intention movements of flight in certain Passerines, and their use in systematics. Behaviour *10*, 179–204.

———— 1956 b: Some remarks on behaviour in conflict situations, with special reference to *Emberiza* SPP. British Journal of Animal Behaviour *4*, 41–45.

———— 1956 c: Fear responses in *Emberiza* SPP. British Journal of Animal Behaviour *4*, 125–132.

———— 1962: The situations that evoke vocalization in primates. Annals of New York Academy of Science *102*, 296–315.

———— 1963. The origin and evolution of the calls and facial expressions of the primates. Behaviour *20*, 1–109.

Armitage, K. B. 1962: Social behaviour of a colony of the yellow-bellied marmot *(Marmota flaviventris)*. Animal Behaviour *10*, 319–331.

Armstrong, E. A. 1950: The nature and function of displacement activities. Symposia of the Society for Experimental Biology *4*.

Baerends, G. P. 1941: Fortpflanzungsverhalten und Orientierung der Grabwespe *Ammophila campestris* JUR. Tijdschrift voor Entomologie *84*, 68–275.

—————— 1956: The influence of central nervous mechanisms on the reaction to sensory stimuli. Archives Néerlandaises de Zoologie *11*, 522–524.

—————— 1957: The ethological concept "Releasing mechanism" illustrated by a study of the stimuli eliciting egg-retrieving in the herring gull. The Anatomical Record *128*, 518–519.

—————— 1958: The contribution of ethology to the study of the causation of behaviour. Acta physiologica et pharmacologica neerlandica *7*, 466–499.

—————— 1959: The value of the concept »Releasing mechanism«. Proceedings of the 15th International Congress of Zoology, London.

—————— and J. M. Baerends — van Roon. 1950: An introduction to the study of the ethology of Cichlid fishes. Behaviour Supplement 1.

—————— and G. J. Blokzijl. 1963: Gedanken über das Entstehen von Formdivergenzen zwischen homologen Signalhandlungen verwandter Arten. Zeitschrift für Tierpsychologie *20*, 517–528.

——————, Bril, K. A. and P. Bult. 1965: Versuche zur Analyse einer erlernten Reizsituation bei einem Schweinsaffen *(Macaca nemestrina).* Zeitschrift für Tierpsychologie *22*, 394–411.

Bally, G. 1945: Vom Ursprung und von den Grenzen der Freiheit. Basle.

Barcroft, J. and D. N. Barron. 1939: Movement in the mammalian foetus. Ergebnisse der Physiologie *42*.

Bastock, M. 1956: A gene mutation which changes a behaviour pattern. Evolution *10*, 421–439.

——————, D. Morris and M. Moynihan. 1953: Some comments on conflict and thwarting in animals. Behaviour *6*, 66–84.

Baumgarten, E. 1950: Versuch über die menschlichen Gesellschaften und das Gewissen. Studium Generale *3*, H. 10.

—————— 1951: Versuch über mögliche Fortschritte im theoretischen und praktischen Umgang mit Macht. Studium Generale *4*, 540–558.

Bergman, G. 1964: Zum Problem der gemischten Kolonien: Tonband- und Dressurversuche mit Limicolen und Anatiden. Ornis Fennica *41*, 1–13.

Bertalanffy, L.v. 1933: Theoretische Biologie, Bd I. Berlin.

Bethe, A. 1931: Plastizität und Zentrenlehre. Handbuch der normalen und pathologischen Physiologie *15*, 1175–1220.

—————— and E. Fischer. 1931: Die Anpassungsfähigkeit (Plastizität) des Nervensystems. Handbuch der normalen und pathologischen Physiologie *15*, 1045–1130.

Bierens de Haan, J. A. 1940: Die tierischen Instinkte und ihr Umbau durch Erfahrung. Leiden.

Bilz, R. 1965: Der Subjektzentrismus im Erleben der Angst. In: Aspekte der Angst, Hrsg. H. v. Ditfurth, Stuttgart.

Blumenberg, H. 1952: Philosophischer Ursprung und philosophische Kritik des Begriffs der wissenschaftlichen Methode. Studium Generale, *5*, 113–142.

Bresch, C. 1964: Klassische und molekulare Genetik. Berlin-Göttingen-Heidelberg.

Brunswik, E. and L. Reiter. 1938: Eindruckscharaktere schematisierter Gesichter. Zeitschrift für Psychologie *142*, 67–134.

Bühler, Ch. 1934: Die Reaktionen des Säuglings auf das menschliche Gesicht. Zeitschrift für Psychologie *132*, 1–17.

—————— and H. Hetzer. 1928: Das erste Verständnis für Ausdruck im ersten Lebensjahr. Zeitschrift für Psychologie *107*, 50–61.

Burt, W. H. 1943: Territoriality and home range concepts as applied to mammals. Journal of Mammalogy *24*, 346–352.

Buytendijk, F. J. J. 1933: Wesen und Sinn des Spieles. Berlin.

Calhoun, J. B. 1962: Population density and social pathology. Scientific American *206*, 139–148.

—————— 1963 a: The ecology and sociology of the Norway rat. Public Health Service Publication No. 1008, U. S. Department of Health, Education and Welfare.

—————— 1963 b: The social use of space. In: Physiological Mammalogy I, W. B. Mayer and R. G. van Gelder eds.; Academic Press, New York.

Carpenter, C. R. 1934: A field study of the behavior and social relations of howling monkeys. Comparative Psychology Monographs *10*, 1–168.

—————— 1935: Behavior of the red spider monkey (*Ateles geoffroyi*) in Panama. Journal of Mammalogy *16*, 171–180.

Chance, M. R. A. 1953: The social life of a macaque colony. Film, made for the Zoological Society of London.

—————— 1959: What makes monkeys sociable? The New Scientist *5*, 520–523.

—————— 1962: An interpretation of some agonistic postures; the role of »cut-off« acts and postures. Symposia of the Zoological Society of London *8*, 71–89.

—————— 1963: The social bond of the primates. Primates *4*, 1–22.

—————— and Mead, A. P. 1953: Social behaviour and primate evolution. Symposia of the Society for Experimental Biology *7*, 395–439.

Clara, M. 1942: Das Nervensystem des Menschen. Leipzig.

Cofer, C. N. and M. H. Appley. 1964: Motivation: Theory and research; Wiley, New York-London-Sydney.

Cohen, R. 1965: Versuche zur Quantifizierung von Angst. In: Aspekte der Angst, Hrsg. H. v. Ditfurth, Stuttgart.

Craig, W. 1918: Appetites and aversions as constituents of instincts. Biological Bulletin *34*, 91–108.

Crinis, M. de. 1943: Das vegetative System in seinen Beziehungen zu den klinischen Krankheitserscheinungen. Leipzig.

Curio, E. 1959: Verhaltensstudien am Trauerschnäpper. Zeitschrift für Tierpsychologie, Beiheft 3, Berlin.

Darwin, C. 1871: The descent of man, and selection in relation to sex.

—————— 1872: The expression of the emotions in man and animals. University of Chicago Press (new edition 1965).

Dasmann, R. F. and R. D. Taber. 1956: Behavior of Columbian black-tailed deer with reference to population ecology. Journal of Mammalogy *37*, 143–164.

Davis, D. E. 1942: The phylogeny of social nesting habits in the *Crotophaginae*. Quarterly Review of Biology *17*, 115–134.

—————— 1957: The use of food as a buffer in a predator-prey system. Journal of Mammalogy *38*, 466–472.

Davitz, J. R. 1964: The communication of emotional meaning. New York.

Demoll, R. 1933: Instinkt und Entwicklung. Munich.

Diebschlag, E. 1941: Psychologische Beobachtungen über die Rangordnung bei der Haustaube. Zeitschrift für Tierpsychologie *4*, 173–188.

Dobzhansky, T. 1939: Die genetischen Grundlagen der Artbildung. Jena.

Drees, O. 1952: Untersuchungen über die angeborenen Verhaltensweisen bei Springspinnen (*Salticidae*). Zeitschrift für Tierpsychologie *9*, 170–207.

Drever, J. 1961: Perception and action. Bulletin of the British Psychological Society *45*, 1–9.

Dücker, G. 1957: Farb- und Helligkeitssehen und Instinkte bei Viverriden und Feliden. Zoologische Beiträge (Neue Folge) *3*, 25–99.

—————— 1962: Brutpflegeverhalten und Ontogenese des Verhaltens bei Surikaten (*Suricata suricatta* Schreb., *Viverridae*). Behaviour *19*, 305–340.

Eccles, J. C. 1964: The physiology of synapses. Berlin-Gottingen-Heidelberg.

Eibl-Eibesfeldt, I. 1950: Über die Jugendentwicklung eines männlichen Dachses (*Meles meles* L.) unter besonderer Berücksichtigung des Spieles. Zeitschrift für Tierpsychologie *7*, 327–355.

—————— 1951: Beobachtungen zur Fortpflanzungsbiologie und Jugendentwicklung des Eichhörnchens (*Sciurus vulgaris* L.). Zeitschrift für Tierpsychologie *8*, 370–400.

—————— 1953 a: Biologie des Hamsters I; Paarungsverhalten und frühe Jugendstadien (Text accompanying Film C 646 of Institut für den Wissenschaftlichen Film, Göttingen).

—— 1953 b: Zur Ethologie des Hamsters (*Cricetus cricetus* L.). Zeitschrift für Tierpsychologie *10*, 204–254.

—— 1955 a: Angeborenes und Erworbenes im Nestbauverhalten der Wanderratte. Die Naturwissenschaften *42*, 633–634.

—— 1955 b: Zur Biologie des Iltis (*Putorius putorius* L.) mit Filmvorführung C 697. Verhandlungen der Deutschen Zoologischen Gesellschaft, 304–314.

—— 1956: Angeborenes und Erworbenes in der Technik des Beutetötens (Versuche am Iltis, *Putorius putorius* L.). Zeitschrift für Säugetierkunde *21*, 135–137.

—— 1957: Ausdrucksformen der Säugetiere. Handbuch der Zoologie *8/10*, 1–26.

—— 1958 a: Das Verhalten der Nagetiere. Handbuch der Zoologie *8/10* (13).

—— 1958 b: *Putorius putorius* (L.): Beutefang I (Töten von Wanderratten); Film E 106 der Encyclopaedia Cinematographica, Göttingen.

—— 1960: Darwin und die Ethologie. Hundert Jahre Evolutionsforschung, 355–367.

—— 1963: Angeborenes und Erworbenes im Verhalten einiger Säuger. Zeitschrift für Tierpsychologie *20*, 705–754.

—— 1967: Ethologie, die Biologie des Verhaltens. Handbuch der Biologie Bd. II, Frankfurt a. M.

Elsenhans-Giese. 1939: Lehrbuch der Psychologie. 3rd Ed. Tübingen.

Esser, A. H. 1965: Social contact and the use of space in psychiatric patients. American Zoologist *5*, 231.

——, A. S. Chamberlain, E. D. Chapple, and N. S. Kline, 1964: Territoriality of patients on a research ward. Recent Advances in Biological Psychiatry *7*, 37–44.

Ewer, R. F. 1963: The behaviour of the meerkat, *Suricata suricatta*. Zeitschrift für Tierpsychologie *20*, 570–607.

Ewert, O. M. 1965 a: Sematologie des Ausdrucks. Handbuch der Psychologie *5*, (Ausdruckspsychologie), 220–254.

—— 1965 b: Zur Ontogenese des Ausdrucksverstehens. Handbuch der Psychologie *5*, (Ausdruckspsychologie), 289–308.

Fentress, J. C. 1965: Classification and analysis of selected motivational systems in voles (*Microtus agrestis* and *Clethrionomys britannicus*). IXth International Ethological Conference, Zürich.

Fiedler, W. 1964: Die Haut der Säugetiere als Ausdrucksorgan. Studium Generale *17*, 362–390.

Fischer, H. 1965: Triumphgeschrei der Graugans (*Anser anser*). Zeitschrift für Tierpsychologie *22*, 247–304.

Fisher, A. E. and E. B. Hale. 1957: Stimulus determinants of sexual and aggressive behavior in male domestic fowl. Behaviour *10*, 309–323.

Foley jr., J. P. 1935: Judgment of facial expression of emotion in the Chimpanzee. Journal of Social Psychology *6*, 31–67.

Freedman, D. G. 1964: Smiling in blind infants and the issue of innate vs. acquired. Journal of Child Psychology and Psychiatry *5*, 171–184.

Frijda, N. H. 1965: Mimik und Pantomimik. Handbuch der Psychologie *5* (Ausdruckspsychologie), 351–421.

Frisch, K.v. 1914: Der Farbensinn und Formensinn der Biene. Zoologische Jahrbücher: Allgemeine Zoologie und Physiologie, *35*, 1–188.

—— 1939: Schreckstoffwirkung bei der Elritze. Institut für den Wissenschaftlichen Film, Göttingen, Film C 654.

Fröhlich, W. D. 1965: Angst und Furcht. Handbuch der Psychologie *2* (Motivation), 513–568.

Fuller, J. L. 1964: The K-puppies. Discovery *25*, 18–22.

Gardner, B. T. 1965: Shapes of figures identified as a baby's head. Perceptual and Motor Skills *20*, 135–142.

Gause, G. F. 1942: The relation of adaptability to adaptation. Quarterly Review of Biology *17*, 99–114.

Gehlen, A. 1941: Der Mensch, seine Natur und seine Stellung in der Welt. 2nd Ed. Berlin.

Gesell, A. 1929: Maturation and infant behaviour pattern. Psychological Review 36.
Goethe, F. 1937: Beobachtungen und Untersuchungen zur Biologie der Silbermöwe (*Larus a. argentatus* Pontopp.) auf der Vogelinsel Memmertsand. Journal für Ornithologie 85, 1–119.
––––––– 1940 a: Beobachtungen und Versuche über angeborene Schreckreaktionen junger Auerhühner (*Tetrao u. urogallus* L.). Zeitschrift für Tierpsychologie 4, 165–167.
––––––– 1940 b: Beiträge zur Biologie des Iltis. Zeitschrift für Säugetierkunde 15, 180–223.
––––––– 1950: Vom Leben des Mauswiesels (*Mustela n. nivalis* L.) (Ein Beitrag zur Ethographie der heimischen Musteliden). Der Zoologische Garten (Neue Folge) 17, 193–204.
Goodall, J. 1962: Nest building behavior in the free-ranging chimpanzee. Annals of the New York Academy of Science 102, 455–467.
––––––– 1963: Feeding behaviour of wild chimpanzees. A preliminary report. Symposia of the Zoological Society of London 10, 309–407.
––––––– 1964: Chimpanzees in the Gombe Stream Reserve. In: Primate Behavior, Field studies of monkeys and apes, ed. DeVore, 53–110.
Gottschaldt, K. 1958: Handlung und Ausdruck in der Psychologie der Persönlichkeit. Zeitschrift für Psychologie 162, 206–222.
––––––– 1960: Das Problem der Phänogenetik der Persönlichkeit. Handbuch der Psychologie 4 (Persönlichkeitsforschung und Persönlichkeitstheorie), 222–280.
Graf, W. 1956: Territorialism in deer. Journal of Mammalogy 37, 165–170.
Grant, E. C. 1965: An ethological description of some schizophrenic patterns of behaviour. Proceedings of the Leeds Symposium on behavioural disorders, Chapter 12.
Graumann, C. F. 1956: »Social perception«. Die Motivation der Wahrnehmung in neueren amerikanischen Untersuchungen. Zeitschrift für experimentelle und angewandte Psychologie 3, 605–661.
––––––– 1966: Nicht-sinnliche Bedingungen des Wahrnehmens. Handbuch der Psychologie 1 (Allgemeine Psychologie), 1031–1098.
Greenberg, B. 1947: Some relations between territory, social hierarchy, and leadership in the green sunfish (*Lepomis cyanellus*). Physiological Zoology 20, 267–299.
Grzimek, B. 1943: Zum Erkennen vertrauter Menschen durch Tiere. Zeitschrift für Tierpsychologie 5.
––––––– 1944: Das Erkennen von Menschen durch Pferde. Zeitschrift für Tierpsychologie 6.
––––––– 1956: Einige Beobachtungen an Wildtieren in Zentral-Afrika. Zeitschrift für Tierpsychologie 13, 143–150.
Guggisberg, C. A. W. 1961: Simba. London.
Gwinner, E. 1964: Untersuchungen über das Ausdrucks- und Sozialverhalten des Kolkraben (*Corvus corax corax* L.). Zeitschrift für Tierpsychologie 21, 657–748.
––––––– und J. Kneutgen. 1962: Über die biologische Bedeutung der »zweckdienlichen« Anwendung erlernter Laute bei Vögeln. Zeitschrift für Tierpsychologie 19, 692–696.
Haas, A. 1962: Phylogenetisch bedeutungsvolle Verhaltensänderungen bei Hummeln. Zeitschrift für Tierpsychologie 19, 356–370.
Haecker, V. 1900: Der Gesang der Vögel, seine anatomischen und biologischen Grundlagen. Jena.
Hall, K. R. L. 1962 a: Numerical data, maintenance activities and locomotion of the wild Chacma baboon, *Papio ursinus*. Proceedings of the Zoological Society of London 139, 181–220.
––––––– 1962 b. The sexual, agonistic and derived social behaviour patterns of the wild Chacma baboon, *Papio ursinus*. Proceedings of the Zoological Society of London 139, 283–327.
Haltenorth, Th. 1953: Die Wildkatzen der Alten Welt. Leipzig.

Hartmann, M. 1939: Geschlecht und Geschlechtsbestimmung im Tier- und Pflanzenreich. Berlin.
Hassenstein, B. 1954: Abbildende Begriffe. Verhandlungen der Deutschen Zoologischen Gesellschaft, Tübingen, 197–202.
—— 1960: Die bisherge Rolle der Kybernetik in der biologischen Forschung. Naturwissenschaftliche Rundschau 13, 349–355, 373–382, 419–424.
Hediger, H. 1946: Mäuse und Menschen. Schweizer Annalen 3, 103–106.
—— 1948: Kleine Tropenzoologie. Acta Tropica Suppl. 1, Basle.
—— 1949: Säugetierterritorien und ihre Markierung. Bijdragen tot de dierenkunde 28, 172–184.
—— 1951: Observations sur la psychologie animale dans les parcs nationaux du Congo Belge. Brussels (Institut Parcs Nationaux Belges).
—— 1959: Die Angst des Tieres. In: Die Angst, Studien aus dem C. G. Jung-Institut, Zürich, 10, 7–33.
—— 1961: Beobachtungen zur Tierpsychologie im Zoo und Zirkus. Basle.
Heilgenberg, W. 1963: Ursachen für das Auftreten von Instinktbewegungen bei einem Fisch (Pelmatochromis subocellatus kribensis Boul., Cichlidae). Zeitschrift für vergleichende Physiologie 47, 339–380.
—— 1964: Ein Versuch zur ganzheitsbezogenen Analyse des Instinktverhaltens eines Fisches (Pelmatochromis subocellatus kribensis Boul., Cichlidae). Zeitschrift für Tierpsychologie 21, 1–52.
Heinemann, F. 1958: Stille Brunst und Orgasmus weiblicher Rinder als verhaltensbiologische und züchterische Probleme. Zuchthygiene 2, 235–265.
Heinroth, O. 1910: Beiträge z. Biologie, namentlich Ethologie und Psychologie der Anatiden. Verhandlungen des Internat. Ornithologenkongresses, Berlin, 615.
—— 1930: Über bestimmte Bewegungsweisen der Wirbeltiere. Sitzungsberichte der Gesellschaft Naturforschender Freunde, Berlin, 333–343.
Heiss, R. 1956: Allgemeine Tiefenpsychologie. Bern.
Held, R. and A. Hein. 1963: Movement-produced stimulation in the development of visually guided behaviour. Journal of Comparative and Physiological Psychology 56, 872–976 .
Helson, H. 1964: Adaptation level theory. New York.
Hendrichs, H. 1965: Vergleichende Untersuchung des Wiederkauverhaltens. Biologisches Zentralblatt 84, 681–751.
Hess, E. 1959: Imprinting. Science 130, 133–141.
Hess, W. R. 1943 a: Teleokinetisches und ereismatisches Kräftesystem in der Biomotorik. Helvetica Physiologica Acta 1, C62–C63.
—— 1943 b. Das Zwischenhirn als Koordinationsorgan. Helvetica Physiologica Acta 1, 549–565.
—— 1954: Das Zwischenhirn. 2nd Ed. Basle.
—— 1957: Die Formatio reticularis des Hirnstammes im verhaltens-physiologischen Aspekt. Archiv für Psychiatrie und Zeitschrift für die Gesamte Neurologie 196, 329–336.
—— und M. Brügger. 1943: Das subkortikale Zentrum der affektiven Abwehrreaktion. Helvetica Physiologica Acta 1, 33–52.
Hinde, R. A. 1956: Ethological models and the concept of »drive«. British Journal of Philosophical Science 6, 321–331.
—— 1958: The nest-building behaviour of domesticated canaries. Proceedings of the Zoological Society of London 131, 1–48
—— 1959: Unitary drives. Animal Behaviour 7, 130–141.
—— 1960: Energy models of motivation. Symposia of the Society for Experimental Biology 14 (Models and Analogues in Biology), 199–213.
Hörmann, S. v. 1955: Über den Erbgang von Verhaltensmerkmalen bei Grillenbastarden. Die Naturwissenschaften 42, 470–471.
Hofstätter, P. R. 1956: Dimensionen des mimischen Ausdrucks. Zeitschrift für experimentelle und angewandte Psychologie 3, 505–529.

Holst, E. v. 1935 a: Erregungsbildung und Erregungsleitung im Fischrückenmark. Pflügers Archiv *235*.

———— 1935 b: Über den Prozeβ der zentralnervösen Koordination. Pflügers Archiv *236*.

———— 1935 c: Alles oder nichts, Block, Alternans, Bigemini und verwandte Phänomene als Eigenschaften des Rückenmarks. Pflügers Archiv *236*.

———— 1936 a: Versuche zur Theorie der relativen Koordination. Pflügers Archiv *237*, 93–121.

———— 1936 b: Vom Dualismus der motorischen und der automatisch-rhythmischen Funktionen im Rückenmark und vom Wesen des automatischen Rhythmus. Pflügers Archiv *237*, 356–378.

———— 1936 c: Über den »Magnet-Effekt« als koordinierendes Prinzip im Rückenmark. Pflügers Archiv *237*.

———— 1937: Vom Wesen der Ordnung im Zentralnervensystem. Die Naturwissenschaften *25*, 625–631.

———— 1938: Über relative Koordination bei Säugern und beim Menschen. Pflügers Archiv *240*.

———— 1939 a: Entwurf eines Systems der lokomotorischen Periodenbildungen bei Fischen. Ein kritischer Beitrag zum Gestaltproblem. Zeitschrift für vergleichende Physiologie *26*, 481–528.

———— 1939 b. Über die nervöse Funktionsstruktur des rhythmisch tätigen Fischrückenmarks. Pflügers Archiv *241*.

———— 1939 c: Die relative Koordination als Phänomen und als Methode zentralnervöser Funktions-Analyse. Ergebnisse der Physiologie *42*, 228–306.

———— 1943: Über relative Koordinationen bei Arthropoden. Pflügers Archiv *246*.

———— 1948: Von der Mathematik der nervösen Ordnungsleistung. Experientia *IV*.

———— 1950 a: Die Tätigkeit des Statolithenapparates im Wirbeltierlabyrinth. Die Naturwissenschaften *37*.

———— 1950 b: Die Arbeitsweise des Statolithenapparates bei Fischen. Zeitschrift für vergleichende Physiologie *32*.

———— 1957: Aktive Leistungen der menschlichen Gesichtswahrnehmung. Studium Generale *10*, 232–243.

———— und H. Mittelstaedt. 1950: Das Reafferenzprinzip (Wechselwirkungen zwischen Zentralnervensystem und Peripherie). Die Naturwissenschaften *37*, 464–476.

———— und U. v. St. Paul. 1960: Vom Wirkungsgefüge der Triebe. Die Naturwissenschaften *47*, 409–422.

Holzapfel, M. 1938: Über Bewegungsstereotypien bei gehaltenen Säugern I–II. Zeitschrift für Tierpsychologie *2*, 46–72.

———— 1939 a: Über Bewegungsstereotypien bei gehaltenen Säugern IV. Zeitschrift für Tierpsychologie *3*, 151–160.

———— 1939 b: Die Entstehung einiger Bewegungsstereotypien bei gehaltenen Säugern und Vögeln. Revue Suisse de Zoologie *46*, 567–580.

———— 1940: Triebbedingte Ruhezustände als Ziel von Appetenzhandlungen. Die Naturwissenschaften *28*, 273–280.

Holzkamp, K. 1965: Zur Geschichte und Systematik der Ausdruckstheorien. Handbuch der Psychologie *5* (Ausdruckspsychologie), 39–116.

Hückstedt, B. 1965: Experimentelle Untersuchungen zum »Kindchenschema«. Zeitschrift für experimentelle und angewandte Psychologie *12*, 421–450.

Hugger, H. 1941: Zur objektiven Auswertung des Elektroencephalogramms unter besonderer Berücksichtigung der gleitenden Koordination. Pflügers Archiv. *244*.

Huxley, J. 1914: The courtship habits of the great crested grebe *(Podiceps cristatus)*; with an addition to the theory of sexual selection. Proceedings of the Zoological Society of London, 491–562.

Iersel, J. J. A. van. 1953: An analysis of the parental behavior of the male Threespined Stickleback *(Gasterosteus aculeatus* L.). Behaviour Suppl. III.

———— and A. Bol. 1958: Preening of two tern species: A study on displacement. Behaviour *13*, 1–88.

Ilse, D. 1929: Über den Farbensinn der Tagfalter. Zeitschrift für vergleichende Physiologie *8*, 658–692.

Immenroth, W. 1933: Kultur und Umwelt der Kleinwüchsigen in Afrika. Leipzig.

Inhelder, E. 1955 a: Zur Psychologie einiger Verhaltensweisen—besonders des Spiels—von Zootieren. Zeitschrift für Tierpsychologie *12*, 88–144.

———— 1955 b: Über das Spielen mit Gegenständen bei Huftieren. Revue Suisse de Zoologie *62*, 240–250.

Isaac, D. and P. Marler. 1963: Ordering of sequences of singing behaviour of Mistle Thrushes in relationship to timing. Animal Behaviour *11*, 179–188.

Jander, R. 1964: Die Detektortheorie optischer Auslösemechanismen von Insekten. Zeitschrift für Tierpsychologie *21*, 302–307.

Jay, P. C. 1962: Aspects of maternal behavior among langurs. Annals of the New York Academy of Sciences *102*, 468–476.

———— 1963: Écologie et comportement social du Langur commun des Indes, *Presbytis entellus*. La Terre et la Vie No. *1*, 50–65.

Jung, C. G. 1938: Die Beziehungen zwischen dem Ich und dem Unbewußten. 3rd Ed., Zürich und Leipzig.

Jung, R. 1939 a: Vortrag auf dem Deutsch-Schweizerischen Physiologentreffen in Heidelberg am 6. Mai. Pflügers Archiv *241*.

———— 1939 b: Das Elektrencephalogramm und seine klinische Anwendung. I. Methodik der Ableitung, Registrierung und Deutung des EEG. Der Nervenarzt *12*.

———— 1941: Das Elektrencephalogramm und seine klinische Anwendung. II. Das EEG des Gesunden, seine Variationen und Veränderungen und deren Bedeutung für das pathologische EEG. Der Nervenarzt *14*.

Kaila, E. 1932: Die Reaktionen des Säuglings auf das menschliche Gesicht. Annales Universitatis Aboensis Series B, *17*.

Katz, D. 1948: Gestaltpsychologie. 2nd Ed., Basle.

Kaufmann, J. H. 1962: Ecology and social behavior of the Coati, *Nasua narica*, on Barro Colorado Island, Panama. University of California Publications in Zoology *60*, 95–222.

Kiener, F. 1965: Physiognomik der Gesamtleibestektonik. Physiognomik leibestektonischer Teilbezirke. Handbuch der Psychologie *5* (Ausdruckspsychologie), 467–529.

Kirchhoff, R. 1960: Ausdruck und Sprache. Bericht über den 22. Kongress der Deutschen Gesellschaft für Psychologie, 49–61.

———— 1961: Die Umfelder des pathognomischen Ausdrucks. Acta psychologica (Amsterdam) *19*, 482–485.

———— 1962 a: Methodologische und theoretische Grundprobleme der Ausdrucksforschung. Studium Generale *15*, 135–156.

———— 1962 b: Das Verhältnis von Graphologie und Ausdruckskunde. Zeitschrift für Menschenkunde *26*, 320–337.

———— 1963: Ausdruck: Begriff, Regionen und Binnenstruktur. Jahrbuch für Psychologie und Psychotherapie *10*, 197–223.

———— 1965 a: Vorbemerkungen zur historischen Darstellung. Handbuch der Psychologie *5* (Ausdruckspsychologie), 3–8.

———— 1965 b: Zur Geschichte des Ausdrucksbegriffes. Handbuch der Psychologie *5* (Ausdruckspsychologie), 9–38.

Kirchshofer, R. 1953: Aktionssystem des Maulbrüters *Haplochromis desfontainesii*. Zeitschrift für Tierpsychologie *10*, 297–318.

Klages, L. 1936: Grundlegung der Wissenschaft vom Ausdruck. Leipzig.

Klineberg, O. 1954: Social psychology. New York.

Klimpfinger, S. 1952: Kindergartenstudien I und II. Film der Bundesstaatlichen Hauptstelle für den Unterrichtsfilm. Vienna.

Klopfer, P. H. and J. P. Hailman. 1964: Basic parameters of following and imprinting in precocial birds. Zeitschrift für Tierpsychologie *21*, 755–762.

Kluyver, H. N. 1955: Das Verhalten des Drosselrohrsängers, *Acrocephalus arundinateus* (L.), am Brutplatz mit besonderer Berücksichtigung der Nestbautechnik und Revierbehauptung. Ardea *43*, 1–50.

Knappe, H. 1959/60: Beobachtungen über die Aktivität der Hauskatze. Wissenschaftliche Zeitschrift der Humboldt-Universität Berlin, Mathematisch-Naturwissenschaftliche Richtung *IX*, 461–478.

Koch, M. 1959: Wesensunterschiede menschlicher und tierischer Entwicklung. Handbuch der Psychologie *3* (Entwicklungspsychologie), 585–593.

Koehler, O. 1933: Die Ganzheitsbetrachtung in der modernen Biologie. Verhandlungen der Königsberger gelehrten Gesellschaft.

―――― 1943: »Zähl«-Versuche an einem Kolkraben und Vergleichsversuche an Menschen. Zeitschrift für Tierpsychologie *5*, 575–712.

―――― 1949 a: Vorsprachliches Denken und »Zählen« der Vögel. In: Ornithologie als biologische Wissenschaft (Festschrift Stresemann). Heidelberg.

―――― 1949 b: »Zählende Vögel« und vorsprachliches Denken. Verhandlungen der Deutschen Zoologischen Gesellschaft, Mainz.

―――― 1950: Die Analyse der Taxisanteile instinktartigen Verhaltens. Symposia of the Society for Experimental Biology *4*, Animal Behaviour.

―――― 1951: Der Vogelgesang als Vorstufe von Musik und Sprache. Journal für Ornithologie *93*, 3–20.

―――― 1952: Vom unbenannten Denken. Verhandlungen der Deutschen Zoologischen Gesellschaft, Freiburg, 203–211.

―――― 1953: Tierpsychologische Versuche zur Frage des »unbenannten Denkens«. Vierteljahresschrift der naturforschenden Gesellschaft, Zürich, *98*, 242–251.

―――― 1954 a: Das Lächeln als angeborene Ausdrucksbewegung. Zeitschrift für menschliche Verebungs- und Konstitutionslehre *32*, 390–398.

―――― 1954 b: Vom Erbgut der Sprache. Homo *5*, 97–104.

―――― 1954 c: Vorbedingungen und Vorstufen unserer Sprache bei Tieren. Verhandlungen der Deutschen Zoologischen Gesellschaft, Tübingen, 327–341.

―――― 1955 a: Vorformungen menschlicher Ausdrucksmittel im Tierreich. Lebendiges Wissen (Neue Folge) *1*, 218–223.

―――― 1955 b: Tierische Vorstufen menschlicher Sprache. 1. Arbeitstagung über zentrale Regulation der Funktionen des Organismus, Leipzig, 3–37.

―――― and A. Zagarus. 1937: Beiträge zum Brutverhalten des Halsbandregenpfeifers (*Charadrius h. hiaticula*). Beitr. zur Fortpflanzungsbiologie der Vögel *13*, 1–9.

Köhler, W. 1921 a: Intelligenzprüfungen an Menschenaffen. Berlin.

―――― 1921 b: Zur Psychologie des Schimpansen. Psychologische Forschung *1*, 2–46.

Koenig, L. 1953: Beobachtungen am afrikanischen Blauwangenspint (*Merops superciliosus chrysocerus*) in freier Wildbahn und Gefangenschaft mit Vergleichen zum Bienenfresser (*Merops apiaster* L.). Zeitschrift für Tierpsychologie *10*, 180–204.

―――― 1960: Das Aktionssystem des Siebenschläfers (*Glis glis* L.). Zeitschrift für Tierpsychologie *17*, 427–505.

Koenig, O. 1951: Das Aktionssystem der Bartmeise II. Oesterreichische Zoologische Zeitschrift *3*, 247–325.

―――― 1962: Kif-kif. Vienna.

Kohler, I. 1955: Die Methode des Brillenversuchs in der Wahrnehmungspsychologie; mit Bemerkungen zur Lehre von der Adaptation. Zeitschrift für experimentelle und angewandte Psychologie *3*, 381–417.

Konishi, M. 1963: The role of auditory feedback in the vocal behavior of the domestic fowl. Zeitschrift für Tierpsychologie *20*, 349–367.

―――― 1964: Effects of deafening on song development in two species of juncos. Condor *66*, 85–102.

Kortlandt, A. 1938: De uitdrukkingsbewegingen en-geluiden van *Phalacocorax carbo sinensis* (Shaw and Nodder). Ardea *27*, 1–40.

———— 1953: Signal, Ausdruck und Begegnung. Archives Néerlandaises de Zoologie *10*, 65–78.

———— 1955: Aspects and prospects of the concept of instinct (Vicissitudes of the hierarchy theory). Archives Néerlandaises de Zoologie *11*, 155–284.

———— 1962: Observing chimpanzees in the wild. Scientific American *128*.

Kramer, G. 1950: Über individuell und anonym gebundene Gemeinschaften der Tiere und Menschen. Studium Generale *3*, 565–572.

Kretschmer, E. 1946: Medizinische Psychologie. 9th Ed., Stuttgart.

———— 1948: Hysterie, Reflex und Instinkt. 5th Ed., Stuttgart.

———— 1953: Der Begriff der motorischen Schablonen und ihre Rolle in normalen und pathologischen Lebensvorgängen. Archiv für Psychiatrie und Nervenkrankheiten *190*, 1–3.

Krieg, H. 1964: Säugetiere stellen sich nicht tot. Das Tier, H. 6, 25.

Krott, P. 1959: Der Vielfraß (*Gulo gulo* L. 1758). Jena.

———— und G. Krott. 1963: Zum Verhalten des Braunbären (*Ursus arctos* L. 1758) in den Alpen. Zeitschrift für Tierpsychologie *20*, 160–206.

Kruijt, J. P. 1964: Ontogeny of social behaviour in Burmese Red Junglefowl (*Gallus gallus spadiceus*). Behaviour, Supplement XII.

Krummbiegel, J. 1941: Die Persistenz physiologischer Eigenschaften in der Stammesgeschichte. Zeitschrift für Tierpsychologie *4*, 249–251.

Kühme, W. 1961: Beobachtungen am afrikanischen Elefanten (*Loxodonta africana* Blumenbach 1797) in Gefangenschaft. Zeitschrift für Tierpsychologie *18*, 285–296.

———— 1963: Ergänzende Beobachtungen an afrikanischen Elefanten (*Loxodonta africana* Blumenbach 1797) im Freigehege. 2. Teil. Zeitschrift für Tierpsychologie *20*, 66–79.

Kühn, A. 1919: Die Orientierung der Tiere im Raum. Jena.

———— 1949: Grundriß der Allgemeinen Zoologie. 10th Ed., Stuttgart.

———— 1965: Entwicklungsphysiologie. 2nd Ed., Berlin.

Kunz, H. 1965: Zur Anthropologie der Angst. In: Aspekte der Angst, ed. H. v. Ditfurth, Stuttgart.

Kuo, Z. Y. 1929: The net result of the anti-heredity movement in psychology. Psychological Review *36*.

———— 1931: The genesis of the cat's responses to the rat. Journal of Comparative Psychology *11*.

———— 1932: Ontogeny of embryonic behavior in *Aves*, I. and II. Journal of Experimental Zoology *61*, 395–430, *62*, 453–489. III and IV: Journal of Comparative Psychology *13*, 245–272, *14*, 109–122.

Lack, D. 1939: The behaviour of the robin I/II. Proceedings of the Zoological Society of London *109*.

Lashley, K. 1915: Notes on the nesting activity of the Noddy and Sooty Terns. Papers of the Department of Marine Biology, Carnegie Institute, Washington, 7, 61–84.

———— 1938: Experimental analysis of instinctive behavior. Psychological Review *45*, 445–471.

Lehrman, D. S. 1953: A critique of Konrad Lorenz's theory of instinctive behaviour. Quarterly Review of Biology *28*, 337–363.

Leiner, M. 1929: Oekologische Studien an *Gasterosteus aculeatus*. Zeitschrift für Morphologie und Oekologie der Tiere *14*, 360–400.

Leonhard, K. 1949: Ausdruckssprache der Seele. Berlin and Tübingen.

Lersch, P. 1940: Seele und Welt. Leipzig.

———— 1943: Gesicht und Seele. 2nd Ed., Munich.

Lewin, K. 1926: Untersuchungen zur Handlungs- und Affektpsychologie I. Vorbemerkungen über die psychischen Kräfte und Energien und über die Struktur der Seele. Psychologische Forschung *7*, 192.

Leyhausen, P. 1949: Liebhaberaquarium und Tierpsychologie. Deutsche Aquarien- und Terrarien-Zeitschrift *2*, 55–56.

—— 1951: Einführung in die Eindruckskunde. Schola 6, 895–900.*

—— 1952: Das Verhältnis von Trieb und Wille in seiner Bedeutung für die Pädagogik. Ledendige Schule (Schola) 7, 521–542.*

—— 1953 a: *Potos flavus* (Schreb.); Fressen. Film E 23 der Encyclopaedia Cinematographica, Göttingen.

—— 1953 b: *Potos flavus* (Schreb.); Klettern. Film E 24 der Encyclopaedia Cinematographica, Göttingen.

—— 1953 c: Beobachtungen an einer brasilianischen Tigerkatze. Zeitschrift für Tierpsychologie 10, 77–91.

—— 1954 a: Die Entdeckung der relativen Koordination. Ein Beitrag zur Annäherung von Physiologie und Psychologie. Studium Generale 7, 45–60.*

—— 1954 b: Vergleichendes über die Territorialität bei Tieren und den Raumanspruch des Menschen. Homo 5, 116–124.*

—— 1955 a: Über relative Stimmungshierarchie bei Säugern. Paper read at IIIrd International Ethological Conference, Groningen.

—— 1955 b: *Felis (Zibethailurus) viverrina* (Bennet); Abwehrverhalten. Film E 27 der Encyclopaedia Cinematographica, Göttingen.

—— 1956 a: Verhaltensstudien an Katzen. Zeitschrift für Tierpsychologie, Beiheft 2.

—— 1956 b: Das Verhalten der Katzen. Handbuch der Zoologie 8/10, Berlin.

—— 1960: *Clupea harengus* (L.); Schwarmverhalten. Film E 167 der Encyclopaedia Cinematographica, Göttingen.

—— 1961: Über den Begriff des Normalverhaltens in der Ethologie. Paper read at VIIth International Ethological Conference, Starnberg.

—— 1962 a: Domestikationsbedingte Verhaltenseigentümlichkeiten der Hauskatze. Zeitschrift für Tierzüchtung und Züchtungsbiologie 77, 191–197.

—— 1962 b: Smaller cats in the zoo. International Zoo Yearbook 3, 11–21.

—— 1963: Über südamerikanische Pardelkatzen. Zeitschrift für Tierpsychologie 20, 627–640.

—— 1965 a: Über die Funktion der Relativen Stimmungshierarchie. (Dargestellt am Beispiel der phylogenetischen und onotogenetischen Entwicklung des Beutefangs von Raubtieren.) Zeitschrift für Tierpsychologie 22, 412–494.*

—— 1965 b: Das Motivationsproblem in der Ethologie. Handbuch der Psychologie 2 (Motivation), 794–816.

—— 1965 c: The communal organization of solitary mammals. Symposia of the Zoological Society of London 14, 249–263.*

—— 1967: Zur Naturgeschichte der Angst. Politische Psychologie 6, 94–112.*

—— and R. Wolff. 1959: Das Revier einer Hauskatze. Zeitschrift für Tierpsychologie 16, 666–670.

Lind, H. 1961: Studies on the behaviour of the Black-tailed Godwit (*Limosa limosa* L.). Copenhagen.

Lindemann, W. 1952: Zur Psychologie des Igels. Zeitschrift für Tierpsychologie 8, 224–251.

Lissmann, H. W. 1932: Die Umwelt des Kampffisches (*Betta splendens* Regan). Zeitschrift für vergleichende Physiologie 18, 65–111.

Lloyd, D. P. C. 1944: Functional organization of the spinal cord. Physiological Review 24.

Lorenz, K. 1931: Beiträge zur Ethologie sozialer Corviden. Journal für Ornithologie 79, 67–127.**

—— 1932: Betrachtungen über das Erkennen der arteigenen Triebhandlungen der Vögel. Journal für Ornithologie 80, 50–98.

—— 1935: Der Kumpan in der Umwelt des Vogels. Journal für Ornithologie 83, 137–213, 289–413.**

*Included in this volume.

————— 1937 a: Über die Bildung des Instinktbegriffs. Die Naturwissenschaften 25, 289–300, 307–308, 324–331.**

————— 1937 b: Über den Begriff der Instinkthandlung. Folia Biotheoretica Series B II: Instinctus, 17–50.

————— 1939: Vergleichende Verhaltensforschung. Verhandlungen der Deutschen Zoologischen Gesellschaft, Rostock. Zoologischer Anzeiger, Supplement 12, 69–102.*

————— 1940: Durch Domestikation verursachte Störungen arteigenen Verhaltens. Zeitschrift für angewandte Psychologie und Charakterkunde 59, 1–81.

————— 1941: Kants Lehre vom Apriorischen im Lichte gegenwärtiger Biologie. Blätter für Deutsche Philosophie 15, 94–125.

————— 1943 a: Die angeborenen Formen möglicher Erfahrung. Zeitschrift für Tierpsychologie 5, 235–409.

————— 1943 b: Psychologie und Stammesgeschichte. In: Die Evolution der Organismen, 105–127. Jena.***

————— 1950 a: So kam der Mensch auf den Hund. Wien.

————— 1950 b: Ganzheit und Teil in der tierischen und menschlichen Gesellschaft. Studium Generale 3, 455–499.***

————— 1950 c: The comparative method of studying innate behaviour patterns. Symposia of the Society for Experimental Biology IV, Animal Behaviour, 221–254.

————— 1951: Ausdrucksbewegungen höherer Tiere. Die Naturwissenschaften 38, 113–116.

————— 1952 a: Balz und Paarbildung bei der Stockente (Anas platyrhynchos L.). Beiheft zum Wissenschaftlichen Film C626 des Instituts für den Wissenschaftlichen Film, Göttingen.

————— 1952 b: Die Entwicklung der vergleichenden Verhaltensforschung in den letzten zwölf Jahren. Verhandlungen der Deutschen Zoolog. Ges., Freiburg, 36–58.

————— 1953: Über angeborene Instinktformeln beim Menschen. Deutsche Medizinische Wochenschrift, 45–46.

————— 1959: Gestaltwahrnehmung als Quelle wissenschaftlicher Erkenntnis. Zeitschrift für experimentelle und angewandte Psychologie 6, 118–165.***

————— 1961: Phylogenetische Anpassung und adaptive Modifikation des Verhaltens Zeitschrift für Tierpsychologie 18, 139–187.***

————— 1965: Darwin hat recht gesehen. Opuscula 20, Pfullingen.

————— 1966: On aggression. Harcourt, Brace and World, New York.

————— und N. Tinbergen. 1939: Taxis und Instinkthandlung in der Eirollbewegung der Graugans. Zeitschrift für Tierpsychologie 2, 1–29.**

Lorenz, R. 1966: Waschen bei zwei Arten der Gattung Presbytis (Cercopithecoidea, Primates). Folia primatologica 4, 191–193.

Makkink, D. F. 1931: Die Kopulation der Brandente (Tadorna tadorna L.). Ardea 20, 18–21.

————— 1936: An attempt at an ethogram of the European Avocet (Recurvirostra avosetta L.) with ethological and psychological remarks. Ardea 25, 1–63.

Manton, S. M. 1953: Locomotory habits and the evolution of the larger arthropodan groups. Symposia of the Society for Experimental Biology VII, Evolution, 339–376.

————— 1958 a: The evolution of the arthropodan locomotory mechanism, Part 6. Journal of the Linnean Society of London (Zoology) XLIII, 487–556.

————— 1958 b: Habits of life and evolution of body design in Arthropoda. Journal of the Linnean Society of London (Zoology) XLIV, 58–72.

————— 1959: Functional morphology and taxonomic problems of Arthropoda. Systematics Association Publications 3, 23–32.

**English version in: Studies in animal and human behaviour, Vol. 1. Methuen, London 1970.
***English version in: Studies in animal and human behaviour, Vol. 2. Methuen. London 1971.

———— 1960: Concerning head development in the arthropods. Biological Review *35*, 265–282.

———— 1964: Mandibular mechanisms and the evolution of arthropods. Philosophical Transactions of the Royal Society of London *247*, B. *737*, 1–183.

Marler, P. 1955 a: Studies of fighting in chaffinches. (1) Behaviour in relation to social hierarchy. British Journal of Animal Behaviour *3*, 111–117.

———— 1955 b: Studies of fighting in chaffinches. (2) The effect on dominance relations of disguising females as males. British Journal of Animal Behaviour *3*, 137–147.

———— 1956: Studies of fighting in chaffinches. (3) Proximity as a cause of aggression. British Journal of Animal Behaviour *4*, 23–30.

———— 1957: Studies of fighting in chaffinches. (4) Appetitive and consummatory behaviour. British Journal of Animal Behaviour *5*, 29–37.

———— 1960: Bird songs and mate selection. In: Animal sounds and communication. American Institute of Biological Science Publications No. 7, 348–367.

———— 1961: The logical analysis of animal communication. Journal of Theoretical Biology *1*, 295–317.

———— and D. Isaac. 1960 a: Physical analysis of a simple bird song as exemplified by the chipping sparrow. Condor *62*, 124–135.

———— 1960 b: Song variation in a population of brown towhees. Condor *62*, 272–283.

———— 1960 c: Analysis of syllable structure in songs of the brown towhee. Auk *77*, 433–444.

———— 1961: Song variation in a population of Mexican juncos. The Wilson Bulletin *73*, 193–206.

————and M. Tamura. 1962: Song »dialects« in three populations of white-crowned sparrows. Condor *64*, 368–377.

———— 1964: Culturally transmitted patterns of vocal behavior in sparrows. Science *146*, 1483–1486.

————, M. Kreith and M. Tamura. 1962: Song development in hand-raised Oregon juncos. Auk *79*, 12–30.

McDougall, W. 1912: Psychology, the study of behaviour. London.

———— 1933: An outline of psychology. 6th Ed., London.

———— 1939: The group mind. Cambridge.

———— 1947: Aufbaukräfte der Seele. 2nd Ed., Stuttgart.

Meehan, W. R. 1961: Observations on feeding, habits and behavior of grizzly bears. The American Midland Naturalist *65*, 409–412.

Messmer E. and I. Messmer. 1956: Die Entwicklung der Lautäußerungen und einiger Verhaltensweisen der Amsel. Zeitschrift für Tierpsychologie *13*, 341–441.

Metzger, W. 1952: Das Experiment in der Psychologie. Studium Generale *5*, 142–163.

———— 1953: Gesetze des Sehens. Frankfurt/Main.

———— 1954: Psychologie. 2nd Ed., Darmstadt.

Meyer-Holzapfel, M. 1949: Die Beziehung zwischen den Trieben junger und erwachsener Tiere. Schweizer Zeitschrift für Psychologie und ihre Anwendung *8*, 32–60.

———— 1952: Die Bedeutung des Besitzes bei Tier und Mensch. Biel/Switzerland.

———— 1956 a: Über die Bereitschaft zu Spiel- und Instinkthandlungen. Zeitschrift für Tierpsychologie *13*, 442–464.

———— 1956 b: Das Spiel bei Säugetieren. Handbuch der Zoologie *8/10*, 1–63.

———— 1957: Das Verhalten der Bären (*Ursidae*). Handbuch der Zoologie *8/10*.

Michael, R. P. 1960: An investigation of the sensitivity of circumscribed neurological areas to hormonal stimulation by means of the application of oestrogens directly to the brain of the cat. 4th International Neurochemical Symposium, 465–480.

———— 1962 a: Estrogen-sensitive neurons and sexual behavior in female cats. Science *126*, 322–323.

──── 1962 b: The entry of oestrogens into the brain of the female cat. Excerpta Medica, International Congress Series No. 51.

Moewus, F. 1938: Untersuchungen über die relative Sexualität von Algen. Biologisches Zentralblatt *58*.

Morgan, L. 1913: Instinkt und Erfahrung. Berlin.

Morris, D. 1956 a: The feather postures of birds and the problems of the origin of social signals. Behaviour *9*, 75–113.

──── 1956 b: The function and causation of courtship ceremonies. In: L'instinct dans le comportement des animaux et de l'homme.

──── 1957: »Typical intensity« and its relation to the problem of ritualisation. Behaviour *11*, 1–12.

──── 1958: The comparative ethology of grassfinches *(Erythrurae)* and mannikins *(Amadinae)*. Proceedings of the Zoological Society of London *131*, 389–439.

──── 1962: The chimpanzee. Punch *243*, No. 6358, 88–90.

──── 1963: Biologie der Kunst. Düsseldorf.

Motikawa, K. 1950: Field of retinal induction and optical illusion. Journal of Neurophysiology *13*.

Mottershead, G. S. 1959: Experiments with a chimpanzee colony at Chester Zoo. International Zoo Yearbook *1*, 18–20.

Moynihan, M. 1962: Hostile and sexual behavior patterns of South American and Pacific Laridae. Behaviour, Supplement 8.

Murie, A. 1944: The wolves of Mount McKinley, Washington.

Neutra, R. 1956: Wenn wir weiter leben wollen . . . Hamburg.

Nice, M. M. 1941: The role of territory in bird life. The American Midland Naturalist *26*, 441–487.

Nippold, W. 1954: Die Anfänge des Eigentums bei den Naturvölkern und die Entstehung des Privateigentums. s'Gravenhage.

Nissen, H. W. 1931: A field study of the chimpanzee. Comparative Psychology Monographs 8.

Nolte, A. 1955: Field observations on the daily routine and social behaviour of common Indian monkeys with special reference to the bonnet monkey *(Macaca radiata* Geoff.). Journal of Bombay Natural History Society *53*, 177–184.

Ortmann, R. 1956: Über die Musterbildung von Duftdrüsen in der Sohlenhaut der weißen Hausmaus *(Mus musculus alba)*. Zeitschrift für Säugetierkunde *21*, 128–141.

Pearson, O. P. 1964: Carnivore-mouse predation: An examination of its intensity and bio-energetics. Journal of Mammalogy *45*, 177–188.

Peckham, G. W. and E. G. Peckham. 1889: Observations on sexual selection in spiders of the family Attidae. Occasional papers of the Natural History Society of Wisconsin, Milwaukee.

Pelwijk, J.-J. ter und N. Tinbergen. 1937: Eine reizbiologische Analyse einiger Verhaltensweisen von *Gasterosteus aculeatus* L. Zeitschrift für Tierpsychologie *1*, 193–200.

Petermann, B. 1929: Die Wertheimer-Koffka-Köhlersche Gestalttheorie. Leipzig.

Peters, H. M. 1937: Experimentelle Untersuchungen über die Brutpflege von *Haplochromis multicolor*, einem maulbrütenden Knochenfisch. Zeitschrift für Tierpsychologie *1*, 201–218.

Petzelt, A. 1951: Kindheit, Jugend, Reifezeit. Freiburg i. Br.

Piderit, T. 1925: Mimik und Physiognomik. 4th Ed., Detmold.

Pocock, R. I. 1917: The classification of existing Felidae. Annals and Magazine of Natural History 8th Series, *20*, 328–351.

Poglayen-Neuwall, I. 1962: Beiträge zu einem Ethogramm des Wickelbären *(Potos flavus* Schreber). Zeitschrift für Säugetierkunde *27*, 1–44.

Poll, M. 1910: Über Vogelmischlinge. Verhandlungen des 5. Internationalen Ornithologenkongresses, Berlin.

Portmann, A. 1948: Die Tiergestalt. Studien über die Bedeutung der tierischen Erscheinung. Basle.

Precht, H. 1958: Triebbedingtes Verhalten bei Tieren. Zeitschrift für experimentelle und angewandte Psychologie 7, 198–210.

Prechtl, H. 1953: Zur Physiologie der angeborenen auslösenden Mechanismen. I. Quantitative Untersuchungen über die Sperrbewegungen junger Singvögel. Behaviour 5, 32–50.

Quine, D. A. and J. M. Cullen. 1964: The pecking response of young Arctic Terns, Sterna macrura, and the adaptiveness of the »releasing mechanism«. Ibis 106, 145–173.

Randall, W. L. 1964: The behavior of cats (Felis catus L.) with lesions in the caudal midbrain region. Behaviour 23, 107–139.

Reichenbach, H. 1944: The philosophic foundations of Quantum Theory. Berkeley.

Rein, H. 1948: Einführung in die Physiologie des Menschen. 9th Ed., Berlin-Heidelberg.

Remane, A. 1952: Die Grundlagen des natürlichen Systems, der vergleichenden Anatomie und der Phylogenetik. Leipzig.

Remplein, H. 1950: Die seelische Entwicklung in der Kindheit und Reifezeit. 2nd Ed., Munich-Basle.

Rensch, B. and R. Altevogt. 1953: Visuelles Lernvermögen eines indischen Elefanten. Zeitschrift für Tierpsychologie 10, 119–134.

———— 1955: Dressurleistungen indischer Arbeitselefanten. Film B 679 des Instituts für den Wissenschaftlichen Film, Göttingen.

Roberts, W. W. and H. O. Kiess. 1964: Motivational properties of hypothalamic aggression in cats. Journal of Comparative and Physiological Psychology 58, 187–193.

Rohracher, H. 1961: Kleine Charakterkunde. 9th Ed., Vienna.

Rothacker, E. 1941: Die Schichten der Persönlichkeit. 2nd Ed., Leipzig.

Russel, E. R. 1934: The behaviour of animals. London.

Russell, W. M. S. 1963: The behaviour of a mutant clawed frog. Zeitschrift für Tierpsychologie 20, 552–557.

Sauer, F. 1954: Die Entwicklung der Lautäußerungen vom Ei ab schalldicht gehaltener Dorngrasmücken (Sylvia c. communis Latham) im Vergleich mit später isolierten und mit wildlebenden Artgenossen. Zeitschrift für Tierpsychologie 11, 10–93.

Schaffer, J. 1940: Die Hautdrüsenorgane der Säugertiere. Berlin-Vienna.

Schaller, G. 1967: The deer and the tiger. Chicago-London.

Schenkel, R. 1947: Verhaltensstudien an Wölfen (Gefangenschaftsbeobachtungen). Behaviour 1, 81–129.

Schjelderup-Ebbe, T. 1922: Beiträge zur Sozialpsychologie des Haushuhns. Zeitschrift für Psychologie 88, 225–252.

Schlegel, W. 1960: Die Sexualinstinkte des Menschen. Hamburg.

Schleidt, M. 1955: Untersuchungen über die Auslösung des Kollerns beim Truthahn (Meleagris gallopavo). Zeitschrift für Tierpsychologie 11, 417–435.

Schleidt, W. M. 1961 a: Reaktionen von Truthühnern auf fliegende Raubvögel und Versuche zur Analyse ihrer AAMs. Zeitschrift für Tierpsychologie 18, 534–560.

———— 1961 b: Operative Entfernung des Gehörorgans ohne Schädigung angrenzender Labyrinthteile bei Putenküken. Experientia 17, 464.

———— 1962: Die historische Entwicklung der Begriffe »Angeborenes auslösendes Schema« und »Angeborener Auslösemechanismus« in der Ethologie. Zeitschrift für Tierpsychologie 19, 697–722.

———— 1964: Über die Spontaneität von Erbkoordinationen. Zeitschrift für Tierpsychologie 21, 235–256.

Schmeing, K. 1939: Der Sinn der Reifungsstufen. Leipzig.

Schmidt, H. D. 1958: Verhaltenshomologie und Verhaltensanalogie. Ein Grundproblem der vergleichenden Psychologie. Zschr. f. Psychologie 162, 279–300.

Schmidt, W. 1937: Das Eigentum auf den ältesten Stufen der Menschheit 1. Münster i. W.

Schmidt, W. D. 1951: Einführung in die Schematenforschung. Die Neue Volksschule *III/2*.

––––– 1957: Attrappenversuche zur Analyse des Lachens. Psychologische Beiträge *3*, 223–264.

Schulz, H. 1965: quoted from K. Lorenz in: Aspekte der Angst, Hrsg. H. v. Ditfurth, Discussion p. 17, Stuttgart.

Schutz, F. 1963 a: Objektfixierung geschlechtlicher Reaktionen bei Anatiden und Hühnern. Die Naturwissenschaften *50*, 624–625.

––––– 1963 b: Über geschlechtlich unterschiedliche Objektfixierung sexueller Reaktionen bei Enten im Zusammenhang mit dem Prachtkleid des Männchens. Verhandlungen der Deutschen Zoologischen Gesellschaft, 282–287.

Schwangart, F. 1940: Ausstrahlungen der Tierpsychologie, eine programmatische Skizze. Archiv für die gesamte Psychologie *106*.

Scott, J. P. 1962: Critical periods in behavioral development. Science *138*, 949–958.

Seitz, A. 1940: Die Paarbildung bei einigen Cichliden. I. Die Paarbildung bei *Astatotilapia strigigena* Pfeffer. Zeitschrift für Tierpsychologie *4*, 40–84.

Shaw, E. 1965: Studies on the development of the optomotor response in schooling and non-schooling fishes. Unpublished.

Sherrington, C. S. 1906: The integrative action of the nervous system. New York.

Simpson, G. G. 1945: The principles of classification and a classification of mammals. Bulletin of the American Museum of Natural History *85*, New York.

Spencer, H. 1855: Principles of Psychology. London.

Sperry, R. W. 1945: The problem of central nervous reorganization after nerve regeneration and muscle transposition. The Quarterly Review of Biology *20*, 311–369.

Spindler, M. and E. Bluhm. 1934: Kleine Beiträge zur Psychologie des Seelöwen. Zeitschrift für vergleichende Physiologie *21*.

Spindler, P. 1954: Die Bedeutung des menschlichen Verhaltens für die physische Anthropologie. Homo *5*, 111–112.

––––– 1955: Ausdrücke und Verhalten erwachsener Zwillinge. Acta Genetica Medica (Roma) *4*, 32–61.

Spitz, R. A. 1964: The derailment of dialogue: Stimulus overload, action cycles, and the completion gradient. Journal of the American Psychoanalytic Association *12*, 752–775.

––––– and K. Wolf. 1946: The smiling response. A contribution to the ontogenesis of social relations. General Psychology Monographs *24*, 57–125.

Spranger, E. 1924: Psychologie des Jugendalters. 1st Ed., Leipzig.

Spurway, H. 1953: The escape drive in domestic cats and the dog and cat relationship. Behaviour *5*, 81–84.

Stamm, R. A. 1965: Perspektiven zu einer Vergleichenden Ausdrucksforschung. Handbuch der Psychologie *5* (Ausdruckspsychologie), 255–288.

Tembrock, G. 1957: Zur Ethologie des Rotfuchses (*Vulpes vulpes* L.) unter besonderer Berücksichtigung der Fortpflanzung. Der Zoologische Garten (Neue Folge) *23*, 289–352.

––––– 1959: Beobachtungen zur Fuchsranz unter besonderer Berücksichtigung der Lautgebung. Zeitschrift für Tierpsychologie *16*, 351–368.

––––– 1961: Verhaltensforschung: Eine Einführung in die Tier-Ethologie. Jena.

––––– 1963: Mischlaute beim Rotfuchs (*Vulpes vulpes* L.). Zeitschrift für Tierpsychologie *20*, 616–623.

Thielcke, G. 1964: Zur Phylogenese einiger Lautäußerungen der europäischen Baumläufer. Zeitschrift für Zoologische Systematik und Evolutionsforschung *2*, 383–413.

––––– 1965: Gesangsgeographische Variation des Gartenbaumläufers (*Certhia brachydactyla*) im Hinblick auf das Artbildungsproblem. Zeitschrift für Tierpsychologie *22*, 542–566.

––––– und K. E. Linsenmair. 1963: Zur geographischen Variation des Gesanges des

Zilpzalps, *Phylloscopus collybita*, in Mittel- und Südwesteuropa mit einem Vergleich des Gesanges des Fitis, *Phylloscopus trochilus*. Journal für Ornithologie *104*, 372–402.

Thomas, E. und F. Schaller, 1954: Das Spiel der optisch isolierten, jungen Kaspar-Hauser-Katze. Die Naturwissenschaften *41*, 557–558.

Thorp, W. H. 1956: Learning and instinct in animals. London.

Tinbergen, L. 1939: Zur Fortpflanzungsethologie von *Sepia officinalis* L. Archives Néerlandaises de Zoologie *3*, 324–364.

———— and H. N. Kluyver. 1953: Territory and the regulation of density in titmice. Archives Néerlandaises de Zoologie *10*, 265–289.

Tinbergen, N. 1936: Zur Soziologie der Silbermöwe *(Larus a. argentatus* Pontopp). Beiträge zur Fortpflanzungsbiologie der Vögel *12*, 89–96.

———— 1937: Feldbeobachtungen an Zwergmöwen *(Larus minutus* Pall.). Mimosa *10*, 12–21.

———— 1938: Ergänzende Beobachtungen über die Paarbildung der Flußseeschwalbe *(Sterna h. hirundo* L.). Ardea *27*, 247–249.

———— 1940: Die Übersprungbewegung. Zeitschrift für Tierpsychologie *4*, 1–40.

———— 1948: Social releasers and the experimental method required for this study. The Wilson Bulletin *60*, 6–51.

———— 1950: The hierarchical organization of nervous mechanisms underlying instinctive behaviour. Symposia of the Society of Experimental Biology *IV* (Physiological mechanisms in animal behaviour), 305–312.

———— 1951: The study of instinct. Oxford.

———— 1962: The evolution of animal communication—A critical examination of methods. Symposia of the Zoological Society of London *8*, 1–6.

———— und D. J. Kuenen. 1939: Über die auslösenden und die richtunggebenden Reizsituationen der Sperrbewegung von jungen Drosseln *(Turdus m. merula* L. und *Turdus e. ericetorum* Turton). Zeitschrift für Tierpsychologie *3*, 37–60.

————, B. J. D. Meeuse, L. K. Boerema und W. W. Varossieau. 1942: Die Balz des Samtfalters, *Eumenis (= Satyrus) semele* (L.). Zschr. f. Tierpsych. *5*, 182–226.

Tolman, E. C. 1932: Purposive behavior in animals and men. New York.

Topitsch, E. 1962: Phylogenetische und emotionale Grundlagen menschlicher Weltauffassung. Saggi Filosofici (Turin) *9*.

———— 1963: Das Verhältnis zwischen Sozial- und Naturwissenschaften. Eine methodologisch-ideologiekritische Untersuchung. Dialectica *16*, 211–231.

Uexküll. J. v. 1909: Umwelt und Innenwelt der Tiere. 2nd Ed., 1921, Berlin.

Ullricht, W. 1962: Die letzten indischen Löwen *(Panthera leo persica)* im Gir-Reservat. Der Zoologische Garten (Neue Folge) *26*, 287–297.

Verheyen, R. 1954: Monographie éthologique de l'hippopotame. Brussels (Institut des Parcs Nationaux Belges).

Verwey, J. 1930: Die Paarungsbiologie des Fischreihers. Zoologische Jahrbücher (Abteilung Physiologie) *48*, 1–120.

Wacholder, K. 1925: Beiträge zur Physiologie der willkürlichen Bewegung. Pflügers Archiv *209*.

Washburn, S. L. and E. DeVore 1961: The social life of baboons. Scientific American *204*, 62.

Wasman, M. and J. P. Flynn. 1962: Directed attack elicited from hypothalamus. Archive of Neurology *6*, 220–227.

Weidmann, U. 1956: Verhaltensstudien an der Stockente *(Anas platyrhynchos* L.). I. Das Aktionssystem. Zeitschrift für Tierpsychologie *13*, 208–271.

Weigel, I. 1961: Das Fellmuster der wildlebenden Katzenarten und der Hauskatze in vergleichender und stammesgeschichtlicher Hinsicht. Säugetierkundliche Mitteilungen *9*, Sonderheft.

Whitman, C. O. 1898: Animal behavior. Biology lectures of the Marine Biology Laboratory, Woods Hole, Massachusetts.

———— 1919: The behavior of pigeons. Carnegie Institute of Washington Publications *257*, 1–161.

Wickler, W. 1961: Oekologie und Stammesgeschichte von Verhaltensweisen. Fortschritte der Zoologie *13*, 303–365.

Wieser, S. 1957: Enthemmungsphänomene der prämotorischen Rinde. Film C 769 des Instituts für den Wissenschaftlichen Film, Göttingen.

Winkelsträter, K. H. 1960: Das Betteln der Zootiere, Bern.

Witte, W. 1965: Perzeptive Organisation als Weg zur Wahrnehmung. Bericht über den 24. Kongreß der Deutschen Gesellschaft für Psychologie, 92–96.

Wörner, R. 1940: Theoretische und experimentelle Beiträge zum Ausdrucksproblem. Zeitschrift für angewandte Psychologie und Charakterkunde *59*, 257–318.

Wüstehube, C. 1960 a: Beiträge zur Kenntnis, besonders des Spiel- und Beutefangverhaltens, einheimischer Musteliden. Zeitschrift für Tierpsychologie *17*, 579–613.

———— 1960 b: Beutefang von Wieseln und Iltissen. Film, unpublished.

Wundt, W. 1882: Die Aufgaben der experimentellen Psychologie. In: Essays, 187–212.

Wuttke, W. und F. Hoffmeister, 1967: Differenzierungsmöglichkeiten transquillisierender Wirkungen im Tierreich. Naunyn Schmiedebergs Archiv für Pharmakologie und experimentelle Pathologie *257*, 353.

Wynne-Edwards, V. C. 1962: Animal dispersion in relation to social behaviour. Edinburgh and London.

Ziegler, H. 1920: Der Begriff des Instinktes einst und jetzt. 3rd Ed., Jena.

Ziehen, T. 1914: Leitfaden der Physiologischen Psychologie. 10th Ed., Jena.

Author Index

Species and Subject Index

Chapter 19

How It Works

Before we have a look at how the application has been put together, submit the form. You should be presented with a validation message just above the Name field. If you enter your name and click Submit again, you will be presented with a mostly blank page. Pretty boring, huh?

Open the `c:\struts-base\web\index.jsp` file and have a look at what's currently implemented:

```
<html:form action="/test" method="POST">
    <table width="350" border="0" cellpadding="3" cellspacing="0">
    <logic:messagesPresent message="false">
    <tr>
        <td colspan=2><b><bean:message key="errors.global"/></b></td>
    </tr>
    </logic:messagesPresent>
    <logic:messagesPresent property="name">
    <tr>
        <td colspan=2><html:errors property="name"/></td>
    </tr>
  </logic:messagesPresent>
    <tr>
        <td><bean:message key="form.name.title"/></td>
        <td><html:text altKey="form.name.title" property="name" size="30"/></td>
    </tr>
    <tr>
        <td valign="top"><bean:message key="form.comments.title"/></td>
        <td>
            <html:textarea property="comments" cols="30" rows="8"></html:textarea>
        </td>
    </tr>
    <tr>
        <td> </td>
        <td align="center"><html:submit/></td>
    </tr>
    </table>
</html:form>
```

You will notice a simple form that posts to an action: `/test`. The form also has Struts HTML tags for the two fields, Name and Comments, as well as a placeholder for an error message for the Name field. There is a `logic:messagesPresent` test around this.

This form is represented by a `DynaValidatorForm` configured in the `struts-config.xml` file:

```
<form-beans>

    <form-bean      name="testForm"
                    type="org.apache.struts.validator.DynaValidatorForm">
      <form-property name="name" type="java.lang.String"/>
      <form-property name="comments" type="java.lang.String"/>
    </form-bean>

</form-beans>
```